KNOWLEDGE INTEGRATION AND INNOVATION

Knowledge Integration and Innovation

*Critical Challenges Facing International
Technology-based Firms*

Edited by
CHRISTIAN BERGGREN
ANNA BERGEK
LARS BENGTSSON
MICHAEL HOBDAY
JONAS SÖDERLUND

OXFORD
UNIVERSITY PRESS

OXFORD
UNIVERSITY PRESS

Great Clarendon Street, Oxford ox2 6DP

Oxford University Press is a department of the University of Oxford.
It furthers the University's objective of excellence in research, scholarship,
and education by publishing worldwide in

Oxford New York

Auckland Cape Town Dar es Salaam Hong Kong Karachi
Kuala Lumpur Madrid Melbourne Mexico City Nairobi
New Delhi Shanghai Taipei Toronto

With offices in

Argentina Austria Brazil Chile Czech Republic France Greece
Guatemala Hungary Italy Japan Poland Portugal Singapore
South Korea Switzerland Thailand Turkey Ukraine Vietnam

Oxford is a registered trade mark of Oxford University Press
in the UK and in certain other countries

Published in the United States
by Oxford University Press Inc., New York

British Library Cataloguing in Publication Data
Data available

Library of Congress Cataloging in Publication Data
Data available

Typeset by SPI Publisher Services, Pondicherry, India
Printed in Great Britain
on acid-free paper by
MPG Books Group, Bodmin and King's Lynn

ISBN 978-0-19-969392-4

1 3 5 7 9 10 8 6 4 2

Contents

Preface

One of the most intriguing challenges of the contemporary economy is the increasing need for firms to integrate and coordinate knowledge in project groups, diversified organizations, inter-organizational partnerships, and strategic alliances. The increasing awareness of the importance of knowledge integration in businesses and industries is paralleled by the growing recognition of its importance in the academic management literature during the last decade. So far, however, no comprehensive academic book devoted to this highly topical theme has been published, and there is a shortage of research contributions that integrate the themes of innovation and knowledge integration.

This book is a result of several years of dedicated research efforts by a multidisciplinary group of researchers at Linköping University and University of Gävle into 'Knowledge Integration and Innovation in an Internationalizing Economy', supported by core programme funding from Riksbankens Jubileumsfond.

Knowledge integration and innovation have been the key themes of two international workshops organized by the KITE group in Linköping, Sweden, in September 2008 and in May 2010. These workshops provided forums for in-depth discussions on knowledge integration related to project organizing, to outsourcing and offshoring, to technology sourcing, and to strategic partnerships. The intensity and creativity of these discussions convinced us that these are truly important research areas. Drafts of several of the chapters in this book were presented and discussed at the 2010 workshop, and we are grateful for the stimulating and constructive criticism provided by the workshop participants. After a midterm review by Riksbankens Jubileumsfond in 2010, we will have the privilege to further explore these research topics in the period 2011–14. Hopefully, this book will encourage other researchers to extend the research field in new directions. You may keep up-to-date with the activities of the KITE programme on the KITE web site: www.liu.se/kite!

The book presents an overarching framework of the processes and outcomes of knowledge integration, and acknowledges that knowledge integration occurs at different organizational levels and across the individual firms. Among other things, the studies presented discuss individuals as key actors in the knowledge integration processes, projects as arenas for knowledge integration, technology strategies to drive or limit the need for knowledge integration, and the dynamic nature of knowledge integration capabilities within and across individual firms.

In recent academic debates, there has been a strong interest in the micro-foundations of strategies and processes. This, however, remains a largely unexplored area in the research on knowledge integration. Thus, this book will fill an important void, as it includes several chapters devoted to the micro-organizational level, for example group-based knowledge generation and the role of individuals such as inventors, innovators, and consultants in the integration processes. At the other end of the spectrum, several chapters address knowledge integration between firms in inter-organizational alliances and in the case of outsourced operations. While previous studies of strategic alliances and partnerships have concentrated on knowledge transfer, this book provides a different perspective, that of knowledge integration, for research into these issues.

The KITE group is deeply grateful for the continued support from Riksbankens Jubileumsfond and the feedback provided by its evaluators of the KITE programme: Erhard Friedberg (Sciences Po, Paris), Marius T. H. Meeus (Tilburg University), and Walter W. Powell (Stanford University). From the very beginning, the KITE research programme has enjoyed the support of an active international advisory group consisting of Mike Hobday (CENTRIM, University of Brighton), Lars Hultman (Thin Film Physics Division, Linköping University), Kristian Kreiner (Department of Organization, Copenhagen Business School), Jacky Swan (Industrial Relations & Organisational Behaviour, Warwick Business School), and Andy Van de Ven (Carlson School of Management, University of Minnesota). We very much appreciate their encouragement and contribution.

Linköping   Christian Berggren and Fredrik Tell
November 2010   Director and Co-director of the KITE
                                    research programme

List of Figures

List of Tables

List of Contributors

Editors

Lars Bengtsson, Professor, Faculty of Engineering and Sustainable Development, University of Gävle, Sweden

Anna Bergek, Associate Professor, Department of Management and Engineering, Linköping University, Sweden

Christian Berggren, Professor, Department of Management and Engineering, Linköping University, Sweden

Michael Hobday, Professor, Centre for Research in Innovation Management (CENTRIM), University of Brighton, UK

Jonas Söderlund, Associate Professor, Department of Management and Engineering, Linköping University, Sweden; and Professor, Department of Leadership and Management, BI Norwegian School of Management, Norway

Other Contributors

Hans Andersson, Assistant Professor, Department of Management and Engineering, Linköping University, Sweden

Mattias Axelson, Assistant Professor, Centre for Innovation and Operations Management, Stockholm School of Economics, Sweden

Marie Bengtsson, Assistant Professor, Department of Management and Engineering, Linköping University, Sweden

Karin Bredin, Assistant Professor, Department of Management and Engineering, Linköping University, Sweden

Mandar Dabhilkar, Research Fellow, Department of Management and Engineering, Linköping University, Sweden; and Assistant Professor, Department of Industrial Economics and Management, KTH, Sweden

Cecilia Enberg, Assistant Professor, Department of Management and Engineering, Linköping University, Sweden

Robin von Haartman, PhD Candidate, Faculty of Engineering and Sustainable Development, University of Gävle, Sweden

Mattias Johansson, Research Fellow, Department of Management and Engineering, Linköping University, Sweden

Nicolette Lakemond, Associate Professor, Department of Management and Engineering, Linköping University, Sweden

Lars Lindkvist, Professor, Department of Management and Engineering, Linköping University, Sweden

Thomas Magnusson, Associate Professor, Department of Management and Engineering, Linköping University, Sweden

Fredrik Tell, Professor, Department of Management and Engineering, Linköping University, Sweden

Linnea Wahlstedt, PhD Candidate, Department of Management and Engineering, Linköping University, Sweden

Part I

Introduction

1

Exploring Knowledge Integration and Innovation

Christian Berggren, Anna Bergek, Lars Bengtsson, and Jonas Söderlund

This chapter explains the book's rationale and primary purpose. It also presents the book's theoretical and empirical background and provides an overview of its twelve chapters.

1.1 WHAT MAKES MICRONIC FLY?

Micronic Laser System is not a household name; few people have seen its products, and even fewer understand its technology. Yet Micronic, located outside Stockholm, Sweden, could be seen as a symbol of a competitive technology firm from an advanced economy which thrives in the global economy: an innovation-based, growing company that employs people with skills ranging from PhDs in optical acoustics and micro-lithography to advanced prototype builders. Trebling its sales in the period of 2002–5, Micronic is a world leader in laser pattern generators, a key technology for producing the photo masks its customer firms in Japan, Korea, Taiwan, and the United States need to manufacture large flat displays for TVs and computers. When Micronic developed its new Spatial Light Modulation-technology for semiconductor chips, each with 1 million individually controlled micro-mirrors that change direction at a frequency of 2,000 Hertz, the company spent more than 25 per cent of its turnover on this platform project involving both cutting-edge internal research and demanding development partnerships with distant suppliers. Micronic's main R&D facility is located north of Stockholm, close to its manufacturing plant. Here, engineers and technicians spend thousands of hours assembling heavy and complex machines from 3,500 to 5,000 components, as well as testing and calibrating them in clean rooms, collaborating tightly with customer engineers. In many ways, Micronic symbolizes the highly agile, technologically sophisticated firms, small and large, which lead the advanced nations as they attempt to move up the value and technology chain to cope with global low-cost competition.

So what makes Micronic fly? What enables this company to integrate a wide array of internal and external knowledge sources and how does it augment its internal expertise in external partnerships? What are the organizational and technical means required for successful management of knowledge integration in technology-based firms in general, and how can arenas and actors at different levels contribute to this process? These are some of the issues discussed in this book.

1.2 INNOVATION AND KNOWLEDGE INTEGRATION IN TECHNOLOGY-BASED INDUSTRIES: TRENDS AND CHALLENGES

As indicated by the case of Micronic Laser Systems, the central theme of this book is the role of knowledge integration for innovation in globally operating technology-based companies. In contrast to prominent contributions in the previous literatures (see overview in Chapter 2), which primarily focus on the mechanisms by which knowledge integration occurs in companies' day-to-day (or 'routine') activities, the principal idea behind this book is that knowledge integration is a vital part of the dynamics of the innovation process. Innovation processes involve the exploration and exploitation of opportunities for new or improved products, systems, processes, or services through the generation of knowledge, the transformation of knowledge into artefacts, and the continuous matching of these artefacts to market needs and demands (Pavitt, 2005).[1] In these processes, different knowledge bases – well-established as well as newly generated – have to be combined and integrated in order to achieve new, functional products or solutions. Indeed, it has been argued that it is mainly through the product development process that organizations perform their critical role of integrating knowledge (cf. Henderson and Cockburn, 1994; Helfat and Raubitschek, 2000). Thus, companies in technology-based industries need to master knowledge integration (Hoopes, 2001; Carlile and Rebentisch, 2003) to gain and sustain competitive advantage in the global market (Verona and Ravasi, 2003).

The main empirical focus of the book is on large firms in industries that are reliant on advanced technologies, often in complex combinations, for exploiting business opportunities (cf. Granstrand, 1998; Licht and Nerlinger, 1998). These include, for example, the automotive, heavy electrical equipment, packaging machinery, telecom, tooling, and aerospace industries. Companies in such industries, which are subject to fierce technology-based competition in global markets, can be seen as 'critical' cases for the study of knowledge integration. They are under the influence of three major trends that deeply affect the conditions for innovation in general and knowledge integration in particular: (*a*) the internationalization of R&D and production, (*b*) the transformation of national

---

[1] We are, therefore, not primarily concerned with innovation in terms of the development of new business models, the creation of new organizations, or other possible innovation types, although these of course may both precede and follow from product and process innovation.

and global markets, and (*c*) changes in the character of developments in science and technology.

The first trend is the increasing *internationalization of R&D and production*. The share of R&D performed outside the home country has increased – not only for OECD (Organisation for Economic Co-operation and Development) countries in Europe and North America (Bruche, 2009) but also for new economies such as China, Taiwan, and India (Engardio et al., 2005) – creating new types of multinationals and locations for knowledge generation. Emerging economies are also becoming increasingly important as markets for products and services. China, for example, overtook the United States as the world's premier automobile market in 2009 and has become the major manufacturing centre in a range of industries from electronics to textiles to solar cells. Combined with the growth of other low-cost industrializing nations in Asia and the enlarged European Union, this is putting enormous pressure on manufacturing in the OECD core, resulting in a drastic increase in the offshoring of production (Bengtsson et al., 2005). In order to develop new products and processes, companies need to make use of knowledge from both R&D and manufacturing (Kline and Rosenberg, 1986). The increasing dispersion of these activities implies that, to a greater extent than ever, knowledge integration has to take place over vast geographical distances and across cultural and national borders.

The second trend is the *transformation of national and global markets*. Deregulation, re-regulation, and privatization are creating new market conditions and breaking up established ways of developing and manufacturing products and systems. The traditional so-called 'development pairs' (Fridlund, 1999), in which national champions in complex technologies developed new systems in close collaboration with public users and procurement bodies, are being dissolved, forcing firms to find new ways to organize their innovative activities, combining internal development with alliances and partnerships. Thus, innovation hinges on knowledge integrated across an increasing number of organizational borders. There are also changes with regard to the type of products offered in deregulated markets, from water treatment to power generation and telecommunications. In these industries, companies are striving to increase the value of their sales by offering clients 'functions', instead of 'products'. This generally tends to imply a focus on 'integrated solutions', which requires boundary-spanning knowledge integration activities, such as integrating R&D with after sales and services in conjunction with advanced cross-organizational coordination (Davies, 2003, 2004; Windahl, 2006).

The third trend relates to *changes in the character of science and technology*, in particular in terms of increasing speed, specialization, and complexity.

With respect to *speed*, there is evidence that in a number of industries, the time available to develop and launch new products is becoming shorter with each new generation (Doz et al., 2001).

With respect to *specialization*, a reinforced tendency to focus on core competences and outsourcing has resulted in an increasing division of labour between companies in the supply chain and a specialization on delineated tasks. This tendency is strengthened by efforts to modularize products and services, to facilitate a further decoupling of activities, from financial services to software programming and clinical testing. At first glance, this may seem to be resulting in a 'neatly' specialized innovation infrastructure, in which product/system designers, component specialists, and manufacturers work together through market relations (Pavitt, 2005). In reality, however, innovation in technology-based industries tends to be quite demanding in terms of coordination of processes and adaptation of interfaces: R&D management in focal firms needs to integrate knowledge that is both broad and deep (Brusoni et al., 2001, 2005), to balance often contradictory requirements from downstream units (Olausson, 2009), and to handle a variety of cooperative R&D, alliances, mergers, and other collaborative efforts between specialized units inside or outside the organization. Indeed, new product development in these industries requires the coordination of a larger number of participating organizations than ever before.

With respect to *complexity*, products, systems, processes, and services embody an increasing number of rapidly evolving components and subsystems and draw on a broadening range of technologies and knowledge fields, and their development and commercialization require more complex organizational forms and practices (Hobday, 2000). It is increasingly difficult for firms to master advances in all relevant knowledge fields, and external sourcing in terms of contract development and manufacturing of components and subsystems becomes increasingly important. This in turn implies that knowledge integration to a larger extent than before has to take place across organizational borders.

To sum up, these three trends result in higher levels of specialization and separation of activities in industrial value chains, and have profound implications for the innovation process, making it more interdisciplinary, collaborative, interorganizational, and international. In particular, these trends imply that there is an increasing need to integrate knowledge across disciplinary, organizational, and geographical boundaries. As a consequence, a firm's ability to integrate knowledge within the company, as well as between the company and external actors, has a major influence on its innovative capability (Lazonick, 2005) and, thus, on its ability to prevail in the escalating time-to-market competition.

1.3 OVERALL AIM

Against this background, the aim of this book is to provide new in-depth empirical evidence of the dynamics of knowledge integration (KI) as a crucial process and capability in modern firms, to define and conceptualize KI in a systematic way, and to present multilevel studies of challenges and ways of managing KI. Based on original empirical investigations in different technology-based industries, we describe and analyse the forms, practices, outcomes and trade-offs of KI, as well as the contextual and organizational factors influencing the process. The book demonstrates how the study of KI augments the understanding of innovation and the ability of organizations to manage the processes of KI. 'An organization cannot improve that which it does not understand' (Teece, 2009: 129).

In the remainder of this chapter, we elaborate in more detail the concept of 'knowledge integration', in terms of what it is and why it is important, and identify important gaps in extant research on KI (for a detailed analysis of this research, see

Chapter 2). Based on this, we formulate a more precise purpose and describe the contributions this book makes to the research field and to managers facing the challenges of KI.

1.4 THE CONTENT AND CONTEXT OF KNOWLEDGE INTEGRATION

As we are interested in how firms can manage distributed knowledge, we analyse KI as a goal-oriented process, or as part of a goal-oriented process, aspiring to achieve a significant organizational outcome. Mainstream understanding of KI claims that it is about problem-solving (Okhuysen and Eisenhardt, 2002) to accomplish the integration of specialist knowledge needed to perform discrete productive tasks (Grant, 1996a). In this book, we go beyond this understanding to show the dynamics of KI as a process of collaborative and purposeful combination of complementary knowledge, underpinned by specific and focused personal, team, and organizational capabilities, a process that usually involves significant elements of new knowledge generation. (See Chapter 2 for contrasts with definitions found in the literature.)

In our detailed empirical investigations into the development of products, systems, and services, we focus primarily on technology-based firms and the integration of technological knowledge. This includes applied scientific knowledge, knowledge about the overall function of technical systems, 'structural' knowledge of the assembly and interplay of components and subsystems (including component knowledge as well as architectural knowledge (cf. Henderson and Clark, 1990), manufacturing knowledge, and application knowledge, i.e. knowledge about the specific contexts in which a product or process will be used (cf. Ropohl, 1997). Although our main focus is on the integration of technological knowledge, several of the chapters in this book show that innovation requires the integration of many other types of knowledge as well, such as marketing and organizational knowledge.

In contrast to most definitions (see Chapter 2), we show that KI is not only a process of combining and fusing different knowledge bases but also a process of creating new knowledge needed for this integration to succeed. KI goes beyond identifying, communicating, and transferring information. It differs from the concepts of 'knowledge transfer', that is, a unidirectional flow from unit A to unit B, and 'knowledge sharing', the process of developing trans-specialist understanding through the creation of overlapping knowledge fields (cf. Postrel, 2002).[2] Instead, we see KI as the bringing together and combining of all the different types of knowledge required for developing new products, systems, and solutions and generating the requisite complementary knowledge. This type of integration includes determining what should be integrated in a product and how (concept development), as well as the implementation of this concept through detailed product and process design and engineering (cf. Iansiti, 1997). In the empirical

---

[2] Thus, even though knowledge transfer and knowledge sharing can exert an influence on knowledge integration, as defined by us, we treat them as conceptually different processes.

contexts we analyse in this book, new knowledge is regularly required for this integration to happen. This means we are not merely interested in the *application* (coordination and adaptation) of existing knowledge but also in the *creation* of new knowledge and the acquisition of knowledge from external sources. Thus, within a specific product, process, or system development project, knowledge sourcing, knowledge creation, and knowledge integration are closely related and often interdependent processes. We can therefore see a functional product or process as a manifestation or embodiment of a successful KI process.

Several authors have emphasized the importance of KI for competitive advantage (e.g. Henderson and Clark, 1990; Grant, 1996*a*, 1996*b*; Grandori, 2001; Okhuysen and Eisenhardt, 2002), and the rapidly increasing number of studies devoted to KI implies there is now great interest in this subject from scholars and practitioners (see Chapter 2). The new definition we develop through our empirical studies deepens our understanding of the meaning of KI and indicates that there is a need to study:

1. KI as a process, with several different types of inputs and outputs;
2. KI in an innovation context with its specific system or product challenges;
3. KI as a multilevel phenomenon, including the role of individuals, teams, projects, wider organizational settings, and corporate strategies;
4. the broad repertoire of organizational and technical means required for successful management of KI in technology-based firms;
5. how KI across organizations is related to the creation of internal integration capabilities;
6. the resources and costs for KI and their implications for strategic decisions, business orientations, and business outcomes.

1.4.1 Knowledge integration as process

The majority of the literature tends to treat KI as an undifferentiated concept. In this book, however, we find it important to distinguish between the KI *process* (or processes), the *inputs* and *outcomes* of that process, the *contextual and organizational factors* influencing the process, and the *capabilities* underlying the process (see Figure 1.1). This simplified model is also a starting point for further analysis in the book concerning the development of KI capabilities, KI as a strategic choice, and the management of KI as a multilevel challenge.

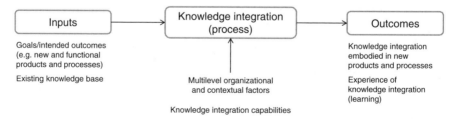

Figure 1.1 A simple model of knowledge integration

The main *inputs* to the KI process are the goals or intended outcomes (e.g. new products, systems, services, and solutions) in addition to the characteristics of the knowledge bases which are to be integrated, in terms of their complexity, uncertainty, tacitness, proximity, speed of change, and interdependencies (cf. Polanyi, 1966; Grant, 1996a; von Hippel and Tyre, 1996; Grandori, 2001; Allan and Henn, 2006). Typically, these inputs come from a variety of internal and external specialist sources.

The *processes* of KI include the combination and integration of complementary knowledge bases which, in turn, may require both internal knowledge creation and absorption of knowledge from external sources. The processes may vary in several different ways and occur dynamically over extended periods of time. First, the composition and number of actors involved may vary, from the minimum number $n = 1$ (implying that a single individual may accomplish a KI process), to a vast number of different types of actors located in various settings. Second, the type of collaboration may also vary, from sequential coordination to intensive and iterative parallel interaction.

A primary *outcome* of the KI process is the physical or informational integration of knowledge in products, processes, systems, services, and solutions. In relation to the goals, this can be successful or not. For example, the resulting products/processes can be more or less innovative in terms of performance. In addition, outcomes relate closely to the degree of novelty, which can range from small, novel increments to radically new system solutions or processes. Another central outcome of the process of KI is organizational experience, learning and new knowledge, and the cumulative building of KI capability (see Dutta et al., 2005); existing capabilities often change as a result of the integration process.

The need for KI is further influenced by technological configurations, type of relations with outside partners, firm strategy (e.g. mode of knowledge sourcing), as well as the structure and location of the involved units. These factors are related to the innovation *context*, as KI may be applied to the refining of existing generations of products/systems or may be concerned with the integration of knowledge in pursuit of new generations of products/systems (see Prencipe, 2003). The latter requires more knowledge creation, experimental activities and innovative organizational forms, and more intensive interaction with suppliers/outside partners. Throughout the book, we show how KI processes are situated within different types of project and broader organizational forms, requiring careful, deliberate, and purposeful management.

The integration process is influenced by existing KI capabilities and the firm's capacity to generate new capabilities. *Knowledge integration capability* can be defined as the attributes which enable integration to be performed and is a major explanatory factor in how well a KI task can be conducted. Attributes include experience, skills, and knowledge (tacit and explicit), which may evolve over long periods of time. Combined, these attributes will tend to grow and mature over time if similar tasks are repeated, incentivized, expanded, and/or deliberately invested in (Helfat and Raubitschek, 2000; Helfat and Peteraf, 2003). As such, the KI capability of a firm is a major factor in explaining its performance, although other factors also influence performance (e.g. industrial trends, competition, synergies with users, and leadership changes). KI capabilities can be subdivided into four major areas: (*a*) strategic

capabilities, including leadership and management, (*b*) organizational structures, (*c*) systems and procedures for managing KI, both formal and informal,
and (*d*) people, including the key individuals and teams which shape and/or
interact with (*a*)–(*c*). Recent research (e.g. Hobday, 2000; Davies and Hobday,
2005), building on earlier studies (Leonard-Barton, 1992; Hamel and Prahalad,
1994; Teece and Pisano, 1994), shows the importance of distinctive and
dynamic capabilities in sustaining technology-based firms' competitive advantage. This book shows that KI is one such distinctive capability essential to
performance in a variety of areas.

KI capability-building, as shown in Figure 1.1, is a critical dimension of the KI
process and an important theme in several of the chapters in this book, such as
Chapter 8 on the P-form organization, Chapters 9 and 10 on outsourcing and
knowledge integration, and Chapter 11 on creative accumulation, where strategies
building on advanced integration capabilities are compared to modular innovation strategies. Another important aspect of KI, suggested in the process approach,
is its *multilevel character*. In this book, we analyse micro-processes of knowledge
generation and integration at the individual and team levels (Chapters 3 and 4), as
well as higher order processes at both the project and firm level (Chapters 6 and 8)
and the inter-firm level (Chapters 7, 9, 10, and 11). In Chapter 12, we return to the
importance of understanding and managing KI as a multilevel process.

As these chapters also illustrate, KI capability-building is an important *strategic
issue*, for example, regarding supply chain management (whether to combine
outsourcing with investments in knowledge and capabilities to be able to reinte-
grate the extended supply chain); or in technology strategy (whether to invest in
internal R&D and manufacturing to build advanced integration capabilities in
complex products, or to minimize such investments by a strategy of modular
product development and supplier collaboration).

1.4.2 The particular context of innovation

As described above, this book focuses on the role KI plays for technology-based
innovation. This is a context which tends to be characterized by varying degrees of
complexity and uncertainty, where actors do not know from the start exactly
which technologies will actually work, what elements of knowledge will be crucial,
or what the end result will actually be (Van de Ven et al., 1999). This context is
different from the one discussed by Grant (1996*a*: 112) in his analysis of the
knowledge-based theory of the firm, which assumes that 'the primary role of the
firm is the application of existing knowledge to the production of goods and
services'. The context of innovation implies that application of existing and
creation of new knowledge are always intertwined, and also key attributes of KI
processes. By necessity, these processes involve experimentation, from the lab to
the field (Kline and Rosenberg, 1986; Pavitt, 1987, 1990, 2005), from internal
sources, from competitors, suppliers, users, or from universities. Innovation, as
studied in this book, requires the ability to integrate knowledge, which is dispersed
across disciplinary, functional, and geographical boundaries, within the firm as
well as between the firm and external sources (Henderson and Cockburn, 1994).

This implies that in an innovation context, firms are faced both with the interdependencies that follow from combination of resources (knowledge as well as artefacts), for example when sourcing components or manufacturing services from external partners, and with the interdependencies involved in collective action among holders of different elements of knowledge. Whereas integration in the context of knowledge application is often solved by rather simple forms of coordination, for example routines and sequencing (Grant, 1996*a*), more advanced forms of integration tend to require more complex mechanisms (Grant, 1996*b*). The collaboration across different organizations or units within an organization for the purpose of innovation 'cannot realistically be reduced to designing flows of codified information across functional boundaries. It also involves coordinated experimentation . . . and the interpretation of ambiguous or incomplete data, where tacit knowledge is essential' (Pavitt, 1998: 444). To handle these different types of interactions and interdependencies, firms need to master several different sets of mechanisms, and change them over time, as analysed in detail in the book.

1.4.3 Knowledge integration as a multilevel process

Much of the current literature in the field of organization and management theory focuses on the integration of knowledge held by individuals. For example, although Grant (1996*a*) as well as Nonaka et al. (2000) recognize that 'knowledge absorption' may take place at both individual and organizational levels, they assume that knowledge creation is 'an individual activity' (Grant, 1996*a*: 112). Other researchers analyse knowledge processes as predominantly collective (e.g. Spender, 1998; Tsoukas and Vladimirou, 2001; Teece, 2009). By contrast, we understand knowledge creation and knowledge integration to be multilevel processes, where individual exploration and creation take place in an intersubjective, often collective context, and collaborative processes play an important role (see in particular Chapters 3 and 4). This multitude of knowledge creation and integration processes follows from the specialized and distributed nature of knowledge bases which characterizes advanced product development and manufacturing processes. As we show, KI occurs not only among individuals but also within and across teams, projects, functional units, and organizations. Indeed, capabilities in integrating knowledge from both internal and external sources are becoming increasingly important, and hence also 'the successful exploitation of the knowledge of other firms' (Kogut, 2000: 406; see also Section 3.5). We argue that building a multilevel KI capability is one of the core capabilities that provide competitive advantage to technology-based firms.

1.4.4 Managing knowledge integration

The existing literature has suggested a number of KI 'mechanisms'. Examples range from rules, directives, and sequencing activities (Grant, 1996*a*) to problem-solving in communities of practice (Grandori, 2001), multifunctional product development projects (Ancona and Caldwell, 1992; Dougherty, 1992), management teams with members from different functional areas (Eisenhardt, 1989), and teams for process improvements (Tyre and Orlikowski, 1994). Even though these suggestions represent important contributions, there is a need to reconsider this discourse in the context of the complexities facing technology-based companies engaged in innovation. Most of the suggestions tend to be generic rather than context-specific; they do not include the strategic aspects of KI; and, with only a few exceptions, they are not designed to handle the specific context of technology-based innovation.

The book reveals and analyses KI in an innovation context as a multilevel process often characterized by uncertainty and complexity. The degree of uncertainty and the requirements of integration vary greatly, however, in relation to time restrictions and to the maturity and novelty of the products and solutions to be developed. In the context of incremental refinement of an established product or architecture, uncertainty tends to be low, and integration requirements are condensed to coordination, following organizational routines and using previously developed technical or organizational interfaces. In contrast, in a context of developing radically new technologies or architectures, new forms of intensive person-to-person, group-to-group, and firm-to-firm interaction are often required to establish the necessary common knowledge base and define the necessary interfaces. Because these integrative mechanisms tend to be costly, firms following a predictable trajectory tend to develop formalized alternatives over time.

If sufficient integration can be achieved through the use of routines, rules, and standards, an emphasis on collaborative knowledge-creating group-processes would not be justified. Yet, when interdependencies and uncertainties are high, and new forms of technology are required, the need for direct interaction and deep integrative solutions increases. This need is associated with the breadth and depth of the knowledge to be integrated, and its speed of change. A combination of high degrees of knowledge differentiation and interdependencies requires a correspondingly high level of integration efforts.

Therefore, a major contribution of this book is to provide an in-depth understanding of the broad repertoire of strategies, structures, and capabilities needed to manage KI, from coordination processes building on standardized interfaces to intensive interaction between holders of dispersed knowledge bases aimed at exploring new territories and creating new knowledge.

1.4.5 Knowledge integration as interplay between external and internal knowledge

As knowledge is increasingly distributed among the various partners in value chains, effective forms of inter-organizational knowledge development and integration are becoming increasingly important. Thus, there is a need to further analyse the interaction between internal and external knowledge and competencies.

Some studies have shown that effective external collaboration requires specific internal competencies. In contrast to traditional appreciations of absorptive capability or capacity (cf. Cohen and Levinthal, 1990), our work demonstrates that KI capabilities are dynamic and evolve over time. The ability to make use of external knowledge may be explained to a great extent by internal mechanisms and capabilities. From a dynamic perspective, there is a need to understand how the development of these internal capabilities may change the capacity to absorb and integrate knowledge from external sources (Wagner and Boutellier, 2002; Lane et al., 2006; Azadegan et al., 2008). Lane and Lubatkin (1998) have introduced the notion of 'relative absorptive capacity' and imply that there needs to be some degree of similarity of knowledge and organizational mechanisms among firms to make their collaboration successful. In their study, they refer to 'knowledge transfers' but, as noted above, KI cannot be reduced to knowledge transfer. Instead, we need to understand what kind of correspondence between knowledge sources and integration mechanisms across firms is essential for successful inter-organizational knowledge integration and creation. Our insights into the interplay between the mechanisms of KI and knowledge itself, both internal and external, are critical for understanding what capabilities firms need to achieve effective inter-organizational KI, and how these capabilities evolve over time.

1.4.6 The limits of knowledge integration

The importance of KI for successful innovation in technology-based firms and its various forms and implications are central to this book. But it is also relevant to discuss the limits and challenges of KI. A key question for firms developing complex products and systems is the costs of designs that are dependent on integrating diverse knowledge sources, compared to other design alternatives. This question is discussed in detail in Chapter 11 on 'creative accumulation', where technology strategies in the automotive industry aiming at architectural innovation are compared to the pros and cons of modular product strategies.

The resources required to achieve KI are also important considerations in relation to structural decisions, such as outsourcing. While mechanisms for KI have attracted increasing interest in recent years, few have analysed the business side of the coin, that is, the costs of KI, especially in cases where integration is needed across organizations. These costs have several implications. They affect the selection of integration mechanisms and, by implication, the effectiveness of the integration effort. They also affect the outcome of strategic choices regarding organizational structures and supply chains that can create new knowledge gaps and needs of KI. The size of the costs for closing knowledge gaps in new value chains is often underestimated, which may mean that the realized benefits of the outsourcing decision fall short of expectations (see further Chapter 9).

In this book, we demonstrate the choices, trade-offs, and alternatives firms face when having to balance the requirements of KI against other competitive pressures. We show that dynamic KI organizational capabilities need to incorporate an in-depth understanding of the benefits and trade-offs of different strategic decisions, for example in relation to outsourcing decisions.

As we show, efficient KI requires sustained investments in specific types of integration capabilities. But akin to innovation processes in general, these types of core capabilities can become core rigidities, which block firms from acquiring and integrating novel types of knowledge. Leonard-Barton (1992) asserts that innovation processes simultaneously require investments in core capabilities and avoidance of core rigidities. Hence, she claims that the core capabilities for mastering the innovation processes of today can easily turn into core rigidities. Previous investments in technology and knowledge create path dependencies that, over time, may turn competitive advantages into disadvantages, when existing capabilities become obsolete. The dual innovation challenge of mastering both learning and unlearning also applies to KI. In this book, we offer examples of how the processes of building KI capabilities may include the abandoning of other capabilities. We also point out some of the key factors that affect this reconfiguration process. But as the centrifugal forces towards differentiation of knowledge bases are so strong in the contemporary global economy, our main focus is on the challenges, forms, and new mechanisms for achieving effective KI where this is a key factor in competitive advantage.

1.5 AN OVERVIEW OF THE BOOK

The book consists of twelve chapters that together provide a systematic multilevel understanding of the process of KI and its prerequisites and outcomes in various

Table 1.1 Outline of the book

Introduction		
Chapter 1	Exploring Knowledge Integration and Innovation	Berggren, Bergek, Bengtsson, Söderlund
Chapter 2	Knowledge Integration and Innovation: A Survey of the Field	Tell
Part I: People and Processes		
Chapter 3	Knowledge Integration and Creation in Projects: Towards a Progressive Epistemology	Lindkvist, Bengtsson, Wahlstedt
Chapter 4	Inventors as Innovators and Knowledge Integrators	Andersson, Berggren
Chapter 5	Participants in the Process of Knowledge Integration	Söderlund, Bredin
Part II: Projects and Partnerships		
Chapter 6	Knowledge Integration Processes in New Product Development: On the Dynamics of Deadlines and Architectures	Magnusson, Lakemond
Chapter 7	Knowledge Integration in Inter-firm R&D Collaboration: How do Firms Manage Problems of Coordination and Cooperation?	Johansson, Axelsson, Enberg, Tell
Chapter 8	Knowledge Integration in a P-form Corporation: Project Epochs in the Evolution of Asea/ABB, 1945–2000	Söderlund, Tell
Part III: Strategies and Outcomes		
Chapter 9	Knowledge Integration Challenges when Outsourcing Manufacturing	Bengtsson, Dabhilkar, von Haartman
Chapter 10	Trade-offs in Make–Buy Decisions: Exploring Operating Realities of Knowledge Integration and Innovation	Dabhilkar, Bengtsson
Chapter 11	Creative Accumulation: Integrating New and Established Technologies in Periods of Discontinuous Change	Bergek, Berggren, Magnusson
Conclusion		
Chapter 12	Lessons and Insights for Managers	Hobday, Bergek

contexts (see Table 1.1). Chapter 2 in this introductory part provides an overview and analysis of existing literature on KI. It critically assesses previous contributions to the field, identifying strengths, weaknesses, and research needs. This is followed by three parts which investigate core areas where there are critical gaps in current understanding of KI and a need for further empirical and conceptual research:

1. Part I addresses the very core of KI by analysing how *people and processes* organize to meet KI needs and challenges.

2. Part II reveals how KI challenges are managed in *projects and partnership* efforts, the principal organizational forms of KI efforts.

3. Part III examines *strategies and outcomes* where different approaches to KI play a crucial role in corporate strategies and prospects for delivering new products, systems, and services, as well as building capabilities for the future.

Finally, Chapter 12 identifies implications and lessons learnt for managers and practitioners arising from our findings.

Part I consists of three chapters. The aim is to provide a far better grasp of the corresponding and complementary roles of individuals and groups in knowledge creation and integration processes. It also demonstrates the conceptual value of an evolutionary, dynamic perspective on KI. This part starts with Chapter 3 by Lindkvist, Bengtsson, and Wahlstedt which shows how knowledge integration and knowledge creation are closely entwined, with knowledge integration leading to creation and vice versa. The authors examine the Nonaka knowledge creation theory, where knowledge creation mainly features as a matter of individual tacit knowing and articulation. To complement and broaden this individual perspective, they turn to evolutionary epistemology, to account for collaborative interaction and knowledge growth in a project context, and use excerpts from product development projects in the telecom and pharmaceutical industries to illustrate the framework empirically.

In Chapter 4 on inventors as innovators and integrators, Andersson and Berggren add further insights into the significance of collaborative individuals for the micro-processes of KI. Building on patent analysis as well as in-depth interviews, the chapter analyses individual innovators in large technology-based firms, a group of people which tends to be neglected in the literature on new product development. The chapter illustrates the practices of these innovative individuals, such as spanning knowledge across different fields, combining individual exploration with collaborative search, and participating in formal projects but using them as permeable entities to further their own innovative ideas. Together, this demonstrates their key integrative role in various innovation efforts, from ideas and patents to testing and realizing new products and processes.

In Chapter 5, Söderlund and Bredin analyse the importance of individuals for KI by focusing on the particular positions and roles of mobile engineers who move between projects in different firms. The chapter explores the strategies of engineers as they make use of and develop new skills as professional participants in complex integration efforts.

Taken together, Chapters 3, 4, and 5 illustrate the importance of individuals and collaborative processes for KI, and the need to adopt an evolutionary perspective on knowledge growth.

Part II addresses a critical gap in the field by analysing the key organizational forms which typically underpin KI. This section moves from people and process issues to how they are organized (a 'bottom-up perspective'), providing new in-depth knowledge of organizational options and managerial challenges, the way KI processes are organized in practice, and the dynamics in different types of project. A central feature in projects is the deadline. This is very much the focus in Chapter 6, where Magnusson and Lakemond explore the management of cross-functional integration and the implications of extendable time limits – two important aspects of KI in projects. The authors start out with a framework of four ideal–typical situations to identify the effects of time limits and product system characteristics; in a longitudinal approach, they show the dynamics of these factors, and how these dynamics influenced the outcomes.

While Magnusson and Lakemond investigate the cross-functional dimensions of KI, Johansson, Axelson, Enberg, and Tell investigate R&D collaboration across firms in Chapter 7. This is particularly relevant in a time when more R&D work is carried out across organizational boundaries, leading to choice and problems associated with such cross-organizational collaborations. An important theme in this chapter is how firms simultaneously tackle the twin challenges of cooperation (e.g. potential expropriation of knowledge by a partner) and coordination (i.e. the challenge of integrating the know-how of different specialists). Johansson et al. examine three cases of R&D collaboration, taking into account differences in governance structures, the tacitness and complexity of R&D knowledge, uncertainty, and knowledge spillovers from one firm to another, showing the need for strategies to treat cooperation and coordination problems together to achieve effective integration processes and outcomes.

In Chapter 8, Söderlund and Tell turn to the firm level to investigate how KI develops over time. The data presented are taken from a historical study of Asea Brown Boveri over a period of fifty years. They identify four major 'project epochs' that represent different configurations of knowledge and argue that one critical factor in the development of this technology-based organization was the capability it developed to shift project epochs and accumulate new relevant skills. The chapter offers a dynamic framework for KI, shows what mechanisms were important, and explains why these integration mechanisms changed over time.

Part III is devoted to the firm level and overall *innovation strategies and outcomes* of KI. The chapters examine KI strategies, dealing with the hard choices firms need to make, as well as the difficulties, the costs of getting it wrong, and the benefits of building up strong KI capabilities. Together, they deal with three critical research needs in this field.

In Chapter 9, Bengtsson, Dabhilkar, and von Haartman evaluate strategies for outsourcing against possible alternatives. The chapter elaborates on three major KI challenges when outsourcing manufacturing. The authors introduce the concept of manufacturing absorptive capacity to inform the understanding of KI challenges when outsourcing. The cross-organizational issues are discussed further in Chapter 10 on trade-offs by Dabhilkar and Bengtsson. The authors show that trade-offs occur in two distinct ways: between different performance objectives and between different make-or-buy decision factors within the same performance objective. This has major implications for management, not yet appreciated in the KI field.

In Chapter 11, Bergek, Berggren, and Magnusson continue on the track of dynamic interpretation and historical analysis. Their study of technology-based firms confronting eras of discontinuity shows that incremental innovation is insufficient and theories of 'creative destruction' are not applicable. A cross-industry comparison of recent shake-outs in the gas turbine industry with the current competition in the automotive industry to develop hybrids and other fuel efficient power trains provides new insights into processes of innovation and knowledge integration when large 'mature' companies enter eras of turbulence and uncertainty. The authors develop the concept of creative accumulation, showing how it is particularly relevant for complex technologies, emphasizing both its creative and cumulative aspects to allow us to understand how firms sustain or lose competitiveness in sometimes dramatic ways.

Finally, in Chapter 12, Hobday and Bergek summarize the major new insights into KI and provide a series of practical lessons for industrial managers and practitioners facing the contemporary challenges of KI.

REFERENCES

Allen, T. and Henn, G. (2006) *The Organization and Architecture of Innovation: Managing the Flow of Technology*, Cambridge, MA: Butterworth-Heinemann.

Ancona, D. and Caldwell, D. (1992) Bridging the Boundary: External Activity and Performance in Organizational Teams, *Administrative Science Quarterly*, 37(4): 634–66.

Azadegan, A., Dooley, K. J. and Carter, P. L. (2008) Supplier Innovativeness and the Role of Interorganizational Learning in Enhancing Manufacturer Capabilities, *Journal of Supply Chain Management*, 44(4): 14–35.

Bengtsson, L., Berggren, C. and Lind, J. (eds.) (2005) *Alternativ Till Outsourcing*, Malmö: Liber.

Bruche, G. (2009) The Emergence of China and India as New Competitors in MNCs' Innovation Networks, *Competition and Change*, 13(3): 269–90.

Brusoni, S., Prencipe, A. and Pavitt, K. (2001) Knowledge Specialization, Organizational Coupling and the Boundaries of the Firm: Why Do Firms Know More Than They Make? *Administrative Science Quarterly*, 46: 597–621.

—— Criscuolo, P. and Genua, A. (2005) The Knowledge Bases of the World's Largest Pharmaceutical Groups: What Do Patent Citations to Non-patent Literature Reveal? *Economics of Innovation and New Technology*, 14(5): 395–415.

Carlile, P. R. and Rebentisch, E. S. (2003) Into the Black Box: The Knowledge Transformation Cycle, *Management Science*, 49(9): 1180–95.

Cohen, W. M. and Levinthal, D. A. (1990) Absorptive Capacity: A New Perspective on Learning and Innovation, *Administrative Science Quarterly*, 35: 128–52.

Davies, A. (2003) Integrated Solutions: The Changing Business of Systems Integration, in: A. Prencipe, A. Davies and M. Hobday (eds.), *The Business of Systems Integration*, New York: Oxford University Press, pp. 333–68.

—— (2004) Moving Base into High-Value Integrated Solutions: A Value Stream Approach, *Industrial and Corporate Change*, 15(5): 727–56.

—— Hobday, M. (2005) *The Business of Projects: Managing Innovation in Complex Products and Systems*, Cambridge: Cambridge University Press.

Dougherty, D. (1992) Interpretive Barriers to Successful Product Innovation in Large Firms, *Organization Science*, 3(2): 179–202.

Doz, Y., Santos, J. and Williamson, P. (2001) *From Global to Metanational: How Companies Win in the Knowledge Economy*, Boston: Harvard Business School Press.

Dutta, S., Narasimhan, O. and Surendra, R. (2005) Conceptualizing and Measuring Capabilities: Methodology and Empirical Application, *Strategic Management Journal*, 26(3): 277–85.

Eisenhardt, K. M. (1989) Making Fast Strategic Decisions in High-Velocity Environments, *Academy of Management Journal*, 32(3): 543–76.

Engardio, P., Einhorn, B., Kripalani, M., Reinhardt, A., Nussbaum, B. and Burrows, P. (2005) Outsourcing Innovation, *Business Week*, March 21, 2005, Issue 3925: 84–94.

Fridlund, M. (1999) *Den gemensamma utvecklingen*, PhD thesis, Stockholm: Royal Institute of Technology.

Grandori, A. (2001) Neither Hierarchy nor Identity: Knowledge-Governance Mechanisms and the Theory of the Firm, *Journal of Management and Governance*, 5(3–4): 381–99.

Granstrand, O. (1998) Towards a Theory of the Technology-based Firm, *Research Policy*, 27(5): 465–89.

Grant, R. M. (1996*a*) Toward a Knowledge-based Theory of the Firm, *Strategic Management Journal*, 17(Winter Special Issue): 109–22.

—— (1996*b*) Prospering in Dynamically-Competitive Environments: Organizational Capability as Knowledge Integration, *Organization Science*, 7(4): 375–87.

Hamel, G. and Prahalad, C. K. (1994) *Competing for the Future*, Boston: Harvard Business School Press.

Helfat, C. E. and Peteraf, M. A. (2003) The Dynamic Resource-Based View: Capability Lifecycles, *Strategic Management Journal*, 24: 997–1010.

—— Raubitschek, R. S. (2000) Product Sequencing: Co-Evolution of Knowledge, Capabilities and Products, *Strategic Management Journal*, 21: 961–79.

Henderson, R. and Clark, K. B. (1990) Architectural Innovation: The Reconfiguration of Existing Product Technologies and the Failure of Established Firms, *Administrative Science Quarterly*, 35: 9–30.

—— Cockburn, I. (1994) Measuring Competence? Exploring Firm Effects in Pharmaceutical Research, *Strategic Management Journal*, 15: 63–84.

Hobday, M. (2000) The Project-based Organization: An Ideal Form for Management of Complex Products and Systems? *Research Policy*, 29: 871–93.

Hoopes, D. G. (2001) Why are There Glitches in Product Development? *R&D Management*, 31(4): 381–9.

Iansiti, M. (1997) From Technological Potential to Product Performance: An Empirical Analysis, *Research Policy*, 26(3): 345–65.

Kline, S. J. and Rosenberg, N. (1986) An Overview of Innovation, in: R. Landau and N. Rosenberg (eds.), *The Positive Sum Strategy. Harnessing Technology for Economic Growth*, Washington, DC: National Academy Press.

Kogut, B. (2000) The Network as Knowledge: Generative Rules and the Emergence of Structure, *Strategic Management Journal*, 21(3): 405–25.

Lane, P. J. and Lubatkin, M. (1998) Relative Absorptive Capacity and Interorganizational Learning, *Strategic Management Journal*, 19(5): 461–77.

—— Koka, B. R. and Pathak, S. (2006) The Reification of Absorptive Capacity: A Critical Review and Rejuvenation of the Construct, *Academy of Management Review*, 31(4): 833–63.

Lazonick, W. (2005) The Innovative Firm, in: J. Fagerberg, D. C. Mowery and R. R. Nelson (eds.), *The Oxford Handbook of Innovation*, Oxford: Oxford University Press, pp. 29–55.

Leonard-Barton, D. (1992) Core Capabilities and Core Rigidities: A Paradox in Managing New Product Development, *Strategic Management Journal*, 13: 111–25.

Licht, G. and Nerlinger, E. (1998) New Technology-based Firms in Germany: A Survey of the Recent Evidence, *Research Policy*, 26(9): 1005–22.

Nonaka, I., Toyama, R. and Konno, N. (2000) SECI, Ba and Leadership: A Unified Model of Dynamic Knowledge Creation, *Long Range Planning*, 33: 5–34.

Okhuysen, G. A. and Eisenhardt, K. M. (2002) Integrating Knowledge in Groups: How Formal Interventions Enable Flexibility, *Organization Science*, 13(4): 370–86.

Olausson, D. (2009) *Facing Interface Challenges in Complex Product Development*, PhD thesis, Linköping: Linköping University.

Pavitt, K. (1987) The Objectives of Technology Policy, *Science and Public Policy*, 14(4): 182–8.

—— (1990) What We Know about the Strategic Management of Technology, *California Management Review*, 32(3): 17–26.

—— (1998) Technologies, Products and Organization in the Innovating Firm: What Adam Smith Tells Us and Joseph Schumpeter Doesn't, *Industrial and Corporate Change*, 7(3): 433–52.

—— (2005) Innovation Processes, in: J. Fagerberg, D. C. Mowery and R. R. Nelson (eds.), *The Oxford Handbook of Innovation*, Oxford: Oxford University Press, pp. 86–114.

Polanyi, M. (1966) *The Tacit Dimension*, New York: Anchor Day Books.

Postrel, S. (2002) Islands of Shared Knowledge: Specialization and Mutual Understanding in Problem-Solving Teams, *Organization Science*, 13(3): 303–20.

Prencipe, A. (2003) Corporate Strategy and Systems Integration Capabilities. Managing Networks in Complex Systems Industries, in: A. Prencipe, A. Davies and M. Hobday (eds.), *The Business of Systems Integration*, Oxford: Oxford University Press.

Ropohl, G. (1997) Knowledge Types in Technology, *International Journal of Technology and Design Education*, 7: 65–72.

Spender, J.-C. (1998) Pluralist Epistemology and the Knowledge-based Theory of the Firm, *Organization*, 19(2): 233–56.

Teece, D. (2009) *Dynamic Capabilities and Strategic Management*, Oxford: Oxford University Press.

—— Pisano, G. (1994) The Dynamic Capabilities of Firms: An Introduction, *Industrial and Corporate Change*, 3(3): 537–56.

Tsoukas, H. and Vladimirou, E. (2001) What is Organizational Knowledge? *Journal of Management Studies*, 38(7): 973–93.

Tyre, M. J. and Orlikowski, W. J. (1994) Windows of Opportunity: Temporal Patterns of Technological Adaptation in Organizations, *Organization Science*, 5(1): 98–118.

Van de Ven, A., Polley, D. E., Garud, R. and Venkataraman, S. (1999) *The Innovation Journey*, Oxford: Oxford University Press.

Verona, G. and Ravasi, D. (2003) Unbundling Dynamic Capabilities: An Exploratory Study of Continuous Product Innovation, *Industrial and Corporate Change*, 12(3): 577–606.

von Hippel, E. and Tyre, M. (1996) The Mechanisms of Learning by Doing: Problem Discovery During Process Machine Use, *Technology and Culture*, 37: 312–29.

Wagner, S. M. and Boutellier, R. (2002) Capabilities for Managing a Portfolio of Supplier Relationships, *Business Horizons*, 45(6): 79–88.

Windahl, C. (2006) *Integrated Solutions*, PhD thesis, Linköping: Linköping University.

2

Knowledge Integration and Innovation: A Survey of the Field

Fredrik Tell

This chapter gives an overview of previous contributions on knowledge integration (KI). It surveys definitions and empirical operationalizations of the concept of 'knowledge integration', reviews the main empirical findings related to inputs to and outputs of the KI process and identifies avenues for further studies of KI and innovation.

2.1 INTRODUCTION

The general economic benefits and consequences of the specialization of labour and knowledge were recognized in economic thinking by, for example, Smith (1776) and Babbage (1835), and in sociology by, for example, Tönnies (1887) and Durkheim (1933). The coordination and integration of specialized and distributed knowledge were discussed in economic terms by, for example, Hayek (1945). In more recent literature, it has been argued that knowledge integration is fundamental in explaining the existence of firms (Kogut and Zander, 1992; Grant, 1996a; Grandori, 2001; Nickerson and Zenger, 2004) and that firms which succeed in knowledge integration will outperform competitors financially (Grant, 1996b; Nesta and Saviotti, 2006). Moreover, research suggests that the extent to which firms succeed in integrating distributed knowledge helps to explain differences in product development performance (e.g. Hoopes, 2001; Carlile and Rebentisch, 2003). In this chapter, we review the literature on knowledge integration with the aim of clarifying possible interpretations and definitions of the concept, and discuss the implications for research into knowledge integration and innovation. We investigate both the theoretical core of studies of knowledge integration and their empirical application in terms of operationalizations, measurements, and findings.

The outline of the chapter is as follows. The second section reviews the definitions of knowledge integration in previous literature. Here, definitions from some of the most quoted studies are used to highlight three main interpretations, that is, knowledge integration as (a) knowledge sharing, (b) knowledge relatedness, and (*c*) knowledge combination. The third section provides an overview of empirical studies into knowledge integration, with a focus on summarizing the factors that influence the knowledge integration process and its outcomes. The fourth section identifies some gaps in this literature and also discusses some methodological issues related to the study of knowledge integration, most notably how the concept of knowledge integration has been operationalized in the contributions reviewed. The chapter is wrapped up in the fifth section by a discussion of possible implications for studies on knowledge integration and suggestions for future research.

2.2 THE CONCEPT OF KNOWLEDGE INTEGRATION IN THE LITERATURE

The concept of 'knowledge integration' has been studied in various contexts – both theoretically and empirically – and in different areas of inquiry. In our review, we have found publications ranging the fields of Organization Theory, New Product Development (NPD), Information Systems, Project Management, Human Resource Management, and International Business (see Appendix 2.2 for an overview of these publications). This section aims to trace different definitions of knowledge integration as suggested by the literature in order to identify the concept's distinguishing characteristics.

2.2.1 The research problem: knowledge integration as a consequence of knowledge specialization

The general problem addressed in the literature on knowledge integration is one of division and integration/coordination of knowledge (which may not coincide with division of labour/activities, cf. Pavitt, 1998; Brusoni et al., 2001; Takeishi, 2001; Brusoni and Prencipe, 2006; Parmigiani and Mitchell, 2009; Zirpoli and Camuffo, 2009). Most authors on the subject tend to agree with Steven Postrel's general characterization of the knowledge specialization problem underlying the need for knowledge integration:

> If the traditional problem of the division of labor is to trade off the superior task efficiency of specialization against its inferior coordination properties, the fundamental tension in the division of knowledge is between the superior learning efficiency of specialization and its inferior integration properties. (Postrel, 2002: 306)

Thus, the literature on knowledge integration does not primarily deal with the economic 'problem of cooperation', that is, problems of incentive alignment between economic agents, but focuses on the 'problem of coordination', that is, how differentiated knowledge can be effectively integrated in economic activities (cf. Grant, 1996*a*; Roberts, 2004; see also Chapter 7).

2.2.2 Tracing the heritage of the current literature on knowledge integration

One route to a further investigation of the concept of knowledge integration is to study the main sources of inspiration for the published studies of this concept. Of the forty-six selected publications on knowledge integration identified in our bibliographic study (see Appendix 2.3), we will focus on the most cited papers. The most cited author, who also explicitly uses the concept of knowledge integration, is Robert Grant. Grant (1996*a*) attempts to design a knowledge-based theory of the firm in general, drawing upon the concept of knowledge integration as the core foundation of an analysis of knowledge application and coordination in the firm. In defining knowledge integration, Grant (1996*a*) stresses that 'Given the efficiency gains of specialization, the fundamental task of organizations is to coordinate the efforts of many specialists. [. . .] But *transferring* knowledge is not an efficient approach to *integrating* knowledge. If production requires the integration of many people's specialist knowledge, the key to efficiency is to achieve effective integration while minimizing knowledge transfer through cross learning by organizational members' (pp. 113–14, italics in original). The subsequent argument builds on Thompson's classification (1967) of three types of interdependencies (pooled, sequential, reciprocal), adding Van de Ven et al.'s notion (1976) of team interdependencies, and suggests four knowledge integration mechanisms (rules and directives, sequencing, routines, group problem-solving and decision-making) that are appropriate to solve knowledge integration problems under different degrees of interdependence.

In the analysis presented in Grant (1996*b*: 377), the capabilities of the firm are essentially related to the ability effectively to integrate specialist knowledge: 'Integration of specialist knowledge to perform a discrete productive task is the essence of organizational capability, defined as a firm's ability to perform repeatedly a productive task which relates either directly or indirectly to a firm's capacity for creating value through effecting the transformation of inputs into outputs.' He suggests three relevant characteristics of knowledge integration: (*a*) the efficiency of integration; (*b*) the scope of integration; and (*c*) the flexibility of integration. The efficiency of integration according to this analysis is determined by the level of common knowledge, the frequency and variability of task performance, and structure. The scope of integration is affected by complementarities and substitutability of specialized knowledge and causal ambiguity. Flexibility of integration and renewal of knowledge can take place through extension of capabilities to encompassing new knowledge and/or by reconfiguration of existing types of knowledge.

Another early use of knowledge integration is Okhuysen and Eisenhardt (2002). This is an experimental study of effects of interventions on knowledge integration in groups, where the authors distinguish between knowledge integration and the knowledge integration process: 'In particular, the knowledge integration process involves the actions of group members by which they share their individual knowledge within the group and combine it to create new knowledge. By contrast, knowledge integration is the outcome of this process, consisting of both the shared knowledge of individuals and the combined knowledge that emerges from their interactions' (Okhuysen and Eisenhardt, 2002: 371). They also distinguish between 'knowledge sharing' (i.e. individuals identify and communicate their uniquely held information) and 'knowledge integration' (i.e. several individuals combine their information to create new knowledge) (Okhuysen and Eisenhardt, 2002: 383).

Other studies often referred to in work on knowledge integration are less explicit about the concept itself. Cohen and Levinthal (1990) argue that outside sources of knowledge are often critical to the innovation process and that the ability of a firm to recognize the value of new, external information, assimilate it, and apply it to commercial ends is accordingly critical to its innovative capabilities. They label this ability 'absorptive capacity' and argue that it is a function of the firm's level of prior related knowledge. However, they also argue that knowledge diversity facilitates innovation since it increases the probability that incoming knowledge will relate to what is already known and also increase the organization's capacity to make novel linkages and associations between different pieces of knowledge.

Henderson and Clark (1990) distinguish between architectural and component knowledge, where the former emphasizes 'the ways in which components are integrated and linked together into a coherent whole' (Henderson and Clark, 1990: 11). They argue that as product designs get established, organizational practices and communication channels tend to mirror architectural knowledge, making architectural innovation – that is, changes in linkages between components and the overarching core concept – more cumbersome since knowledge specialization attuned to specific architectures constrains organizational search. Henderson (1994) extends this argument to discuss the integrative capabilities necessary for attaining architectural innovations. In a similar vein, Kogut and Zander (1992) identify a paradox of replication, that is, speed of replication determines growth but at the same time, making knowledge replicable by making it more information-like increases the risk of imitation by competitors. They suggest the notion of combinative capabilities to acknowledge the path-dependent nature of knowledge accumulation and innovation in firms.

Also Nonaka (1994; Nonaka and Takeuchi, 1995) is concerned with the relationship between knowledge integration and innovation. In line with Kogut and Zander (1992), their argument draws upon the distinction between tacit and explicit knowledge, and Nonaka suggests that knowledge is created in the conversion of tacit into explicit knowledge.[1] Continuing on the replication paradox identified by Kogut and Zander (1992) and the distinction between tacit and explicit knowledge, and absorptive capacity, Szulanski (1996) provides an analysis of stickiness in internal knowledge transfer. The general thrust of his argument is that knowledge factors such as absorptive capacity of the recipient, causal ambiguity, and quality of social relationships (rather than motivational factors) create stickiness, that is, barriers to knowledge transfer. Systematizing these and other findings, Teece et al. (1997) extend the analysis of firm capabilities and knowledge integration to introduce the notion of dynamic capabilities. This notion tries to embrace both the path-dependent nature of knowledge accumulation and integration, while at the same time addressing the requisite generation of new

---

[1] This conversion model is denoted SECI (Socialization, Externalization, Combination, Internalization).

knowledge combinations outside established paradigms and trajectories under dynamic market and industry conditions. Accordingly, they define dynamic capabilities as: ' . . . the firm's ability to integrate, build, and reconfigure internal and external competences to address rapidly changing environments' (Teece et al., 1997: 516).

Summarizing the most cited references in the literature on knowledge integration, it is worth noting that only a few of them explicitly use the concept of knowledge integration. Upon closer scrutiny, however, it becomes evident that the majority of them discuss problems of knowledge integration, and that several also acknowledge knowledge integration in their core constructs. In particular, the cited references are concerned with knowledge integration and its relation to innovation. It is recognized that knowledge specialization and path dependence are important cornerstones in capability accumulation, but that the ability to absorb, recombine, and integrate external or in other respects unfamiliar knowledge is crucial for innovation. Such foundations open up for the question of how the literature more specifically concerned with knowledge integration and innovation has chosen to define this concept.

2.2.3 Approaches to knowledge integration

Despite the general claim that knowledge integration is important, there is a striking lack of a general perspective on what the concept actually entails. Appendix 2.5 presents a collection of over thirty definitions of knowledge integration. These definitions share the basic understanding of the problem of knowledge integration as outlined by Postrel (2002) above. Many of them also agree that knowledge integration is part of a goal-directed (rational) process and involves collaboration among economic agents (e.g. individuals, groups, organizations).[2]

However, notwithstanding these similarities, the definitions differ substantially in their characterization of what the process of knowledge integration consists of. We have organized them into three main approaches to knowledge integration:

1. Knowledge integration as *sharing* or *transferring* knowledge.
2. Knowledge integration as *use of similar/related* knowledge.
3. Knowledge integration as the *combination* of *specialized, differentiated*, but *complementary* knowledge.

In the reviewed literature, most authors define knowledge integration according to categories 1 and 3.[3] In the following subsections, the main characteristics of each approach and some criticism pertaining to each approach are discussed.

---

[2] The second feature draws upon Lawrence and Lorsch's definition (1967: 11) of integration: 'the quality of the state of collaboration that exists among departments that are required to achieve unity of effort by the demands of the environment'.

[3] The distinction between a definition and a research approach to knowledge integration is seldom entirely clear-cut; Appendix 2.4 also indicates when researchers have combined different definitional approaches. However, for the subsequent discussion of knowledge characteristics and the relation between knowledge integration and innovation, we have found the three categories quite useful.

Knowledge integration as sharing or transferring knowledge

In his seminal contribution to the concept of knowledge integration, Grant (1996*a*) pointed out that: 'While these mechanisms for knowledge integration are necessitated by the individuals' stocks of specialized knowledge, all depend upon the existence of common knowledge for their operation' (Grant, 1996*a*: 115). This statement has been used as a vantage point for quite a substantial number of studies of knowledge integration that focus on the sharing and transferring of knowledge in order to draw upon, obtain, or sustain such common knowledge. Such definitions include defining knowledge integration as knowledge transfer (e.g. Frost and Zhou, 2005; Marsh and Stock, 2006; Mitchell, 2006), joint construction of shared beliefs (e.g. Huang and Newell, 2003; Newell et al., 2004), the activity of sharing knowledge (e.g. Willem et al., 2008), or all of these (e.g. Yang, 2005). See further Appendix 2.4 (category i).

One argument for this understanding of knowledge integration is that some basic sameness is a structural condition for the occurrence of any sharing and subsequent integration of specialized knowledge. In its most general formulation, this assumption is also shared by those proposing definitions of knowledge integration that emphasize the differentiated nature of specialized knowledge in the knowledge integration process. However, especially if organizational knowledge is conceived as practice (e.g. Brown and Duguid, 1991; Lave and Wenger, 1991; Wenger, 2000), that seems to imply a more profound argument for knowledge integration as sharing and transferring knowledge. As practices are conceived as collective endeavours where organizational members belong to communities that are integrated by knowledge-base similarity (cf. Lindkvist, 2005), integration of knowledge by shared practices and transfer of knowledge can be advocated to be a strong form of integration. Brown and Duguid (1991) even argue that such communities may be conducive for innovation. Such a line of reasoning could be supported by research on innovation which argues that successful innovation requires both depth and breadth in search activities (e.g. Prencipe, 2000; Brusoni et al., 2005; Laursen and Salter, 2006).

Critics of this category of definitions may argue, in line with Grant (1996*a*), that knowledge transfer is hardly an efficient way of integrating knowledge. Another, more trivial objection to this definitional category would be the argument that two individuals having exactly the same knowledge initially cannot share or transfer such knowledge between them, since they already possess it. In such an extreme situation, knowledge integration would thus be an irrelevant option.

Knowledge integration as use of similar/related knowledge

Fundamental to this argument is that also specialization (denoted depth by Brusoni et al., 2005; Brusoni and Cassi, 2009) entails an aspect of knowledge integration because individuals specialized in certain areas (communities) will integrate their knowledge more easily, and by searching 'small worlds' (Stuart and Podolny, 1996; Kodama, 2009) they may be able to probe further into a specialized field of knowledge than a more general search over a range of different specialties of knowledge (i.e. what is called breadth) would achieve. An extension of this argument is that knowledge integration of this 'specialized' kind could be understood and measured by investigating the relatedness between integrated fields of knowledge. In line with this, Nesta and Saviotti (2006) use the 'coherence' of a group or firm's knowledge base as a proxy for the degree of knowledge integration achieved.

While also this perspective in its most general form is easy to grasp and accept (it is easier to integrate related than unrelated knowledge), this approach to knowledge integration can be criticized on a couple of counts. Perhaps the most serious objection is that it conflates integration with specialization. For instance, in suggesting the notion of corporate coherence in explaining the non-random-ness of knowledge in diversified firms, Teece et al. (1994) took pains to point out that coherence (relatedness) meant something different than specialization. While such a relatedness argument is fairly easy to pursue across knowledge domains (knowledge integration breadth), it is more difficult to address know-ledge integration depth as an issue of knowledge relatedness but not of knowledge specialization (the latter being a precondition in almost all definitions of the *ex ante* knowledge integration problem). There is a risk that the argument merely says that the more related (and integrated) a certain knowledge base becomes, the more specialized it will also become. A more promising avenue may be to operationalize vertical knowledge integration with respect to a range between basic/general knowledge and specific/applied knowledge (Criscuolo and Nesta, 2008; Brusoni et al., 2010). A second problem with this approach (at least as pursued this far) is that it does not really account for the process of knowledge integration, but rather infers processes from measured outcomes. It is therefore not surprising that studies, which have attempted to study knowledge integration so conceived, have had difficulties in coming up with conceptual definitions that are aligned with their empirical approach to knowledge integration.

Knowledge integration as the combination of specialized, differentiated, but complementary knowledge

As the problem of knowledge integration is usually conceived as a consequence of the benefits of specialization, it is not surprising to find that many definitions characterize knowledge integration as a process/activity whereby such specialized knowledge is combined (rather than shared or transferred). Several definitions recognize the existing or potential complementarities of knowledge that is integrated (e.g. Lin and Chen, 2006; Enberg, 2007). Although some knowledge-sharing activities may be involved in knowledge integration, definitions in this category recognize the distinctiveness of different actors' (e.g. individuals or organizations) specialized knowledge (e.g. Tiwana and McLean, 2005; Bhandar et al., 2007; Tiwana, 2008). The economic inefficiency of cross-learning is also recognized, calling for knowledge integration mechanisms to minimize such costs (e.g. Becker and Zirpoli, 2003; Enberg et al., 2006; Schmickl and Kieser, 2008).

Two major rationales can be discerned for the argument of knowledge integra-tion as the combination of specialized knowledge. One is the static efficiency argument emphasized by Grant (1996a) and Postrel (2002). Basically, this argu-ment is driven by cost concerns in the application of knowledge, where the ultimate goal is to minimize such costs through the use of effective knowledge integration processes and mechanisms. This approach to the definition of knowledge integration still seems to be predominant in the literature on knowledge integration. The second rationale is more dynamic and also involves the generation of new knowledge. This rationale can be traced back to Schumpeter (1934) and Hayek (1945) in their theories on how knowledge is used, coordinated, and created in capitalistic economic systems through combinations of knowledge. In more modern formulations, it has been argued that recombinant search (Fleming and Sorensen, 2001, 2004) is an important determinant of innovations. Accordingly, the creation of innovations requires agents to exit local search behaviour and instead search 'far away' (Rosenkopf and Nerkar, 2001; Katila and Ahuja, 2002; Rosenkopf and Almeida, 2003). This implies that in more innovative settings, knowledge integration takes place in knowledge collectivities that are integrated despite knowledge-base dissimilarities (Lindkvist, 2005).

Despite the attractiveness and promises of this approach to defining knowledge integration, it does entail some conceptual problems. First, empirical studies seem to indicate that integration of specialized knowledge is far from easy (Dougherty, 1992; Hoopes and Postrel, 1999). Second, and taking the knowledge specialization argument to the extreme, it may even be argued that knowledge integration of completely specialized knowledge is not possible, since the required common knowledge is lacking (as recognized by Grant, 1996a; Postrel, 2002). Third, drawing upon, for example, March's distinction (1991) between exploration and exploitation, it may be argued that the barriers in incentives and cognitive frames between short-term and long-term behaviour constitute an irreconcilable trade-off between exploiting familiar knowledge and exploring unchartered territory.

Defining knowledge integration: Implications for this book

Although all three identified approaches to defining knowledge integration are fraught with some difficulties, the studies of knowledge integration and innovation presented in this book use a coherent set of definitions of knowledge integration. These definitions are in line with the third approach presented here: knowledge integration as combining specialized but complementary knowledge. One important reason for adopting this approach is the understanding of current changes in the global competitive landscape outlined in Chapter 1.

This means that when studying and conceptualizing knowledge integration on the level of people and processes, projects and partnerships, and strategies and outcomes, the fundamental problem of knowledge integration lies in understanding the process involving the combination of specialized knowledge bases (embodied in people and/or groups/organizations). This does not entirely exclude other approaches to knowledge integration (indeed, the review presented suggests certain complementarities among them). However, instead of presenting an eclectic array of studies, there is a focus on how firms deal with an increasing specialization of knowledge in the global economy.

The remainder of this chapter outlines some previous research contributions in order to identify potential research gaps and challenges to which the studies presented in this book can be related.

2.3 EMPIRICAL RESEARCH ON KNOWLEDGE INTEGRATION

Table 2.1 outlines the main characteristics of previous empirical research on knowledge integration, based on whether knowledge integration is the explanans, that is, an independent variable, or the explanandum, that is, a dependent variable.[4] Studies of the former kind have investigated what positively (or

Table 2.1 Overview of some empirical studies of knowledge integration

	Factors influencing knowledge integration	Outcomes of knowledge integration
Project/group level of analysis	Okhuysen and Eisenhardt (2002), Huang and Newell (2003), Scarbrough et al. (2004), Newell et al. (2004), Bhandar et al. (2007), Enberg et al. (2006), Ordanini et al. (2008), Boh et al. (2007), Kleinschmidt et al. (2007), Bresnen et al. (2008), Lillieskiöld and Taxén (2008), Schmickl and Kieser (2008), Bouty and Gomez (2009), Deltour and Sargis Roussel (2009), Mahmoud-Jouini and Charue-Duboc (2009), Panourgias et al. (2009), Kleinsmann et al. (2010)	Iansiti (1995), Tiwana and McLean (2005), Mitchell (2006), Rui et al. (2008), Subramanian and Soh (2008), Gupta (2009), Mengis et al. (2009)
Firm/ organizational level of analysis	de Boer et al. (1999), D'Adderio (2001), Ravasi and Verona (2001), Carlile (2002), Carlile and Rebentisch (2003), Frost and Zhou (2005), Sabherwal and Becerra-Fernandez (2005), Woiceshyn and Daellenbach (2005), Becker and Zirpoli (2003), Marsh and Stock (2006), Subramanian (2006), Andersson (2008), Willem et al. (2008), Magnusson and Berggren (2009), Ruuska et al. (2009)	Lessard & Zaheer (1996), Verona and Ravasi (2003), Yang (2005, 2008), Nesta and Saviotti (2006), Patnayakuni et al. (2007), Criscuolo and Nesta (2008), Singh (2008), Antonacopoulou et al. (2009), Brusoni and Cassi (2009), Söderlund and Tell (2009)
Industry/inter-organizational level of analysis	Takeishi (2001, 2002), Bannert and Tschirky (2004), DiBiaggio (2007), Grunwald and Kieser (2007), Robertson (2007), Acworth (2008), Bengtsson et al. (2008*b*), Bergek et al. (2008), Harryson et al. (2008), Stock and Tatikonda (2008), Sutherland-Olsen (2008), Evans et al. (2009), Martinsuo (2009), Moreira Ottani and Bou Alameda (2009), Zirpoli and Camuffo (2009)	Brusoni et al. (2001), Brusoni and Geuna (2003), Swan and Scarbrough (2005), Lin and Chen (2006), Tsekouras (2006), Bengtsson et al. (2008*a*), Tiwana (2008), Dibiaggio and Nasiriyar (2009), Kodama (2009)

---

[4] 'By the *explanandum*, we understand the sentence describing the phenomenon to be explained (not that phenomenon itself); by the *explanans*, the class of those sentences which are adduced to account for the phenomenon' (Hempel and Oppenheim, 1948: 152).

negatively) influences knowledge integration,[5] whereas the latter have examined the effects on knowledge integration of some other variable. As indicated by the overview of various attempts to operationalize knowledge integration in Appendix 2.5, the measurement of knowledge integration poses particular challenges for empirical research. There is no common operationalization available in the literature, but depending on the focus of the study conducted, knowledge integration has been measured using proxies that for instance identify structures (e.g. teams, agreements), processes (e.g. routines, learning, codification, transformation), patterns of patent classes and citations (e.g. specialization, relatedness), or other outcomes (e.g. shared knowledge, process performance). This observed variation is hardly surprising, since a number of methodologies have been used in the empirical studies reported (e.g. surveys, patent data panels, retrospective case studies, ethnographies, experiments, etc.).

2.3.1 Factors influencing knowledge integration

Studies of what affects knowledge integration range over a multitude of data and research designs, with a slight overrepresentation of the use of qualitative case studies. They also range over all levels of analysis. Table 2.2 classifies factors influencing knowledge integration found in the empirical literature. Although the picture is fragmented, many of the identified variables correspond quite well to previous conceptualizations. The findings are organized around the three groups of characteristics that have been argued to affect knowledge integration: task characteristics, knowledge characteristics, and relational characteristics. In the exposition below, we have also opted to discuss some empirical findings in conjunction with theoretical propositions and conjectures.

Task characteristics

Using notions of complexity suggested in the previous literature, such as decomposability (Simon, 1962), interdependencies (Thompson, 1967), and analysability (Perrow, 1970), one way of framing the problem of knowledge integration is to argue that knowledge integration needs to address the complexity of tasks and artefacts (Grant, 1996a; Grandori, 2001). In general, propositions based on this assertion suggest that more complex tasks need more elaborate (in terms of time-consuming and communication-intensive) knowledge integration mechanisms. Studies investigating the influence of product architecture on knowledge integration (e.g. Zirpoli and Camuffo, 2009) are examples of this approach.

The uncertainty and novelty involved is another influencing variable that has been studied (Takeishi, 2001; Carlile and Rebentisch, 2003; Enberg et al., 2009). This variable often pertains to the radicalness of new knowledge to be developed. In particular, in line with innovation literature in general, many studies focusing on uncertainty and novelty tend to investigate the breadth and depth of

---

[5] We also include studies here which assert that knowledge integration is a mediating or moderating variable but study the effects of knowledge integration on some other variable, as well as studies where knowledge integration is one of several independent variables in the theoretical model used.

Table 2.2 Task, knowledge, and relational characteristics that influence knowledge integration

Task characteristics	Knowledge characteristics	Relational characteristics
• Complexity and decomposability • Uncertainty • Novelty • Frequency • Heterogeneity	• Internal vs. external • Tacit vs. explicit • Shared vs. differentiated • Related vs. unrelated • Complement vs. substitute	• Social capital • Normative social structures • Level of interaction • Collective identity and aspirations • History

knowledge required for knowledge integration under uncertainty conditions (cf. Brusoni et al., 2001; Brusoni and Cassi, 2009). Surveying forty-five supplier–manufacturer product development projects reported by nine supplier firms in the Japanese automotive industry, Takeishi (2001) studies the knowledge requirements of automakers when outsourcing component development. He found that in regular projects, it is important for automakers to have architectural knowledge of product performance (measured as component design quality), whereas when projects involve new technology the relative importance of automakers' component knowledge increases. Using a cross-sectional dataset obtained from a *survey* of ninety-one external technology integration project managers, Stock and Tatikonda (2008) investigate the impact of uncertainty and organizational interaction on knowledge integration. They find support for their hypothesis that external technology integration will be most successful when the level of interaction between the source of the technology and its recipient is appropriately matched, or fitted, to the characteristics of the technology to be integrated.

Uncertainty and complexity may also be related to the frequency and heterogeneity with which tasks are conducted in an organization (cf. Perrow, 1970). For instance, Zollo and Winter (2002) suggest that less frequent and homogeneous tasks call for more articulated and codified knowledge integration processes (cf. also Grant, 1996a). Studying distributed individual knowledge in a product development project, Enberg et al. (2006) suggest that knowledge integration can be characterized by iterations between individual acting and collective interacting. They propose that such iterations economize on cognitive resources in task situations where there is a high degree of frequency, homogeneity, and causal ambiguity.

Knowledge characteristics

The underlying characteristic of the knowledge to be integrated is another source for hypothesizing on which factors influence knowledge integration. Often expressed in dualities, this dimension emphasizes that there may be continuum variables. It can be argued that an organization's boundaries constitute barriers for knowledge integration or that integration mechanisms may differ between and within organizations. Whether the knowledge to be integrated is internal or external to the organization has been investigated by, for example, Woiceshyn and Dallenbach (2005), Mitchell (2006), and Dibiaggio (2007). Becker and Zirpoli (2003) studied the consequences of knowledge dispersion for knowledge integration in the NPD process at FIAT Auto. They show how the Italian car manufacturer, through further decomposition into organizational units (which alleviates the knowledge integration problem in the short run), runs the risk of 'hollowing' out its knowledge integration capabilities in the long run when the firm starts outsourcing decomposed activities.

Grant (1996a), for instance, discusses the underlying tacitness of knowledge as one determinant of the knowledge integration mechanisms that can be used effectively. In general terms, his suggestion is that less explicit knowledge requires more elaborate knowledge integration. Due to the difficulty of operationalizing tacit knowledge, few studies have been able to confirm or refute this hypothesis.

Another influencing variable, emphasized by Grandori (2001) and Lindkvist (2005), is knowledge differentiation, that is, the degree to which the knowledge to be integrated is shared or differentiated. As argued by Grant (1996b), common knowledge is a prerequisite for knowledge integration. In a comparative case study using qualitative data on two projects, one in IT/insurance and the other in biotechnology, Mengis et al. (2009) argue that the development of common ground among specialized practices serves as an important means towards achieving knowledge integration.

On the other hand, Enberg et al. (2006, 2009) and Schmickl and Kieser (2008) find that shared knowledge may be kept to a minimum, maintaining efficient knowledge integration. Knowledge relatedness (Breschi et al., 2003; Tanriverdi and Venkatraman, 2005; Winter and Bryce, 2007) is another factor that has been suggested to influence knowledge integration. The degree of similarity and relatedness required has been studied by, for example, Nesta and Saviotti (2006). Knowledge complementarity is also emphasized in many definitions of knowledge integration (cf. Appendix 2.4). For instance, Postrel (2002) has also suggested that common (integrated) knowledge and distributed knowledge may be substitutes for each other. Few empirical studies have pursued the relationship between complementarity and substitution further using the concept of knowledge integration. However, Dibiaggio and Nasiriyar (2009) study industry architecture and the effects of knowledge integration capabilities on firms' innovative performance in the semiconductor industry. They find that while complementarities among knowledge increase the performance of all firms in the industry, systems-integrating firms in particular invest in interface development, which benefits their innovative position.

Relational characteristics

The third category of influencing factors consists of relational characteristics between agents, such as individuals, groups, or organizations. One conceived determinant is the strength and patterns of interaction. Of course, several empirical studies also use this very factor as the variable for measuring knowledge integration (see Appendix 2.6), which makes it a suspect candidate for circular reasoning. However, since activities and knowledge may be (at least partly) independent (cf. Brusoni and Prencipe, 2006), it is possible to envisage how activities structured in interactions will influence knowledge processes and consequently the integration of knowledge. D'Adderio's study (2001) of integrative routines in a consumer electronics firm is a case in point. In suggesting what determines the boundaries of the firm in a knowledge-based theory of the firm,

Kogut and Zander (1996) argued that identity is a viable candidate. Along these lines, in a study of two firms, Willem et al. (2008) argue that a coherent company-wide social identity facilitated knowledge integration in the more successful case.

Of the relational characteristics, it is probably the notion of social capital that has received most attention as regards the impact on knowledge integration (see e.g. Huang and Newell, 2003; Newell et al., 2004; Frost and Zhou, 2005; Bhandar et al., 2007). In a single case study of an inter-organizational information systems project, Bhandar et al. (2007) found that social capital positively influenced knowledge integration. Also on the project-level of analysis, Huang and Newell (2003) made a comparative case study of four cross-functional projects. Drawing upon Grant's distinction (1996b) between the efficiency, the scope, and the flexibility of knowledge integration, they found that social capital, past integration experience, and embedded practices influenced coordination and the scope of knowledge integration achieved.

As the elusive concept of social capital can be used to denote a resource that manifests itself in norms, trust, and power, there are obvious implications for the partitioning and integration of knowledge. This means that it also embraces other social normative structures (both formal and informal) that have been studied in relation to knowledge integration, such as structural ambiguity. Ravasi and Verona (2001) analysed changes in structural organizational mechanisms at Oticon A/S and their influence on knowledge integration. They found that introducing a more loosely coupled structure involving increased structural ambiguity, defined in terms of multipolarity, fluidity, and interconnectedness, had positive effects on the efficiency, scope, and flexibility of knowledge integration (using the terminology provided by Grant (1996b)). Ordanini et al. (2008) studied two projects at EMI Music aiming at launching new products into the market. They argue that organizing in project-based structures enabled integration of functionally located knowledge through mechanisms of synchronization and the establishment of joint decision-making rules. Using patent data, Frost and Zhou (2005) conducted an empirical analysis of 'reverse' (subsidiary to headquarters) knowledge integration in two sectors – automotive and pharmaceuticals – over a twenty-one-year period and found that R&D co-practice (joint technical activities between units) increased levels of absorptive capacity and social capital among participating units, increasing the likelihood that they will share knowledge in future time periods.

Other relational variables that have been studied include strategic objectives/aspirations and historical accumulation. Based on a study of task partitioning and knowledge integration in two co-development projects (between supplier and manufacturer) in the auto industry, Zirpoli and Camuffo (2009) suggest that firm-specific factors such as technological capabilities, strategic objectives, and history of the firms involved are more important determinants of patterns of partitioning and integration of knowledge than product architecture.

2.3.2 Outcomes of knowledge integration

Table 2.3 distinguishes three different sets of outcomes associated with knowledge integration suggested in the empirical literature. These outcomes are grouped into

Table 2.3 Measured outcomes of knowledge integration in the literature

Efficiency	Effectiveness	Innovation
• R&D productivity	• Effective strategic response	• Team creativity
• Timely project completion	• Stock valuation	• New product performance
• Task completion/solution	• Financial performance	• Innovation
• Industry structure	• Product timeliness	• Dynamic capabilities
	• User satisfaction	
	• Alliance ambidexterity	

the categories: efficiency, effectiveness, and innovation/novelty. Although there are a few case studies investigating the effects of knowledge integration on some other variable, most studies in this field use quantitative data, such as surveys or various panels (e.g. patents). In some studies, hypotheses are posed both on certain variables' effects on knowledge integration, and on the effects of knowledge integration on outcome variables (e.g. Lin and Chen, 2006; Patnayakuni et al., 2007; Tiwana, 2008). In this overview, such studies have been placed in the category of outcomes of knowledge integration.

Categorizing the literature this way emphasizes that measures used in studying the outcomes of knowledge integration do indicate that knowledge integration can be viewed as a means towards different ends.

Efficiency measures indicate that the problem of knowledge integration is conceived in static terms, or as denoted by Grant (1996a, 1996b), as 'knowledge application'. Utilizing effectiveness measures can be viewed as an attempt to capture effects of organizational adaption processes whereby knowledge integrated is conceived as conducive to organizational performance in relation to its environment. Finally, knowledge integration as measured by innovation or novelty suggests that there is an intrinsic relationship between knowledge integration, innovation, and knowledge generation, and that knowledge integration, besides making it possible for firms to adapt to external environments, renders endogenous change attainable.

Knowledge integration contributing to efficiency

One example of studies utilizing efficiency outcomes of knowledge integration is Iansiti (1995), a field study of twenty-seven product development projects and sixty-one problem-solving attempts. Measuring R&D performance in terms of development lead time, R&D productivity, and technical product improvement, the study showed that differences in R&D performance among projects could be explained by skills and routines developed to achieve technology integration. Relating knowledge integration to project performance, several studies have found a positive relationship between knowledge integration and timeliness in project completion (e.g. Mitchell, 2006; Patnayakuni et al., 2007; Rui et al., 2008). Also on the group/project level, Subramanian and Soh (2008) and Gupta (2009) find that knowledge integration enhances the efficiency with which tasks are solved. On the industry level, the contributions in Brusoni et al. (2009) indicate that there are efficiency properties of knowledge integration, where knowledge integration across firm boundaries is a challenge, but that knowledge integration may be a determinant of the degree of industry architecture and vertical integration.

Knowledge integration contributing to effectiveness

The impact of knowledge integration on effectiveness and adaptation has been measured in various ways. Taking into account the financial environment of firms, Nesta and Saviotti (2006) find that knowledge integration positively influences stock valuations of biotechnology firms; they use panel data on patents from eighty-four biotechnology firms during 1989–97 and measure knowledge integration as knowledge relatedness in terms of the coherence among the technological classes where firms patent. Using stock valuation as a dependent variable, they find that knowledge integration positively affects stock valuations of the biotechnology firms in the sample. Further, the impact of knowledge integration on financial performance is studied by Yang (2005).

On the product level, studies have shown that knowledge integration is positively correlated to product timeliness (Yang 2008) and the satisfaction of users (Lin and Chen, 2006; Patnayakuni et al., 2007). Lessard and Zaheer's study (1996) of responses to exchange rate fluctuations suggests that knowledge integration positively affects strategic managerial decision-making and responses to changes in the external environment. They suggest a model of the integration of distributed knowledge for effective strategic responses, where knowledge integration is constituted of three factors: framing of experts, incentives for knowledge integration, and processes of knowledge integration. They used a survey of managers at selected forty-eight Fortune 500 firms to test their model and found that all three factors significantly affected decision-making with regard to responses to foreign-exchange rate exposure. Moreover, using data on forty-two innovation-seeking strategic alliances, Tiwana (2008) argues that there exists a complementary relationship between weak and strong ties in alliances and that this supports alliance ambidexterity (i.e. the ability to both explore and exploit simultaneously) because in conjunction they facilitate knowledge integration at the project level in these alliances.

Knowledge integration contributing to innovation

Relating knowledge integration to the creation of new knowledge, Tiwana and McLean (2005) find that knowledge integration is positively correlated with team creativity. On the product level, several studies indicate that knowledge integration influences product performance (which may be an indication of how innovative a product is) (Iansiti, 1995; Takeishi, 2001; Marsh and Stock, 2006). More generally, measuring the relationship between knowledge integration and innovation, one group of studies utilizing patent citations reveals a positive relationship (e.g. Criscuolo and Nesta, 2008; Singh, 2008; Dibiaggio and Nasiriyar, 2009). Another group assesses the relationship more generally or with regard to specific products (e.g. Tsekouras, 2006; Schmickl and Kieser, 2008; Brusoni and Cassi, 2009). Finally, on the firm level, some studies reveal that knowledge integration positively impacts dynamic capabilities (e.g. D'Adderio, 2001; Verona and Ravasi,

2003; Söderlund and Tell, 2009). Drawing upon survey data from 128 plants of engineering firms that have outsourced manufacturing, Bengtsson et al. (2008*a*) find that supplier involvement and integration is particularly beneficial for innovation-oriented outsourcing. Tsekouras (2006) made a comparative case study of eight firms in the Greek food-processing industry and argues that knowledge integration critically affected the innovative and competitive performance of these firms.

2.4 IMPLICATIONS FOR RESEARCH ON KNOWLEDGE INTEGRATION AND INNOVATION

This chapter has reviewed studies of knowledge integration and innovation. In concluding, we point to a number of opportunities and challenges for future research that may be derived from the overview of the conceptual and empirical literature on knowledge integration and innovation. We also point to specific contributions in this book that seek to improve our understanding of certain identified white spots.

2.4.1 Understanding the context of knowledge integration

The present book constitutes one of the first attempts to systematize the literature on knowledge integration and innovation and to conduct studies of knowledge integration in a wide range of contexts. While it is obviously necessary to test the importance of knowledge integration more generally, the uncertainty regarding the concept that is indicated by this literature review suggests that more exploratory research is needed. There is a lack of integrated work that provides insights into the activities conducted by organizational members in carrying out knowledge integration. This calls for in-depth case studies and inductive analyses of knowledge integration in order to obtain more insight into what underlying processes are at work.

A particular challenge indicated by the literature review concerns the level of analysis that is selected for analysing knowledge integration and innovation. In short, who is conducting knowledge integration? Most studies suggest that both individualistic and collectivistic approaches are possible, and that knowledge integration is part of an organizational and collective effort. Not only can key individuals function as gatekeepers (Allen, 1977; Tushman and Katz, 1980) or knowledge brokers (Hargadon and Sutton, 1997) in organizations, but individuals themselves may also conduct knowledge integration. However, the literature review indicates a shortage of studies on the level of the individual. Such studies could analyse the roles individuals play in organizational and inter-organizational knowledge integration processes and also disentangle possible knowledge integration processes that primarily take place on the individual level. In this book, the individual level in knowledge integration processes is analysed in a couple of contributions.

The literature suggests that knowledge integration also involves collaborative efforts and elements. But this review has also indicated that the processes and dynamics of such collaborations are poorly understood. Too little is still known about activities that are undertaken to integrate knowledge through collaboration among individuals and organizations. One of this book's ambitions is to add evidence of how knowledge integration is pursued in different innovative settings. It therefore presents studies of knowledge integration on a range of levels of analysis in firms. For instance, this means that individuals as knowledge integrators are presented (Chapters 4 and 5). Moreover, as identified in the conceptual and empirical literature on knowledge integration, much knowledge integration and innovation goes on in projects. Hence, the book also includes a number of studies of knowledge integration in group and project settings (e.g. Chapters 3, 6, and 7). However, any integrated work on knowledge integration and innovation needs to take into account the entire organizational context, hence several studies involve knowledge integration and the firm, including the boundaries of the firm (e.g. Chapters 8, 9, and 11).

2.4.2 The creative side of knowledge integration and innovation

As indicated above, one conclusion from the review of the literature is that there is a shortage of studies of knowledge integration processes. This contention can be expanded to a more general call for studies explicitly discussing the dynamics involved in knowledge integration and innovation. As recognized in the review, some of the most developed and cited arguments on the importance of knowledge integration (e.g. Grant, 1996a; Grandori, 2001; Postrel, 2002) still rely heavily on steady-state analysis, assessing the efficiency properties of knowledge integration. However, as indicated by the review of empirical studies into the outcomes of knowledge integration, it has been shown that knowledge integration is also related to knowledge creation and innovation.

Conceptually, this indicates that combination and recombination constitute an important facet of knowledge integration processes that lead to the 'new combinations' alluded to by Schumpeter (1934) in his analysis of innovation and economic change. Besides paying more attention to knowledge integration as 'knowledge application' (Grant, 1996a), research needs to extend the analysis of knowledge integration to include knowledge combination (Kogut and Zander, 1992) and recombination (Fleming and Sorensen, 2001, 2004), in particular over time.

This book paves the way in this direction by providing analyses of the relationship between knowledge integration and generation in a manner that goes beyond mere problem-solving. For instance, Chapter 3 explicitly discusses knowledge generation in project groups. The analysis provided in Chapter 7 on three collaborative R&D projects also acknowledges the role of technological novelty and knowledge generation as influencing the choice of governance structure and integration mechanisms. Moreover, Chapter 8 presents an analysis of the dynamic and generative capabilities associated with knowledge integration in project-based organizations. Furthermore, the cumulative processes of knowledge integration and innovation are penetrated in depth in Chapter 11, which concerns innovation in mature industries.

2.4.3 Managing knowledge integration in project-based settings

Both the contributions in this book and in the literature reviewed have been particularly concerned with knowledge integration in competitive firms. The notion of knowledge integration is perceived as useful for understanding and promoting the effective and successful management of firms. The organization of the current review into variables that influence knowledge integration and its outcomes also indicates the need to identify variables that are manageable. As indicated above, a primary setting for the present work has been project-based organizations.

One avenue for future research implied by the literature review is to further investigate the relationship between the organizational design of activities and knowledge integration (see e.g. Brusoni and Prencipe, 2006). While both mechanisms (Grant, 1996a) and governance structures (Grandori, 2001) conducive to knowledge integration under certain conditions have been identified in the conceptual literature, we still lack a systematic framework of knowledge integration mechanisms that can be studied and used in a broader range of industries. The review of the empirical literature also suggests that while the relationship between organizational design and knowledge integration is acknowledged (e.g. Ravasi and Verona, 2001), each study of such relationships has developed rather idiosyncratic terminology and operationalizations.

Many of the studies in this book zoom in on the management of knowledge integration and innovation in project-based settings. Every chapter obviously has managerial implications but many of the studies presented also deal with managerial activities aimed at knowledge integration and innovation. For instance, in the first part of the book, Chapter 4 deals with the management of knowledge integration in invention and the relationship between individual inventors and the organization. Chapter 5 discusses how individual consultants act as knowledge integrators in temporary settings and the strategies that are used to cope with this situation. Extending the analysis to the project level, Chapters 6 and 7 add time and conflict of interests to traditional dimensions of the management of knowledge integration in project settings. On the more aggregate level, Chapters 8, 9, 10, and 11 discuss strategic and organizational design issues arising in the management of knowledge integration and innovation.

2.5 CONCLUDING REMARKS

In searching for a foundation of knowledge integration and innovation, this chapter has identified an emerging stream of literature concerned with the challenges involved in knowledge integration and innovation. A number of theoretical and empirical strands of research literature have been identified, suggesting that this field of inquiry is still in its infancy. The lack of dynamic analysis and poor understanding of underlying processes and mechanisms of knowledge integration are two major concerns about the extant literature that need attention in future research. The studies underlying the present book constitute the first systematic attempt to address some of these concerns. Of the various approaches to knowledge integration suggested in the literature, the focus on knowledge integration as a combination of specialized and complementary knowledge has been highlighted. Moreover, rather than focusing on factors influencing knowledge integration or the outcomes of knowledge integration – two of the dominant features of previous research – the present work aims to aid in improving our understanding of the dynamic processes underlying knowledge integration and innovation, which entails going beyond static analysis.

Having said this, some emerging themes are identified that can be useful for building future research. The ambition of this chapter has been to outline some possible foundations for an important and emerging field in the study of innovation management. As the empirical studies that follow this survey show, this is an exciting area, providing opportunities for many important contributions and insights.

ACKNOWLEDGEMENTS

In drafting and developing this chapter, I have benefited tremendously from numerous discussions of early versions within the KITE group, presentations at the EGOS conference in Barcelona, the University of Bologna, Bocconi University, and St. Anna School of Advanced Studies, Pisa, during 2009, and at Imperial College in 2010. The incisive suggestions of the book editors Anna Bergek and Mike Hobday have been instrumental in crafting the emerging structure of the argument. I also want to express my gratitude to Linus Dahlander for invaluable assistance and discussions when I conducted the bibliometric study during my visit to SCANCOR, Stanford University, in the summer of 2009. Financial support from Handelsbanken's research foundations and Riksbanken's Jubileumsfond is greatly appreciated.

Appendix 2.1 Keywords used for narrowed search on knowledge integration

Keyword	No. of articles	
Knowledge integration	30	
Integration of knowledge	9	(+2 overlapping with knowledge integration)
Technology integration	2	
Integration of technology	2	
Integration of learning	1	
Integrative capability	1	(+1 overlapping with knowledge integration)
Knowledge specialization	1	
Learning integration	0	
Skill integration	0	
Integration of skills	0	
Learning specialization	0	
Knowledge innovation and integration	0	
Knowledge creation and integration	0	
Total	46	

Appendix 2.2 Journals where studies of knowledge integration were found

Journal	No. of articles
International Journal of Technology Management	5
Industrial and Corporate Change	4
Organization Science	4
IEEE Transactions on Engineering Management	3
Journal of Management Studies	3
Organization Studies	3
Research Policy	3
Human Relations	2
Journal of Product Innovation Management	2
Strategic Management Journal	2
Technology Analysis & Strategic Management	2
Technovation	2
Journal of Management Information Systems	2
Administrative Science Quarterly	1
British Journal of Management	1
International Journal of Human Resource Management	1
International Journal of Operations Product Management	1
Journal of International Business Studies	1
Management Learning	1
Management Science	1
MIS Quarterly	1
Organization	1
Total	46

Appendix 2.3 Top fourteen cited papers on knowledge integration in the search conducted

Ranking by total citations		Ranking by number of citations per year since publication	
Paper	Total citations	Paper	Citations per year since publication
Grant (1996*b*)	17	Grant (1996*b*)	1.31
Henderson and Clark (1990)	14	Okhuysen and Eisenhardt (2002)	1.29
Cohen and Levinthal (1990)	14	Carlile (2002)	1.00
Kogut and Zander (1992)	14	Harryson et al. (2008)	1.00
Nonaka (1994)	11	Szulanski (1996)	0.85
Szulanski (1996)	11	Teece et al. (1997)	0.83
Teece et al. (1997)	10	Kogut and Zander (1992)	0.82
Nelson and Winter (1982)	9	Henderson and Clark (1990)	0.74
Okhuysen and Eisenhardt (2002)	9	Cohen and Levinthal (1990)	0.74
Nonaka and Takeuchi (1995)	9	Nonaka (1994)	0.73
Dougherty (1992)	9	Zollo and Winter (2002)	0.71
Eisenhardt (1989)	8	Nonaka and Takeuchi (1995)	0.64
Barney (1991)	8	Grant (1996*a*)	0.62
Grant (1996*a*)	8	Hansen (1999)	0.60

One top citation in each list was omitted due to particular circumstances. Eisenhardt (1989) is a methodology paper, indicating that many studies of knowledge integration use a case study methodology, but the article itself does not entail any argument pertaining to the issue of knowledge integration. Harryson et al. (2008) had one citation which made it score very high, whether this is a significant trend or not is impossible to say based on one-year citation analysis. Three publications in each list that did not overlap (Nelson and Winter, 1982; Barney, 1991; Dougherty, 1992 vs. Hansen, 1999; Carlile, 2002; Zollo and Winter, 2002) were all among the top 100 in the other ranking list (most often significantly higher), making the two 'lists' quite comparable.

Appendix 2.4 Definitions of knowledge integration sampled from the literature, in three main categories (and combinations of categories)

Knowledge integration view	Knowledge integration concept	Definition of knowledge integration
(i)	Integrative capability (Mitchell, 2006)	'Access to external knowledge represents an external-to-internal transfer of knowledge, while internal knowledge integration captures an internal-to-internal transfer of knowledge. Amassing and synthesizing specialized knowledge from multiple sources is a pivotal factor in

		resolving the technical and operational uncertainties that impede timely project completion.' (p. 923)
(i)	Intertemporal integration (Marsh and Stock, 2006)	'Intertemporal integration, or the application of knowledge developed in prior projects, contributes to new product development performance because it enables exploitation of existing knowledge to solve the problems encountered in new product development. When an organization draws on prior knowledge, it reduces the costs of search associated with the problem-solving activities of new product development.' (p. 427)
(i)	Knowledge integration (Huang and Newell, 2003)	'For the purpose of clarity, we adopt the definition of knowledge integration as "an ongoing collective process of constructing, articulating and redefining shared beliefs through the social interaction of organizational members"' (p. 167)
(i)	Knowledge integration (Newell et al., 2004)	'[. . .] people need to communicate, assimilate cognitive frameworks and develop shared understandings (Becker 2001). So, the integration of knowledge within the project team does not simply involve the mechanistic pooling of the various "pieces" [. . .]. Rather, the integration of knowledge depends on joint knowledge generation.' (p. 45)
(i)	Knowledge integration (Patnayakuni et al., 2007)	'[. . .] focuses on how organizations integrate and apply dispersed, specialized knowledge to organizational activities through the process of knowledge integration [. . .]. We propose that formal and informal organizational integrative practices influence the extent to which specialized organizational knowledge is integrated in the ISD process through the development and use of boundary objects, and that the application of this integrated knowledge influences the performance of the ISD process.' (p. 287)
(i)	Knowledge integration (Scarbrough et al., 2004)	'[Knowledge integration] can be viewed as the synthesis of specialized knowledge into situation-specific systemic knowledge (Alavi and Tiwana 2002). From a practice-based perspective, knowledge integration within a project involves overcoming barriers to the flow and transfer of knowledge arising from pre-existing divisions of practice among team members.' (p. 1582)
(i)	Knowledge integration (Subramanian, 2006)	'[. . .] effective knowledge integration requires that multisource knowledge not only gets transferred but also applied into design features and, ultimately, embodied into products. (p. 542) [. . .] Enhanced knowledge integration manifests as transnational product development capabilities as it directly influences its core attributes:

(continued)

Appendix 2.4 Continued

Knowledge integration view	Knowledge integration concept	Definition of knowledge integration
		consistency, frequency, simultaneous launches, and market success.' (p. 546)
(i)	Knowledge integration (Willem et al., 2008)	'Knowledge integration includes sharing and transferring knowledge, but also the collective application of knowledge in cooperative activities. This integration exists on different levels in the organization; namely within teams, subunits, units, communities, or the organization.' (p. 371)
(i)	Knowledge integration (Yang, 2005)	'Knowledge integration is defined as creating, transferring, sharing and maintaining information and knowledge. Knowledge integration is the task of identifying how new and prior knowledge interacts while incorporating new information into a knowledge base.' (p. 123)
(i)	Reverse knowledge integration (Frost and Zhou, 2005)	'We define knowledge integration as the utilization by one multinational subunit of knowledge originating in another.' (p. 676)
(i)	Knowledge integration (Rui et al., 2008)	'Knowledge integration is the effective creation and use of specific knowledge throughout the firm [. . .]' (p. 100)
(i) and (ii)	Knowledge integration (Criscuolo and Nesta, 2008)	'[. . .] we define knowledge integration as the activity of combining dispersed pieces of knowledge in order to achieve a given productive task.' (p. 4)
(i) and (iii)	Knowledge integration (Subramanian and Soh, 2008)	'Knowledge integration is the fusion and combination of knowledge from sources that are multiple, distributed and heterogeneous. [. . .] if diverse specialised knowledge is a critical input to the production process, the primary role of a firm is to integrate the diverse knowledge possessed by individuals.' (p. 141)
(i) and (iii)	Knowledge transformation cycle (Carlile and Rebentisch, 2003)	'A core challenge of any organization is to create new knowledge (i.e., solutions to problems, new products, etc.) through the integration of knowledge from different sources. The study of knowledge transfer is an important area of prior research that supports this inquiry because the movement of knowledge from one location to another is central to integration activities. [. . .] In circumstances of strong specialization individuals who do not share enough background or common methods may have difficulty setting conflicts that arise across knowledge domains. Organizations or individuals who seek knowledge integration, therefore, face both the challenge of learning about what is new and the challenge of

		changing their current knowledge to accommodate the creation of solutions across specialized domains.' (pp. 1181–2)
(ii)	Knowledge integration depth (Brusoni et al., 2005)	'Specialization as breadth and knowledge integration (integrative capability) as depth (following Prencipe, 1997, 2000). This section measures firms' integrative capabilities calculating an indicator of the depth of the capabilities maintained by an organisation in any given discipline. The intuition behind this indicator is that if a corporate group has a positive specialisation in a given scientific field for each typology of research (e.g., it has a positive specialisation both in clinical observation/investigation and in basic research in the field of pharmacology and pharmacy), it has a knowledge base of greater depth in that scientific field compared with the other groups.' (p. 408)
(ii)	Knowledge integration (Nesta and Saviotti, 2006)	'Knowledge integration is understood as the expression of some form of organizational practices, structures, and strategies and fundamentally differs from the knowledge capital approaches by pointing out the non-random character of knowledge accumulation and articulation (Henderson, 1994).' (p. 626)
(ii) and (iii)	Knowledge integration (Brusoni and Cassi, 2009)	'By knowledge integration, we mean exactly this ability of defining the relational architecture of a group. We shall argue that knowledge integration capabilities are necessary to make search less local and more goal-directed.' (p. 11)
(ii) and (iii)	Knowledge integration (Brusoni and Geuna, 2003)	'[. . .] the integration of different types of research plays a crucial role in the process of innovation. [. . .] Engineering disciplines are commonly stressed as being powerful, although often overlooked, enablers of such integration. They provide the problem-solving techniques to handle complex problems by decomposing them into simpler sub-tasks, which can be solved and then integrated back into a consistent whole. [. . .] Consistent with the results of micro-level studies of technical change, we argue that the successful exploitation of such combinations requires the existence of capabilities spanning a range of disciplines that go beyond the traditional boundaries of scientific endeavour.' (pp. 1900–1)
(iii)	Knowledge integration (Becker and Zirpoli, 2003)	'From a management perspective, the central challenge in the organization of the [New Product Development] process is therefore how to integrate and co-ordinate the specialist knowledge and competences of the participants in the [New Product Development] process. (pp. 1035–6) In the case of knowledge, it is not possible to know

(*continued*)

Appendix 2.4 Continued

Knowledge integration view	Knowledge integration concept	Definition of knowledge integration
		about the knowledge that has to be integrated and co-ordinated for its utilization with [*sic!*] having that very knowledge. But in that case there will be no specialization advantages realized through the coordination of specialists, due to the duplication of the specialist knowledge in question.' (p. 1039)
(iii)	Knowledge integration (Bhandar et al., 2007)	'This study furthers the process perspective and conceptualizes knowledge integration as the process of combining, applying, and assimilating disparate specialized knowledge.' (p. 264)
(iii)	Knowledge integration (de Boer et al., 1999)	'For reasons of analytical simplicity, the multilevel integration process is reduced to two levels. At the bottom of the knowledge hierarchy lie three types of component knowledge, namely knowledge related to products (or services), production processes and markets. At the top lies architectural knowledge. In line with Grant (1996b), the knowledge integration process is characterized using three dimensions. These three dimensions are efficiency, scope and flexibility. Efficiency of knowledge integration refers to the way in which the architectural knowledge accesses and utilizes component knowledge. Scope of knowledge integration refers to the breadth of component knowledge the architectural knowledge draws upon. Flexibility of knowledge integration, finally, refers to the extent to which the architectural knowledge can access additional component knowledge and integrate existing component knowledge.' (pp. 381–2)
(iii)	Knowledge integration (Enberg et al., 2006)	'From the perspective of the knowledge-based theory of the firm, the main problem lies in assuring the most effective integration of individuals' specialized knowledge at the lowest attainable cost.' (p. 145)
(iii)	Knowledge integration (Enberg, 2007)	'define[s] knowledge integration as the processes of goal-oriented interrelating with the purpose of benefiting from knowledge complementarities existing between individuals with differentiated knowledge bases.' (p. 8)
(iii)	Knowledge integration (Grant, 1996a)	'Given the efficiency gains of specialization, the fundamental task of organizations is to coordinate the efforts of many specialists. [. . .] But transferring knowledge is not an efficient approach to integrating knowledge. If production requires the integration of many people's specialist knowledge, the key to efficiency is to

		achieve effective integration while minimizing knowledge transfer through cross learning by organizational members.' (pp. 113–14)
(iii)	Knowledge integration (Lin and Chen, 2006)	'We thus can define "knowledge integration" as the integration of complementary assets and knowledge across organizational boundaries for developing market-oriented new products and services through an information-sharing and communication process.' (p. 159)
(iii)	Knowledge integration (Okhuysen and Eisenhardt, 2002)	'In particular, the knowledge integration process involves the actions of group members by which they share their individual knowledge within the group and combine it to create new knowledge. By contrast, knowledge integration is the outcome of this process, consisting of both the shared knowledge of individuals and the combined knowledge that emerges from their interactions. (p. 371) [. . .] Differentiate between "knowledge sharing" (i.e., individuals identify and communicate their uniquely held information) and "knowledge integration" (i.e., several individuals combine their information to create new knowledge).' (p. 383)
(iii)	Knowledge integration (Tiwana, 2008)	'[. . .] we define knowledge integration as the process of jointly applying specialized knowledge held by various alliance partners at the project level. In this perspective, knowledge integration creates value through the application of alliance partners' specialized knowledge to project specific activities.' (p. 255)
(iii)	Knowledge integration (Verona and Ravasi, 2003)	'Knowledge integration refers to the capacity to shape and manage a context that stimulates latent and dispersed knowledge resources, so that they can jointly contribute to developing and launching new products.' (p. 579)
(iii)	Knowledge integration (Yang, 2008)	'[. . .] this study defines knowledge integration as a reflection of a firm's capability of integrating different individual knowledge into a new configuration.' (p. 232)
(iii)	Knowledge transfer reduction (Schmickl and Kieser, 2008)	'Two approaches provide insight into how [technically demanding innovations] is achieved: the dominating cross-learning approach assumes that the specialists of different knowledge domains have to intensively learn from each other in order to be able to jointly develop the new product. This cross-learning implies that groups of specialists transfer their specific knowledge, which encompasses different concepts (theories), methods and world views, among each other. However, some researchers argue that intensive cross-learning between specialists is a considerable expense in time and effort and, therefore, inefficient. They insist that integration of specialists' knowledge is

(continued)

Appendix 2.4 Continued

Knowledge integration view	Knowledge integration concept	Definition of knowledge integration
		achieved through structural mechanisms that significantly reduce the need for cross-learning. This article is based on one of the latter approaches.' (p. 473)
(iii)	Knowledge translation (Carlile, 2002)	'I start with the premise that knowledge in organizations is problematic; specifically, in new product development, knowledge is both a source of and a barrier to innovation. The characteristics of knowledge that drive innovative problem solving within a function actually hinder problem solving and knowledge creation across functions. It is at these "knowledge boundaries" that we find the deep problems that specialized knowledge poses to organizations. The irony is that these knowledge boundaries are not only a critical challenge, but also a perpetual necessity because much of what organizations produce has a foundation in the specialization of different kinds of knowledge.' (p. 442)
(iii)	Technology integration (Iansiti, 1995)	'Technology integration consists of the set of knowledge-building activities through which novel concepts are explored, evaluated and refined to provide the foundation for product development. The process is integrative since managing the relationship between new and old knowledge may require the combination of a variety of sources of information, from fundamental science to the details of the manufacturing environment.' (pp. 521–2)
(iii)	Knowledge integration (Dibiaggio and Nasiriyar, 2009)	'Knowledge integration refers to the capabilities to bring together and combine knowledge elements to perform innovative activities. [. . .] At any stage along the value chain, the production of goods and services relies on a large range of specialized knowledge, widely distributed throughout the organization. However, knowledge elements within a knowledge base are not disseminated randomly. While some elements are highly connected to each other, others are more dispersed and isolated. When the combined use of knowledge elements provides complementary services in order to perform a specific task, their combination generates new value and is productive and useful (Nesta and Saviotti, 2006). The strength of complementarities relies on the level of cross-fertilization and on the synergies of knowledge combinations. The more frequently knowledge combinations provide useful

		solutions, the higher is the level of complementarity between the elements.' (p. 268)
(iii)	Knowledge integration (Ravasi and Verona, 2001)	'Effective knowledge integration depends on the extent to which the organisation accesses and exploits individual knowledge, the breadth of specialised knowledge that the organisation draws upon, and the extent to which the organisation can access additional knowledge and reconfigure existing knowledge (Grant, 1996*a*).' (p. 62)
(iii)	Expertise integration (Tiwana and McLean, 2005)	'Building on Grant's [1996*b*] initial conceptualization and recent team-level extensions of Grant's definition [Alavi and Tiwana, 2002; Okhuysen and Eisenhardt, 2002], we define expertise integration as the coordinated application of individually held specialist expertise in the accomplishment of tasks at the project level.' Expertise is integrated when at least one piece of knowledge from one individual is used together with expertise from another team member to accomplish a project task.' (p. 17)

Appendix 2.5 Operationalizations of knowledge integration found in empirical studies

Knowledge integration variable	Operationalization of knowledge integration (variables: number)
Expertise integration (Tiwana and McLean, 2005)	Synthesis of individually held specialist expertise at the project level (4 items/variables)
Integration of distributed knowledge (Lessard and Zaheer, 1996)	Framing of problems by experts (functional-, service-, time-orientation: 3) Incentives facilitating integration (index of 3 disincentives to cooperate) Processes facilitating integration (7 items on cross-functional work, 4 variables on planning flexibility)
Integrative capability (Mitchell, 2006)	Access to external knowledge (3 items/variables) Internal knowledge integration (7 items/variables)
Intertemporal integration (Marsh and Stock, 2006)	5 items: acquisition of information about technologies developed in prior projects; acquisition of information about marketing developed in prior projects; good at applying information and know-how gained in prior projects to current projects; 2 reverse codings
Knowledge (Takeishi, 2001)	Component-specific knowledge and Architectural knowledge (18 elements)
Knowledge integration (Becker and Zirpoli, 2003)	Specific New Product Development process solutions corresponding to knowledge integration mechanisms
Knowledge integration (Bhandar et al., 2007)	'From all the data collected, key knowledge integration activities were identified and categorized into three chronological phases, following a time-ordered matrix (Miles and Huberman, 1984). The three phases identified

(continued)

Appendix 2.5 Continued

Knowledge integration variable	Operationalization of knowledge integration (variables: number)
	were Negotiations and Planning, Design and Implementation, and Postimplementation . . . (p. 266). 8 knowledge integration activities identified: Business integration (pre-project phase); Achieving buy-in, cost-negotiations, project planning (Negotiations and Planning phase); Requirements gathering, Prototype building and refining (Planning, Design and Implementation phase); System usage and review, Reconfiguration of work practices (Postimplementation phase).'
Knowledge integration (Brusoni and Geuna, 2003)	Relative specialization index (using journal classification system as proxy for specialization)
Knowledge integration (Criscuolo and Nesta, 2008)	Using USPTO data Vertical knowledge integration: dispersion index of a firm's research activities across the spectrum of basic and applied research (VKI measure over four research categories) Horizontal knowledge integration: computing the average relatedness across all technologies held by the firm (WAR)
Knowledge integration (de Boer et al., 1999)	Efficiency, Scope, and Flexibility of Knowledge integration (Grant, 1996*a*)
Knowledge integration (Dibiaggio and Nasiriyar, 2009)	'Knowledge integration refers to the extent to which a firm exploits its knowledge base productively. It demonstrates the firm's capacity to combine different technological knowledge components in order to exploit their complementarities. The intensity of the joint utilization of two components may reflect the strength of the complementarity between them. Knowledge integration can be measured by the average level of complementarity exploited by the firm.' (p. 271) Weighted Average Complementarity (WAR): measuring exploited combinations of technologies (represented by frequency of co-occurrence of classification codes in patents)
Knowledge integration (Huang and Newell, 2003)	Efficiency, scope, and flexibility of knowledge integration (Grant, 1996*a*)
Knowledge integration (Lin and Chen, 2006)	4 items: access to partners' knowledge resources, synergy created by combining knowledge among participating firms, creating capabilities beyond individual firms, and creating new business opportunities exceeding individual firms' expectations
Knowledge integration (Nesta and Saviotti, 2006)	Knowledge integration is measured as the extent to which the technologies used by a firm are related to one another. The measure of knowledge integration (coherence) is computed as the mean degree of knowledge relatedness within the firm. Technology variables are constituted by patent classes.
Knowledge integration (Newell et al., 2004)	'appropriate and be able to use the knowledge from their wider networks' (p. 55).

Knowledge integration (Patnayakuni et al., 2007)	Knowledge transfer (codification across syntactic boundaries); knowledge translation (common meanings across semantic boundaries); knowledge transformation (shared understanding across pragmatic boundaries) (Carlile, 2002)
Knowledge integration (Ravasi and Verona 2001)	Improved performance of the innovation process (p. 45)
Knowledge integration (Rui et al., 2008)	'Based on extensive interviews with academic scholars and executives. The measure of knowledge integration emphasises team establishment for knowledge integration, cooperative agreements between firms and their suppliers, and project-related knowledge integration.' (p. 102)
Knowledge integration (Scarbrough et al., 2004)	Shared practices seen in: intra-project learning; transfer of learning to organization or other projects
Knowledge integration (Subramanian and Soh, 2008)	Efficiency (number of forum messages; number of messages on the mailing list: 2) Flexibility (the number of other projects that are license compatible with the focal project of interest: 1) Scope (software languages and no. of operating systems: 2)
Knowledge integration (Subramanian, 2006)	'The dependent variable, transnational new product development capability, was measured using five indicators on a scale from 1 to 7 developed based on the construct's key attributes outlined in the definition: (1) frequency of new product introductions; (2) simultaneous entry in multiple markets; (3) being both responsive to market requirements and competitive in terms of price; (4) early market entry; and (5) penetration in new overseas markets.' (p. 549)
Knowledge integration (Tiwana, 2008)	3 items: members of this team: (1) competently blend new project-related knowledge with what they already know, (2) span several areas of expertise to develop shared project concepts, (3) synthesize and integrate their individual expertise at the project level.
Knowledge integration (Verona and Ravasi, 2003)	Actors (Loose affiliation of technical experts, eclectic skills of employees), physical resources (New workplace layout, mobile workstations, easily accessible electronic archive), structures and systems (cross-functional teams, competence centres, professional areas, 'multi-job' systems, hiring mechanisms, self-participation in projects), culture (openness to creativity, absence of departmental identification, interaction and dialogue encouraged).
Knowledge integration (Willem et al., 2008)	Example: 'The identification of the employees with this company and its working style led to a high level of informal coordination and discourse through the socialization of shared ways of thinking [. . .]. This identification gave people a common goal, which resulted in very low rivalry and in high levels of trust and cooperation; a situation that is required for a high level of knowledge integration. Clearly, more and strong cooperative behaviour to reach the common organizational goal, the development of organizational knowledge in implicit routines and mental models, are caused by a strong coherent social identity. A high level of knowledge integration was reached, and this occurred

(*continued*)

Appendix 2.5 Continued

Knowledge integration variable	Operationalization of knowledge integration (variables: number)
	seemingly spontaneously, not enhanced by formal systems or incentives. There was knowledge integration through the collective application of knowledge in composing the internet and paper versions of the advertising paper, requiring the integration of marketing, publishing and editorial knowledge. The knowledge that was shared involved, for example, knowledge about customers, knowledge on new human resources (HR) trends, new internet techniques, and editing techniques.' (p. 379)
Knowledge integration (Yang, 2005; 2008)	3 items: existence of knowledge integration teams, existence of buyer–supplier cooperative agreements, integration of knowledge in projects
Knowledge integration mechanisms (Enberg et al., 2006)	Experience accumulation and Articulation/Codification (Zollo and Winter, 2002) as knowledge integration mechanisms.
Knowledge transfer reduction (Schmickl and Kieser, 2008)	Knowledge exchange and transfer. Use of identified knowledge transfer reduction mechanisms (transactive memory, prototyping, modularization).
Knowledge transformation cycle (Carlile and Rebentisch, 2003)	Storage, retrieval, transformation.
Knowledge translation (Carlile, 2002)	'Objects' refer to the collection of artefacts that individuals work with—the numbers, blueprints, faxes, parts, tools, and machines that individuals create, measure, or manipulate. 'Ends' are outcomes that demonstrate success in creating, measuring, or manipulating objects—a signed sales contract, ordering prototype parts, an assembly process certification, or a batch of high-quality parts off the production line. The work itself is an ongoing process of moving an object from its current state to a required end state.' (p. 446)
Knowledge translation (D'Adderio, 2001)	Emergence of translation routines (such as CAD/CAM).
Reverse knowledge integration (Frost and Zhou, 2005)	'We use a citation by a headquarters patent to a prior subsidiary patent as the basis for our measure of reverse knowledge integration.' (p. 679)
Technology adoption (Woiceshyn and Dallenbach, 2005)	External integration: generating options by sampling external information sources and evaluating those options with regard to existing capabilities Internal integration: sharing the external information within the organization and facilitating the implementation of the new technology
Technology integration (Iansiti, 1995)	System focus (index of 14 variables); problem-solving breadth.

APPENDIX 2.6

2.6 Methodological comment

Figure 2.1 illustrates the publication of academic articles (as registered in Thomson ISI Web of Science under the heading Management) over twenty years (1989–2008). The search was done on the concepts of knowledge AND integration (not necessarily in conjunction but when both occurred) in titles, abstracts, and keywords of articles in the ISI Web of Science database. In total, we found 431 articles that fitted this description. These articles were parsed into a database. Figure 2.1 shows the yearly counts of the articles, with a low of a single article in both 1989 and 1990 and a high of sixty-six articles in 2007.

In order to control for the increase of knowledge and integration publications being not just an artefact of an increase of the total number of publications in the database, we also normalized the results with respect to the fraction of knowledge integration publications in relation to the total number of publications in the 'Management' category in the ISI Web of Science database. As shown graphically in Figure 2.1, the results are similar, although with an earlier 'levelling out' after 2005. Notably, 83 per cent of the articles (357) were published during the last decade. Hence, bibliographic evidence seems to suggest that there has been a mounting interest in knowledge and integration in the management research community over the last ten years.

However, scrutinizing these 431 articles showed that only a few of them actually used the concept of knowledge integration. Therefore, the abstracts of each article were read and a new search was done in the database on the narrow concept of 'knowledge integration'.[6] This new search resulted in forty-six articles (see Figure 2.2 for their distribution over the

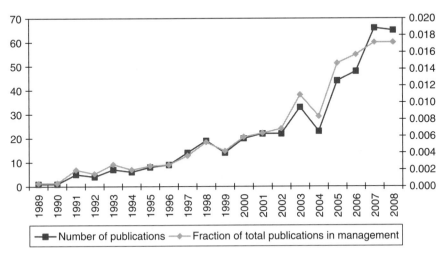

Figure 2.1 Publications in ISI Web of Science 1989–2008, containing the words 'knowledge' and 'integration' anywhere in titles, abstracts, or keywords

---

[6] In order to capture variations in formulations, a number of keywords were used in this search. See Appendix 2.1 for the results.

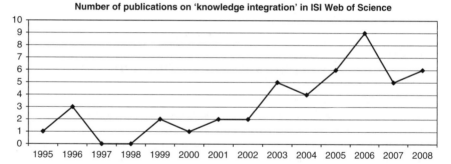

Figure 2.2 Publications in ISI Web of Science between 1989–2008, containing the phrase 'knowledge integration' anywhere in titles, abstracts, or keywords

period). These forty-six articles were printed and read in their entirety and served as a basis for Sections 2.2 (The concept of knowledge integration in the literature) and 2.3 (Empirical research on knowledge integration).[7]

REFERENCES

Acworth, E. B. (2008) University-Industry Engagement: The Formation of the Knowledge Integration Community (KIC) Model at the Cambridge-MIT Institute, *Research Policy*, 37: 1241–54.

Alavi, M. and Tiwana, D. E. (2002) Knowledge Integration in Virtual Teams: The Potential Role of KMS, *Journal of the American Society for Information Science and Technology*, 53(12): 1029–37.

Allen, T. J. (1977) *Managing the Flow of Technology: Technology Transfer and the Dissemination of Technological Information within the R&D Organization*, Cambridge, MA: MIT Press.

Andersson, H. (2008) The Role of Patenting Knowledge in New Product Development Work, Paper presented at the KITE Advanced Workshop, Linköping, 15–16 September 2008.

Antonacopoulou, E., Geary, S. and Konstantinou, E. (2009) *Knowledge Dis-Integration Matters to Organizational Innovation: New Evidence from Knowledge Management Practices*, Paper presented at the EGOS Colloquium, Barcelona.

Babbage, C. (1835/1993) *On the Economy of Machinery and Manufactures*, 4th ed., London: Routledge.

Bannert, V. and Tschirky, H. (2004) Integration Planning for Technology Intensive Acquisitions, *R&D Management*, 34(5): 481–94.

---

[7] Obviously, there are limitations to this methodology. For instance, Grant (1996*a*), a seminal contribution to the theory of knowledge integration, did not show up in the search. Moreover, the ISI database does not contain all relevant journals. In order to remedy these limitations, we conducted a similar search in the Scopus database, searched for articles with similar content in reference lists in the articles read, and read the working papers presented at the KITE Advanced Workshops *Integrating Knowledge: A challenge for R&D Management* in Linköping, 15–16 September 2008, *Knowledge Integration and Innovation* in Linköping, 24–25 May 2010, at the sub-theme 'Knowledge Integration and Innovation' at the *EGOS Colloquium* in Barcelona, 2–4 July 2009, and in the Special Issue on Industry Architecture and Knowledge Integration published in *European Management Review* in 2009 (Brusoni et al., 2009). We also conducted an analysis of the most cited references in our database containing the forty-six articles on knowledge integration.

Barney, J. (1991) Firm Resources and Sustained Competitive Advantage, *Journal of Management*, 17(1): 99–120.

Becker, M. (2001) Managing Dispersed Knowledge: Organizational Problems, Managerial Strategies and their Effectiveness, *Journal of Management Studies*, 38(7): 1037–51.

Becker, M. C. and Zirpoli, F. (2003) Organizing New Product Development: Knowledge Hollowing-out and Knowledge Integration – The FIAT Auto Case, *International Journal of Operations & Production Management*, 23(9): 1033–61.

Bengtsson, L., Dabhilkar, M. and von Haartman, R. (2008*a*) *Exploring the Outcomes of Four Outsourcing and Integration Strategies in Manufacturing Plants*, Paper presented at the KITE Advanced Workshop, Linköping, 15–16 September 2008.

—— Niss, C. and von Haartman, R. (2008*b*) *Being Both Master and Apprentice: Promoting Knowledge Integration in a Distributed Industrialization Process*, Paper presented at the KITE Advanced Workshop, Linköping, 15–16 September 2008.

Bergek, A., Tell, F., Berggren, C. and Watson, J. (2008) Technological Capabilities and Late Shakeouts: Industrial Dynamics in the Advanced Gas Turbine Industry, 1986–2002, *Industrial and Corporate Change*, 17(2): 335–92.

Bhandar, M., Pan, S-H. and Tan, B. C. Y. (2007) Towards Understanding the Roles of Social Capital in Knowledge Integration: A Case Study of a Collaborative Information Systems Project, *Journal of the American Society for Information Science and Technology*, 58(2): 263–74.

de Boer, M., Van Den Bosch, F. A. J. and Volberda, H. (1999) Managing Organizational Knowledge Integration in the Emerging Multimedia Complex, *Journal of Management Studies*, 36(3): 379–98.

Boh, W. F., Ren, Y., Kiesler, S. and Bussjaeger, R. (2007) Expertise and Collaboration in the Geographically Dispersed Organization, *Organization Science*, 18(4): 595–612.

Bouty, I. and Gomez, M-L. (2009) *Creating in Organizations as an Occasion for Integration*, Paper presented at the EGOS Colloquium, Barcelona.

Breschi, S., Lissoni, F. and Malerba, F. (2003) Knowledge-relatedness in Firm Technological Diversification, *Research Policy*, 32: 69–87.

Bresnen, M., Newell, S., Robertson, M. and Swan, J. (2008) *Integrating Knowledge in Biomedical Projects and the Role of Project Organisation*, Paper presented at the KITE Advanced Workshop, Linköping, 15–16 September 2008.

Brown, J. S. and Duguid, P. (1991) Organizational Learning and Communities-of-Practice: Toward a Unified View of Working, Learning, and Innovation, *Organization Science*, 2(1): 40–57.

Brusoni, S. and Cassi, L. (2009) *Re-inventing the Wheel: Knowledge Integration in Fast-Changing Environments*, Working paper, Bocconi University.

—— Geuna, A. (2003) An International Comparison of Sectoral Knowledge Bases: Persistence and Integration in the Pharmaceutical Industry, *Research Policy*, 32(2003): 1897–912.

—— Principe, A. (2006) Making Design Rules: A Multidomain Perspective, *Organization Science*, 17(2): 179–89.

—— Principe, A. and Pavitt, K. (2001) Knowledge Specialization, Organizational Coupling and the Boundaries of the Firm: Why Do Firms Know More than They Make? *Administrative Science Quarterly*, 46: 597–621.

—— Criscuolo, P. and Geuna, A. (2005) The Knowledge Bases of the World's Largest Pharmaceutical Groups: What Do Patent Citations to Non-patent Literature Reveal? *Economics of Innovation and New Technology*, 14(5): 395–415.

—— Principe, A. and Jacobides, M. (2009) Strategic Dynamics in Industry Architectures and the Challenges of Knowledge Integration, *European Management Review*, 6: 209–16.

—— Criscuolo, P. and Nesta, L. (2010) *Knowledge Integration and Innovative Performance in the Pharmaceutical Industry*, Paper submitted to the KITE Advanced Workshop, Linköping, 24–25 May 2010.

Carlile, P. R. (2002) A Pragmatic View of Knowledge and Boundaries: Boundary Objects in New Product Development, *Organization Science*, 13(4): 442–55.

——— Rebentisch, E. S. (2003) Into the Black Box: The Knowledge Transformation Cycle, *Management Science*, 49(9): 1180–95.

Cohen, W. M. and Levinthal, D. A. (1990) Absorptive Capacity: A New Perspective on Learning and Innovation, *Administrative Science Quarterly*, 35: 128–52.

Criscuolo, P. and Nesta, L. (2008) *Horizontal and Vertical Knowledge Integration in Chemical and Pharmaceutical Research*, Paper presented at the 12th International Joseph A. Schumpeter Society Conference, Rio de Janeiro, 2–5 July 2008.

D'Adderio, L. (2001) Crafting the Virtual Prototype: How Firms Integrate Knowledge and Capabilities Across Organisational Boundaries, *Research Policy*, 30: 1409–24.

Deltour, F. and Sargis Roussel, C. (2009) *Understanding Dynamics of Knowledge Integration in Process Innovation Projects: Political Challenges of IT Projects*, Paper presented at the EGOS Colloquium, Barcelona.

Dibiaggio, L. (2007) Design Complexity, Vertical Disintegration and Knowledge Organization in the Semiconductor Industry, *Industrial and Corporate Change*, 16(2): 239–67.

——— Nasiriyar, M. (2009) Knowledge Integration and Vertical Specialization in the Semiconductor Industry, *European Management Review*, 6: 265–76.

Dougherty, D. (1992) Interpretive Barriers to Successful Product Innovation in Large Firms, *Organization Science*, 3(2): 179–202.

Durkheim, E. (1933/1893) *The Division of Labor in Society*, New York: The Free Press.

Eisenhardt, K. (1989) Building Theories from Case Study Research, *Academy of Management Review*, 14(4): 532–50.

Enberg, C. (2007) *Knowledge Integration in Product Development Projects*, PhD thesis, Linköping: Linköping University.

——— Lindkvist, L. and Tell, F. (2006) Exploring the Dynamics of Knowledge Integration: Acting and Interacting in Project Teams, *Management Learning*, 37(2): 143–65.

——— ——— ——— (2009) *Knowledge Integration at the Edge of Technology: On Teamwork and Complexity in New Turbine Development*, Paper presented at the IRNOP IX Conference, Berlin, 11–13 October 2009.

Evans, S., Robertson, M. and Swan, J. (2009) *Challenges for Knowledge Integration within the Clinical Research Process: Networked Innovation within a Regulatory Regime*, Paper presented at the EGOS Colloquium, Barcelona.

Fleming, L. and Sorensen, O. (2001) Technology as a Complex Adaptive System: Evidence from Patent Data, *Research Policy*, 30(2001): 1019–39.

——— ——— (2004) Science as a Map in Technological Search, *Strategic Management Journal*, 25: 909–28.

Frost, T. S. and Zhou, Z. (2005) R&D Co-practice and 'Reverse' Knowledge Integration in Multinational Firms, *Journal of International Business Studies*, 36: 676–87.

Grandori, A. (2001) Neither Hierarchy Nor Identity: Knowledge-Governance Mechanisms and the Theory of the Firm, *Journal of Management and Governance*, 5(3–4): 381–99.

Grant, R. M. (1996a) Toward a Knowledge-Based Theory of the Firm, *Strategic Management Journal*, 17(Winter Special Issue): 109–22.

——— (1996b) Prospering in Dynamically-Competitive Environments: Organizational Capability as Knowledge Integration, *Organization Science*, 7(4): 375–87.

Grunwald, R. and Kieser, A. (2007) Learning to Reduce Inter-organizational Learning: An Analysis of Architectural Product Innovation in Strategic Alliances. *Journal of Product Innovation Management*, 24: 369–91.

Gupta, N. (2009) *Knowledge Distribution in Transactive Memory: Effects on Group Performance*, Paper presented at the EGOS Colloquium, Barcelona.

Hansen, M. T. (1999) The Search-Transfer Problem: The Role of Weak Ties in Sharing Knowledge across Organization Subunits, *Administrative Science Quarterly*, 44(1): 82–111.

Hargadon, A. and Sutton, R. I. (1997) Technology Brokering and Innovation in a Product Development Firm, *Administrative Science Quarterly*, 42(4): 716–49.

Harryson, S. J., Dudkowski, R. and Stern, A. (2008) Transformation Networks in Innovation Alliances – The Development of Volvo C70, *Journal of Management Studies*, 45(4 June): 745–73.

Hayek, F. A. (1945) The Use of Knowledge in Society, *The American Economic Review*, 35(4): 519–30.

Hempel, C. G. and Oppenheim, P. (1948) Studies in the Logic of Explanation, *Philosophy of Science*, XV: 135–75.

Henderson, R. M. (1994) The Evolution of Integrative Capability: Innovation in Cardio-vascular Drug Discovery, *Industrial and Corporate Change*, 3: 607–30.

—— Clark, K. B. (1990) Architectural Innovation: The Reconfiguration of Existing Product Technologies and the Failure of Established Firms, *Administrative Science Quarterly*, 35(1): 9–30.

Hislop, D. (2003) Knowledge Integration Processes and the Appropriation of Innovations, *European Journal of Innovation Management*, 6: 159–72.

Hoopes, D. G. (2001) Why are There Glitches in Product Development? *R&D Management*, 31(4): 381–9.

—— Postrel, S. (1999) Shared Knowledge, 'Glitches', and Product Development Performance, *Strategic Management Journal*, 20(9): 837–65.

Huang, J. and Newell, S. (2003) Knowledge Integration Processes and Dynamics within the Context of Cross-functional Projects, *International Journal of Project Management*, 21: 167–76.

Iansiti, M. (1995) Technology Integration: Managing Technological Evolution in a Complex Environment, *Research Policy*, 24: 521–42.

Katila, R. and Ahuja, G. (2002) Something Old, Something New: A Longitudinal Study of Search Behavior and New Product Introduction, *Academy of Management Journal*, 45(6): 1183–94.

Kenney, J. and Gudergan, S. (2006) Knowledge Integration in Organizations: An Empirical Assessment, *Journal of Knowledge Management*, 10: 43–58.

Kleinschmidt, E. J., de Brentani, U. and Salomo, S. (2007) Performance of Global New Product Development Programs: A Resource-based View, *Journal of Product Innovation Management*, 24: 419–41.

Kleinsmann, M., Buis, J. and Valkenburg, R. (2010) Understanding the Complexity of Knowledge Integration in Collaborative New Product Development Teams: A Case Study, *Journal of Engineering and Technology Management*, 27(1): 20–32.

Kodama, M. (2009) Boundaries Innovation and Knowledge Integration in the Japanese Firm, *Long Range Planning*, 42: 463–94.

Kogut, B. and Zander, U. (1992) Knowledge of the Firm, Combinative Capabilities, and the Replication of Technology, *Organization Science*, 3(3): 383–97.

—— —— (1996) What Firms Do? Coordination, Identity and Learning, *Organization Science*, 7(5): 502–18.

Laursen, K. and Salter, A. (2006) Open for Innovation: The Role of Openness in Explaining Innovation Performance among U.K. Manufacturing Firms, *Strategic Management Journal*, 27(2): 131–50.

Lave, J. and Wenger, E. (1991) *Situated Learning: Legitimate Peripheral Participation*, Cambridge: Cambridge University Press.

Lawrence, P. R. and Lorsch, J. W. (1967) *Organization and Environment: Managing Differentiation and Integration*, Boston: Division of Research Graduate School of Business Administration Harvard University.

Lessard, D. R. and Zaheer, S. (1996) Breaking the Silos: Distributed Knowledge and Strategic Responses to Volatile Exchange Rates, *Strategic Management Journal*, 17(7): 513–53.

Lillieskiöld, J. and Taxén, L. (2008) *Knowledge Integration: Balancing between Anarchy and Despotism*, Paper presented at the KITE Advanced Workshop, Linköping, 15–16 September 2008.

Lin, B-W. and Chen, C-J. (2006) Fostering Product Innovation in Industry Networks: The Mediating Role of Knowledge Integration, *International Journal of Human Resource Management*, 17(1): 155–73.

Lindkvist, L. (2005) Knowledge Communities and Knowledge Collectivities: A Typology of Knowledge Work in Groups, *Journal of Management Studies*, 42(6): 1189–210.

Magnusson, T. and Berggren, C. (2009) Entering an Era of Ferment – Radical vs. Incrementalist Strategies in Automotive Power Train Development, forthcoming in *Technology Analysis and Strategic Management*.

Mahmoud-Jouini S. B. and Charue-Duboc, F. (2009) *Internal and External Knowledge Integration in Concept Generation Process*, Paper presented at the EGOS Colloquium, Barcelona.

March, J. G. (1991) Exploration and Exploitation in Organizational Learning, *Organization Science*, 2(1): 71–87.

Marsh, S. J. and Stock, G. N. (2006) Creating Dynamic Capability: The Role of Intertemporal Integration, Knowledge Retention, and Interpretation, *Journal of Product Innovation Management*, 23: 422–36.

Martinsuo, M. (2009) *External Integration during Radical Innovation Projects*, Paper presented at the EGOS Colloquium, Barcelona.

Mengis, J., Nicolini, D. and Swan, J. (2009) *Working Together in the Space between Expertise and Ignorance*, Paper presented at the EGOS Colloquium, Barcelona.

Miles, M. A. and Huberman, A. M. (1984) *Qualitative Data Analysis A Sourcebook of New Methods*, Newbury Park, CA: Sage.

Mitchell, V. L. (2006) Knowledge Integration and Information Technology Project Performance, *MIS Quarterly*, 30(4): 919–39.

Moreira Ottani, S. and Bou Alameda, E. (2009) *Bridging Old Worlds and Building New Ones: The Challenge of Integrating Knowledge in Networks*, Paper presented at the EGOS Colloquium, Barcelona.

Nelson, R. R. and Winter, S. G. (1982) *An Evoluationary Theory of Economic Change*, Cambridge, MA: The Belknap Press of Harvard University Press.

Nesta, L. and Saviotti, P-P. (2006) Firm Knowledge and Market Value in Biotechnology, *Industrial and Corporate Change*, 15(4): 625–52.

Newell, S., Tansley, C. and Huang, J. (2004) Social Capital and Knowledge Integration in an ERP Project Team: The Importance of Bridging and Bonding, *British Journal of Management*, 15: S43–S57.

Nickerson, J. A. and Zenger, T. R. (2004) A Knowledge-based Theory of the Firm – The Problem-Solving Perspective, *Organization Science*, 15(6): 617–32.

Nonaka, I. (1994) A Dynamic Theory of Organizational Knowledge Creation, *Organization Science*, 5(1): 14–37.

—— Takeuchi, H. (1995) *The Knowledge Creating Company*, New York: Oxford University Press.

Okhuysen, G. A. and Eisenhardt, K. M. (2002) Integrating Knowledge in Groups: How Formal Interventions Enable Flexibility, *Organization Science*, 13(4): 370–86.

Ordanini, A., Rubera, G. and Sala, M. (2008) Integrating Functional Knowledge and Embedding Learning in New Product Launches: How Project Forms Helped EMI Music, *Long Range Planning*, 41: 17–32.

Panourgias, N., Scarbrough, H. and Nandhakumar, J. (2009) *Knowledge Integration and Innovation in Computer Games Design and Development*, Paper presented at the EGOS Colloquium, Barcelona.

Parmigiani, A. E. and Mitchell, W. (2009) Complementarity, Capabilities, and the Boundaries of the Firm: The Impact of Within-Firm and Inter-Firm Expertise on Concurrent Sourcing of Complementary Components, *Strategic Management Journal*, 30: 1065–91.

Patnayakuni, R., Rai, A. and Tiwana, A. (2007) Systems Development Process Improvement: A Knowledge Integration Perspective, *IEEE Transactions on Engineering Management*, 54(2): 286–300.

Pavitt, K. (1998) Technologies, Products and Organization in the Innovating Firm: What Adam Smith Tells Us and Joseph Schumpeter Doesn't, *Industrial and Corporate Change*, 7: 433–52.

Perrow, C. (1970) *Organizational Analysis: A Sociological Review*, London: Tavistock.

Postrel, S. (2002) Islands of Shared Knowledge: Specialization and Mutual Understanding in Problem-Solving Teams, *Organization Science*, 13(3 May–June): 303–20.

Prencipe, A. (2000) Breadth and Depth of Technological Capabilities in CoPS: The Case of the Aircraft Engine Control System, *Research Policy*, 29: 895–911.

Ravasi, D. and Verona, G. (2001) Organising the Process of Knowledge Integration: The Benefits of Structural Ambiguity, *Scandinavian Journal of Management*, 17: 41–66.

Roberts, J. (2004) *The Modern Firm: Organizational Design for Performance and Growth*, Oxford: Oxford University Press.

Robertson, M. (2007) Translating Breakthroughs in Genetics into Biomedical Innovation: The Case of UK Genetic Knowledge Parks, *Technology Analysis & Strategic Management*, 19(2): 189–204.

Rosenkopf, L. and Almeida, P. (2003) Overcoming Local Search Through Alliances and Mobility, *Management Science*, 49(6): 751–66.

—— Nerkar, A. (2001) Beyond Local Search: Boundary Spanning, Exploration and Impact on the Optical Disk Industry, *Strategic Management Journal*, 22: 287–306.

Rui, M., Yang, J., Hutchinson, J. and Wang, J. (2008) Managing Knowledge for New Product Performance in the High Technology Industry, *International Journal of Technology Management*, 41(1&2): 96–108.

Ruuska, I., Lehtonen, P., Martinsuo, M. and Artto, K. (2009) *Knowledge Integration across Intra-organizational Project Boundaries – A Case Study in a Service Development Portfolio*, Paper presented at the EGOS Colloquium, Barcelona.

Sabherwal, R. and Becerra-Fernandez, I. (2005) Integrating Specific Knowledge: Insights from the Kennedy Space Center, *IEEE Transactions on Engineering Management*, 52(3): 301–15.

Scarbrough, H., Swan, J., Laurent, S., Bresnen, M., Edelman, L. and Newell, S. (2004) Project-based Learning and the Role of Learning Boundaries, *Organization Studies*, 25(9): 1579–600.

Schmickl, C. and Kieser, A. (2008) How Much Do Specialists Have to Learn from Each Other when They Jointly Develop Radical Product Innovations? *Research Policy*, 37(3): 473–91.

Schumpeter, J. A. (1934) *The Theory of Economic Development*, Cambridge, MA: Harvard University Press.

Simon, H. (1962) The Architecture of Complexity, *Proceedings of the American Philosophical Society*, 106(6): 467–82.

Singh, J. (2008) Distributed R&D, Cross-regional Knowledge Integration and Quality of Innovative Output, *Research Policy*, 37(1): 77–96.

Smith, A. (1776) *The Wealth of Nations*, London: Dent (1910).

Söderlund, J. and Tell, F. (2009) Exploring the Dynamics of the P-form Organization: Project Epochs in Asea/ABB 1950–2000, *International Journal of Project Management*, 27(2): 101–12.

Stock, G. N. and Tatikonda, M. V. (2008) The Joint Influence of Technology Uncertainty and Interorganizational Interaction on External Technology Integration Success, *Journal of Operations Management*, 26: 65–80.

Stuart, T. and Podolny, J. (1996) Local Search and the Evolution of Technological Capabilities, *Strategic Management Journal*, 17(Special Issue Summer): 21–38.

Subramanian, M. (2006) Integrating Cross-Border Knowledge for Transnational New Product Development, *Journal of Product Innovation Management*, 23: 541–55.

Subramanian, A. M. and Soh, P-H. (2008) Knowledge Integration and Effectiveness of Open Source Software Development Projects, *IIMB Management Review*, June: 139–48.

Sutherland-Olsen, D. (2008) *Does Integrated Knowledge Require Collaborative Learning? The Challenge of Developing Anti-viral Nanomaterials to Combat Bird-flu*, Paper presented at the KITE Advanced Workshop, Linköping, 15–16 September 2008.

Swan, J. and Scarbrough, H. (2005) The Politics of Networked Innovation, *Human Relations*, 58(7): 913–43.

Szulanski, G. (1996) Exploring Internal Stickiness: Impediments to the Transfer of Best Practice within the Firm, *Strategic Management Journal*, 17(Winter Special Issue): 27–43.

Takeishi, A. (2002) Knowledge Partitioning in the Interfirm Division of Labor: The Case of Automotive Product Development, *Organization Science*, 17(3): 321–38.

Tanriverdi, H. and Venkatraman, N. (2005) Knowledge Relatedness and the Performance of Multibusiness Firms, *Strategic Management Journal*, 26: 97–119.

Teece, D., Rumelt, R., Dosi, G. and Winter, S. (1994) Understanding Corporate Coherence: Theory and Evidence, *Journal of Economic Behavior and Organization*, 23: 1–30.

—— Pisano, G. and Shuen, A. (1997) Dynamic Capabilities and Strategic Management, *Strategic Management Journal*, 18(7): 509–33.

Thompson, J. D. (1967) *Organisations in Action*, New York: McGraw-Hill.

Tiwana, A. (2008) Do Bridging Ties Complement Strong Ties? An Empirical Examination of Alliance Ambidexterity, *Strategic Management Journal*, 29: 251–72.

—— McLean, E. R. (2005) Expertise Integration and Creativity in Information Systems Development, *Journal of Management Information Systems*, 22(1): 13–43.

Tönnies, F. (1887/1955) *Community and Association*, London: Routledge & Kegan Paul.

Tsekouras, G. (2006) Gaining Competitive Advantage through Knowledge Integration in a European Industrialising Economy, *International Journal of Technology Management*, 36(1/2/3): 126–47.

Tushman, M. and Katz, R. (1980) External Communication and Project Performance: An Investigation into the Role of Gatekeepers, *Management Science*, 26(11): 1071–108.

Van de Ven, A. H., Delbecq, A. L. and Koenig, R. (1976) Determinants of Coordination Modes within Organizations, *American Sociological Review*, 41: 322–38.

Verona, G. and Ravasi, D. (2003) Unbundling Dynamic Capabilities: An Exploratory Study of Continuous Product Innovation, *Industrial and Corporate Change*, 12(3): 577–606.

Wenger, E. (2000) Communities of Practice and Social Learning Systems, *Organization*, 7(2): 225–46.

Willem, A., Scarbrough, H. and Buelens, M. (2008) Impact of Coherent Versus Multiple Identities on Knowledge Integration, *Journal of Information Systems*, 34(3): 370–86.

Winter, S. G. and Bryce, D. (2007) *Capabilities Overlap and Diversification*, Paper presented at the DRUID Summer Conference, Copenhagen, 18–20 June 2007.

Woiceshyn, J. and Dallenbach, U. (2005) Integrative Capability and Technology Adoption: Evidence from Oil Firms, *Industrial and Corporate Change*, 14(2): 307–42.

Yang, J. (2005) Knowledge Integration and Innovation: Securing New Product Advantage in High Technology Industry, *The Journal of High Technology Management Research*, 16(1): 121–35.

—— (2008) Unravelling the Link between Knowledge Integration and New Product Timeliness, *Technology Analysis and Strategic Management*, 20(2): 231–43.

Zirpoli, F. and Camuffo, A. (2009) Product Architecture, Inter-Firm Vertical Coordination and Knowledge Partitioning in the Auto Industry, *European Management Review*, 6: 250–64.

Zollo, M. and Winter, S. G. (2002) Deliberate Learning and the Evolution of Dynamic Capabilities, *Organization Science*, 13(3): 339–51.

Part II

People and Processes

3

Knowledge Integration and Creation in Projects: Towards a Progressive Epistemology

Lars Lindkvist, Marie Bengtsson, and Linnea Wahlstedt

Product development projects typically involve collaborative knowledge integration and new knowledge creation. This chapter focuses on the progression of such processes and suggests how they may be modelled within a framework grounded in evolutionary epistemology.

3.1 INTRODUCTION

Creative individuals as well as processes of creative interaction are important for advancing development projects. While the creativity of individuals has been researched extensively, the question of how individuals create new knowledge in collective settings has received rather scant attention. Knowledge integration often involves a high level of new knowledge creation. The attempts of specialists in project teams to integrate their knowledge result in the creation of new knowledge, and attempts to integrate this new knowledge result in the creation of more new knowledge. Knowledge creation and integration typically occur simultaneously throughout the early stages of new product and system development projects, as well as during the move from one generation of products or systems to another. In a sense, all the efforts made in knowledge integration settings will generate some new knowledge, whether this is an intended or serendipitous outcome. In a product development context, which involves the use of a combination of diverse knowledge bases in order to achieve a specific goal, we can think of knowledge integration and knowledge creation as two sides of the same coin. When investigating such processes, we can focus on various issues, such as the interface problems encountered as different knowledge bases are integrated, or how new knowledge is generated. In this chapter, and in the context of product development projects, we focus on the latter aspect with a view to understanding new knowledge integration and creation as a 'progressive' process whose outcome may be a successfully concluded project, but also a failed one.

The focus of this chapter is on 'interaction' as a knowledge creation and integration process. In addition, reflecting the distinctiveness of projects as future-oriented and time-limited endeavours, we propose a framework that enables their trajectory to be envisaged as a progressive knowledge process, that is, as a process that over time generates increasingly useful knowledge in relation to the tasks or goals that need to be managed. Thus, instead of focusing on organizational project practices per se, in this chapter we try to identify some of the underlying epistemological features of these practices.

Section 2 reviews recent literature on knowledge creation. Section 3 provides a brief account of why individual knowledge work needs to be complemented by collective or group-level processes of creation and integration. In addressing this, we draw on Nonaka's influential way of modelling knowledge creation, grounded in the epistemology of Polanyi. We discuss Nonaka's and Polanyi's views on the significance of tacit knowledge and articulation processes, and their ways of focusing on the individual as the origin of new knowledge. However, their ideas do not cast much light on the question of how processes of social interaction contribute to knowledge creation; thus, we propose an extension to Nonaka's model.

Section 4 focuses on the 'interaction' component of this model. We discuss our understanding of the knowledge generation process as Janus-faced, that is, as a process that relies on both creative imagination and discipline. We elaborate this idea within an evolutionary epistemology framework, featuring the roles of preselection, variation, and selective retention. We use excerpts from two case studies to support this framework and suggest a set of core epistemological assumptions to support our understanding of knowledge creation–integration processes within projects as progressive.

3.2 KNOWLEDGE CREATION IN PROJECTS: A REVIEW

Product development projects often allow its project members a high degree of freedom to decide how goals should be achieved. The existence of a significant diversity of team members' knowledge and experience in such settings provides fertile soil for creativity and innovation (Scarbrough et al., 2004; Sydow et al., 2004; DeFillippi et al., 2006). Yet, as noticed by Cross and Sproull (2004: 447), 'we know little regarding how actionable knowledge is created through interaction with others' and 'we know little about important features of the relationships within which these interactions occur'. Kurzberg and Amabile (2001: 285) summarize the state of creativity research as heavily focused on the individual, with relatively 'little attention paid to team level creative synergy', and Hargadon and Bechky (2006) advocate the development of interactive approaches to creativity. In a similar vein, Dunbar (1997: 463) concludes that 'little is known about the way in which groups reason'. There appears to be not all that much to build on regarding the growth of knowledge in projects and the epistemological issues involved.

However, a few studies are informative in the more general sense of 'what goes on' in these settings. Cross and Sproull (2004) point out that within short-term projects, problem-solving is directed towards acquiring or creating 'actionable knowledge', that is, knowledge that leads to immediate progress on the current assignment. In their study of consultancy practices in a Big Five accounting firm, they found that the cultivation of different kinds of information relationships allowed for the generation of five types of helpful actionable knowledge, '(1) solutions (both know-what and know-how), (2) referrals (pointers to other people or databases), (3) problem reformulation, (4) validation, and (5) legitimation' (Cross and Sproull, 2004: 446). Similarly, Lindkvist (2004) shows how short-term projects (lasting one to two years) in a research and development unit contributed to an action–orientation among project workers, promoting the image of 'brico- lage', of people using 'whatever resources and repertoire one has to perform whatever task one faces' (Weick, 1993a: 63). In these settings, people are required to react immediately to the actions of others and to emerging contingencies, which favours a swift exchange of intuitions. In order to solve problems, team members approach each other, analyse each other's ideas, extract feedback on their strengths and weaknesses, and generally use others in the co-evolution of new knowledge. Hargadon and Bechky (2006: 484) refer to the sudden emergence of new knowledge as 'the fleeting coincidence of behaviours that triggers *moments* when creative insights emerge'. In their study of project work in three consultancy firms, Hargadon and Bechky identified four sets of interrelating activities that play a role in triggering such moments: help seeking, help giving, reflective reframing, and reinforcing.

Novelty may thus result from helping activity and behavioural coincidence. In a project context, such processes are subject to the simultaneous presence and operation of structuring and disciplining forces. A salient, structuring feature of project processes is the different kinds of tests and assessments that are part of the process. As Gersick (1989) shows, self-organizing groups with a deadline tend to stop around midway through the project to reflect, take in new information, and conduct a means–ends analysis before continuing. These bracketing activities help to 'break the spell, facilitating strategic reorientation' (Gersick, 1995: 145). Simi- larly, Lindkvist et al. (1998) argue that the use of deadlines, milestones, and other kinds of time-based controls tends to produce a 'rationalistic break' that serves to promote more global concerns, and to moderate behaviour that has become overly imaginative. There is a great deal of evidence of adherence to a multitude of 'time-related' mechanisms (deadlines, tollgates, milestones, etc.) and tools (time charts, project models, etc.) in project contexts (see Räisänen and Linde, 2004). Hence, the process of knowledge creation in projects is based on the generation of new ideas within a process that is constrained by predefined structures (goals, norms, rules, procedures, etc.) as well as structures that emerge as the project gets underway.

As this brief review of the literature indicates, many spontaneous and unregu- lated processes occur where the problems encountered are ill-defined. When time is scarce, people tend to turn to one another for help and advice and to get a new angle on their problems. Rather than falling back on codified knowledge, they prefer face-to-face interaction with members of their information network or others suggested by them. While this is informative in terms of how we think about knowledge integration and knowledge creation in projects, it does not tell us much about the progressive nature of project processes or the epistemology associated with such progression.

3.3 MODELLING KNOWLEDGE CREATION

Individuals do have the power to create knowledge. This was forcefully argued already by Polanyi who pointed to our formidable powers of tacit knowing, the 'great and indispensable power by which all knowledge is discovered, and once discovered, is held to be true' (Polanyi, 1966: 6). This power is rooted deeply in the constitution of our mental faculties and skilfully exploited from earliest childhood. Nonaka (1994) builds on this argument in proposing his theory of knowledge creation, and argues that while the role of the individual is to create knowledge, the role of the organization is to articulate and amplify it. A similar appreciation of individual knowing can be seen in Simon's comment (1991: 125) that all learning 'takes place within human individual heads . . .' and Grant's idea (1996: 112) that 'knowledge creation is an individual activity'. Also, the cognitive psychology literature acknowledges that individuals cannot but be creative:

> The human mind is an enormously creative instrument. Our ability to go beyond concrete experiences to produce novel ideas is one of our most salient characteristics. Whether it be a scientist proposing a theory, an author imagining a character, a parent dreaming up an activity to entertain children, or a speaker seeking a figurative way to express a thought, humans are constantly about the business of constructing and modifying new mental representations that are relevant to some goal. (Ward et al., 1997: 1)

However, as observed by Dunbar (1997: 483) in a study of molecular biology laboratories, it is also the case that, left to themselves, individuals do not easily change their interpretations: 'Individuals have great difficulty generating alternative inductions from data and also have great difficulty limiting and expanding inductions'.

Dunbar sees this as indicating a need for 'distributed reasoning' that is able to provide new premises, representations, or models that the individual alone may not be able to generate. Moreover, as discussed by Popper (1972), human beings have strong inclinations to form beliefs in regularities and it is not uncommon for one observation to be sufficient to generate law-like expectations. We want to stick to our 'theories' and are more interested in verifying than falsifying them. Similar human 'weaknesses' in the context of organizations are acknowledged by March (1995: 29): 'They are inclined to see historical events as necessary events, . . . They use extremely simple rules for attributing causality, . . . They tend to conserve beliefs by interpreting ambiguous histories as confirmation of their own prior understandings'.

It is hence important to expose our ideas and conjectures to collective discussion and critical examination in order to promote reflection, sense-making, and learning. Rather than thinking alone, people 'need a little help from their friends'[1] and need to think together and apply their knowledge bases in a concerted effort to reach project goals.

3.3.1 The Nonaka model of knowledge creation

Nonaka et al.[2] are some of the best known and most cited authors in the recent organizational literature addressing the issue of knowledge creation. Their placing of Polanyi's epistemology at the centre led them to suggest the way that tacit knowledge can be made explicit, facilitating communication. They also proposed the novel theory of the knowledge-creating firm. As discussed in Lindkvist and Bengtsson (2009), it is mainly the externalization component in Nonaka and Takeuchi's SECI-model (Socialization, Externalization, Combination, Internalization) (1995), which is often referred to as the 'engine', that is associated with a significant amount of creative power. For Nonaka (1994: 20), 'tacit knowledge held by individuals . . . lie[s] at the heart of the knowledge creating process', something that makes the conversion of personal, tacit knowledge into useful organizational knowledge the main challenge: 'Among the four modes of knowledge conversion, externalization holds the key to knowledge creation, because it creates new, explicit concepts from tacit knowledge' (Nonaka and Takeuchi, 1995: 66).

Like Polanyi, Nonaka (1994) recognizes that much or most of what people know is only tacitly known, and explicitly refers to Polanyi's famous maxim (1966: 4) that 'we can know more than we can tell'. This tacit knowledge is seen as highly personal and hard to formalize (Nonaka et al., 2000: 7), deeply rooted in action and commitment, and involving both body and mind.

Nonaka (1994: 24) also suggests that 'the cross-functional team . . . serves as the basic building block for structuring the organizational knowledge creation process' in firms. Such teams serve as a social context or a 'field' for interaction where individual perspectives can be articulated and turned into higher level concepts: 'In the business organization, the field for interaction is often provided in the form of an autonomous, self-organizing "team" made up of several members coming from a variety of functional departments' (Nonaka, 1994: 23).

This interaction process, Nonaka explains, comprises two steps, a first socialization-like step, where individual tacit knowing is homogenized and shared among team members, and a second step where this knowledge is articulated. Face-to-face communication is proposed as the main channel for bringing about these conceptions. The use of face-to-face communication is justified generally by reference to well-known ideas about the virtues of such close interaction, and a set of rules that encourage a positive dialectic process. Such a dialogic externalization

---

[1] For reasons of scope, in this chapter, we refer to knowledge processes in the narrow sense. The use of the term 'friends' here signifies that all act in good will and engage in 'respectful interaction' (Weick, 1993b). Hence, we leave power, conflict, opportunism, trust, etc., out of the discussion. For the same reasons, we do not explicitly consider the important role of information technology, or other tools and artefacts in such processes.

[2] We use 'Nonaka et al.' to refer generally to the work of Nonaka and his co-authored articles and books.

process is portrayed as involving abductive thinking and the use of metaphors. Also, the outcome is assumed to be in the form of (explicit) metaphors that constitute the 'new knowledge' that is created.

Overall, there is considerable unity in the way that Nonaka et al. and Polanyi think about articulation and externalization. Both tend to see the individual as the primary or sole source of new knowledge. Both also believe the move from tacit to explicit knowledge to be difficult, but do not rule it out that it may sometimes be a possible and worthwhile undertaking. These authors, however, do not say much about the collaborative nature of these processes or the further proliferation of such explicit knowledge. Polanyi acknowledges the importance of conversational processes, but shows little interest in exploring their nature or trying to place them on a par with individual tacit knowing. Nonaka (1994) puts his faith in face-to-face communication and dialogue. These recommendations, however, appear to lack a firm ground in any specific epistemology but rather to mirror what is often suggested in more general organization theory.

3.3.2 An extended model

In our view, taking a complementary point of departure in the notion of 'unfathomable knowledge' as discussed by Bartley (1987, 1990) represents a fruitful way to think of knowledge as less personal. This is based on the idea that once created, knowledge takes on a life of its own. While its generation involves 'knowing subjects', the knowledge produced takes on the character of 'objective knowledge', that is, something that is freed from its creators into an exosomatic artefact. From there on, it loses its relationship with the specific knowing subjects and can embark on a developmental trajectory of its own. Once theories have been proposed, their authors lose control over them.

> Bodies of knowledge, while created and explored by men, do not bend and yield like slaves to those who would create and master them... After their birth, bodies of knowledge remain forever unfathomed and unfathomable. They remain forever pregnant with consequences that are unintended and cannot be anticipated. (Bartley, 1987: 32)

It would be fruitless, therefore, for the authors of theories to try to spell out their ramifications; what happens to them will depend on what others do to them in the future. Some new ideas die in silence, others may provide great inspiration for further theorizing, as exemplified by, for example, Einstein's theories. These events are unforeseeable and unimaginable, beyond the reach of the intentionality of the knowledge producers. Thus, in a sense, we may 'tell more than we can know' as suggested by Lindkvist (2005). While Polanyi's maxim (1966) that 'we can know more than we can tell' motivated Nonaka to focus on how we convert tacit knowledge into explicit knowledge, this complementary maxim points instead to knowledge's own dynamics and proliferation as it circulates among interacting individuals.

In cross-functional projects, where ambiguity prevails, and where deadlines are tight, team members rely heavily on the processes of trial-and-error, spontaneous interaction, and communication (Lindkvist, 2004). As people interact and make their thoughts explicit, they may unknowingly and unintentionally inspire new thoughts in their fellow team members. Hence, a good conversation might be one where 'the meaning is open, being transformed by a recipient into a more interesting message than was anticipated by the sender. Precision destroys conversation; misunderstandings enrich it' (March and Weil, 2005: 59).

If such 'connectivity' is a key to achieving new knowledge collaboratively, it would seem that knowledge which can be 'released' from its creator has its virtues. As phrased by Bartley (1987: 440): 'In their interaction, the various participants can bring to bear their dispersed, specialized, individual, and different knowledge on the unknown and unfathomable object-product, and in this process they may discover more of its potentialities and utilize it accordingly', and Popper (1975: 75): 'the tentative adoption of a new conjecture... invariably opens up many *new* problems, for a new revolutionary theory is exactly like a new and powerful sense organ'.

Relying on the complementary maxim 'we tell more than we can know', we would suggest that *interaction* processes should be recognized as another source of new knowledge. The three processes of tacit knowing, articulation, and interaction presumably occur simultaneously and spiral – upwards or downwards – into a mode of knowing that brings collective work to a successful conclusion. However, it may also simply stop when a deadline has been reached and little has been accomplished.

The models discussed above show that knowledge creation in project practices can originate at the individual level as well as in interactive processes. While these processes tend to be closely intertwined and mutually reinforcing, we focus next on what happens as people interact. Our interest is in how we may think of these processes as constituting goal-oriented and time-related knowledge creation, that is, as processes that over time generate more and/or better knowledge in relation to the tasks or goals that have to be managed. In doing so, we locate the discussion in evolutionary epistemology, represented primarily by Campbell (1960) and Popper (1972).

3.4 INTERACTIVE KNOWLEDGE CREATION AS A PROGRESSIVE PROCESS

Descriptions of evolutionary processes commonly identify the phases of variation, selection, and retention. This sequence is analogous to the rich and spontaneous variation of biological species that are selected on the basis of how well they manage to adapt to fit their environment. However, if this means variation first and then selection, the analogy does not fully apply to the firm and project context. In order to make room for and incorporate intentionality, Lovas and Ghoshal (2000) talk about 'guided evolution', March (1994) uses 'evolutionary engineering', and Weick (1989) refers to 'artificial' rather than natural selection. In similar vein, Lindkvist and Söderlund (2002) and Lindkvist (2008) suggest that the notion of 'preselection' should be incorporated to account specifically for the goal-oriented nature of project processes.

We develop the idea of three fundamental epistemological elements – preselection, variation, and selective retention – and illustrate them using two case studies taken from the literature.[3] The first one is a project to develop a new mobile telephone system (Mobile), and the second one a preclinical drug development project (Pharma).

The Mobile case features an engineering-based, incremental innovation project, in which the time goal had a rather strong preselecting impact throughout the project. Continuous collaborative creativity was needed to enable a swift response to interface errors, and the choice of best options was made serially in the light of the approaching deadline. In this highly time-critical project, safeguarding the appropriate operation of the preselection and selective-retention elements was the responsibility mainly of the project managers. The Pharma case is an example of a very different, 'science-based' project, involving radical innovation. Here, project goals played a more limited preselecting role. The generation of creative solutions was highly dependent on trial-and-error-based work in the various sub-units and sub-disciplines, combined with regular opportunities to 'think together' in collaborative settings. Here, the selection of 'best' activity options was based much more on the intuitions and gut feelings of experienced project members, while at the same time recognizing that no project can go on forever.

3.4.1 Preselection: problems and 'searchlights'

Seen through an evolutionary lens, humans, like animals, are engaged in a relentless struggle to survive and prosper by trying to solve their problems in a process consisting of trials and the elimination of errors. Popper (1963) sees these processes typically as progressing through the formulation of generalized predictions based on single initial experiences that subsequently can be changed as new experience and observations occur. Rather than waiting for the accumulation of a substantial number of positive 'verifying' observations before acting, we often have to engage in 'guesswork' and act on what we currently know.

In order to embark on an observation, we must establish a point of departure in a chosen problem, task, interest, perspective, or prediction. Popper (1974) describes all knowledge creation processes as presupposing a guiding 'searchlight'. Without a point of view, we can see nothing. In the project context, we can think of the searchlight function as being fulfilled by project plans and goals, which 'enlighten' and 'enact' (Weick, 1989) a specific solution or action space, and 'envision' a preferred position therein. Like a torch, they would cast a selecting light onto a dark and unknowable future, and inform project members about the terrain and their direction. Such a vision, 'held and cherished' (Asch,

---

[3] The telecommunication illustration comes from a comprehensive study of Ericsson, conducted by Lindkvist et al. (1998), based on thirty interviews with division management, functional line managers, and project leaders/members. The pharmaceutical illustration comes from a study of four preclinical development projects in two large international pharmaceutical firms, reported in Vik and Lindkvist (2001), and is based on forty-seven interviews with project leaders/members and research directors.

1952) in common by those involved, may facilitate self-organized collaborative effort (Weick and Roberts, 1993). The existence of an a priori searchlight will set the knowledge creation process in motion and enable the observation of feedback and the assessment of the results achieved in functional units and their combined effects. Such goals or searchlights are basically 'guesses' or predictions about the future that for the moment are held to be true, but may change as people engage in interaction and when disturbances occur (Kreiner, 1995). Hence, in projects with high levels of complexity and uncertainty, project

---

Box 3.1: Mobile

The aim of this project was to develop a new mobile phone system for the Japanese market. During the contract negotiations, the Japanese customers made it clear that they wanted the system, including switches and radio base stations, installed and ready for commercial operation in Tokyo, by a particular date or it would consider another supplier. This was a challenging task because it meant that the system had to be developed in half the time required for the previous development of the GSM standard for the European market. Hence, the project deadline was definitive and the project leaders made it clear that deadlines and milestones would be focused throughout the project. Those involved were carefully selected on the basis of prior experience with this kind of development effort. Team members realized the strategic importance of this project, making project goals a collective commitment.

Although everything that happened in the project had to be aligned to the time goal, there was room for compromises related to the system's technical sophistication and there was much discussion among project team leaders and members about the level of perfection required and feasible within the deadline. Frequent discussions about what would be 'good enough' were thus needed. Hence, while the project goals provided a strong preselecting force, there was much interaction and communication affecting the formation of parts of these goals.

Box 3.2: Pharma

In the Pharma case the ultimate goal was a highly motivating force, but considered far too distant and uncertain to be effective for guiding and structuring the project process. The development of a candidate drug (CD) that can be certified to enter the next phase of clinical trials is a process that typically combines periods of progress with periods of standing still or even retrogression. Moreover, achieving a viable CD is often plainly denied by Mother Nature.

In the absence of a clearly manageable and guiding goal, the direction of the development work was imposed from within the project by the various sub-disciplinary departments involved. The more precise meaning of the general CD goal was formed locally and sequentially through interaction and communication. However, the ultimate goal was always present, and senior research managers visited the project on a regular basis, which served as a reminder that no project can go on indefinitely. While these visits were not seen as very helpful for guiding the knowledge generation process, they affected decisions about what could and could not be investigated within the flexible, and sometimes extendable, but nevertheless approaching, deadline.

members will engage in a continuous 'co-construction' of project goals and plans. At times, however, the initial project goals and plans will have a lasting influence and benefit processes of trial-and-error learning throughout the life-time of the project. Boxes 3.1 and 3.2 illustrate the above in the cases of Mobile and Pharma respectively.

3.4.2 Variation: imagination and 'unfathomable knowledge'

Seen through the evolutionary lens, the generation of new ideas, theories, or conjectures is a creative endeavour that has little relation to the use of a specific method. To quote Popper (1975: 78): 'Scientific discovery is akin to explanatory storytelling, to myth making and poetic imagination'. As noticed by Campbell (1974: 142), 'if one is expanding knowledge beyond what one knows, one has no choice but to explore without the benefit of wisdom (gropingly, blindly, stupidly, haphazardly)'. Thus, these processes are often very much a matter of 'blind' or 'unjustified' variation.

Ensemble improvisation, as discussed by Sawyer (2000), describes the inter-active nature of such processes. In a setting where there is no structured plan or strong leader to guide the performance, there are many paths that a participant can take at each turn and, in the beginning in particular, a vast number of options are available. As the performing act proceeds, some options are closed off, but new ones will open up. These types of interaction imply that members constantly, more or less strongly, influence each other, build on each other's ideas, and help each other out when their own power of imagination weakens. This process of 'collaborative emergence' is described by Sawyer (1999: 448) as 'not additive, not predictable from knowledge of its components, and not decomposable into those components'. Hence, in the context of ensemble improvisation, we cannot identify the creativity of the entire performance through the actions of a single performer. This example illustrates yet again the importance of the social context and the necessity of a little help from one's friends in the collaborative creation of new knowledge. Sawyer (2000: 182) describes it this way: 'Although each member of the group contributes material, a musician's contributions only make sense in terms of the way they are heard, absorbed and elaborated by the other musicians. The performance that results *emerges* from the interactions of the group'.

Variation may thus be increased as people engage in an interactive and com-municative process wherein they help each other imagine new ideas and expand on one another's ideas. 'People need one another . . . to help probe and objectify their ideas and other products – and thereby to discover their potentialities' (Bartley, 1990: 46). The growth of knowledge in such settings would seem to depend critically on the circulation of 'unfathomable knowledge' (Bartley, 1990). Hence, a major concern for project managers must be to secure the availability of suitable meeting points and arenas for interactivity that will set this key dynamic element in motion. See Boxes 3.3 and 3.4.

Box 3.3: Mobile

To complete the task in time, it was necessary to carry out many activities simultaneously, which required frequent interaction and communication among members of different functional units. While many project activities and sub-parts of the product were allocated to separate functional teams, the kinds of problems that would emerge when the pieces were integrated could not be anticipated.

Errors and deviations typically occurred at functional interfaces. Many different means were used to try to identify and resolve these problems, such as a 'systems emergency ward', daily stand-up meetings, and prototyping. In these collective arenas, 'interface' problems were identified and diagnosed. They enabled teams to engage in collective efforts to find new ways of doing things, or to set up ad hoc inter-functional teams to manage the more serious problems. In this fast-moving project, those involved needed to collaborate and be creative and to propose solutions that effectively and rapidly cleared away the intra-functional and inter-functional problems as they emerged in the process.

Box 3.4: Pharma

As would be expected, informal discussions were seen by project managers and team members as valuable for promoting creativity. However, many also pointed to the significance of the regular progress meetings. As one group leader stated, the possibility for sharing ideas and 'thinking together' in intra- as well as interdepartmental settings was a major stimulus to imagination and knowledge creation.

The lion's share of the development work was conducted in highly specialized sub-units and laboratories, for example in pharmacology and chemistry departments, and great efforts were made to interpret the results of trials. Sometimes results and deviations were easy to interpret, basically confirming previous hunches of ideas, while other-times they rather increased ambiguity. In particular when severe setbacks were encountered, and there was great uncertainty as to what to do next, trial-and-error experimentation was a means for searching for clues. Such processes could produce results that were completely unimaginable, but provided 'raw material' vital for new thinking. Hence, deviations from plans were often something deliberately sought after to feed the process of generating novel ideas.

3.4.3 Selective retention: comparison and 'critical enquiry'

Seen through an evolutionary lens, knowledge growth presupposes the elimination of errors and subsequent new trials. Unlike animals, who often have to pay with their lives for errors, humans can communicate their conjectures, and if mistaken, let them die in their stead (Popper, 1999: 12). While the elimination of errors would improve the survival potential of the (animal) race, for humans, choosing among superior and inferior ideas or conjectures implies a communicative process through which still better knowledge is generated. This Popperian view thus reflects a strong belief in the value of 'critical enquiry', that is, in our ability to use our argumentative powers to make choices.

As already pointed out, all new trials will to an extent be 'blind' or 'unjustified'. Popper's view (1975: 84) is that great ideas may well be 'guided by an inspiration of a decidedly aesthetic character, rather than rational thought'. However, this is not to say that the result cannot be considered rationally; we can rationally assess whether a new theory that contradicts the old one produces better results. Acknowledging the possibility of such comparisons is a vital feature of an evolutionary understanding. Considering the difficulty for individuals to assess their own ideas and achievements critically, as discussed initially, such comparisons should be institutionalized as collective undertakings. In such a process of 'progressive discourse' (Bereiter, 1994), the selection of best theory is a matter of 'decision' (Popper, 1972), since we can never know anything for certain. Empirical

---

Box 3.5: **Mobile**

The project was special in that development time was half that for the earlier GSM project. To manage this, a simultaneous engineering approach was adopted, without clear preset exit and entry criteria to regulate exchanges and 'deliveries' between functional sub-projects. As a consequence, it was particularly important to check that the work of these sub-units was contributing to an integrated and well-functioning system. This called for the use of multiple arenas for immediate and frequent interaction to prevent the project from escalating along a faulty course of action.

Furthermore, a variety of test activities (software tests, simulation modelling, prototypes) could be used to assess progress and how best to proceed. These options enabled regular assessment of the overall project, what still remained to be done, how it could be accomplished in the time remaining, and whether more resources should be invested to guarantee quality or speed up the process. Most of these assessments were conducted collaboratively, allowing participants to contribute ideas, make conjectures, and consider pragmatically how to achieve the best technical solution as well as the impact of resource and time constraints.

Box 3.6: **Pharma**

Progress in Pharma projects tends to originate in the achievement of sub-unit departments and be the result of meticulous work on the properties of certain substances particular to each sub-unit. Setbacks can occur suddenly, and late in the process, making it difficult to see if the project is moving in the right direction and how much is left to do. Hence, the unit's selection of best conjectures was very much an internal and far from linear process.

Integrating the 'results' achieved by the different sub-units working autonomously was notoriously difficult. Much of the knowledge integration happened within an emergent process, when the different units met to exchange and align their findings. As often stated, project managers with a strong multidisciplinary competence and long experience could fulfil a significant role as 'knowledge integrators'. Nevertheless, they had to work hard to construct a comprehensive 'picture' of project progress that would impress superior level research managers at biannual evaluations. Moreover, unlike in the Mobile project, managers had little possibility to speed up the process by investing additional resources or suggesting trade-offs between optimal and 'good enough' quality. Achieving acceptance of a new CD is a very demanding process, where only perfection and few or no side effects are tolerated.

observations are important here, but what we might regard as 'fact' is also fundamentally a matter of decision. However, in project settings, there are often 'hard facts' that are too salient to be ignored or theorized away.

This means that at each point in time there is a need to compare prevailing 'best guesses' with novel experiences and conjectures to decide which one is preferable. In a project context, such 'critical enquiry' is mirrored in the frequent use of tests, prototypes, etc., in order to assess (pragmatically) whether new ideas and solutions are aligned with quality standards and production requirements. It can also be found in the common practice of relying on regular assessments in collective settings, such as tollgate and milestone meetings (see Boxes 3.5 and 3.6).

3.4.4 A summary model

Boxes 3.1–3.6 provide a sequential description of the three elements. It should be remembered, however, that these elements operate more or less simultaneously. Hence, preselection, variation, and selective retention are three elements in a single process of knowledge integration and creation; taken together, they provide a set of assumptions for a progressive evolutionary epistemology. The case study examples from two very different product development projects can be seen as a set of features, which taken together illustrate this framework empirically, and underline that the generation of new knowledge in a project context involves imagination embedded in a variety of guiding and structuring forces. The pedagogy of presenting simultaneously operating elements sequentially is far from ideal; however, in order to give the reader a sense of the 'holistic' nature of the framework, we summarize its elements in a simplified model (Figure 3.1).

This model summarizes our exploration of the issue of interactive knowledge creation using projects as our empirical anchor. In a traditional project management terminology, this anchoring means that, in a background manner, we have had a context in mind where practices, such as planning, goal setting, team

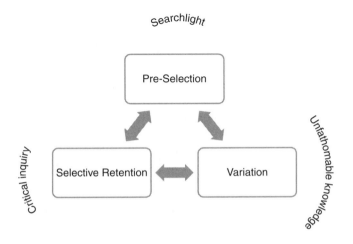

Figure 3.1 Interactive knowledge creation in projects

composition, brainstorming, problem-solving, and milestone assessments, are significant features. In the inner layer of the model are the basic elements of the evolutionary framework, including the complementing of preselection with the traditional elements of variation and selective retention. This addition seems to be particularly fitting in a project context. The outer layer of the model represents our choice of core epistemological assumptions associated with each of the three elements described above.

For preselection, we propose that the *searchlight* idea is the core epistemological assumption. Without some enlightening point of view, the operating terrain cannot be seen, the future preferred position cannot be envisioned, work cannot begin, and feedback information cannot be generated. For variation, we propose that the idea of *unfathomable knowledge* is a core assumption. The view of knowledge as set free from its creators and as something that proliferates (unfathomably) as it circulates, provides a conception of what would be a dynamic force in interactive settings. Finally, for selective retention, we propose that *critical enquiry* is a core assumption. This acknowledges the need to engage in collective discussion, use arguments, and refer to facts in order to assess which theories and conjectures are 'better' for us. At least in the context of project work, where selection and retention choices are made on a continuous basis, this last assumption seems essential.

Together, these three epistemological assumptions outline a framework for the knowledge creation in projects as a progressive process. A preselecting searchlight guides and sets the process in motion, unfathomable knowledge generates variety and new ideas, and critical enquiry provides a means to select and retain the best choices.

3.5 CONCLUSIONS

Collaborative knowledge creation and integration in projects has received scant attention in the literature, but the works of Nonaka et al. are prominent exceptions. In their theory of organizational knowledge creation, they take a point of departure in the epistemology of Polanyi. However, both Nonaka et al. and Polanyi focus on the individual origins of new knowledge and consider knowledge to be something that people 'dwell in', and something that is closely integrated with their bodies and personalities. None of these authors shed much light on how processes of social interaction may constitute a source of new knowledge. Hence, a somewhat extended model, featuring the process of 'interaction', and the role of 'unfathomable knowledge', was proposed.

We then elaborated the 'interaction' part of this model to show how such knowledge processes can be seen as comprising imagination and discipline simultaneously, and outlined a three-pronged progressive epistemology of knowledge creation and integration processes in project settings. Such processes, we suggest, are fundamentally 'searchlight-guided', depend critically on the circulation and proliferation of 'unfathomable' knowledge, and presuppose 'critical enquiry' in determining best options.

This chapter contributes by proposing that the Nonaka/Polanyi framework should be complemented by an evolutionary epistemology view. It also suggests that the traditional evolutionary framework, comprising variation and selective retention, should be complemented with a third element, preselection, which appears appropriate to the project context. Finally, it contributes by identifying three core epistemological assumptions, which are associated with these three elements, and taken together provide a basis for understanding the processes of knowledge creation–integration within projects as progressive.

REFERENCES

Asch, S. E. (1952) *Social Psychology*, New York: Prentice-Hall.

Bartley, W. W. (1987) Alienation Alienated. The Economics of Knowledge Versus the Psychology and Sociology of Knowledge, in: G. Radnitzky and W. W. Bartley (eds.), *Evolutionary Epistemology, Rationality and the Sociology of Knowledge*, La Salle, IL: Open Court.

—— (1990) *Unfathomed Knowledge, Unmeasured Wealth*, La Salle, IL: Open Court.

Bereiter, C. (1994) Implications of Postmodernism for Science, or, Science as Progressive Discourse, *Educational Psychologist*, 29(1): 3–12.

Campbell, D. T. (1960) Blind Variation and Selective Retention in Creative Thought as in Other Knowledge Processes, *The Psychological Review*, 67: 380–400.

—— (1974) Unjustified Variation and Selective Retention in Scientific Discovery, in: F. J. Ayala and T. Dobzhansky (eds.), *Studies in the Philosophy of Biology: Reduction and Related Problems*, London/Basingstoke: Macmillan.

Cross, R. and Sproull, L. (2004) More Than an Answer: Information Relationships for Actionable Knowledge, *Organization Science*, 15(4): 446–62.

DeFillippi, R., Arthur, M. and Lindsey, V. (2006) *Knowledge at Work. Creative Collaboration in the Global Economy*, Malden, MA: Blackwell Publishing.

Dunbar, K. (1997) How Scientists Think: On-line Creativity and Conceptual Change in Science, in: T. B. Ward, S. M. Smith and J. Vaid (eds.), *Creative Thought: An Investigation of Conceptual Structures and Processes*, American Psychological Association, Washington, DC.

Gersick, C. J. G. (1989) Marking Time: Predictable Transitions in Work Groups, *Academy of Management Journal*, 32(2): 274–309.

—— (1995) Everything New Under the Gun – Creativity and Deadlines, in: C. M. Ford and D. A. Gioia (eds.), *Creative Action in Organizations*, Thousand Oaks, CA: Sage, pp. 142–8.

Grant, R. M. (1996) Toward a Knowledge-based Theory of the Firm, *Strategic Management Journal*, 17(Winter Special Issue): 109–22.

Hargadon, A. B. and Bechky, B. A. (2006) When Collections of Creatives Become Creative Collectives: A Field Study of Problem Solving at Work, *Organization Science*, 17(4): 484–500.

Kreiner, K. (1995) In Search of Relevance: Project Management in Drifting Environments, *Scandinavian Journal of Management*, 11(4): 335–46.

Kurzberg, T. R. and Amabile, T. M. (2001) From Guilford to Creative Synergy: Opening the Box of Team Level Creativity, *Creativity Research Journal*, 13: 285–94.

Lindkvist, L. (2004) Governing Project-based Firms. Promoting Market-like Processes within Hierarchies, *Journal of Management and Governance*, 8(1): 3–25.

—— (2005) Knowledge Communities and Knowledge Collectivities. A Typology of Knowledge Work in Groups, *Journal of Management Studies*, 42(6): 1189–210.

—— (2008) Project Organization: Exploring Its Adaptation Properties, *International Journal of Project Management*, 13: 13–20.

—— Bengtsson, M. (2009) *Extending Nonaka's Knowledge Creation Theory. How We Know More than We Can Tell and Tell More than We Can Know*, Paper presented at the EGOS Colloquium, Barcelona.

Lindkvist, L., Söderlund, J. (2002) What Goes on in Projects? On Goal-directed Learning Processes, in: K. Sahlin-Andersson and A. Söderholm (eds.), *Beyond Project Management. New Perspectives on the Temporary-Permanent Dilemma*, Malmö: Liber Ekonomi.

—— Tell, F. (1998) Managing Product Development Projects – On the Significance of Fountains and Deadlines, *Organization Studies*, 19(6): 931–51.

Lovas, B. and Ghoshal, G. (2000) Strategy as Guided Evolution, *Strategic Management Journal*, 21: 875–96.

March, J. G. (1994) The Evolution of Evolution, in: J. Baum and J. Singh (eds.), *The Evolutionary Dynamics of Organizations*, Cambridge, MA: Oxford University Press.

—— (1995) *Learning Processes are Powerful Tools of Organizational Adaptation*, Helsinki: Tvön Tuuli Aikakauskirja.

March, J. D and Weil, T. (2005) *On Leadership*, Malden, MA: Blackwell Publishing.

Nonaka, I. (1994) A Dynamic Theory of Organizational Knowledge Creation, *Organization Science*, 5(1): 14–37.

—— Takeuchi, H. (1995) *The Knowledge Creating Company*, New York: Oxford University Press.

—— Toyama, R. and Konno, N. (2000) SECI, Ba and Leadership: A Unified Model of Dynamic Knowledge Creation, *Long Range Planning*, 33: 5–34.

Polanyi, M. (1966) *The Tacit Dimension*, Gloucester, MA: Peter Smith.

Popper, K. (1963) *Conjectures and Refutations*, London: Routledge & Kegan Paul.

—— (1972) *Objective Knowledge: An Evolutionary Approach*, Oxford: Clarendon Press.

—— (1974) *The Open Society and Its Enemies*, Vol. 2, London: Routledge & Kegan Paul.

—— (1975) The Rationality of Scientific Revolutions, in: R. Harré (ed.), *Problems of Scientific Revolutions*, Oxford: Clarendon Press.

—— (1999) *All Life is Problem Solving*, London: Routledge.

Räisänen, C. and Linde, A. (2004) Technologizing Discourse to Standardize Projects in Multi-project Organizations: Hegemony by Consensus? *Organization*, 11(1): 101–21.

Sawyer, R. K. (1999) The Emergence of Creativity, *Philosophical Psychology*, 12(4): 447–69.

—— (2000) Improvisational Cultures: Collaborative Emergence and Creativity in Improvisation, *Mind, Culture and Activity*, 7(3): 180–5.

Scarbrough, H., Swan, J., Laurent, S., Bresnen, M., Edelman, L. F. and Newell, S. (2004) Project-based Learning and the Role of Learning Boundaries, *Organization Studies*, 25(9): 1579–600.

Simon, H. (1991) Bounded Rationality and Organizational Learning, *Organization Science*, 2: 125–34.

Sydow, J., Lindkvist, L. and DeFillippi, R. (2004) Project-based Organizations, Embeddedness and Repositories of Knowledge: Editorial, *Organization Studies*, 25: 1475–89.

Vik, M. and Lindkvist, L. (2001) Styrning av prekliniska utvecklingsprojekt, in: C. Berggren and L. Lindkvist (eds.), *Projekt. Organisation för målorientering och lärande*, Lund: Studentlitteratur.

Ward, T. B., Smith, S. M. and Vaid, J. (1997) Conceptual Structures and Processes in Creative Thought, in: T. B. Ward, S. M. Smith and J. Vaid (eds.), *Creative Thought: An Investigation of Conceptual Structures and Processes*, American Psychological Association, Washington, DC.

Weick, K. E. (1989) Theory Construction as Disciplined Imagination, *Academy of Management Review*, 14: 516–31.

—— (1993a) Organizational Redesign as Improvisation, in: G. P. Huber and W. H. Glick (eds.), *Organizational Change and Redesign. Ideas and Insights for Improving Performance*, Oxford: Oxford University Press.

—— (1993b) The Collapse of Sensemaking in Organizations: The Mann Gulch Disaster, *Administrative Science Quarterly*, 38(4): 628–52.

—— Roberts, K. H. (1993) Collective Mind in Organizations: Heedful Interrelating on Flight Decks, *Administrative Science Quarterly*, 38: 357–81.

4

Inventors as Innovators and Knowledge Integrators

Hans Andersson and Christian Berggren

This chapter illustrates how individual innovators in large technology-based firms support both knowledge integration and knowledge creation, for example, by spanning knowledge across different fields, by pursuing individual exploration as well as collaborative search, and by participating in formal projects but simultaneously using them as permeable entities to further their own innovative ideas.

4.1 INTRODUCTION

Chapter 3 examined how groups act collaboratively to create and integrate knowledge. This chapter focuses on the role of certain key individuals as knowledge creators and integrators. In our study of inventors in three large, technology-based firms in three industries, a pattern emerged where a small number of individuals in each organization consistently developed more technical inventive ideas, as documented in patent applications, than the majority of their colleagues.

Figure 4.1 shows the number of patents applied for by the twenty-five most productive inventors in each of the three firms in the study, here called North, South, and West.

In each of the three firms, there are a relatively small number of inventors that outperform the majority of their colleagues.[1] Previous research (Andersson and Berggren, 2007) has shown how individual inventors are also important in the R&D organizations of large firms competing on mature markets, where there is a strong emphasis on resource efficiency and predictable project flows. However, what characterizes much of the literature on New Product Development (NPD), innovation, and knowledge integration is their focus on strategies, structures, and processes. We want to complement these perspectives not by exploring

---

[1] For each firm, individual 1 represents the single inventor who had applied for most patents, individual 2 the second most productive, etc. The vertical differences between the firms have more to do with different propensities to patent across industries, not that West's inventors are much more creative than those at South.

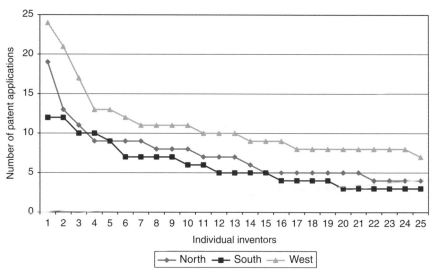

Figure 4.1 Number of patents applied for by the twenty-five most productive inventors in each of the three firms during the five years before the study, using 'whole counts' unadjusted for co-inventions by two or more inventors (Narin and Breitzman, 1995: 232). The tails of the curves (not shown) are long, including up to 150 individuals

Source: Internal company data from North, South, and West

individuals in isolation but by studying individual inventors as innovators and knowledge integrators in their organizational contexts. Other studies have emphasized the key roles of project managers (Söderlund, 2005) or chief engineers (Brusoni and Cassi, 2009) for knowledge integration. As formally recognized agents for coordination and project integrity, they are certainly important for the integration that is necessary in innovation processes. In this chapter, however, we argue that knowledge integration is not just an organizational and team-level practice but concerns the everyday activities of inventive engineers and researchers involved in development activities. Therefore, we are particularly interested in innovative individuals in non-directive, non-managerial positions: engineers, product developers, or researchers in the R&D departments of large, technology-based industrial firms.

The purpose of the chapter is to investigate and illustrate the practices of inventors as innovators and knowledge integrators, individually and in collaboration with others. We will not study the personalities or individual dispositions of the inventors/integrators, neither do we attempt to ascertain their relative importance compared to mainstream means and methods in the NPD process; to do so properly would require longitudinal case studies over an extended period of time. The focus is on inventors-cum-innovators who generate ideas and scan new knowledge fields to complement deep knowledge in their own domains, and turn ideas into new solutions. By illustrating their activities and practices, the chapter contributes to a deeper understanding of what knowledge integration is about in technology-based firms, how innovative individuals combine knowledge from different fields; pursue individual exploration as well as collaborative search; and not only participate in time-paced projects but also use them to further their own innovative ideas.

This could be seen as a micro-level perspective of individuals, interactions, and integration behaviours in the sense recently discussed by Foss (2009). We are aware that *micro* often refers to the firm level, but it may also be used to denote the level of individuals and their '... face-to-face conduct' (Layder, 1994: 6), while *macro* according to Layder is then used for the more impersonal.

In the following section, we will briefly discuss individual roles in the extant literature on innovation, creativity, and knowledge integration; the new interest in individual innovators; and the research gap this study will address. After that we state our way of selecting firms and inventors for this study, before presenting the empirical results which illustrate the innovators' practices in three different areas. The concluding section elaborates on the action-oriented dimension of knowledge integrators; their interplay of individual and collaborative activities; and how formal structures can be perceived as permeable entities surrounded by horizontal innovative space.

4.2 INDIVIDUAL ROLES IN THE LITERATURE ON INNOVATION AND KNOWLEDGE INTEGRATION

Back in the early 1960s, Machlup wrote that 'invention has become the business of organized, large-scale research and development in specialized departments of large corporations' (1961: 1464). That is still true but in the meantime the requirement that those 'specialized departments' handle and integrate complementary fields of technology has increased considerably (cf. Kleinschmidt et al., 2007). Thus, product development in technology-based firms has become a common empirical context in recent studies on knowledge integration. Development of turbines and stackers (Enberg, 2007), software and hardware innovation (Schmickl and Kieser, 2008), and information systems development (Tiwana and McLean, 2005) are just a few examples. According to Schmickl and Kieser (2008), cross-learning among the specialists involved in the process is the dominant approach to knowledge integration in technically demanding product innovation. Extensive cross-learning is expensive and time-consuming, however, and a number of ways have been proposed for reducing the learning required for knowledge integration. Grant (1996: 114) argues that 'If production requires the integration of many people's specialist knowledge, the key to efficiency is to achieve effective integration while minimizing knowledge transfer through cross-learning by organizational members.' Grant, like Schmickl and Kieser and many others, clearly acknowledges the organizational members, their competence, and awareness of others' specialized knowledge. However, in the bulk of the knowledge integration literature, the focus is on means and mechanisms for achieving knowledge integration. When discussed at all, individuals are recognized as sources of knowledge but not studied as potentially important agents in the integration process.

4.2.1 NPD teams and fuzzy front end inventors

The NPD literature resembles the knowledge integration literature in this respect. Processes and project groups, in particular cross-functional teams, are seen as key elements and the smallest relevant unit of analysis. As Brown and Eisenhardt (1995) emphasize, although project members do the actual work, the focus of most research is on the team and the project. In general, the project members are regarded as 'generic engineers' (Steiner, 1995) with no other distinguishing traits than the field of technology they represent. This is understandable when NPD is defined as a process starting *after* invention or concept definition, and is mainly about implementing what is then known and specified (cf. Griffin, 1997). The more general innovation literature has identified a number of roles as important for success: product champions (Schon, 1963), gatekeepers (Allen, 1970), heavyweight project managers (Clark and Wheelwright, 1992), and leaders (Mumford and Licuanan, 2004). Most of these roles are related to the problem of selecting and acquiring external knowledge (e.g. the gatekeeper role); to the much-discussed problem of overcoming internal resistance and inertia by building networks, alliances, and high-level support (champions); or to the challenge of maintaining project momentum and product integrity (leaders, heavyweight project managers). Few have studied the role of non-managerial individuals for overcoming 'non-political' knowledge-related challenges, for building knowledge networks, and refining inventive ideas before or in parallel to formal product processes. For example, Clark and Fujimoto (1990), as well as Nonaka and Takeuchi (1995), do recognize the importance of 'ordinary' engineers' knowledge-related activities, but their main focus is on management, not inventors.

Another stream of literature has been devoted to general studies of creativity and inventiveness, from the organizational level (e.g. studies of 'creative climate') (Amabile et al., 1996; Hemlin et al., 2008) 'down' to the level of individuals. Traditionally, the latter have been in focus, but increasing attention is being paid to the influence of social and contextual factors (Ford and Gioia, 1995). While there are obvious connections between creativity and innovation in general (e.g. Kanter, 1988; West and Farr, 1990; Gupta et al., 2007), few authors relate creative and inventive activities to knowledge integration and innovation in the context of technology-based firms, where multiple technologies and processes need to be merged in order to implement new inventions successfully. One reason may be that knowledge integration involves several different domains of knowledge, whereas creative contributions are normally assessed, and recognized, in relation to a specific domain, that is, a specific system of rules and procedures that define permissible actions, 'presented to the organization members as "given knowledge", the basic factors of the profession' (Csikszentmihalyi and Sawyer, 1995: 169). From a knowledge-integration point of view, the creative contribution is contingent upon an integrative moment across domains, and thus both encompasses and transgresses the single domain view (as described in 'The systems view of creativity', cf. Csikszentmihalyi, 1988, 1999; Montuori and Purser, 1995). Another reason for the lack of interest in individuals as knowledge integrators in the creativity literature may be that, in keeping with the NPD literature, creative aspects are thought of as confined to the early, 'fuzzy' phase of innovation and product development. Knowledge integration, on the other hand, is related to the entire ideation and development process in technology-based firms. It is important as a guide to preselection and focused creativity, and also as a basis for implementing inventions in products and solutions, which may call for just as much creativity as the front end (Mumford et al., 2002).

4.2.2 From inventors to innovators and knowledge integrators

In the following section, we will present our study of inventors who have successfully applied for several patents in their firms and been involved in implementing their ideas, that is, in turning something new (the invention) into something new and useful (an innovation). By doing so, they become *innovators*, being involved in several phases of the innovation process. In the literature, innovators have been described in rather general terms as change agents who not only introduce but also carry out an idea and thus link creativity to organization (Knight, 1967). Rothwell (1975) defines the 'technical innovator' as one who makes important contributions on the technical side, even if s/he is not the inventor of the product/process. In our study, however, the interviewed individuals are both inventors and innovators.

As noted above, a significant literature discusses individual roles related to acquisition of external knowledge or overcoming organizational obstacles to innovation. We know less of roles and practices needed to overcome the knowledge barriers to successful innovation in technology-based firms. Recently, however, there has been an increasing interest in the specific roles of individual innovators. Sim et al. investigated innovators within an engineering services firm and write that a body of research has begun to identify what characterizes innovators and 'how innovators span the innovation process in its entirety' (2007: 426). Griffin et al. recently studied 'exceptional industrial innovators' who had been instrumental for breakthrough technologies (2009: 223). While both these studies provide a lot of information about innovators, neither of them has a focus on practices related to knowledge integration.

To sum up and simplify, the NPD literature has mainly focused on project teams, staffed by generic engineers representing functional areas; the knowledge integration literature has analysed mechanisms and forms for handling individuals perceived as carriers of specialized knowledge; the innovation literature has discussed individual roles mainly of a managerial and political character and sometimes also extraordinary individuals (Edison, etc.); and the creativity literature has above all been interested in early phases of ideation and invention. Recently, however, an interest in individual innovators and their activities has emerged. The present study will address a gap in this new literature by specifically focusing on knowledge-related and integrative practices of innovative individuals, and how they add to a broader understanding of knowledge integration in technology-based firms.

Table 4.1 A comparison of South, North, and West

	South	North	West
Product system scope (Hobday et al., 2005)	Medium- to high-tech product systems – 'COPS'	Mainly medium-tech system components based on high-tech research and manufacturing processes	Composite products comprising several details and materials, both simple and advanced
R&D focus	Engineering	Basic research and engineering	Research and engineering
Main management background	Engineers	Engineers and/or scientists (many of them inventors)	Engineers and/or market
Innovation focus	Incremental	Incremental *and* discontinuous	Incremental *and* discontinuous

4.3 PATENT-INTENSIVE INDIVIDUALS IN THREE PATENT-INTENSIVE FIRMS

The starting point of this study is patent-intensive individuals in patent-intensive firms. To file for a patent in a large company means that the invention involves not just what is regarded internally as an inventive step, that is, its novelty exceeds what is obvious to those skilled in the art (EPO, 2005), it must also be accepted internally as representing a potential value to the company. Thereby patent applications, even if not quite to the same degree as granted patents, provide some kind of objective measure of inventive or creative activity (Ford, 1995; Oldham and Cummings, 1996; Huber, 1998; Dewett, 2007). Moreover, using patent applications makes it possible to draw on more recent data than is possible with granted patents.

Public statistics on patent applications filed in Sweden in 2000–4 revealed that a small number of companies consistently applied for more patents than others. Three firms, here called North, South, and West, were selected on the basis of their high patenting intensity and their focus on R&D effectiveness. All three are large companies, competing on several continents in mostly mature markets, but doing so in very different industries (see Table 4.1).

4.3.1 Three large technology-based firms

South develops and manufactures heavy vehicles of an integrated, product systems character (Hobday et al., 2005). Inventions in a new component or subsystem have to be integrated with a multitude of other components and systems, hard- and software. This is related to the European way of developing heavy trucks, where all major subsystems and components, such as cabins, engines, gearboxes, or rear axles, are developed and integrated by the final assemblers. This differs from the US model, where these components are developed by independent specialists. The complex product character thus leaves relatively little room for radical or discontinuous innovations (Garcia and Calantone, 2002). Most of the patents obtained by South in recent years represent 'small steps', minor but ingenious improvements, according to the VP of R&D. This can also be seen as a consequence of a company policy of launching incremental improvements in a continuous fashion. Larger steps are achieved by integrating many small patentable inventions into a non-patentable product system. The company regards itself as innovative, and top management encourages its engineers to patent, supported by a patent department working more proactively than in previous decades. At the same time, a lot of managerial effort is devoted to streamlining the project flow in the image of the 'R&D factory'. Manufacturing the vehicles is a complex process involving many entities, but R&D is located adjacent to the main manufacturing facilities, and close interaction between development and production is strongly emphasized.

North is a tool producer that successfully competes worldwide by combining inventions in materials science with in-depth mechanical knowledge, and high-precision and high-volume manufacturing. North's products are different from those of South, they are components or subsystems, and closer to advances in basic science. These products are integrated into complex systems by their customers, with very high demands for reliability and trouble-free operation. This limits the space for innovative departures if the new solutions cannot match these requirements early on. It does not limit the overall inventive activity, however. In recent years, the two R&D departments at North have obtained an increasing number of patents. Management describes patenting as strategically important and all new products should enjoy some kind of patent protection. To support this ambition, patent officers are located next to R&D engineers. The company's R&D sites include facilities for testing and laboratory work. Manufacturing takes place in all important market areas worldwide, but the central manufacturing site is located between the two R&D units involved in this study. New products are introduced to the market twice a year, which sets clear deadlines for development projects, which normally run for two to three years. North's so-called competence projects are not subject to deadlines in the same way. They are initiated to explore new technologies, a new process, or a new type of material. The degree of freedom is larger and the goal is to learn and evaluate the new technology. Many R&D staff are engaged in both kinds of project in order to facilitate transfer of solutions as well as problems between different kinds of activities across time and space.

West develops branded consumer goods. Unlike many other consumer goods firms, West puts a lot of emphasis on innovation and patent protection of new products. On the basis of a platform of related technologies, West develops products that target a wide variety of customers and consumers. This makes West's market situation more complex than that of South and North. Often considered not to be 'high-tech', R&D activities at West nevertheless comprise both advanced materials knowledge, the design of sophisticated physical shapes, and adaptation to demanding manufacturing requirements, as the products are produced at high speed in large volumes. Accordingly, development engineers need to understand both customer and production requirements. While the products are sold in more than ninety countries and manufacturing is dispersed across the world, R&D operations are centralized and co-located with the market organization and the patent department. As with the other two firms, West has increased its managerial focus on process efficiency within R&D.

4.3.2 The importance of individual inventors

In the histories of technology-based companies, some individual inventors often figure prominently as examples, role models, or myths. These roles of inventors as examples and role models were salient also in the studied firms. As Figure 4.1 shows, the distribution of inventive activity across individuals in terms of patent applications was highly uneven in all three firms. In each of the three companies, a small group of inventors consistently outperformed their colleagues in terms of patents applied for and were considered highly important for the success of the firm. One manager commented on Figure 4.1 as follows:

> There are five individuals that form the first five [referring to an ice hockey term describing the team's strongest formation] that you have to take care of. (Top manager, North)

Inventors were publicly recognized in various ways. At South, the VP of R&D (himself an inventor) had created a 'Wall of Fame', with signs bearing the names of all inventors/patentees, and instituted an annual Patentees' Party to celebrate recent progress. At one of North's R&D operations, new employees were expected to submit a patent application within two years of being hired, and a manager referred to one of the interviewed R&D engineers as being critical for the company's financial success over the years.

> Yes, I think he has accounted for a great deal of our company's profitability. A great deal. (Middle manager, North)

West organized an annual 'Innovation Day' to emphasize the importance of innovation and to publicly celebrate creative contributions from various employees.

4.3.3 Methodology: from patent-intensive firms to patent-intensive individuals

After selecting the firms, the next step in the study was to select inventors for interviews. Based on internal company statistics on patent applications, eight to ten of the most active inventors in each R&D department were selected for in-depth interviews. As North's R&D activities are undertaken in two units, not only with different orientations but also located in different parts of the country, twice as many North inventors were interviewed; this is reflected in the number of quotes used in the empirical section of the chapter. Discussions with R&D and patent managers added quality and relevance aspects, interpreted as value and usefulness of the inventors' contributions (cf. Ernst et al., 2000). According to these evaluations, almost all the productive inventors had generated highly valuable innovations. In addition to inventors, we have interviewed managers at different organizational levels, some of them repeatedly, and a number of informative meetings have also provided valuable information.

The interviews started with one or a few particular patents applied for by the interviewee, and how these inventions had been realized (or failed to be realized) in competitive products. All interviews were transcribed verbatim and read and coded independently. We started with detailed knowledge of the product development process in one of the firms (the vehicle producer); in the other two, our pre-understanding was rudimentary, and the study had an essentially inductive character. Irrespective of the starting point, we were able to identify a number of company practices which reinforced the view of inventors and inventing as highly important.

In recent years, the companies had developed their patent offices from corporate legal departments into also being supportive units close to the R&D operations, staffed by experienced engineers/researchers with patenting expertise.

The interviewees illustrated the importance of this reorientation, and how the patent officers actively helped inventors to identify new, unexplored areas for further inventive activity.

These inventive individuals were seldom content to produce more patents, but were also active in realizing their inventions. This brings us to the key question of the study, how these inventors-cum-innovators developed personal, more or less informal practices to test, refine, and integrate their new knowledge elements with other important knowledge domains inside and outside their firms.

4.4 FROM LAB EXPERIMENTS TO USER INTERACTION: INVENTIVE INDIVIDUALS AS KNOWLEDGE INTEGRATORS

A recurrent theme when interviewing R&D executives was the importance of 'unplanned' creative activities, where individuals could explore the unexpected. As the VP of R&D at the heavy vehicle producer explained:

> I expect people in R&D to experiment informally, in what you may call skunk works. In a way, it's a self-adjusting system. Most ideas won't catch on. You have to be lucky and have the right timing. With experimenting going on, the ideas that have survived the pre-selection process are reasonably good, and enjoy some degree of established trust. When you start a systematic evaluation, the basic technical idea development is already finished. (VP R&D, South)

At the tooling company, the attitude was similar and one top manager described the important zone between the formalized product- and competence projects:

> There is a zone in between which we call skunk works. This denotes work that is not scheduled and not sanctioned all the way, but still takes place with our consent. Especially if you have that profile [of being extra innovative], you have more room for skunk work. Actually, it is to sanction the testing of ideas and trying to bring more input into the big treadmill.... Most innovations probably come from competence- and skunk work and I think that is where we have time and space for creativity. In product development there is more control and time restrictions. (VP R&D, North)

In this way, inventors were expected not only to come up with new ideas but also to start to test and realize them, that is, they were expected to become innovators. These activities tended to be more important as the technological level of the invention increased, and so the firm's reluctance to take risks. One of the ingenious inventors, specializing in mechanical design, was very aware of the split requirements posed by this situation:

> Yes, I think you should run the projects by the book. At the same time it is important to explore some other ideas, so you should also be able to follow a side track and test something different. And sometimes I have felt that it was really a stroke of luck that I did that, since it was this sidetrack which became so good. (Inventor, North)

All the firms in the study had invested heavily in developing efficient project structures and methods, to create streamlined R&D with a flow of new products and upgrades arriving in a timely fashion. At the same time, inventing, probing, testing, and integrating activities by creative individuals continued to play an important role and the more innovative the solution, the more important these individual integrative efforts tend to be. To give the reader a flavour of these efforts, below we present excerpts from the stories and reflections collected in the innovator interviews, grouped under three subheadings: (*a*) Spanning several knowledge domains and types of activity; (*b*) Discussing ideas broadly, and consulting different types of experts; (*c*) Informal testing and integration prior to or parallel with formal projects.

The first two can be seen as activities aimed at building and integrating knowledge; the third is also a knowledge-integrating activity but pursued in a particular action- and implementation-oriented mode. The headings are generated inductively from our empirical material, but as demonstrated below they can be related to other studies of individual innovators, for example Griffin et al. (2009).

4.4.1 The importance of spanning several knowledge domains

A central aspect of the effectiveness of the interviewed innovators had to do with their way of fusing deep knowledge in a particular domain and its critical tools, be it mechanical design and CAD systems, or thermodynamics and programmes for thermodynamic and phase diagram calculations, with broader insights into related but different fields. Thus, when the innovators select and develop new ideas, they make use of broader knowledge, especially of downstream processes. Some of them emphasize the importance of close insights into the manufacturing process, as seen in the following quote:

> The way I think, when I come up with a solution for something, I have almost always the [manufacturing] process in mind. Mostly that's what it is about, finding a solution that can be produced in our process and I know how the processes work. I have an interest in the processes. The integration of product and process, I have always been interested in that. When I get the chance I am out in the factory, I study the machine in detail and make sure I understand everything from the material roll to the finished product. (Development engineer, West)

Others stress the value of personal knowledge of customer use. Sometimes, this could be acquired in far-away locations:

> My background is thermodynamics and alloy design, which was the subject of my PhD thesis. But what is really good at this company is that you are supposed to have

direct contact with those who actually are using our products. So you are part of the projects, which realize new products; you can go out on field tests and participate when our tools are actually cutting metal. We are standing close to some milling machine in a mechanical workshop in northern Italy and just observe. (R&D engineer, North, PhD in materials science)

In other cases, the innovators acquired this knowledge by personal use of the company's products, as stated below:

I use the vehicle as inspiration, I don't say I'm the one who uses our test trucks most of all, but I think I'm one of the most frequent users. It is so rewarding to use the stuff, to understand the driver's everyday work. That's when I get ideas. That's where I realize where we suck. (Product developer, South)

The quotes add to the observation in the study of industrial innovators by Griffin et al. about their intuition which '. . . is based on their core deep technical understanding of one area, supported by learning peripheral technologies, which they can then combine into new configurations' (2009: 232). The innovators in our study specifically emphasized the importance of covering several knowledge fields in the innovation process, from idea generation to customer presentation. In some cases, the organizational structure by itself facilitated a holistic view and close contacts between different functions, as in the quote below:

What I like a lot is that we have an overview of the whole product. When I worked at X-company you were stuck with your part of the car and you were pretty far from the final consumer. Here we verify and test against consumers and try to understand. You are really close both to the market and consumers. I think it is exciting to hear about the consumers' problems. / . . . / I am triggered by 'consumer insight' – to make myself acquainted with the situation, 'how does s/he think, what situations do they experience, what is required of the product, what is it exposed to, what are the everyday problems encountered' – trying to get acquainted. . . . Then, based on the consumers' problems – how can we take care of them in the product? Then we have to build, a lot of practical work. (Development engineer, West)

The ability to span several knowledge fields was also related to the possibilities for innovators to participate in the entire innovation process, including customer launch, instead of being dedicated to pre-development projects:

It is a creative thing to be part of the entire process, from idea to product launch, when the new product can be found in the catalogue. Animations and stuff like that, which are used to describe the product, well I'm happy to do that also. I can give a helping hand to the/marketing/guys here since I have the basic material in my CAD model. That's part of the idea generation process for me to participate later on and spread the message about the new product. (Development engineer, mechanical design, North)

Being part of the entire process from idea to product launch is more or less the definition of innovators. But whereas the literature tends to focus on the innovator's activities to overcome organizational obstacles for the new product idea, our study points to the importance for the knowledge-integrative efforts of 'being part of the entire process'. As the above quote illustrates, it could be about integrating the knowledge of the innovators into the marketing approach, but it could also be the other way around, a means for the innovators to integrate new knowledge about user responses into new generation of products.

4.4.2 Discussing ideas broadly, and consulting
different types of experts

The ability of the studied innovators to personally combine deep knowledge in their core field with detailed insights in related areas was a key factor for their effectiveness, but seldom enough to succeed. Again and again they emphasized the importance of discussing their ideas broadly and engaging in repeated dialogues with others. One of the most productive inventors at North, for example, stressed the importance of this type of informal collaboration to develop new patents:

> If you look at my patents, you will find quite a lot with several co-inventors, and that is because it is so important to be willing to share your ideas. For example, [after my own experiments] I need someone who is skilled at materials analysis, someone who is doing the microscope study, or something else, and who provides the explanations you need to write a solid patent. (Experienced 'serial inventor', North)

Another inventor, with a very different educational background and at a different department in the same company, also stressed the value of taking advantage of his colleagues' particular skills:

> But I'm not particularly good at doing computation and simulations and that stuff. Well I know a bit of engineering formulas which I can handily use, but often there are geometrical limits anyway.... Or I can ask someone else, I can kindly ask someone to have a look at these parts, and do some calculations to find out if there are any critical spots. This can provide very important information in some special cases, especially for embedded tooling systems.... There are some guys who are really good at that, and they will handle the computational problems very well, and I have well developed contacts with them. So I know who I can ask for help, colleagues in other parts of the organization. (Development engineer, mechanical design, North)

Others emphasized the advantage of having not only personal knowledge in downstream processes but also personal contacts with downstream departments, for example manufacturing plants:

> I have really good contacts with the manufacturing facility (located several hours away). This goes back many years to the 1980s when I worked quite closely with them, and I have later refined these contacts to get a high quality input in my own work. To have this good communication is a real strength in the product projects where it is very important that everything works fine in the last phase, full-scale manufacturing. We know of competitors who have launched products which they had to withdraw after six months or so, because they could not guarantee reliable deliveries. In a recent project, which I did not take part in, this happened to us, too many defects, no reliable deliveries, which is a thing customers really hate, our stuff works well, but the next order we cannot deliver on time. So we had to withdraw that product. (Development engineer, North, PhD in metallography)

Personal contacts in service departments could also be important, as in the quote below:

> I ride and drive trucks a lot with a number of friends and customers who I have got to know over the years. I have a friend in the service department who works extra as a truck driver and if I have two equally good possible solutions to a problem he has more

authority than anyone else here at the company. He weighs the disadvantages of the solutions and I do as he says. (Product developer, South)

Informal relations with sales and applications departments were another source of knowledge and a possibility to test out and iteratively develop ideas:

> Maybe we got some new materials to play with, let's say I've got a new type of coating. Then I can bandy ideas with the guys developing new substrates in this field. Listen, listen! Here, something is looking fishy! Can we use a new coating here? Are there any weak spots in the materials where a new coating can help? So you have to talk around and discuss with various people. When I gather I have a reasonable grasp on it, then I may talk a little with my boss to ask if it's ok if I continue to spend time on this idea. Then we do a couple of try-outs and test the new stuff; our workshop for technological testing is quite good. And then there is the sales department. They have some really good customers, where we can test new product ideas. I know if I call someone there, I've got a few names, I can sound out what they are doing, where they have tested similar type of materials before, and I can tell them I got a few ideas and wonder if they will go to these places within a certain time. (R&D engineer, North)

The importance of networks was a recurrent theme, not primarily as a means to overcome resistance and inertia but as a vehicle to probe and refine new concepts, and to expand and integrate new knowledge:

> Your network is very important.' Will everything work?' You want to know before you have worked too much on something as ideas can turn out as real disappointments. You really believe in something, but when you have your prototype you realize it wasn't very good. Then it's good to bandy with different people to get an understanding how much time it's worth. Ideally there should be more time for this. You have to weigh it against other things. (Development engineer, West)

A common trait of the successful innovators was their combination of having deep and broad personal knowledge and being able to 'kindly ask for help' – to refine ideas via dialogue and to mobilize the knowledge of others to analyse crucial aspects. As Van de Ven (1986) has observed, innovations in industrial firms are collective achievements. Our study illustrates that there is more to say about this: individual innovators continue to be important, and are successful both on the basis of their own deep knowledge and inventive minds, and because they are diligent in collaborating and mobilizing collective inputs, that is, operating in a collective context.

4.4.3 Informal testing and integration prior to or parallel with formal projects

According to Gaynor (2001), being 'doers', not just 'idea people', is one of the aspects that separates innovators from inventors. Ideas and skills are necessary but not sufficient for an innovator, it also takes an action orientation not restricted to the boundaries of formal projects (Griffin et al., 2009). In our study, this action orientation often meant that innovators informally used their participation in official projects to advance more long-term innovative activities:

> We became famous for our extremely short lead times (in this technology development study). Did we steal resources from the others? No we did not, but we knew people and

we went to the right places so we could make our stuff fit in. For example, instead of filing a formal order for a particular production run at the manufacturing facility, we liaised directly with the operators at the pressing and forming machines and asked them: When you are going to produce this particular type of tool, and start the set-up procedure in the machines, please call me directly! It will take you two hours to run that production order, and at the end I will be there with my dishes, and then you can insert them just before finishing, so you don't have to rig the machine just for this little order. So in this way we could piggyback on regular production runs and get our results and feedback at the blink of an eye. Of course, after doing this a couple of times, we bought a big cake to the guys at our next visit. (Previous inventor, now R&D executive, North)

In another case, a development engineer stressed the importance of being able to collaborate informally with the prototype facilities and physically try out new product ideas:

There is a prototype centre in another building where they produce all items we send to consumers for testing, doing it by hand if there are no suitable machines. But there is all the equipment you need to build, cut, paste something into a new product. Or, I ask for help from those who work there. It as a rather large share of our product development work: building [prototypes] that are evaluated against each other before you decide which path to chose. (Development engineer, West)

The value of being part of several types of projects, and simultaneously advancing his own ideas, was explicitly emphasized by another R&D engineer at one of the R&D departments at North:

However, these time-focused product realization projects are also fun to be part of. Then you have a real target to aim at. So I work in both types: technology development and product development. Then you can make a little manoeuvre to include a few 'specials' in these product projects. In that way you can gain time if you have any ideas of your own. (R&D engineer, PhD in materials chemistry, North)

In line with previous literature, our interviews thus illustrate that collaborative abilities and action competence (cf. Talke et al., 2006) are needed to create the required room for innovative manoeuvre. Importantly, however, this 'informal' space for innovation is not created at the expense of official projects and structures. The studied innovators do both: they participate in the product projects, contributing their knowledge and learning new things at the same time as they use these projects to test, refine, and integrate knowledge needed for the next product or product generation.

4.5 CONCLUSIONS

After a long period when the innovation and knowledge integration literatures tended to focus on strategies, structures, and organizational arrangements, a new interest in exploring the role of individual inventors in the innovation process has emerged (Henderson, 2004; Andersson and Berggren, 2007; Giuri et al., 2007). More needs to be done, however, to understand the interaction between idea generation and implementation, and between individual agents and formal structures, especially in technology-based firms. The literature on knowledge integration emphasizes the integration of many people's specialist knowledge. By investigating the practices of inventors-cum-innovators in the organizational context of large technology-based firms, the study adds several insights to the process of actually doing so.

4.5.1 Knowledge integrators are doers

Knowledge integration is an abstract concept that researchers operationalize in various ways, with different interpretations (see Chapter 2). So what is knowledge integration in the context of innovation in technology-based firms, and what concrete activities constitute a knowledge integration process? This study can be seen as a partial empirical answer to that question. When innovators span different knowledge fields, combine their own core knowledge with crucial insights in other areas, when they test and probe and adjust their initial solutions, mobilize the knowledge of colleagues to analyse and scrutinize different properties, involve operators or sales engineers or customer representatives to find out what does or does not work and what needs to be modified, they are pursuing key practices of knowledge integration at a *micro level*.

According to Brusoni et al. (2009: 210), 'exchange of information and ideas among individuals' is a foundational activity of knowledge integration. Our study demonstrates that these 'foundational activities' consist of more than exchange, and include exploring and implementing, acting in multiple roles and arenas, formal project roles, and informal technology development. In short, knowledge integration also calls for different kinds of action. Like innovators, knowledge integrators seem to be doers.

4.5.2 Individual inventiveness and collaborative processes

All the innovators in this study were considered to be creative and innovative far above the average. Nevertheless, their practices illustrated a keen awareness of the importance of collaborative processes, of sharing ideas broadly, testing solutions with other colleagues, and exposing solutions to the gauntlet of technological testing or manufacturing runs. The acquisition of broader and, in some cases, 'peripheral' knowledge served to refine their idea generation process, and facilitate dialogue, but was no substitute for 'kindly asking' colleagues for assistance in other specialist fields. Thus, the study illustrates the importance of innovators as individuals in collectives, involved in collaborative efforts, both in early creative efforts and in later phases of implementation. This is very much in line with the discussion on collaborative processes by Lars Lindkvist et al. in Chapter 3.

4.5.3 Permeable projects and horizontal integration space

On an organizational level, the findings can be summarized in terms of the ideas of permeable projects and horizontal integration space. The studied innovators tended to be involved in more than one type of process, to be part of several groups or teams, and to fulfil different roles inside and outside different projects.

But their informal activities should not be seen as an opposition or alternative to formalized, time-paced projects. Rather, the innovators' activities embed the structured development projects in a broader web of innovative activities. Whereas project managers tend to privilege a view of projects as separated systems, it seems fruitful in this context to perceive them as permeable entities.

Formal processes and structured projects are critical for a predictable flow of new products. But as vehicles for innovation and knowledge integration, they need to be surrounded by less formal practices driven by inquisitive, creative, and collaborative individuals. The study points to the importance for managers of being aware of the fine balance between formal and informal practices and also of recognizing that excessive process-mapping and controls might erode the informal activities, a point made by one R&D executive at company North:

> Sure, you can take this culture out by too much organizational control. I think it is a much smaller challenge to take it out than to make it happen. Most of these guys don't feel good about too many structures, frameworks, and static demands. . . . It is really a very delicate system.

Like other successful innovators, those in this study knew 'how to work the system' (O'Connor and McDermott, 2004) and how to leverage their organizations' capabilities to get things going (Verona, 1999). However, the study demonstrates how the innovators not only make use of existing mechanisms and capabilities but also create new arenas and patterns for interaction. When this combination is maintained, the innovators contribute to official projects but also use them for testing their own ideas, informally collaborating with colleagues outside the project. They are involved in a stream of permeable projects and other types of development activities in parallel, and pursue patenting activities as an important sideline to retain knowledge for future use. In this way, they create a horizontal space for innovation and knowledge integration. We denote this space horizontal as it is created in a non-hierarchic and informal fashion, in contrast to formal structures with appointed project leaders and chief engineers. In a long-term perspective, this horizontal innovative space may be critical for the development of creative ideas and technologies.

4.5.4 Discussion: individual innovators and the evolutionary creation of knowledge

An evolutionary framework for knowledge creation in collaborative processes was presented in Chapter 3. Such a framework may also be applied to the practices of the innovators studied in this chapter. The innovator's personal integration of different knowledge fields acts a guide to preselection in the creation process and helps to avoid false starts, such as products that will be impossible to manufacture or service. Then, when the development process starts, it involves several moments of selection and integration. But the evolutionary model with its three steps – variation, selection, and retention – derived from the study of 'blind' biological processes needs to be complemented to take account of the more complex choices that are present in these types of purposive action. Even when the new knowledge is of no direct value in current product development projects, inventors can patent their findings or 'store' them in other ways for future use. In contrast to biological evolution, these elements of newly created knowledge are not simply either discarded or selected, but can be 'retained', and may be of significance in a much later development process. Studying the activities and practices of innovators in technology-based firms can inform both the understanding of knowledge integration and the interpretation of knowledge creation.

REFERENCES

Allen, T. J. (1970) Communication Networks in R & D Laboratories, *R&D Management*, 1(1): 14–21.

Amabile, T. M., Conti, R., Coon, H., Lazenby, J. and Herron, M. (1996) Assessing the Work Environment for Creativity, *Academy of Management Journal*, 39(5): 1154–84.

Andersson, H. and Berggren, C. (2007) Individual Inventors in the R&D Factory, *Creativity and Innovation Management*, 16(4): 437–46.

Brown, S. L. and Eisenhardt, K. M. (1995) Product Development – Past Research, Present Findings, and Future-Directions, *Academy of Management Review*, 20(2): 343–78.

Brusoni, S. and Cassi, L. (2009) *Re-inventing the Wheel: Knowledge Integration in Fast-changing Environments*, Working paper, Bocconi University.

—— Jacobides, M. G. and Prencipe, A. (2009) Strategic Dynamics in Industry Architectures and the Challenges of Knowledge Integration, *European Management Review*, 6(4): 209–16.

Clark, K. B. and Fujimoto, T. (1990) The Power of Product Integrity, *Harvard Business Review*, 68(6): 107–18.

—— Wheelwright, S. C. (1992) Organizing and Leading Heavyweight Development Teams, *California Management Review*, 34(3): 9–28.

Csikszentmihalyi, M. (1988) Society, Culture and Person: A Systems View of Creativity, in: R. J. Sternberg (ed.), *The Nature of Creativity – Contemporary Psychological Perspectives*, Cambridge: Cambridge University Press.

—— (1999) Implications of a Systems Perspective for the Study of Creativity, in: R. M. Sternberg (ed.), *Handbook of Creativity*, New York: Cambridge University Press, pp. 313–35.

Sawyer, K. (1995) Shifting the Focus from Individual to Organizational Creativity, in: D. A. Gioia, and C. M. Ford (eds.), *Creative Actions in Organizations*, Thousand Oaks, CA: Sage.

Dewett, T. (2007) Linking Intrinsic Motivation, Risk Taking, and Employee Creativity in an R&D Environment, *R&D Management*, 37(3): 197–208.

Enberg, C. (2007) *Knowledge Integration in Product Development Projects*, PhD thesis, Linköping: Linköping University.

EPO (2005) *Guidelines for Examination in the European Patent Office*, Munich: European Patent Office.

Ernst, H., Leptien, C. and Vitt, J. (2000) Inventors Are not Alike: The Distribution of Patenting Output among Industrial R&D Personnel, *IEEE Transactions on Engineering Management*, 47(2): 184–99.

Ford, C. M. (1995) Striking Inspirational Sparks and Fanning Creative Flames: A Multi-domain Model of Creative Action Taking, in: D. A. Gioia, and C. M. Ford (eds.), *Creative Actions in Organizations*, Thousand Oaks, CA: Sage.

—— Gioia, D. A. (eds.) (1995) *Creative Action in Organizations: Ivory Tower Visions and Real World Voices*, Thousand Oaks, CA: Sage.

Foss, N. (2009) Alternative Research Strategies in the Knowledge Movement: From Macro Bias to Micro-foundations and Multi-level Explanation, *European Management Review*, 6(1): 16–28.

Garcia, R. and Calantone, R. (2002) A Critical Look at Technological Innovation Typology and Innovativeness Terminology: A Literature Review, *Journal of Product Innovation Management*, 19(2): 110–32.

Gaynor, G. H. (2001) Innovator: What Does It Take to Be One? *Antennas and Propagation Magazine, IEEE*, 43(3): 126–30.

Giuri, P., Mariani, M., Brusoni, S., Crespi, G., Francoz, D., Gambardella, A., Garcia-Fontes, W., Genua, A., Gonzales, R., Harhoff, D., Hoisl, K., Le Bas, C., Luzzi, A., Magazzini, L., Nesta, L., Nomaler, Ö., Palomeras, N., Patel, P., Romanelli, M. and Verspagen, B. (2007) Inventors and Invention Processes in Europe: Results from the PatVal-EU Survey, *Research Policy*, 36(8): 1107–27.

Grant, R. M. (1996) Toward a Knowledge-based Theory of the Firm, *Strategic Management Journal*, 17: 109–22.

Griffin, A. (1997) PDMA Research on New Product Development Practices: Updating Trends and Benchmarking Best Practices, *Journal of Product Innovation Management*, 14: 429–58.

——— Price, R. L., Maloney, M. M., Vojak, B. A. and Sim, E. W. (2009) Voices from the Field: How Exceptional Electronic Industrial Innovators Innovate, *Journal of Product Innovation Management*, 26(2): 222–40.

Gupta, A. K., Tesluk, P. E. and Taylor, M. S. (2007) Innovation at and Across Multiple Levels of Analysis, *Organization Science*, 18(6): 885–97.

Hemlin, S., Allwood, C. M. and Martin, B. R. (2008) Creative Knowledge Environments, *Creativity Research Journal*, 20(2): 196–210.

Henderson, S. J. (2004) Product Inventors and Creativity: The Finer Dimensions of Enjoyment, *Creativity Research Journal*, 16(2–3): 293–312.

Hobday, M., Davies, A. and Prencipe, A. (2005) Systems Integration: A Core Capability of the Modern Corporation, *Industrial and Corporate Change*, 14(6): 1109–43.

Huber, J. C. (1998) Invention and Inventivity is a Random, Poisson Process: A Potential Guide to Analysis of General Creativity, *Creativity Research Journal*, 11(3): 231–41.

Kanter, R. M. (1988) When a Thousand Flowers Bloom – Structural, Collective, and Social Conditions for Innovations in Organizations, *Research in Organizational Behavior*, 10: 169–211.

Kleinschmidt, E. J., de Brentani, U. and Salomo, S. (2007) Performance of Global New Paroduct Development Programs: A Resource-based View, *Journal of Product Innovation Management*, 24(5): 419–41.

Knight, K. E. (1967) A Descriptive Model of the Intra-Firm Innovation Process, *Journal of Business*, 40(4): 478–96.

Layder, D. (1994) *Understanding Social Theory*, London: Sage.

Machlup, F. (1961) Patents and Inventive Effort, *Science*, 133(3463): 1463–6.

Montuori, A. and Purser, R. E. (1995) Deconstructing the Lone Genius Myth: Toward a Contextual View of Creativity, *Journal of Humanistic Psychology*, 35(3): 69–112.

Mumford, M. D. and Licuanan, B. (2004) Leading for Innovation: Conclusions, Issues, and Directions, *The Leadership Quarterly*, 15(1): 163–71.

——— Scott, G. M., Gaddis, B. and Strange, J. M. (2002) Leading Creative People: Orchestrating Expertise and Relationships, *Leadership Quarterly*, 13(6): 705–50.

Narin, F. and Breitzman, A. (1995) Inventive Productivity, *Research Policy*, 24(4): 507–19.

Nonaka, I. and Takeuchi, H. (1995) *The Knowledge-Creating Company*, New York: Oxford University Press.

O'Connor, G. C. and McDermott, C. M. (2004) The Human Side of Radical Innovation, *Journal of Engineering and Technology Management*, 21(1–2): 11–30.

Oldham, G. R. and Cummings, A. (1996) Employee Creativity: Personal and Contextual Factors at Work, *Academy of Management Journal*, 39(3): 607–34.

Rothwell, R. (1975) Intracorporate Entrepreneurs, *Management Decision*, 13(3): 142–54.

Schmickl, C. and Kieser, A. (2008) How Much Do Specialists Have to Learn from Each Other When They Jointly Develop Radical Product Innovations? *Research Policy*, 37(6–7): 1148–63.

Schon, D. A. (1963) Champions for Radical New Inventions, *Harvard Business Review*, 41(2): 77–86.

Sim, E. W., Griffin, A., Price, R. L. and Vojak, B. A. (2007) Exploring Differences between Inventors, Champions, Implementers and Innovators in Creating and Developing New Products in Large, Mature Firms, *Creativity & Innovation Management*, 16: 422–36.

Söderlund, J. (2005) What Project Management Really is about: Alternative Perspectives on the Role and Practice of Project Management, *International Journal of Technology Management*, 32(3–4): 371–87.

Steiner, C. J. (1995) A Philosophy for Innovation: The Role of Unconventional Individuals in Innovation Success, *Journal of Product Innovation Management*, 12(5): 431–40.

Talke, K., Salomo, S. and Mensel, N. (2006) A Competence-based Model of Initiatives for Innovations, *Creativity and Innovation Management*, 15(4): 373–84.

Tiwana, A. and McLean, E. R. (2005) Expertise Integration and Creativity in Information Systems Development, *Journal of Management Information Systems*, 22(1): 13–43.

Van de Ven, A. H. (1986) Central Problems in the Management of Innovation, *Management Science*, 32(5): 590–607.

Verona, G. (1999) A Resource-based View of Product Development, *Academy of Management Review*, 24(1): 132–42.

West, M. A. and Farr, J. L. (eds.) (1990) *Innovation and Creativity at Work: Psychological and Organizational Strategies*, Chichester: John Wiley & Sons.

5

Participants in the Process of Knowledge Integration

Jonas Söderlund and Karin Bredin

Based on in-depth research of technical consultants, this chapter identifies and theoretically positions five interrelated activities that are critical to ensure effective knowledge integration in engineering work settings characterized by collaboration between 'strangers' and 'unknowns'. It, thus, brings the operational work condition back into the analysis of knowledge integration.

5.1 PEOPLE IN KNOWLEDGE INTEGRATION

Building on the model presented in Chapter 1, this chapter examines knowledge integration as a process by which several actors (e.g. individuals) combine their uniquely held knowledge to create new knowledge (Okhuysen and Eisenhardt, 2002: 383). The core argument developed here is that knowledge integration depends on the individual actors' abilities to participate in knowledge integration processes and, hence, that the individuals' behaviour and skills are central for the analysis of such processes. It is at this level that different areas of expertise and problem-solving cycles typically are being integrated. This is perhaps especially true for complex R&D and engineering projects (Dougherty, 1992) found in, for instance, the telecom and aerospace sectors, which are the present chapter's primary industry focus.

Two factors appear to be pertinent to accurately address contemporary knowledge integration in engineering work from the viewpoint of the individual engineer. First, R&D and engineering projects in some industries are to a growing extent carried out by contracted engineers or various kinds of 'mobile engineers'. This generally affects the possibilities to build knowledge integration on established 'common knowledge', that is, 'a shared body of knowledge that allows for communication between actors' (see Carlile, 2004: 566). Second, the mounting complexity of technologies and systems involving fundamental interdependencies and group problem-solving modes typically calls for collaborative work across knowledge areas and disciplines, making 'multi-technology' a key feature in the integration activities at the team, project, and firm levels (cf. Granstrand et al.,

1997). These two factors highlight a series of important subsequent enquiries into knowledge integration at work, including the skills that engineers need to be able to work with relative strangers and swiftly establish relationships and the work roles and collaboration among the people involved in the knowledge integration process. Individuals accordingly also need to possess the skills to work with professionals representing diverse backgrounds and engineering expertise – to understand how to make use of other people's knowledge, to know how, and, not least, when to contribute their own uniquely held knowledge to other people's problem-solving processes. Although not applicable to all R&D and engineering contexts, knowing how to move into new projects and become a participant in knowledge integration seems to be critical for the individual engineer.

The overall aim of this chapter is to advance the understanding of engineering work and knowledge integration in technology-based firms where project organization is the order of the day, and where projects and project teams constitute the operational setting for knowledge integration. We focus on one particular group of engineers – a borderland consultant-type of engineer that, so far, has received marginal scholarly attention – in a company that employs highly educated and skilled engineers. The company is Combitech – formally a subsidiary of the Saab aerospace and defence industrial group but with assignments not only for Saab but also for a range of technology-based companies throughout Sweden, such as Ericsson, ABB, and Volvo. In that sense, the company is a modern form of work and knowledge pool, employing people who are project-oriented and hired to do a project together with other technical consultants from Combitech and others, and, to a large extent, with experts from the client organization. There are several firms with a role similar to Combitech's, such as Semcon and ÅF and a range of IT consultancies, that play a critical role for the supply of competencies and resources to development, implementation, and integration projects in technology-based firms. In some industries and regions, they have come to play a critical role, complementing the conventional line organizations and internal work pools to supply additional resources in temporary upswings or crisis situations, or expertise that the company for other reasons does not have in-house. Important explanations for the growth of technical consultancies are the 'flexibilization' of the workforce of corporate giants (cf. Smith, 1997) and the need to reduce transaction costs for knowledge-based services and contracts. The latter has led to clients entering the so-called 'framework contracts' with selected suppliers of IT specialists and technical consultants. Consequently, it has made the entire industry of technical consultancies and IT specialists an important resource and work reservoir for most advanced technology-based firms and, not least, important workplaces for a cadre (junior as well as senior) of engineers. Accordingly, this industry, the consultancies and their employees, also plays a critical part for knowledge development and knowledge integration in technology-based firms in general.

Of course, these engineers do a number of different things: they assume various resource, expertise, and specialist roles and, in some cases, take on coordinative and managerial duties. The engineers in whom we are particularly interested are involved in rather complex development and engineering projects. One example is engineering work for the Gripen air fighter – a development programme with numerous sub-projects which over the years has involved quite a few Combitech engineers. These engineers and their experience from project assignments give us novel insights into the work and worries of people who regularly take part in knowledge integration in technology-based firms, and thereby improve our understanding of knowledge integration at work.

To explore the work and worries of members in complex knowledge integration, we draw upon methodological ideas presented in influential discourses on work studies that touch upon matters similar to those treated in the present chapter. Most important is the work by Barley and Kunda (2006) on technical consultants in Silicon Valley and Tara Fenwick's investigation (2007) of network identities among change management consultants. The point of departure in both cases was a large number of detailed and in-depth interviews with experienced consultants; based on that empirical material, they were able to generate interesting reflections on and insights into the life of the modern project-oriented engineer and knowledge worker. Their primary focus was, however, on work-life issues and identity construction. The study reported here has a different tack. It attempts to delve deeper into the knowledge integration problem – specifically how engineers enter and become part of knowledge integration processes. Above all, we find it interesting to talk about and analyse how the engineers in our study look upon their role generally as technical consultants and project workers and how they handle the early stages of assignments. In that respect, we direct our attention towards what they believe is important in order to swiftly establish knowledge integration preconditions and locate themselves in the knowledge integration processes. The chapter identifies a set of interrelated activities that seem to be crucial for achieving knowledge integration.

5.2 PARTICIPANTS IN KNOWLEDGE COLLECTIVITIES

Traditionally, knowledge integration in development teams and R&D projects has been viewed as a process involving tight coordination, strong mutuality, and shared understanding among those concerned. Although many engineers are still working in this kind of extended group longevity (Katz, 1982), the post-industrial organizational form tends to reduce the strong mutuality and limit the extensive history of common collaborative work (Boltanski and Chiapello, 1999). This is particularly true for the people who participated in our study and just as true for employees in an increasing number of technology-based firms and other technical consultancies. Typically, these engineers work in teams that do not correspond to the conventional idea of the 'well-developed team'. On the contrary, engineering work takes place in less developed groups operating at a limited level of shared understanding in strongly project-oriented settings, characterized by rapid socialization, speedy deliveries, and tough deadlines. Due to high mobility, changing circumstances, travelling inside and across organizations, the engineers' working context is therefore perhaps better described, to draw on Lindkvist (2005), as resembling the 'knowledge collectivity' (see also Hargadon and Bechky, 2006). The knowledge collectivity stands in sharp contrast to the 'knowledge community' – tightly knit teams that have been working together long enough to develop into a cohesive community with relationships of mutuality and shared understandings, often representing similar knowledge areas (Brown and Duguid, 1991; Lindkvist, 2005: 1189). In the knowledge community, knowledge integration thus builds on a deep understanding of each other, resulting from shared, often extensive common experience, shared examples, and work procedures, leading to relatively strong ties between the people involved (Hansen, 1999). This notion, however, seems ill-fitted to the analysis of many contemporary situations of knowledge integration in R&D contexts, where teams and projects exhibit dynamic, mobile, and temporary characteristics. Typically, as argued by Lindkvist (2005: 1189), these teams and projects consist of diversely skilled individuals, most of whom have not met before, who have to solve a problem or carry out a pre-specified and technically challenging task within tightly set limits as to time and costs. Consequently, teams are less well developed and knowledge integration has to operate on a minimal basis of shared knowledge and understandings. Indeed, this allows for greater flexibility and opens up for a kind of 'expertise organization' that is targeted for the specific purpose and equipped to solve the problems at hand. Nevertheless, this kind of organization entails a number of challenges – two of them being the arrangements for knowledge integration and the possibilities of transferring more complex knowledge (Hansen, 1999). Additionally, it requires that the individual engineer becomes part of knowledge integration, understands the context, and makes use of contextual resources, besides activating certain kinds of knowledge capital within as well as outside the team context (cf. Nahapiet and Ghoshal, 1998). One might thus assume that the organizational fluidity in knowledge-intensive work requires a more elaborate form of knowledge integration compared to knowledge integration in ongoing teams in established organizations. At the same time, one would also assume that the mobile engineer learns particular skills over time that are associated with participation in knowledge integration, such as establishing swift trust, understanding socialization processes, living with uncertainties, forming new relationships, making use of external contacts, etc. These skills are then generally assumed to be important for knowledge creation and knowledge integration in a fluid, project-based economy.

The matter of context is essential for the theoretical and empirical framing of the present study, especially in terms of the social connections between the actors involved. In addition, the contextual focus has a more wide-ranging implication because it positions knowledge integration as primarily a social and ongoing, even emergent, activity. Consequently, knowledge integration processes contain important elements of co-participation that are defined in relation to their 'actional contexts' (Hanks, 1991). This indicates the nature of knowledge integration as a process involving improvisation, actual cases of interaction, and emergent processes, making, in Hanks' terms, negotiation, strategy, and unpredictable aspects of action salient ingredients of knowledge integration. What is suggested here is thus a perspective on knowledge integration at work on technological, complex problems that views knowledge integration as being relational, negotiated, and situated (cf. Lave and Wenger, 1991). By addressing knowledge integration accordingly, we are able to locate the individual at its midpoint, yet simultaneously acknowledge the important role of knowledge integration's context and situatedness. Continuing with the idea of situated knowledge integration, which calls for closer scrutiny of the individual engineer's activities and interaction, we would however still argue that the individual engineer can possess some portable skills and activate different kinds of knowledge capital during problem-solving processes, to draw on networks (Barley and Kunda, 2004), connections, and statuses to gain control of problem-setting and problem-solving situations (Schön, 1983).

5.3 SOCIAL AND TECHNICAL DIMENSIONS
OF KNOWLEDGE COLLECTIVITIES

If knowledge collectivities are playing an increasingly important role for knowledge integration and problem-solving in technology-based companies, it seems imperative to address how individual engineers relate to less developed groups and new organizational contexts, and how they cope with increasingly higher demands for flexibility and mobility. Our study takes special interest in the so-called 'interrelated activities' that engineers rely on to participate in knowledge integration processes. In project-based organizations, for instance, one could think of the engineer, who moves from project to project, from team to team, and even from one client organization to another, as not having solid roots in one team or department but continually travelling from temporary projects and teams and still being able to take part in situated knowledge integration processes.

We start from a pattern observed in the empirical accounts, namely the perception of problem-solving situations as displaying both social and technical attributes. This pattern surfaced as an important distinction for making sense of many of the interviews in our fieldwork and was also brought up by the managers in meetings as being essential to satisfy clients and foster motivation among engineers. In other words, engineers enter problem-solving situations that are technically difficult and have to be sorted out in interaction with other engineers, often representing technical domains with which the engineer has not previously collaborated. This typically leads to difficulties of more social kinds, requiring interpretation, communication, interaction, and negotiation. The distinction suggested here between technical and social difficulties is by no means unique – it was already emphasized in classic works in socio-technical studies (Emery and Trist, 1960) and accordingly builds on a long, strong tradition of organizational-behaviour research. In our interpretation, this implies that engineers working in project settings may experience problems primarily as either a technical or a social difficulty. The two-sided nature of complex problem-solving thus echoes the well-known debate about two forms of group development: the social group development as laid out by Tuckman (1965) and the task-oriented group development more recently elaborated by, among others, Gersick (1989). At first sight, the distinction may seem obvious and straightforward. However, closer consideration reveals a rather important theoretical implication. Let us elaborate a bit further on this.

Experts typically begin to 'abstract and simplify their understanding of tasks' (Hinds and Pfeffer, 2003: 6) in highly technical terms, despite the strong evidence that higher order competence involves an ability to position the technical difficulties in their social setting (Sandberg, 2000) and that social ties of various kinds are critical for solving technical problems (Hansen, 1999). Empirical studies also reveal that engineers tend to ignore the social dimension of problem-solving despite the overwhelming evidence that successful technical consultants out-compete their competitors primarily in social terms (Barley and Kunda, 2004), indicating also that decision-makers evaluate technical solutions to a great extent in their interpersonal and social context. Viewing technical issues in their social setting has a number of advantages. Hansen (1999), for instance, convincingly shows that problem solvers need to master a great variety of mechanisms and personal ties to improve their abilities to effectively integrate complex knowledge. It may also lead to a better understanding of knowledge integration per se, since to a large extent in the context addressed here, the process of knowledge integration is a social process, involving communication, interaction, situation awareness, mutual trust, and respect.

A second observation concerns the distinction between active and passive stances or orientations in problem-solving situations. This distinction emerged as important in our data and has considerable support in research on organizational behaviour, with particular reference to the intentional actions pursued by participants in problem-solving situations. The active orientation generally signifies the value of enactment, trial-and-error, and agency in problem-solving situations. The passive orientation encompasses a different modus operandi that relies to a great extent on perception, observation, and reflection. To some degree, these different orientations also represent contrasting 'styles of learning' that serve as a basic distinction in research on experiential learning (Kolb, 1984). Although the distinction builds on somewhat contrasting views of agency – its possibilities and restrictions – the point we are trying to make is that individuals have freedom to act within certain limits and that problem-solving situations are never completely fixed. On the contrary, problem-solving situations are seldom given, emerging instead through a combination of active and passive orientations in the following two ways: (*a*) looking at the technical aspect, through a combination of trial-and-error (active) and reflection (passive) (Weick, 1995), and (*b*) looking at the social dimension, through combinations of role taking (active) and role making (passive) (cf. Turner, 1990). The latter signals that social interaction could be seen as a combination of role taking and role making where the actor actively creates and recreates her role as she progresses through problem-solving situations (Hilbert, 1981).

In sum, combining the idea of knowledge collectivity with the two aforementioned theoretical distinctions, we seek to explore the interrelated activities that people engage in to participate in knowledge integration processes in complex R&D projects. The latter emphasizes not only the emergent nature of problem-solving but also the need to interact with experts from other knowledge domains – of understanding what the problem is, what knowledge is important to connect with, and knowing who possesses that knowledge. It also indicates the significance of the individual activities for gaining a position such that people trust each other, share knowledge and that they have some kind of basic understanding of where to locate relevant knowledge and information, and simultaneously locate other persons' knowledge requirements, for instance knowing whom and when to help out.

Contrary to conventional analyses of technical consultants as knowledge integrators and/or knowledge brokers, the primary idea here is not to portray the engineers as integrators or brokers of knowledge per se. As an alternative, this chapter argues for an analysis that considers them as project workers and as such participants in knowledge integration processes. Accordingly, these experts must be able to activate different kinds of knowledge capital to make use of other expertise and thereby effectively integrate knowledge; the key issue thus becomes that of participating in knowledge integration processes.

We would, however, not posit that these engineers, although in many cases extremely talented and skilled, possess the unique technical specialist knowledge that is critical for the problem-solving situation either on their own or by distributing tasks and information to others. On the contrary and to a great extent, they have similar technical expertise to many of the resident engineers in their client organizations; yet, their experience from a frequent shifting of assignments and from a diverse number of settings could lead one to expect that they have learned something different from resident engineers, and that the client organizations need to consult this expertise; otherwise, the entire idea of mobile engineers becomes merely one of numerical employee flexibility. Numerical flexibility is far from the only and perhaps not even the primary reason for hiring engineers from technical consultancies. Our argument instead is that mobile engineers possess certain unique skills and experience; their skills relate, among other things, to the ability to swiftly enter knowledge integration processes and become participants in knowledge integration. In analysing their participation in knowledge integration, we discern a number of activities, practices, and mechanisms which together substantiate the identified planned and patterned behaviour of significance to knowledge integration. Drawing on adjacent research in work psychology and organizational behaviour, we refer to these activities as ways to enter and improve participation in knowledge integration. In that respect, we align ourselves with a tradition of social psychology that explores the process of managing troublesome, exacting, and tedious circumstances (Horney, 1942) and that frames the work of the engineer to a great extent as that of problem-solving in technical and social settings (cf. Schön, 1983). In general, the activities are then used to master, minimize, reduce, and/or tolerate knowledge integration problems – in our study of complex problems, requiring group problem-solving modes that have both social and technical features. Primarily, as discussed here, the activities work to establish some kind of 'common ground' with the intended recipients and co-creators of their knowledge (Hinds and Pfeffer, 2003) and allow for the activation of certain kinds of capital and knowledge resources.

5.4 RESEARCH SETTING AND METHODS

Combitech is one of Scandinavia's leading engineering consultancies. The company employs technical consultants and experts within the areas of information security, systems security, logistics, systems integration, systems development, and mechanics. Its employees are typically located at customer sites and involved in client projects with members from other consultancies and client resources. Combitech has grown considerably in recent years and at present has almost

1,000 employees, of whom approximately 20 per cent are women. Their average age is roughly 37 and almost 80 per cent have a master's degree in engineering.

Combitech is known for its skilled employees and knowledge within a number of specialist disciplines. It is a popular employer, competing for newly graduated engineers on even terms with Sweden's other most popular employers, including Ericsson, Scania, Saab, Volvo, and ABB. Its relatively rapid growth has tended to weaken the corporate culture, although managers have tried to reinforce shared values, for instance, through various attempts to strengthen the learning environment – 'we offer better learning opportunities than our competitors' and 'we invest more in personal and competence development compared to other employers and technical consultancies' are expressions repeatedly heard from the managers at Combitech. Equally important, as stated in job advertisements and public websites, are the value of 'on-the-job training' and that this requires a certain attitude, thereby fostering a psychological contract between employers and employees that builds on the supply of 'new and challenging assignments' and a willingness to enter new 'problem situations' and take on new challenging project assignments. The latter is vital for the development of competence among people working at Combitech, although quite a few of the informants tell us that these are complicated matters.

Top management has invested a lot of time and resources to establish support functions and development programmes for enhancing the skills of the engineers. For instance, a learning lab has been set up and a series of seminars are regularly held to build networks and relationships to improve the problem-solving capabilities of the engineers – to make it easier for them to get in contact with other specialists working with other assignments but with related technologies. Various internal development projects are also important. These projects generally aim to stimulate experimentation with new methods, work procedures, and advanced technologies. An important initiative, implemented already in the 1990s, is the so-called 'dialogue seminar', a training programme originally designed in collaboration with a group of researchers at the Royal Institute of Technology, but later becoming a part of Combitech's own offerings to clients. The dialogue seminar has also come to be associated with the corporate culture – it is not shared values and common rituals that stand in the fore, rather it is the common interest in continuous learning and skill development that is singled out as critical. Talking and articulating are critical activities, emphasized by managers and frequently mentioned to newcomers, clients, and visitors as part of the company's way of working. The stated importance, however, is not with whom one talks but that one continuously talks with other people, with senior managers, colleagues, and mentors.

The data presented in this chapter consist of interviews with twenty engineers at Combitech and a large number of documents, reflection reports, and books written by its employees and researchers involved in a collaborative research programme on knowledge, experience, and skills among development engineers (see Fock, 2004). The written material and documents span almost fifteen years and thousands of pages. Of particular importance is the *Playground* report series, in which Combitech employees document their reflections about their work and job roles, in particular with regard to skills and knowledge processes. These employees are relatively experienced consultants and the series deals with such topics as collective improvisation, tacit knowledge, trial-and-error processes, creativity, articulation, reflection, leadership, and teamwork. Besides the analysis of the written material, the transcripts from interviews with managers at various levels and engineers were analysed in-depth to ensure sufficient data on the entry into knowledge integration processes.

In the first phase of our fieldwork, we interviewed the managers and studied different sorts of corporate documents and internal material to get an overall understanding of the firm, its history and culture; the organizational structure, responsibilities and roles; and the various knowledge bases residing within the organization. Important here were activities linked to mobility and competence development, and the processes, skills, and behaviours that the managers thought were important to be able to do a good job as an engineer/technical consultant. The interviewed managers all have a background as technical consultants, and a few of them still have part-time consulting assignments parallel to their managerial obligations at Combitech. Thus, they were able to give us an initial understanding of the experience from the senior consultant's perspective along with the experience from being managers for several years. In this phase, we also collected quite a number of written reports, including reflection reports, working papers, and books about knowledge processes and consulting assignments written by engineers in various kinds of development programmes and courses arranged by Combitech to stimulate reflection and professionalism among their employees.

In the second phase of our fieldwork, we interviewed twenty engineers. The reason for selecting twenty interviewees was based on methodological as well as theoretical literature. For instance, it was supported by methodological recommendations in Kvale (1996) and Griffin and Hauser (1993). The latter demonstrates, for example, that twenty interviews yielded 91 per cent of the theoretically available information, that is, adding one more interview gave only slight improvements, excluding one considerably reduced the theoretically available information. Together with managers from Combitech, we selected employees with extensive experience from work as engineers, representing different knowledge areas and demographics. The interviews followed a standardized guide covering such topics as personal background, professional history and education, work role, assignments, and a series of detailed questions about their current assignments. In that respect, the empirical study was designed in accordance with the recommendations of Barley and Kunda (2006) and Fenwick (2007), mentioned earlier. The engineers were asked to talk about their most recent project and incidents they thought were important for them to be able to carry out their assignment. The intention from our side was to create a trustful conversation about their role and work as engineers, perceived challenges, and obstacles during project assignments. Each interview lasted between 1.5 and 2.5 hours. The interviews were recorded, transcribed, and analysed at the empirical level, listening through the recordings, making notes, and identifying common patterns and differences across the interviews. When quoting from the interviews, we use code names (Manager I, Manager II, etc. and Engineer A, Engineer B, etc.), since some of the information might be sensitive for the individual engineer or manager.

In the third phase, we conducted the analysis of our data and carried out additional, complementary data gathering, such as telephone interviews, e-mail questions, focused follow-up interviews with selected respondents, and collection of additional written material. This process was initiated to add breadth and depth to our investigation and correct any misunderstandings in our preliminary analysis. In this phase, we also analysed in further depth the reflection reports and working papers written by some of the employees. A few of the consultants and managers have even presented their work as part of their doctoral dissertations (e.g. Backlund, 2006; Sjunnesson, 2007) and written extensively in various articles, reports, and papers about their skills, skill development, and role as engineers. In that respect, we believe, this company is almost unique and a rather exceptional source of data for reflecting on the skills and knowledge of engineers and consultants, and, equally, for addressing participation in knowledge integration processes.

5.5 INTERRELATED ACTIVITIES IN COMPLEX KNOWLEDGE INTEGRATION

The analysis of the data from these materials identifies five sets of 'interrelated activities' which together appear to precipitate knowledge integration in project work. Taken together, the activities constitute an alternative framework for understanding and managing the knowledge integration processes within projects. The following activities will be illustrated, discussed, and theoretically positioned: (*a*) Rule following, (*b*) Relating, (*c*) Role carving, (*d*) Reflection, and (*e*) Reframing. The overall intention is to discuss the activities in light of knowledge integration processes – what the interviewees and reflection reports emphasize and what emerges as important for playing their part in the knowledge integration process.

Rule following centres on abilities to make use of existing rules. This activity then acknowledges the importance of rules and directives for knowledge integration (Grant, 1996: 114) but adds an important dimension – that rules exist in a social context and need to be interpreted by individuals and applied wisely in particular situations (Johannessen, 2006). Accordingly, all rules precipitate a certain degree of interpretation and skills, and, not least, tacit understanding. One could argue that rules of various kinds are fundamental for the contexts discussed here: rules abound in software engineering, programming languages, specifications, project models, etc. To make use of this kind of 'structural capital', engineers need to be able to make appropriate interpretations and adaptations of rules to fit the problem situation at hand.

Relating focuses on the social capital of the engineers and the social context of the project team. It centres on the groups of activities tied to resources rooted in intra- and extra-relationships of the focal actional context (cf. Nahapiet and Ghoshal, 1998). In that respect, it refers to a broad set of activities aimed at entering and making use of one's social capital in the focal project, knowing who knows what, whom to ask for guidance, and who might be in need of information, and when this need might arise.

Role carving is an activity of significance in situations where social ambiguity is the key factor. The importance of role carving has also been emphasized in previous research on technical consultants' social situation (Barley and Kunda, 2006: 249). This activity generally highlights the ongoing structuring and dynamics of roles in social settings, and perhaps, most importantly, in dynamic projects. Role carving further supports relating, although it tends to focus more on activities associated with the particular role, not specifically reaching out for knowledge. Accordingly, role carving could play an important role for people to establish appropriate expectations and thus build trust among participants in the knowledge integration process.

Reflection zeroes in on the individual's actions to cope with the task of entering new problem-solving situations with regard to technical solutions. Accordingly, this activity focuses on the technical aspects and is predominantly a passive stance, although it might involve conversations, experimentation, and probing (Schön, 1983: 145). This activity, although associated with experimentation and conversation, focuses primarily on the 'virtual world' (Ibid.). In that respect, it focuses on observing, experimenting, seeing, and listening. The activity also seems to be a matter of preparing for action when things might change or have been sorted by key stakeholders or experts in the project.

Reframing encompasses a broad range of actions, skills, and mechanisms, albeit with a specific focus on the tasks at hand, especially the technical problems. It covers how engineers reinterpret and reformulate system properties, functional specifications, overall task partitioning, and breakdown structure, thereby the task as such and even, in some cases, the entire project. It is viewed here as an active stance because engineers in these situations reinterpret and reformulate complex problems to a greater extent than is common in everyday complex problem-solving.

The remainder of the chapter is structured as follows. The next section gives an inside view of the experiences and stories of the engineers who participated in our study. We will here give a contextual description of Combitech, what is emphasized by management, and try to decipher some aspects of their corporate culture. Then follows a set of examples aimed at illustrating the activities mentioned above. The chapter thereafter proceeds with the analysis and moves into a comparison of the activities, in what situations they are relied upon, what sorts of knowledge are critical, and what knowledge capital is being activated through these activities.

5.6 PATTERNS IN COMPLEX KNOWLEDGE INTEGRATION

So what emerged in our interviews and studied documents? As to the reasons why people want to work for Combitech, many interviewees return to the opportunities of moving across projects and across problem-solving contexts. The typical assignment lasts between one and two years, depending on the area of technology, although the assignments might be divided into a series of short, three-to-four-month, periods after which contract terms and job roles are renegotiated. This creates a particular kind of work dynamic. The respondents seem to be aware of the negative aspects of working as a hired engineer, but still prefer it to working in a more traditional technology-based company, such as the ones represented by their clients. Some refer to the possibility of working with exciting technologies;

others stress the social dimensions of consulting work. In either case, it is the continuous movement that keeps them going and ensures the activation of their abilities and skills, for instance when it comes to entering new teams and seeing patterns across problem-solving situations. The positive effects are also evident among those who state they get bored by being on the same assignment for too long. As one of the engineers told us in an interview:

> To be honest, I can stand around 1.5 years on the same assignment and then I have to get out of there. (Engineer G)

Several of the respondents mention that they 'don't want to end up in the situation where a lot of regular employees end up'. Accordingly, they look upon their work as quite different from that of many other engineers – that it is not a matter of 'holding on desperately to their desks and their tasks' but 'to complete the assignment and then move on to the next one' (Manager II). Being a technical consultant, working at Combitech or one of its competitors, is 'different' and many seem to have the need to accentuate this difference, although the basic technical and operational tasks carried out are typically not very different from those of engineers in general, no matter where they work.

Some informants said it could be somewhat frustrating not knowing whether a project or a new assignment will be coming in, but added that 'it has always worked out well in the past, so I'm not particularly worried'. One of the managers pointed out that for many of the engineers, the biggest worry is actually the reverse. He told us that 'staying too long on the same assignment' and ending up doing 'very dull and routine-oriented job' is what many perceive as 'their biggest threat' (Manager II). In that respect, the continuous movement among projects, tasks, and social contexts forces them to engage in an ongoing interaction with new people, which also leads them to explore new relationships and keep dormant relationships alive, since new problems typically call for a broader range of contacts with people inside and outside the current action locality.

Being a knowledge-intensive firm, a critical issue for Combitech is to recruit the right kind of people with the capacity to relate, to 'network', and to make use of various knowledge bases within Combitech, the client organization, and elsewhere, for instance in professional networks and communities. In interviews, managers argue that they need 'good people' with a 'certain attitude' and 'personality', not just the required technical skills. The reason, they say, is basically that the 'good people' find it much easier to shift assignments, enter new teams and new problem-solving contexts, and they seem to make good use of social capital. Social skills and the ability to communicate are emphasized recurrently, compared to skills considered to be important for engineers in general. In the written documents where the consultants reflect upon their assignments and current job role, many emphasize the critical importance as an engineer of building social capital, learning the skills to get to know the organization in which one is currently working, and also that 'asking for help' is not unprofessional, rather the contrary.

The interviewed engineers also brought this up. Quite a number of our informants referred explicitly to certain kinds of 'social skill' and the ability to communicate – something that was contrasted to the conventional image of the professional engineer.

> The social skills are important. To be able to voice your opinion you need to get an understanding of the situation, what kind of situation it is, what is needed to solve the problems . . . do I need to act, how should I act? And when you have managed a certain number of situations you grow as a person and thereby become a better consultant. (Manager III)

In the reflection reports, the importance of 'situation understanding', 'situational awareness', and familiarity with the client organization are popular topics. In the theoretical analysis of these themes, quite a few talk about 'analogical reasoning', 'analogical thinking', and 'heedful interrelating' as part of the core skills of engineers – and perhaps even more critical for engineers associated with Combitech. The familiarity covers quite a broad range of topics, including that of understanding the power game in the focal project and its surroundings, the local language, and various rules and routines. As one of the interviewed engineers put it, 'you need to know where you are to be able to take part in this kind of development work – the language, and all that – we often talk about some sort of situation understanding – they don't teach you that in school, why?' Several of the informants mentioned the importance of having the 'communication skills so people accept or appreciate what you are trying to say'. To some extent, these are somewhat different matters, although they seem to be more related than one would initially assume. The first could perhaps best be described as 'articulation', which according to the informants involves a range of things, including writing, formulating things at meetings, being able to explain the basic ideas underlying a particular system design. Many return to the responsibilities of communicating and making sure of receiving feedback – both have critical roles to play in knowledge integration in the kind of development work discussed here.

However, communication and articulation all happen in a social context and accordingly are firmly grounded in various social skills and self-confidence. It also, according to several interviewees and report writers, depends largely on one's abilities to assume different roles in different situations and organizations, although certain traits and attributes seem to be generic across all situations. As one of our informants put it:

> They can't look at you as a threat or a person with a big ego. Those people just don't work in our organization. (Manager II)

The latter seems to be a critical issue for Combitech engineers. You need to be competent, you need to know the technology, or at least be willing to learn and do your part of the problem-solving. This is frequently brought up in the reflection reports. Questions abound as to what Combitech engineers know that other engineers do not know. Triggered by various 'impulse texts', a number of them have, as mentioned, gone further into issues like 'situation awareness', 'heedful relating', 'situation understanding', although not in a theoretical language but through examples from their own work.

> It's good that you have the chance to see other places, work with other clients. It is probably only when you have had the opportunity to compare your previous experience with something else that you are able to see what actually works, what doesn't work and why it doesn't work. Through this you might learn what is important in your work as an engineer. (Manager IV, Senior Consultant)

As part of the development of skills and the engineers' abilities to better understand the current problem-solving situation, Combitech has arranged a number of courses and seminars. In addition, consultants have written several individual reflection reports to address this particular issue in further depth. In the reflection reports, a common theme is that of being able to 'learn across examples' and 'search for patterns' to identify problems early and detect system-wide errors of both a technical and a social nature. In seminars with experienced consultants, a great deal of the discussion revolved around the process of 'analogical reasoning' and 'analogical thinking'. To be able to make this work in a team context involving a number of disciplines, participants are required to search for analogies as part of their own reflective work, as part of dialogues with other team members, and as part of discussions with people outside the focal project, such as members in other projects, experts in the line organization, and colleagues working elsewhere within the Combitech organization. Accordingly, there are many ways in which the consultants seek to activate the related experience of themselves and others.

Being a technical consultant is associated with expectations, and these expectations may work in two very different directions. In some cases, expectations are helpful since they allow the engineer to get established quickly, getting people to trust the newcomer and assigning the newcomer a prominent role in the knowledge integration process. In other cases, however, perhaps closely associated with this, unduly high expectations may lead clients to think that the 'hired guru' will solve every technical difficulty, get the project back on track, and infuse the entire project with some magic energy. This could lead to continuous negotiations and some frustration – in some cases even open conflict. The interviewees speak about the importance of adjusting expectations to the right level, but at the same time making use of high expectations to be able to get established in the organization.

We asked our interviewees the following kinds of question: What do you learn as a 'mobile engineer'? What are the key skills you need to acquire? Several of the senior engineers mentioned the importance of having an extended network of contacts in the early stage to build self-esteem and learn the role of consultant and project member. Many returned to such expressions as 'school is good, but it doesn't teach you how to work in projects with real people and real problems'. The more senior informants also told stories about it being 'all about people' and that as a young inexperienced engineer one might be great at programming 'but that's not the important stuff' (Engineer A). One of the informants mentioned the value of building 'one's platform'; this was also mentioned by many of the other consultants, although in slightly different terms, starting with technology and moving on from there and that although technology is not always the most difficult issue, a strong connection to it is critical to becoming a successful Combitech consultant. The metaphor of the 'platform' seemed to combine a number of different skills, resources, and networks involving both technical and social dimensions. One of the engineers told us the following story.

> When you start working as a young, inexperienced engineer, you might be great at programming. But that's not the most important thing./ . . . / You need to keep things simple, do only what the customer wants, but the client doesn't know what he wants. So you just have to work your way through, ask a lot of questions, acquire a feeling for what is good and what is not good, what the client might want. When you get more

experience, you have to be able to identify these things – what the client wants and what he doesn't want. It's definitely not easy. (Engineer D)

Another recurrent metaphor used in reflection reports is that of 'the inner picture' and that as an engineer you over time become better at understanding the inner picture of the system, what the team is to develop, and also identify mismatch among the inner pictures of the people taking part in project work. As one of them wrote in a report, the goal is not to have complete overlap of everyone's inner pictures, but make sure that 'they are sufficiently aligned' and not 'divergent'. These skills also make it possible to better comprehend what a 'good system' in the particular situation is and whether the team is equipped to handle the particular problem at hand.

New assignments tend to be coupled with many positive feelings, particularly with regard to learning new things. At the same time, there is a feeling of novelty that some believe might have negative effects, causing stress and frustration. Before taking a new assignment, the engineers normally get a briefing and a short assignment specification to see if the assignment is something they would be interested in. Important here are role descriptions and task specifications and additional brief information about the client's project. Even so, there is uncertainty and ambiguity. As one informant told us:

> Many assignments are quite fuzzy. You begin with a three-month contract and then you extend the contract, and then you extend it again. You might be there for a couple of years and what you are doing at the end of your assignment could be very different from what they initially hired you to do. (Engineer E)

Project assignments differ in several respects. The projects themselves also differ – some are extensive, complex high-technology projects, others are short, focused task-force assignments, not involving a lot of new technologies. In either case, there is always a need to quite rapidly understand the context, due to time pressure, early deliveries, or major initial design decisions. Connected with this is the continuous need to establish trust in new working situations. Socialization becomes a key issue – entering new situations and building trust in new teams.

> In many projects you need to spend a lot of time getting to know the people, establish trust with the people you are working with and build your role and place to be able to carry out the assignment. You need to socialize, be nice, say the right things, and all that. (Engineer A)

However, not everyone referred to the major problem as strictly social; some framed it primarily in technical language, pointing to problems associated with design features and technical specifications. Often consultants entered projects that had already been running for some time within the client organization, with an established team. This led to the feeling of entering a moving project and having to constantly catch up with what had happened and what was already decided. One of our informants used the metaphor of a moving train to explain the general feeling:

> Quite often the train has sort of left the station when I enter the project. So the first weeks you just have to keep running to catch up, get to know the people and get to know your area. . . . My assignments are typically a year or so . . . and when I enter the

project, it is already rolling and there is some kind of problem in the project, that's why they hired me, so to speak. (Engineer A)

When asked about the typical dynamics of an assignment, the engineers referred to very loose and fuzzy beginnings that over time were sorted out with a variety of techniques and methods. Typically, people said they had a passive role in the early stages of an assignment, listening to other people's conversations and slowly trying to find out whom to talk to, who seemed to have important knowledge, and in what areas to search for new knowledge and information. However, instead of disappearing, in many assignments this fuzziness continued as a consequence of social and technical complexities combined with the social dynamics of people joining the project and others leaving it. Although frustrating at times, many seem to be attracted by such assignments and projects.

> I like assignments that are a bit fuzzy where you don't have the walls around you, where you can seek the opportunities and explore the open areas. But I don't think that the newly recruited can handle these situations. I guess many leave the company because they're not mature enough. (Engineer F)

It seems that dealing with ambiguity and fuzzy assignments is business as usual for the more senior consultant. These skills appear to combine self-confidence and proactive behaviour in problem-solving situations. The fear was of becoming isolated and not a part of everyday conversations, not getting the key information that is needed to do a good job. However, some situations call for a slightly more relaxed, even passive attitude.

> If someone would have given me this assignment two or three years ago, I'm not sure I would have made it. It's a lot more difficult to understand this project and it can easily get people worried, a lot of stress and fear. Now, I'm more like: 'Well it'll get sorted. Later on I'll find out what I'm supposed to do here'. (Engineer A)

Over time, the consultants develop the skills and experience to better cope with complexity and ambiguous situations. This generally is a rather multifaceted issue involving both the skills to deal better with architectural or systemic problems, or, which many stress, knowing when there are other people who are better positioned to solve the underlying architectural problems. However, even though this would indicate a less active stance on behalf of the individual engineer, it still very much emphasizes the role of the individual worker to support and 'take part' in the architectural problem-solving process. In the cases where engineers assume a more central role, this also frequently tends to change the typical assignments for which they are recruited. Several of our interviewees said that over time they developed into a more advice-oriented role. However, this seems to be a delicate matter, of not voicing your opinion too strongly, of listening to the needs of clients and the nature of the atmosphere.

> If you have a very strong opinion about something you can't hesitate, you just have to tell the client. But there are different ways of saying things, you need to get them on board, get them to see the reasons for listening to your ideas. You have to be mindful. (Engineer G)

As mentioned earlier, task specifications and role descriptions are intended to provide clarity, steer expectations among the people involved, and sort out any misunderstandings. Yet, in these dynamic problem-solving settings, specifications and role descriptions will always be incomplete. Many informants give examples of projects where they had to 'sort out the role yourself' and that 'it's muddling work' before the engineer understands his/her task, the environment, and the problem-solving situation. This seems to be part of the everyday issues – and it is made even more difficult since clients typically have less knowledge about the tasks as such and the roles of the consultants, which could lead to quite substantial changes in tasks done and roles assumed by the consultants. Some informants said that those 'who hired me probably didn't know what they wanted', which forced them to 'start sorting things out, working with the specification and explain to the client what we needed to do' (Engineer B). One engineer said:

> When I have gotten a task specification or a role description quite often they have been very wrong. So, I say: 'Hey, but this isn't right, this isn't what you need'. These assignments end up very different from where they started. (Engineer G)

This indistinctness is mentioned in particular when we ask the engineers to speak about their experience from new assignments and the early stages of projects. Here many of the informants provide us with quite vivid stories and interesting examples of what they have done, what problems they have encountered, and how they have solved the problems. These early-stage stories typically deal with topics associated with 'assignment specifications' and 'role descriptions'. Although these documents are far from complete, they seem to play a critical role in the ongoing discussions about what to expect from each other, mutual responsibilities, and provide some kind of materiality in an otherwise rather immaterial work condition. The documents are accordingly important for the consultant to know what to prepare for and to manage the client's expectations. Questions entail such matters as: What has been hired? What is my role? What are the client's needs? Despite the attempts to make assignments as clear and transparent as possible, there is always incompleteness, which one of the engineers expressed in the following way:

> There is never a clear assignment specification when you enter a project. You get things as you go. The client checks out how good you are, what you can do, what you can't do. And then things change and you just have to respond to that – enter a new role because the client needs you to. (Engineer A)

Others speak of assignment specifications as something that is part of a pre-negotiation and that the skilled engineers know what questions to ask. In some cases, they get very brief notes and presentations of assignments, for instance if there is a crisis project that desperately needs help and support. One engineer told us about his latest assignment:

> When I started my most recent assignment I got an oral presentation of what I was supposed to do, and then I received an e-mail that explained a bit more about what they wanted me to do. There were a lot of question marks at that time. (Engineer A)

Although the assignment specification and role description play an important part in the preparation for new assignments and new contexts and both assignments and roles become less ambiguous, there is still some kind of dynamic involved. This typically led the informants to speak in terms of 'clarifying', 'lowering expectations', the 'role of the consultant', and the 'ambiguity of the early phases' and that they relied on various activities and skills to deal with these uncertainties. However, given that they are involved in complex engineering work, a certain degree of uncertainty and complexity will always be involved. What was solved yesterday might become a problem today, the detection and correction of bugs and errors had unexpected consequences and a series of new bugs and errors in other parts of the system. In that respect, 'assignments are not static – they change, constantly' (Engineer B).

5.7 INTERRELATED ACTIVITIES AND KNOWLEDGE INTEGRATION

In this section, we engage in a discussion about the patterns observed in our interview transcripts, the identified interrelated activities presented earlier, and the overall idea of participation in knowledge integration. To start with, let us return to the activities of rule following, relating, role carving, reflection, and reframing. Although obviously nested in practice, for analytical purposes we will try to separate them here. The overall questions concern where these activities are observed, in what situations, and through what practices? We will also discuss the linkages between the activities and the activation of different knowledge capital in problem-solving situations. The latter is important to attain a better understanding of the participants' situation in knowledge integration and for framing the entire problem as one of situatedness but with capital that can be drawn on to act and interact in the spirit of complex problem-solving. We have argued in this chapter that (*a*) an important context for knowledge integration in technology-based companies is the so-called knowledge collectivities, where participants integrate knowledge with only a minimum level of shared experience and common history; (*b*) knowledge integration at work typically involves both social and technical elements; (*c*) knowledge integration, given its situatedness, needs to be addressed at the individual level; and (*d*) individuals' experiences of lived and situated knowledge integration, of entering new technical and social situations, offer unique insights into knowledge integration by drawing attention to the activities in which individuals engage in order to activate certain knowledge bases and 'capital' and become legitimate members of knowledge integration. We will discuss how the activities are used, what capital they activate, and what skills and mechanisms are important to participate in knowledge integration.

Looking at the interviews and the empirical account, informants frequently speak about task specifications and role descriptions as important documents that are used to negotiate and sort out ambiguities in problem-solving situations. Task specifications typically relate to the technical dimensions of knowledge collectivities – this is what should be done, these are the tasks to perform, and these are the objectives to reach. Task specifications are important to initially determine the match between one's skills and the requirements for the new assignment. It is also important to evaluate the challenge involved in the new assignment. To a great extent, these specifications play an important role in linking the engineer with the knowledge collectivity, although, due to technical uncertainties and difficulties in articulating needs and expectations, the specifications are at all times incomplete, in some cases even completely misconceived. Accordingly, the engineers spend much time sorting out the real task specifications involved and the associated expectations, which thus seem to be important parts of the knowledge integration process.

Role descriptions centre primarily on the role and function that the engineer is expected to fulfil. Interestingly, these two critical documents and the various interpretations and viewpoints surrounding them also tell us something about knowledge integration, particularly participation in it. As seen in the interview quotations and the summaries of our observations, participation in knowledge integration revolves around both technical and social features – of assuming a role, of carving out a role for oneself and handling expectations of what could be expected of one's performance, and, additionally, of dealing with technical problems – of trying out new solutions, fixing bugs, and detecting errors. However, as the interviews clearly demonstrated, to be able to participate in knowledge integration one needs to handle uncertainties in relation to what the engineer is supposed to do and what role he/she is to perform. The difficulties were most apparent in the early stages of projects and assignments, since that is when many things are blurred, targets have not been completely set, and solutions are still discussed at a very general level. In addition, entering new problem-solving situations for the engineers often meant meeting new people with whom they have not worked before.

Given our earlier standpoint that knowledge integration at work principally is situated, emergent, relational, and negotiated, sorting out one's position among the members of the team and related teams is a critical concern, which cannot be viewed in isolation from the technical features. Correspondingly, viewing technical problem-solving is to the same extent a matter of social games, of having the trust of other members, of having a reputation of being someone who is competent and someone to rely on. It also involves a great deal of timing – of knowing when the time has come to act, when to wait for more information, and in what situations one should assure that the sufficient level of absorptive capacity has been reached on the interacting party's side, for instance within the client organization or among the rest of the project team.

The above discussion has highlighted the combination of activities for entering and participating in knowledge integration processes. Summarizing a few of these observations, it can be said that the five activities are of course complementary but also seem to be utilized more frequently in some situations than in others; where intentions differ, as do the competencies that are in focus (see DeFillippi et al., 2006). Relating, for instance, typically involves such matters as knowing where, knowing whom, and knowing when, whereas reframing to a greater extent centres on knowing why and knowing what. Table 5.1 presents a few of our observations in an attempt to delineate the differences between the interrelated activities discussed earlier. Table 5.1 also contains an interpretation of what kind of 'capital' is activated through the use of each of the activities. This activation of capital will be discussed in more detail below.

So far, we have primarily dealt with participation in knowledge integration and paid only modest attention to knowledge integration processes as such. While the primary focus and idea of the chapter is to discuss the situatedness and the relationship between the technical and social attributes of knowledge integration, we would

Table 5.1 Activities, competencies, and capital activation in knowledge integration

	Rule following	Relating	Role carving	Reflection	Reframing
Intention	Understand procedures and rules of knowledge integration	Understand context of knowledge integration process	Build trust and clarify expectations, ensure interplay within team	Await signals and integration results from more central players, prepare for action	Reduce complexity, sort out assignments at the overall level to make local problem-solving possible
Competencies	Knowing how	Knowing where, knowing whom, knowing when	Knowing whom, knowing what	Knowing why, knowing what, knowing how	Knowing why, knowing what
Mechanisms and practices relied upon	Development models, project management models, development tools	Conversation, dialogue, informal discussions, management support, meetings	Role descriptions, negotiation, team member interactions	Task specifications, observations, listening, reflection, analogical reasoning	Sensing, communication, convincing, project specifications
Maxim	'Understand the contextual rules, and the applicability of design rules'	'Understand context to know who knows what, and who needs to know'	'Create a role to set expectations and build trust'	'Reflect on problems to position requirements and solutions'	'Reframe problems to create a better problem-solving architecture and team interaction'
Activated capital	Structural capital	Social capital	Role capital	Analogical capital	Human capital

still like to comment upon the knowledge involved and what knowledge seems to be activated through the use of the five interrelated activities. We will refer to this as different kinds of capital on which the individual draws to be able to integrate knowledge. We use the term capital because it is frequently employed in this area of study and seems appropriate, given our earlier definition and view of knowledge. The idea of capital as outlined here is still very much in line with the situated analysis since capital does not exist in isolation but is activated by actors in a specific situation and is successfully activated only when the social situation is arranged accordingly or when the individual is in a position or has the power to use his/her capital. We argue that the activities correspond to five slightly different types of capital and thereby posit that an important role of the activities is to activate various sorts of capital. The activation has two aspects. One relates to the fact that knowledge integration is made possible through various sorts of capital; for instance, individuals need human and social capital to take part in knowledge integration processes. The other aspect concerns the fact that knowledge integration might set free knowledge that otherwise would not be part of the knowledge integration process.

An important issue concerns the ability to follow rules. Theoretically, this particular activity is closely associated to tacit knowing and the individual's understanding of the relevant structural capital for the problem-solving situation at hand. This activity is frequently discussed in the reflection reports; it has also been analysed in further detail in the various published reports from research projects in which Combitech engineers have participated. To some extent, this throws additional light on Grant's notion (1996) of rules as important knowledge integration mechanisms; however, here we identify the importance of acknowledging that rules are not abstract; rather they need to be interpreted and defined in the particular knowledge integration context, be adapted to the situation at hand, and be implemented wisely.

The activities that aim at relating, primarily address social capital (Nahapiet and Ghoshal, 1998). This capital is assured mainly by making use of relationships inside and outside the focal problem-solving situation. In the case studied here, these relationships tend to focus on the social capital of the Combitech organization (e.g. managers, mentors, and colleagues) or of people in the client organization (most notably people in the focal project). In that respect, this is capital on which the individual can draw to gain a better understanding of the actional context, to sort out the significant persons in the organization, the potential social ambiguities involved, and how to solve them. The activity is often aided by managerial support and through other contacts and track records. Although involving some degree of action, the activity tends to be rather passive with regard to the focal team and the problem-solving at hand. Instead, this is typically left to others – other team members and members of the client organization should assign and create a role for the individual engineer so that the newcomer can take part in the knowledge integration process.

The role carving activity resembles the relating activity to some extent, although here we are dealing with a more proactive stance with regard to the focal group – where engineers actively seek to position themselves in relation to other team members – for instance to reduce social uncertainty or to clarify expectations and role obligations. Role carving primarily activates what might be referred to as role capital, which is a resource constituted of networks of relationships that are critical for the conduct of social affairs (Baker and Faulkner, 1991). Role capital is embedded in networks, expectations, previous experience and is of course omnipresent in most problem-solving situations. The point here, however, is that role carving always starts with some kind of general role expectations, but can be influenced by the individual through purposeful actions (see e.g. Meyerson et al., 1996). Role carving thus rests on the understanding that role carving is explained both by an understanding of roles as such and different kinds of role in complex problem-solving situations, and by the trust in the individual to carve out a role that will be good for the entire knowledge integration process.

The reflection activity covers a range of things tied to both individual and collective problem-solving. In this context, we would like to emphasize one interpretation in line with our overall idea of knowledge integration at work. Reflection as interpreted here does not centre so much on the role or on interpreting the social interaction processes. Instead, this activity centres primarily on tasks and technologies, of trying to learn what tasks should be done, why they need to be done, and what is required to solve a particular task. It involves quite substantial technical skills and abilities – in particular those skills associated with comparing experience across problem-solving situations and pattern recognition, which was a common theme in the reflection reports written by the consultants. To a great extent, we argue that the particular skills connected to this activity resemble that of analogical reasoning. Accordingly, one might therefore view this activity as one that activates a kind of 'analogical capital'.

The final activity, reframing, makes use to some extent of all the former kinds of capital, structural capital, role capital, social capital, analogical capital, to understand the basic technology, to establish a certain level of trust as well as a role and 'platform' from which the engineer can act in such a way as to affect the perception of a problem situation. In that sense, this activity is to a large extent oriented towards problem setting in social situations – convincing people of the need of problem setting and combining the various forces to integrate knowledge to better frame and perceive the problem at hand. In addition, however, this activity relies on and activates a fifth kind of capital – the human capital that emerges in the focal situation (Barley and Kunda, 2004) and becomes valuable when there is a certain level of acceptance within the group and the person with access to the capital has gained a position from which he/she can activate it.

In sum, viewing these interrelated activities as ways to make successful participation possible adds to the understanding of knowledge integration at work as being situated. However, the analysis of various kinds of capital being activated through the use of these activities adds another dimension that acknowledges the portable knowledge and skills which engineers can take with them across problem-solving situations and the existence of specific kinds of capital which the individual learns to deploy to become better at solving complex problems together with others.

5.8 CONCLUDING DISCUSSION

The findings presented here are important for a variety of reasons and particularly pertinent to some engineering contexts, primarily because they offer novel interpretations of knowledge integration as a complex problem-solving and creative activity. First, it is important to be able to improve the effectiveness of knowledge collectivities – a type of project organization often relied upon in complex problem-solving settings. The chapter offers suggestions about activities that seem important for people dealing with new problem-solving situations. Second, the data highlight the fact that despite the fluid nature of knowledge integration in knowledge collectivities, situatedness is still a salient and significant feature of knowledge integration. Third, the findings may lead to improvements in the working situation and professional development of project-oriented engineers (cf. Allen and Katz, 1995) and how problem-solving skills relate to both social and technical processes. This then evinces the importance of considering knowledge integration as a critical part of an engineer's job. In order to take part in such processes, the repertoire of action strategies and skills for swiftly entering prob lem-solving situations – to sort out the social and technological games that are critical particularly in the early stages, but which, due to the complexities and uncertainties involved in many of these projects – represent ongoing difficulties. Accordingly, the present study sheds light on the importance of socializing oneself to the organizational contexts in which knowledge integration processes are embedded.

Indeed, the issue of knowledge integration as treated here resembles the classic case of organizational socialization, for instance, in the sense that participants enter new organizational contexts (a new organization and a new team) and must thus learn to speak the local language. In that respect, the individual learns the ropes of 'a particular organizational role' and 'acquires the social knowledge and skills necessary to assume an organizational role' (Van Maanen and Schein, 1977: 1). According to work on socialization, this process where individuals are 'transformed from organization outsiders to participating and effective members' (Feldman, 1981: 309) is often time-consuming, lasting between six and twelve months. The socialization that is relevant for technical consultants is obviously very different, since they initially have a fixed deadline for their assignments, and internal policies to shift assignments after eighteen months. Still, socialization does play an important role but takes forms that differ from conventional organizational socialization. For instance, informants said that as a hired engineer one needs to 'speak their language', 'refer to their examples', 'accept their rules', and 'understand their culture'. What seems to be involved here is a kind of socialization that is more deliberate, conscious, and time-restricted. In that sense, it is perhaps more applicable here to speak of some kind of 'swift' trust and 'cool' socialization. In addition, given that the engineers often have skills and experience that the organization needs and that the action locality is relatively restricted and team-oriented, one might assume that resident team members also would need to respond to the behaviour of the newcomer to allow knowledge to be efficiently integrated. Accordingly, there is more of interactive socialization in these cases than what conventional analysis of socialization would have us believe. Interestingly, however, the fact that socialization is 'cool' can actually foster knowledge integration since deep disagreements will not surface during time-limited collaborations (Harrison et al., 2002). Our data indicate that this cool socialization constitutes an important aspect of knowledge integration at work and allows for a broader search for capital and knowledge that would otherwise not be possible. At the same time, it calls for skilled individuals who believe in themselves, look pragmatically at knowledge processes, and engage and consult whomever necessary to be able to activate the right kind of capital and thereby foster knowledge integration.

Thus, the study offers a view on team processes and socialization efforts that contrasts with what is often presented in management literature. The study reported here emphasizes the importance of the individual becoming socialized to such a degree that he/she becomes a participant in situated knowledge integration processes and is able to understand the social framing of technical problems and the social ambience among the people involved in interdependent problem-solving work. The study, although limited in many respects, may prove important for exploring the combination of organizational capabilities for knowledge integration and individual problem-solving skills. In that respect, this and similar studies may enhance the understanding of both an increasingly important organizational capability and individual problem-solving skills. Such studies would need to focus more on actual project work, in particular since there is a 'dearth of data on what people actually do – the skills, knowledge, and practices' (Barley and Kunda, 2001: 90).

5.9 IMPLICATIONS

The chapter has provided some additional insights into the processes and participants of knowledge integration. It identifies a set of important activities of importance for establishing teams and projects that better integrate knowledge across disciplinary areas and activate relevant knowledge capital. The chapter also emphasizes the importance of individual activities for relating to team members in order to ensure a collective mind and heedful interrelating in the focal problem-solving situations. The chapter takes as its point of departure and develops further the idea of knowledge integration at work as a situated process involving both social and technical dimensions. This accentuates the role of skills that breach technological and social qualities and the need to contextualize the 'competence of the engineer' (Sandberg, 2000), involving such parameters as situational awareness, situation understanding, and, as emphasized through this paper, the necessary skills to take part in knowledge integration process and in that process activate the relevant knowledge capital.

ACKNOWLEDGEMENTS

The research presented here was carried out in collaboration with Elisabeth Borg, doctoral candidate, Linköping University. We are grateful for the support from Combitech, its managers, and consultants who willingly shared their experience with us and to the many researchers who were involved in the dialogue seminars with engineers at Combitech. We also acknowledge the valuable comments from

120   *Knowledge Integration and Innovation*

the participants in the *Project Forum* Seminar, BI Norwegian School of Management, on an earlier version of this chapter.

REFERENCES

Allen, T. J. and Katz, R. (1995) The Project-oriented Engineer: A Dilemma for Human Resource Management, *R&D Management*, 25(2): 129–40.

Backlund, G. (2006) *Om ungefärligheten i ingenjörsarbete*, Dialoger, PhD thesis, Stockholm: Royal Institute of Technology.

Baker, W. E. and Faulkner, R. (1991) Role as Resource in the Hollywood Film Industry, *American Journal of Sociology*, 97(2): 279–309.

Barley, S. R. and Kunda, G. (2001) Bringing Work Back In, *Organization Science*, 12(1): 76–95.

———— (2004) *Gurus, Hired Guns, and Warm Bodies: Itinerant Experts in a Knowledge Economy*, Princeton, NJ: Princeton University Press.

———— (2006) Contracting: A New Form of Professional Practice, *Academy of Management Perspectives*, 20(1): 45–66.

Boltanski, L. and Chiapello, E. (1999) *Le nouvel esprit du capitalisme*, Paris: Gallimard.

Brown, J. S. and Duguid, P. (1991) Organizational Learning and Communities-of-Practice: Toward a Unified View of Working, Learning, and Innovating, *Organization Science*, 2(1): 40–57.

Carlile, P. (2004) Transferring, Translating, and Transforming. An Integrative Framework for Managing Knowledge Across Boundaries, *Organization Science*, 15(5): 555–68.

DeFillippi, R. J., Arthur, M. B. and Lindsay, V. (2006) *Knowledge at Work: Creative Collaboration in the Global Economy*, Oxford: Blackwell.

Dougherty, D. (1992) Interpretive Barriers to Successful Product Innovation in Large Firms, *Organization Science*, 3: 179–202.

Emery, F. E. and Trist, E. L. (1960) Socio-Technical Systems, in: C. W. Churchman and M. Verhulst (eds.), *Management Sciences Models and Techniques*, 2: 83–97, Oxford: Pergamon.

Feldman, D. (1981) The Multiple Socialization of Organization Members, *Academy of Management Review*, 6: 309–18.

Fenwick, T. (2007) Knowledge Workers in the In-between: Network Identities, *Journal of Organizational Change Management*, 20(4): 509–24.

Fock, N. (2004) *Eventyrlyst och risker: en explorativ studie om framväxten av dialogseminariemetoden*, Stockholm: Dialoger Förlag och Metod.

Gersick, C. J. G. (1989) Marking Time: Predictable Transitions in Task Groups, *Academy of Management Journal*, 32(2): 274–309.

Granstrand, O., Patel, P. and Pavitt, K. (1997) Multi-Technology Corporations: Why They Have 'Distributed' rather than 'Distinctive Core' Competencies, *California Management Review*, 39(4): 8–25.

Grant, R. M. (1996) Toward a Knowledge-based Theory of the Firm, *Strategic Management Journal*, 17(Special Issue): 109–22.

Griffin, A. and Hauser, J. (1993) The Voice of the Customer, *Marketing Science*, 12(1): 1–27.

Hanks, W. F. (1991) Foreword in Situated Learning and Legitimate Peripheral Participation, in: J. Lave and E. Wenger (eds.), *Situated Learning: Legitimate Peripheral Participation*, Cambridge: Cambridge University Press.

Hansen, M. (1999) The Search-transfer Problem: The Role of Weak Ties in Sharing Knowledge across Organization Subunits, *Administrative Science Quarterly*, 44: 82–111.

Hargadon, A. and Bechky, B. (2006) When Collections of Creatives Become Creative Collectives: A Field Study of Problem Solving at Work, *Organization Science*, 17(4): 484–500.

Harrison, D. A., Price, K. H., Gavin, J. H. and Florey A. T. (2002) Time, Teams, and Task Performance: Changing Effects of Surface- and Deep-Level Diversity on Group Functioning, *Academy of Management Journal*, 45(5): 1029–45.

Hilbert, R. A. (1981) Toward an Improved Understanding of 'Role', *Theory and Society*, 10(2): 207–26.

Hinds, P. and Pfeffer, J. (2003) Why Organizations Don't 'Know What They Know': Cognitive and Motivational Factors Affecting the Transfer of Expertise, in: M. Acheman, V. Pipek, and V. Wulf (eds.), *Sharing Expertise: Beyond Knowledge Management*, Cambridge, MA: MIT Press.

Horney, K. (1942) *The Collected Works of Karen Horney*, New York: W.W. Norton Company.

Johannessen, K. S. (2006) Rule Following, Intransitive Understanding and Tacit Knowledge: An Investigation of the Wittgensteinian Concept of Practice as Regards Tacit Knowing, in: B. Göranzon, M. Hammarén and R. Ennails (eds.), *Dialogue, Skill and Tacit Knowledge*, Chichester: Wiley.

Katz, R. (1982) The Effects of Group Longevity on Project Communication and Performance, *Administrative Science Quarterly*, 27(1): 81–104.

Kolb, D. (1984) *Experiential Learning: Experience as the Source of Learning and Development*, Englewood Cliffs, NJ: Prentice-Hall.

Kvale, S. (1996) *Interviews: An Introduction to Qualitative Research Interviewing*, Thousand Oaks, CA: Sage.

Lave, J. and Wenger, E. (1991) *Situated Learning: Legitimate Peripheral Participation*, Cambridge: Cambridge University Press.

Lindkvist, L. (2005) Knowledge Communities and Knowledge Collectivities: A Typology of Knowledge Work in Groups, *Journal of Management Studies*, 42(6): 1189–210.

Meyerson, D., Weick, K. E. and Kramer, R. M. (1996) Swift Trust and Temporary Groups, in: R. M. Kramer and T. R. Tyler (eds.), *Trust in Organizations*, Thousand Oaks, CA: Sage.

Nahapiet, J. and Ghoshal, S. (1998) Social Capital, Intellectual Capital, and the Organizational Advantage, *The Academy of Management Review*, 23(2): 242–66.

Okhuysen, G. A. and Eisenhardt, K. M. (2002) Integrating Knowledge in Groups: How Formal Interventions Enable Flexibility, *Organization Science*, 13(4): 370–86.

Sandberg, J. (2000) Understanding Human Competence at Work: An Interpretative Approach, *Academy of Management Journal*, 43(1): 9–25.

Schön, D. (1983) *The Reflective Practitioner: How Professionals Think in Action*, Cambridge: Basic Books.

Sjunnesson, J. (2007) *Erfarenhet och processer: en metod för reflekterande ledarskap*, Dialoger, PhD thesis, Stockholm: Royal Institute of Technology.

Smith, V. (1997) New Forms of Work Organization, *Annual Review of Sociology*, 23: 315–39.

Tuckman, B. W. (1965) Development Sequence in Small Groups, *Psychological Bulletin*, 63(6): 384–99.

Turner, R. H. (1990) Role Change, *Annual Review of Sociology*, 16: 87–110.

Van Maanen, J. and Schein, E. (1977) *Toward a Theory of Organization Socialization*, Working paper, Sloan School of Management, MIT.

Weick, K. (1995) *Sensemaking in Organizations*, London: Sage.

Part III

Projects and Partnerships

6

Knowledge Integration Processes in New Product Development: On the Dynamics of Deadlines and Architectures

Thomas Magnusson and Nicolette Lakemond

This chapter explores how time constraints and product system character-istics affect processes for integration of engineering knowledge in new prod-uct development incorporating new technology. It shows that integration processes take place both at the system level and at the modular level, and that product architectures and time limits are repeatedly reconsidered during NPD projects.

6.1 INTRODUCTION

Following a knowledge-based theory of the firm, the integration of different specialized fields of knowledge is at the core of a firm's activity (Grant, 1996). This chapter sets its focus on knowledge integration processes in the context of new product development (NPD) projects. In particular, we focus on processes for integration of different fields of engineering knowledge. Even the development of seemingly simple products relies on integration of engineering knowledge (e.g. integration of product and production engineering), and more complex products are often an integrated outcome of several specialized fields of engineering (e.g. mechanics, software, electronics, fluid dynamics, combustion engineering, tribo-logy). Devising appropriate processes for engineering knowledge integration thus remains a critical challenge in most NPD projects (Iansiti, 1995; Sehdev et al., 1995; Swink, 2003; Vandevelde and Van Dierdonck, 2003; Bengtsson and Berg-gren, 2008). Several studies have pointed out the virtues of using cross-functional team structures to accomplish such integration (Eisenhardt and Tabrizi, 1995; Griffin, 1997; Lynn et al., 1999; Filippini et al., 2004). Cross-functional teams represent a fertile soil for integration as they provide both a channel for knowl-edge flows among individuals and a platform for changing and improving those flows (cf. Okhuysen and Eisenhardt, 2002). However, engineering knowledge integration can take different forms, depending on the specific requirements on knowledge integration. In turn, these requirements are influenced by situational factors such as system scope, complexity, and technological novelty (Shenhar and Dvir, 1996; Lindkvist et al., 1998).

The introduction of new and untried technological concepts in mature products faces managers with a particular NPD integration dilemma. While knowledge integration remains critical in such projects, technologically uncertain NPD also requires decoupling of tasks to facilitate focused and isolated problem-solving (Lindkvist et al., 1998). Literature on technology strategy and innovation management suggests two particular strategies to overcome this dilemma: modularization of product architectures and sequencing of development steps. Through a priori standardized interfaces, modularization separates uncertain parts from mainstream product development activities. This makes it possible to adapt problem solving routines to specific task requirements and reduces the need for systems-wide knowledge integration (Clark and Fujimoto, 1991; Sanchez and Mahoney, 1996; Baldwin and Clark, 1997; Eldred and McGrath, 1997; Nobelius, 2004). Sequencing enables temporal decoupling of uncertain development tasks through advanced engineering efforts and stepwise verification of new technological concepts. It is thus possible to reduce technological uncertainty in consecutive development steps. Such sequential processes are, however, associated with prolonged development lead-times and therefore require extended deadlines (Shenhar and Dvir, 1996; Veryzer, 1998; McDermott and Handfield, 2000).

In this chapter, we argue that recommending sequencing and modularization to facilitate the introduction of new product technologies is of limited use for operative level project managers. The reason for this is that decisions on product architectures and time limits often are based on contingencies that are beyond the control of the individual project. From the project manager's perspective, it is therefore more relevant to consider deadlines and architectures as situational factors that result in different implications for knowledge integration in NPD. Building upon results from four case studies, this chapter explores how deadlines and product architectures affect engineering knowledge integration in development projects incorporating new technology. Based on our findings, we outline different ways to manage integration, following the implications given by deadlines and product architectures. Furthermore, we illustrate how perceptions of product architectures and deadlines may change during the course of NPD projects, something that calls for continuous questioning and revision of knowledge integration processes. Such sense-making of conditions that affect deadlines and product architectures and applying this sense to the project by revising the processes for knowledge integration are based on retrospective interpretations of ongoing activities (Weick et al., 2005). We further discuss implications of such dynamic processes for project management.

The next section elaborates an analytical framework, emanating in a 2×2 matrix, describing a typology of four different kinds of knowledge integration challenges. The subsequent section describes how we used this matrix as a basis for case selection and also describes our research methods. This is followed by descriptions of the individual cases and a cross-case analysis, contrasting observations from the case studies. A closing section summarizes the main conclusions and discusses managerial implications emanating from our studies.

6.2 DEADLINES AND ARCHITECTURES: AN ANALYTICAL FRAMEWORK

6.2.1 Deadlines in new product development

The importance of deadlines for NPD is evident in literature on product development management. Development speed is regarded as a key source of competitive advantage that may result in larger market shares and higher product profitability (Langerak and Hultink, 2006). Therefore, milestones and hard deadlines are important issues for organizing and speeding up NPD projects (Eisenhardt and Tabrizi, 1995).

In general, non-negotiable hard deadlines serve as an important control mechanism that functions as a trigger for action and collaboration in projects (Söderlund, 2002). Hard deadlines call for tight time-based controls and testing in combination with time-compressed, overlapping stages and rapid iterations (Eisenhardt and Tabrizi, 1995).

Hard deadlines serve not only to compress development processes but also to synchronize the work of team members. As Takeuchi and Nonaka (1986: 140) explain:

> Although the team members start the project with different time horizons – with R&D people having the longest time horizon and production people the shortest – they all must work toward synchronizing their pace to meet deadlines. Also, while the project team starts from 'zero information', each member soon begins to share knowledge about the marketplace and the technical community. As a result, the team begins to work as a unit. At some point, the individual and the whole become inseparable. The individual's rhythm and the group's rhythm begin to overlap, creating a whole new pace. This pace serves as the driving force and moves the team forward.

Söderlund (2002) also acknowledges this dynamic aspect, arguing that time-based controls serve an important function in synchronizing the activities in the project. Several arenas, such as quality demonstrations, supplier gatherings, and practical try-outs, play an important role in pacing the project within the given deadlines.

However, studies differ about the alleged effects of hard deadlines (Calantone and Di Benedetto, 2000; Griffin, 2002; Langerak and Hultink, 2006; Langerak et al., 2008). Especially in technologically uncertain NPD projects, there seem to be good reasons for keeping the product under development for longer, until it can offer customers a genuine benefit (Ali et al., 1995; Calantone and Di Benedetto, 2000). Similarly, the longer the market window is open, the less pressure there is to rush the product to market (Calantone and Di Benedetto, 2000). There are also compelling arguments for reducing risk exposure by applying serial or sequential processes (McDermott and Handfield, 2000). Design freeze can be postponed, leaving more time for exploration, testing, and verification of technological concepts (Shenhar and Dvir, 1996; Veryzer, 1998). Consequently, soft deadlines leave more opportunity for iterations, improvisation, interactions, real-time experience, and structured flexibility (Biazzo, 2009). Such deadlines thus help to reduce complexity, enabling action and learning from experience (Lindkvist et al., 1998). Moreover, in reality it seems that pre-announced products are commonly delayed, particularly in technology-intensive industries (Wu et al., 2004). In other words, faster may not always be better and in some projects it may be beneficial to apply soft rather than hard deadlines.

6.2.2 Characterizing product architectures

Assembled products can be described as systems consisting of a number of interlinked subsystems and components. Conceptually, the composition ('architecture') of such product systems can be categorized as either modular or integral (Ulrich, 1995). Products characterized by modular architectures are loosely coupled systems that easily can be decomposed into separate subsystems and components. These subsystems and components can be designed independently as long as designers adhere to the so-called 'visible design rules', which specify the overall architecture of the system, as well as component test standards and interactions between components (Baldwin and Clark, 1997). Modularity can thus be defined as an 'NPD strategy in which the interfaces shared among the components of a given product architecture become standardized and specified' (Mikkola, 2006: 130). NPD will therefore rely on decoupling of tasks, using pre-specified interfaces and standardized verification procedures. That will lessen the necessity of complex system integration processes. In practice, however, innovation in component technologies often affects interfaces between components (Henderson and Clark, 1990) and interdependencies thus seem to remain ubiquitous (e.g. Takeishi, 2002; Staudenmayer et al., 2005). R&D organizations developing modular product systems therefore need to possess extensive skills in systems engineering and planning (Ulrich, 1995).

By contrast, integral product architectures are tightly coupled systems with multiple and systemic interdependencies between different components and subsystems (Ulrich, 1995). Changes in individual components entail corresponding changes in other parts of the product system, and there is a great potential for feedback loops during the development process (Nightingale, 2000). Iansiti (1995) claims that under such circumstances, R&D organizations need to have explicit routines for probing the impact of individual decisions on the complete product system. The ability to discern relationships between different engineering knowledge bases involved in NPD projects is a prerequisite for successful integration. The influence of systemic dependencies is also acknowledged by Lindkvist et al. (1998), who suggest that 'coupling' or 'semi-coupling' logic is beneficial in such development projects. A coupling logic stresses the need for frequent or continuous communication and feedback. Arenas that support system-wide integration are required to combine results from distributed local knowledge processes (Söderlund, 2002). However, in projects addressing tasks that involve both numerous interdependencies and the application of new technology, highly specialized knowledge bases are involved, requiring considerable autonomy, at the same time as there is a great need for integration. Thus, the project organization must correspond to the contradictory requirements of being both differentiated and integrated (cf. Lawrence and Lorsch, 1967).

In R&D organizations, this contradiction is often managed by separating technology development from product development. This means that new technology is developed and verified in applied research or advanced-engineering projects before it is transferred to NPD projects (Clark and Fujimoto, 1991; Wheelwright and Clark, 1992; Eldred and McGrath, 1997). This approach provides an opportunity for local learning by creating buffers to other influences (Lindkvist et al., 1998). However, this strategy has potential drawbacks. Local knowledge processes may lead to oversimplified, rigid mental maps of the individuals, learning limited to the spatial closeness of current actions, and knowledge generation building only on what already exists (Levinthal and March, 1993). Moreover, a high degree of separation may result in problems in integrating technology development and product development and transferring technological knowledge to NPD projects (Clark and Fujimoto, 1991; Nobelius, 2002). As indicated by Nightingale (2000) and Lindkvist et al. (1998), the presence of integral product architectures can be expected to augment these problems.

6.2.3 Deadlines, architectures, and integration processes

Our theoretical framework thus depicts two variables, which may be used to characterize different situations for NPD projects. The first variable refers to deadlines, which can be categorized as either soft or hard. The second refers to product architectures, which can be categorized as either integral or modular. A combination of these variables results in a tentative framework describing four conceptually different situations, which depict different contingencies for NPD projects. Hence, we can expect different kinds of knowledge integration mechanisms to be preferred in these different situations. Figure 6.1 describes different combinations of such mechanisms as four generic integration processes: Sequential, Emergent, Concurrent, and Iterative.

Sequential integration corresponds to situations characterized by soft deadlines and modular product architectures. Literature suggests that projects operating under these conditions experience most freedom in selecting appropriate mechanisms

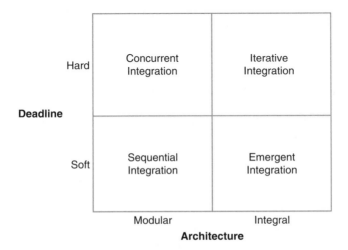

Figure 6.1 Different situations and different integration processes

for integration (Sanchez and Mahoney, 1996; Baldwin and Clark, 1997; McDermott and Handfield, 2000). Several studies have pointed out the virtues of using cross-functional team structures to achieve integration (Eisenhardt and Tabrizi, 1995; Griffin, 1997; Lynn et al., 1999; Filippini et al., 2004). Modular product architectures make it possible to use the product system as a basis for decomposition of the task and assign different (sub)-teams for the development of individual components or subsystems. Cross-functional teams represent a fertile soil for integration as they provide both a channel for knowledge flows among individuals and a platform for changing and improving those flows (cf. Okhuysen and Eisenhardt, 2002). These teams can review project information; conduct team meetings with heads of engineering, marketing, and manufacturing departments; analyse action items from team-staff meetings; review technical quality prototype test reports; and review customer reaction reports to product concepts (Lynn et al., 1999). Modularization further enables the introduction of new component technologies that affect only limited parts of the product, that is, modular innovation (Henderson and Clark, 1990). Organizational separation based upon standardized interfaces between individual components in the product system thus seems to be the underlying logic. Furthermore, with soft deadlines, it will be possible to test and verify new technologies before moving to the next step of development. Thus, it is possible to secure functionality, performance, and reliability stepwise, with gradually increased demands and requirements (Eldred and McGrath, 1997). Consequently, with modular product architectures and soft deadlines, cross-functional team structures, as well as the visible design rules of the product system (Baldwin and Clark, 1997) and the decision gates of the firm's formal NPD model, may function as important knowledge integration mechanisms. Knowledge integration in the project will therefore be primarily local and characterized by temporal and organizational separation.

Emergent integration corresponds to situations characterized by soft deadlines and integral product architectures. With integral architectures, interdependencies in the product system call for a more integrated view of the development process (Nightingale, 2000). Integration under such circumstances comprises continuous challenges of both cross-functional and cross-system integration. Engineers continually have to assess the impact of new component technologies on the entire system (Iansiti, 1995). However, soft deadlines enable later design freeze and flexibility in project execution. Development projects may follow gradually emerging processes with temporarily separated stages. With soft deadlines and integral product architectures, clear goals and responsibilities, specifying the required output from different stages, thus emerge as important knowledge integration mechanisms. The gates will then function as global arenas (Söderlund, 2002) that facilitate system-wide learning and correction.

Concurrent integration corresponds to situations characterized by hard deadlines and modular product architectures. In this case, the modular product architecture makes it possible to decouple component development incorporating new technology, while time pressure forces the development project to seek maximum parallelism. Hence, separation of development tasks is possible using the product architecture as a basis for task partitioning. Technologically uncertain component development may thus be conducted in isolation. Since the product architecture will be considered stable, the need for system-wide integration processes is reduced and knowledge integration processes within the individual development project will be essentially local. Due to hard deadlines, the organization will have to seek possibilities to conduct development tasks concurrently. Consequently, the project will have to apply a flexible development model with 'fuzzy gates' (Cooper, 1994) to ensure that the project is not slowed by formal checkpoints. Hence, with hard deadlines and modular product architectures, cross-functional teams will function as a basis for local knowledge integration. Since there will be limited time for reconsideration, these projects also need to be guided by clear and consistent goals or visions. Flexibility will thus be reduced, corresponding to a process characterized by 'structured rigidity' (Biazzo, 2009).

Iterative integration corresponds to situations characterized by hard deadlines and integral product architectures. This is the most troublesome position for NPD projects, since neither the product architectures nor the character of the deadlines will support focused and isolated problem-solving. The project will experience a continuous pressure to deliver and has to foster a 'short-cycle mentality', constantly looking for possibilities to reduce lead-times through stage overlapping and elimination of gates and decisions (Clift and Vandenbosch, 1999), collapsing formal process models, and established organizational structures. Hence, the organization must establish other arenas that facilitate systems-level knowledge integration. Both system- and component-level knowledge processes will have to be accelerated. Consequently, hard deadlines and integral product architectures demand a great deal of the integrative capabilities of project organization and the available resources; they require highly experienced and educated project managers and project members (Kessler and Chakrabarti, 1999; Filippini et al., 2004). Integration of product and production knowledge has to take place at both a local and a systems level. While cross-functional teams may facilitate local knowledge processes, frequent milestones, prototypes, and system tests are required to integrate the results from these processes, to facilitate feedback and control progress (Eisenhardt and Tabrizi, 1995; Kessler and Chakrabarti, 1999).

The next section explains how we used the 2×2 matrix as a basis for selecting cases and further elaborates the research approach and methods used for the empirical studies.

6.3 RESEARCH METHODS

In order to study how deadlines and architectures affect engineering knowledge integration in NPD projects, we performed in-depth case studies at four different manufacturing companies. These companies all operate on relatively mature markets, and NPD is characterized by a simultaneous focus on effectiveness and efficiency. Even though our study focused on four specific NPD projects, the limited size of the companies meant that we also could develop a comprehensive understanding of the organizational context in which they operated.

All four companies produce products consisting of several components and encompassing a number of different technologies. Moreover, the products are mass-produced. Therefore, design for manufacturability and assembly, as well as production system preparation and production handover, remains critical in all projects. Consequently, NPD needs to integrate product and production engineering knowledge, as well as different product technologies. Stage-Gate systems (Cooper, 1994, 2008) provide a basic structure for NPD at the four companies. The NPD projects selected for study all represented a high degree of technological uncertainty for the companies involved, as they incorporated new, untried technological concepts. At the request of the companies, we refrain from revealing their real names and label the companies and the cases instead with four fictional names: Home, Office, Outdoor, and Automotive.

6.3.1 The companies

Home develops, manufactures, and markets sewing machines for a global market. At the time of the study, the company had 2,246 employees. Its headquarters, the main manufacturing plant, and R&D facilities are all located at the same site. Sewing machines traditionally rely heavily on precision mechanics, but in recent years they have undergone rapid technical development. Advanced electronics and computer controls have made it possible to add new functionality and this has propelled the development of graphical user interfaces and displays. In addition, the amount of integrated software has increased rapidly. As a result, today's most advanced sewing machines rely just as much on electronics and software as on mechanics. The studied project was initiated to replace the existing top model and had many new features, including completely new software.

Office is a worldwide supplier of stapling products and hole-punching equipment. It has about 1,100 employees. The company's product programme includes both manual and electrical products. The products are directed at three main market segments: Office, Tools, and OEM (Original Equipment Manufacturers). The studied project aimed at developing a new stapling system for the OEM segment, which means that the product is integrated in an external customer's product (in this case, a copier machine). It was initiated at the request of an external customer and was based on a new technical principle; no technology or design solutions were at hand and specifications were vague. Product requirements were very challenging in terms of product longevity, reliability, and speed.

Outdoor develops and produces a variety of products for outdoor use. The company has 2,200 employees. The prime production facility is located at the same site as the R&D department. The products are sold worldwide and North America is one of the most important markets. The selected project aimed to develop a new chainsaw, primarily for professional use. The project started as a result of pending emission regulations on the North American market, stipulating a 50 per cent reduction of emissions by a certain date. This entailed a very strict deadline for market introduction. In order to meet the emission requirements, the development engineers had to apply next-generation engine technology. Failure to deliver would lead to the company losing all its sales in North America, which amounted to about one-third of the company's output of chainsaws.

Automotive is a leading supplier of sports utility transportation equipment for cars. It has 3,700 employees and twelve production plants located in different countries. The seasonal character of the company's products makes it very important to finalize development projects on time. The case study is focused on the development of a rear-mounted bike carrier system. This system can be described as a semi-complex mechanical product consisting of several integrated subsystems and components, coupled relatively tightly. Within this product segment, the company renews its products every three years by introducing a completely new generation. In the case study, the development task included a number of important new features, entailing more advanced technological solutions and the use of new materials. An entirely new design also styled the product completely differently from its predecessors.

We intentionally selected the case study projects to mirror different processes for engineering knowledge integration. As a basis for classification, we used records from interviews with project managers, line managers, and engineers on how they actually perceived and managed the projects. Figure 6.2 describes our classification of the case study projects.

This theoretical sampling approach provided us with a possibility to explore and illuminate the specific relationships between deadlines, architectures, and NPD practices. In this way, we aim to extend emergent theory by providing contrary explanations (Eisenhardt, 1989; Yin, 1994; Eisenhardt and Graebner, 2007).

6.4 CASE STUDIES

6.4.1 Case Home: sliding specifications and problems of integration

Case Home was not exposed to serious time pressure initially, and the project manager essentially based the project organization on module teams, applying sequential processes for integration. The original idea for the project was to base much of the design on existing hardware and focus on software development. The

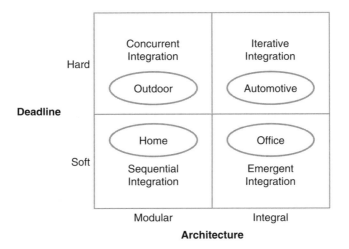

Figure 6.2 Classification of the case studies

project was scheduled for about one and a half years, starting in late 2001 and finishing during the first quarter of 2003. However, in order to achieve a required level of functionality, stipulated from the market analysis, an entirely new software module had to be developed. The extensive software development meant that the project could not deliver until the beginning of 2004. This opened up for changes in the exterior design, resulting in a major redesign effort to make the product more attractive and up-to-date. The project manager recalls:

> We realized that the software had to be rewritten completely. It was impossible to add onto the existing software; if we wanted these functions, we had to start from scratch. Then we considered potential hardware changes: big screen, a more attractive lid, everything. As we counted the number of tools that were affected, our R&D director pleaded: 'the handle can be left untouched, can't it?' All tools were affected, all plastic parts surrounding the machine. In the end 44 tools were affected; in the beginning we had planned for no more than 2 new tools. Only the hand wheel was left untouched – the handle was changed as well. It grew all the time; it took us an entire year before we reached the first gate, accepting that this is the project.

Specification changes also during product development

The NPD project involved almost the entire R&D department, which grew considerably during the course of the project. Since the new personnel did not possess all the necessary background knowledge, demands on communication and learning were extraordinary. The engineers were divided into mechanics, software, and electronics, forming a number of module teams. The software engineer who led the software team describes the organization:

> We had a core group with a project manager and module leaders and we had our own meetings within the modules. We were about 5–6 module teams.

Personnel from Marketing, Production, Verification, and Quality were also included in the project. In particular, production engineers were involved in the mechanical design teams on a continuous basis.

The project manager describes how the specification changed several times during the project:

> In the middle of the project they realised that the floppy was about to be outdated. Then they did a turnaround and used a USB instead. Thus they had to redo the complete front panel tool. This was about one month before R0, release of data for tooling price assessment. So it was quite late. We managed, but the project was a bit delayed (. . .). Then there was another issue that affected the front panel, the illumination. We had a research project on new illumination technology and I promised the sponsor that we could implement this within a month (. . .). We changed two light bulbs for 44 LED with variable temperature. (. . .) This was the single largest change on the machine. It was a separate research project involving a university. It was completely new and unproven and those were also the parts that we eventually had a lot of trouble with. (. . .) the new illumination affected electronics, software and mechanics design. We had to modify, control via the electronics, had to implement a completely new software module.

Hence, integration between different modules became a primary issue during the project. The mechanics design manager describes the key role of the project manager in this process:

It is a common problem that we redefine projects continuously due to changed prerequisites. But you cannot stick your head in the sand stating that we decided to do like this three years ago, irrespective of how the surrounding world changes. So this is both a strength and a weakness and this is where the project manager comes in. To run a project where everything runs according to plan is not difficult. Anybody can do that. But the project manager is important to secure communication and observe relationships when you redefine. Project managers are handy when there are problems, otherwise they are useless.

Time pressure in production handover

The sliding design specification caused problems, especially for software development; in the end, it resulted in severe time pressure, especially during the production preparatory activities and production ramp-up. The project manager elaborates:

> We could not implement any software in the first production machines in order to test them. Thus we could not run the machine. We would have needed the software earlier. Moreover, the electronics were sensitive to electrostatic discharge. The machine disturbed itself and we had to redesign the electronics to protect it better. This was discovered late because we could not run the machine without software. The software team gave us their schedules but we did not sufficiently specify what they were supposed to deliver. For example, we did not know that we had to control the illumination. We knew from the start that the systems integration would be cumbersome, and that was also what happened.

The software group manager recalls the time pressure during the final stages of the project:

> When there is a poor handover from us to production, I would say that the reason is almost always time pressure; there is such hurry in the end and you cannot cope.

6.4.2 Case Office: chasing to catch a moving target

Since it was obvious from the start that the new technology affected the complete product, case Office adopted emergent integration processes. From the outset, the project was intended to run for four years and was headed by a chief design engineer. He was supported by two design engineers and two engineers from the prototype workshop. The initial work in the project focused on technology development. The initial project manager explains:

> We started the project with a clean sheet design. We designed prototypes and experimented with these.

Physical proximity between the prototype department and the product engineers facilitated a close and interactive way of working.

As the customer also started with clean sheet design for the overall product, the specifications were altered many times.

> We got less and less space for our module and also the physical interface with the overall machine changed several times.

The technical challenges and frequent changes in the specifications led to the project always being 'one step behind'.

> Our customer is so eager to receive the prototypes that we hardly manage to test the prototypes on our own.

When the project was approaching its initial launch date, the product concept had still not been verified and many problems remained. Still, seven pre-production series were produced between 2002 and 2004. The initial technically focused project manager was replaced by a production engineer in order to shift focus to production issues. However, with an unstable design, it was difficult to get the product ready for production. Fortunately, the customer also experienced problems with the overall design and decided to delay the project by one and a half years. This allowed Office to initiate a major redesign.

Step 2 – the major redesign

In order to be able to provide the customer with a product that met the specifications for longevity, reliability, and speed, a major redesign was initiated. The project manager at the time explains:

> During the customer's 1.5 years production stop we made a number of important modifications to the machine. So the production stop really made it possible for us to realise the required changes. The new version, which we called step 2, was more thoroughly verified than its predecessor. But still we did not meet the requirements completely.

Moreover, the project manager was replaced by an employee from the sales department. After a while, she was replaced by a consultant and the OEM division manager, and then returned in the project's final phase. As it was recognized that competence in mechatronics was central for the redesign, external consultants were hired to complement the project members' competencies in this field. These worked closely with the product engineers and resolved many of the problematic issues in the project. The more commercially oriented project manager and a technical coordinator were also located close to each other, which facilitated continuous communication about important issues. Otherwise, the project was not co-located:

> In this project we were not co-located. We had two meetings each week in the project, on Tuesdays and Thursday. About 10 persons were involved in these meetings and reported about their areas of responsibility. In addition, we also had project meetings with a smaller core project group.

Finalizing the project

Although a production engineer was involved from the outset, production issues had only a minor influence on the product design. The final project manager explains:

> As the product was so complex, function was prioritized in favour of manufacturability. Moreover, as estimated production volumes are quite low right now we have decided not to implement the necessary changes in the product design to improve manufacturability.

During the project, the relationship between the project and the production department was perceived to be not very smooth on account of differences of opinion about responsibilities. The production department was reluctant to accept responsibility before the project had been completed and formally handed over. In addition, the wish to fulfil the customer's needs by accepting late changes in product requirements resulted in a situation where the gates in the project model were not strictly observed. Several design tools were ordered and produced even though the design had not been settled. This resulted in several tool modifications and also restricted product design. When production started, the product was still not completely verified, and project-related problems in production were solved interactively:

> Problems caused by the project were reported immediately. If someone from the project visited the production, the operator could explain directly how the product design could be improved.

6.4.3 Case Outdoor: disciplined and focused problem-solving

The pending regulation subjected case Outdoor to hard deadlines from the start. The project manager therefore tried initially to buffer technologically uncertain parts from the rest of the project organization, assigning separate module teams to these development engineering tasks while compressing development through *concurrent* integration processes. When the project was initiated, the new engine technology was being developed at a separate research laboratory. A number of prototype tests had been carried out, but the technology had not been fully developed and verified. Still, the definite deadlines forced the decision to start. The project manager explains:

> We knew that production had to start in August 2004. Usually we would have continued technology development for another 1–2 years, but in this case we had to start. The final deadline was settled before we knew what we were supposed to do.

Consequently, technology development had to continue during the course of the project and the project manager thus established a separate engine development group within the project. Apart from the new engine technology, the product was to be quite similar to existing products. The project manager continues:

> In some respects it may even have been easier than other projects. We already had modern products in this segment, so we did not have to take too large risks. If we were to fail on something it was to be the engine (. . .). Many other projects have been forced to reconsider everything and re-design all components. In this case we decided that we will use conventional technology, things that we already have.

In the project, production engineering was represented by an experienced production engineer, committed full-time from the start, and the project was allowed to engage production personnel to run test series. According to the R&D project coordinator, this was the first time the company established such close cooperation between product engineering and production engineering:

> They made the assembly lines and test stations – the complete package – and they did this really well. Moreover, there was a significantly raised level of engagement and more resources, something that was extremely important. Otherwise there is always a fight for resources. Our largest problem is that the departments cannot participate in the projects. People from the line organization come in occasionally, but they rarely commit. In this project we got real attention from production for the first time. This is one of the most important reasons why we were successful in terms of time and quality.

The project used various methods to prepare the product for production, such as Design for Assembly (a DfA coordinator was employed during the project) and production FMEA (Failure Mode and Effect Analysis). Moreover, the project established a special test assembly line, located in the assembly plant. Only this project and a parallel project in the same product segment were allowed to use it. The project executed more rounds of test series than usual, with fewer produced units in each round. Test series production had previously been conducted by the R&D laboratory, but in this case the responsibility lay with the production department. The production engineer elaborates on how this led to the product department becoming more involved in the development project:

> In general, the R&D lab has built the test series. After debugging it, they would consider the chainsaw ready, and hand it over to production engineering and they would build an assembly line. Usually this is not the smartest way to arrange production hand-over. In this project, production engineering built an assembly line in a way that we imagined the production flow.

The test plant became a meeting place for personnel from lab, engineering design, and production and was also used extensively for education and training of assembly operators and production personnel.

Production handover

Handover to production went more smoothly than in previous development projects. The project followed a stepwise process, with a strict division between test series and production pilot run. A production engineer involved in the handover emphasizes the virtues of such a clear structure:

> You cannot have testing and fixing at this stage. We really emphasised that. That is why we did test series production before we started training the assembly personnel. Of course, a few assemblers were engaged in the test series and product debugging, but we did not start training the entire group until the production equipment was completely verified. If you start training people with crude equipment and introduce changes at a later stage, then the training is in vain. The personnel must be introduced when it is all settled. That is why we decided to focus on test series production.

The high priority gave the project preferential treatment within the company. The product owner recalls:

> There was no doubt that we had to do this. The complete organization from senior management down to lab engineers and production personnel agreed (. . .). There was a focus and the project got the highest priority every time.

Series production started as planned and 8,000 of a planned 10,000 units were produced during the autumn of 2004. In the end the project was described as very successful; some even said it was their most successful development project ever.

6.4.4 Case Automotive: accumulating problems and improvised solutions

Due to the seasonal character of the product, the case Automotive project was subjected to severe time pressure. The integral product architecture and hard deadline meant that the project manager had to facilitate *iterative* integration processes to speed up NPD. An important starting point for the development was the preliminary idea of a new technological solution. The initial development of this idea was organized in a separate pre-development project, conducted in advance of the NPD project. As the project manager describes:

> The new technology was the most critical part of the project. We initially developed it in a separate pre-development project. Such pre-development is actually really new for us; we have never before developed a new idea separately.

Several concept solutions were proposed during pre-development, but time pressure prevented a thorough review and verification of each concept.

> In order to be certain, we would have needed more extensive testing. But the overall deadline was concistently pacing our work. Therefore, we just chose one concept from pre-development.

The decision about the concept was made in discussions between the project manager and the main pre-development engineer.

Start of product development

Besides the new technological solution, the new exterior design was an important constraint. An external design firm provided a rough idea that was approved by the product manager and further developed into a more detailed design in-house. At the start, the product development project was manned with members representing the purchasing, marketing, product, and production engineering departments. There were three to four product engineers on the project; with relatively little experience of the specific product segment; two of them were external consultants. Supporting members were from prototype, assembly, and industrial design. From the start, the project group also faced a tough time schedule. The time schedule was tight and actually did not allow any loops in the development process.

The pre-development engineer was part of the project initially, but left after a few months. This resulted in the loss of important competence on the new technological solution. The project manager explains:

> It is not easy to recieve something that is designed by someone else. Maybe if pre-development would have come a bit further, and had performed tests, then we could have understood it better. I thought the concept was more finished than it actually was, and maybe the pre-development engineer thought so too.

Accumulating problems related to new technology

Initially, the project proceeded as planned and the first prototypes were manufactured and presented to the sales representatives from the main market. Just before this meeting, the product manager claimed: *We have a technological solution that is much better than our competitors'*. The meeting with sales representatives resulted in some minor changes in the product design which impacted on the requirements for the new technological solution. Simultaneously, problems relating to the new technological concept accumulated. Six different prototype series were needed to evaluate these problems. Consequently, design evaluation and approval were delayed by six weeks. As the problems had still not been completely solved, it was decided that approval would apply only in parts and that tool engineering would start to prevent further delays.

Intensive interaction between the product engineers was required and was aided by their physical co-location. To further facilitate discussion of detailed technical issues, specific meetings with the product engineers were scheduled at least weekly, separately from the more cross-functionally oriented weekly project meetings.

> It is difficult to discuss everything in one meeting. When discussing detailed technical issues half of the group are yawning because it is not interesting for them.

The project manager also had daily, very intensive interaction with the product manager.

Process and tool design

With a delay of six weeks, an unfinished and partly unapproved design, and the implementation of a new ISO standard during the project, resulting in further changes and delays, process development was initiated. A highly experienced production engineer was involved in the tool design, supported by another one in Sweden and yet another at the production facility in Poland. The production engineer describes the situation as follows:

> When we were supposed to pass the checkpoint after product engineering to have time for the 0- and pre-series, we were not completely ready. Then we released some of the plastic tools, which we thought would not be changed later on. The sheet metal tools were delayed, but when additional problems occurred we needed to start with them anyway. Then I decided, even with incomplete information, to start engineering the tools, keeping them 'on the shelf'. Some had to be modified afterwards, resulting in extra work, but others could be released immediately. In that way we could save about 8 weeks.

This way of working required tight interaction between the product engineers and production engineers. The production engineer describes his role as supporting the product engineers and taking part in brainstorming about potential solutions to solve the problems. Further, he explains that he interacted all the time, came up with ideas, and evaluated others' ideas.

Product launch

A major setback occurred when the product was not approved in a life-time test, just before production approval. This problem was solved within a few weeks but it necessitated another bypass of the formal NPD process. Instead of waiting for formal approval, pre-series volumes were increased and were sold to customers. The late changes and the decision to sell products from the pre-series resulted in an enormous challenge for the project team, which constantly had to decide what could be produced and what needed to be delayed to facilitate changes. In order to facilitate the parallel focus on product changes and product launch, a specific launch team was introduced. This team could handle the specific launch issues that involved the production plants and sales organizations. The team was headed by the product manager; although the project manager belonged to the team, he was able to focus on solving the remaining product problems. In this way, the product could be released on the market in time for the season.

6.5 CROSS-CASE ANALYSIS

We selected the four case studies to match the categories in our 2×2 matrix (Figures 6.1 and 6.2). Cases Outdoor and Home were classified as having modular product architectures. In case Outdoor, we observed that this made it possible to concentrate project efforts on engine development and keep other parts relatively stable. By contrast, in case Home, the perception of a modular product architecture was repeatedly challenged by changes with system-embracing implications. Further, we classified Office and Automotive as cases of integral product architectures and observed the need for frequent system-level integration processes.

In terms of deadlines, we classified Outdoor and Automotive as having hard deadlines; these constraints came from external factors beyond the control of the individual projects. In case Automotive, they were mainly due to the product's seasonal character, while in case Outdoor, they were a result of strict legal requirements. In both projects, design freeze was delayed without delaying production process development. Instead, production process development was partly compressed in time and partly performed concurrently with product engineering. This was achieved by building a separate line for production preparation (case Outdoor), and by ordering tools before design freeze, specific agreements with tool suppliers, and working around formal project routines (case Automotive). This illustrates that when consequences of late product introduction are severe and costly, it may pay to increase risks and costs by compressing production development and working around formal project routines (Clift and Vandenbosch, 1999). A prerequisite for this was that these projects obtained extensive resources and substantial authority within their organizations. As predicted by Söderlund (2002), the definite deadlines seem to have created a high degree of commitment and focus in the organizations, functioning as a trigger for action and collaboration in these specific projects.

By contrast, in the cases with soft deadlines, Home and Office, the project managers exercised discretion in delaying market launch on account of altered specifications. Soft deadlines initially allowed sequential integration, which was especially prevalent in case Office. However, towards the end of these projects, when design specifications were eventually frozen, further postponement of launch dates was not allowed. As a result, production process development had to be compressed; something that was achieved by compressing production preparatory activities (case Home) and through early ordering of tools (case Office). This had negative consequences in terms of reduced time for evaluation, learning, and adjustment between different pre-production test series and it also reduced possibilities for late modifications of product design. In particular, it seems that the market department urged these projects to speed up the later stages of development. A plausible explanation for this is that it may be relatively easy to justify extended time limits by referring to demands from external customers or by adding functionality, making the product more attractive on the market (Calantone and Di Benedetto, 2000); once the design specification is frozen, however, these options are closed, making it difficult to justify further delays. Moreover, as design specifications are based on assumptions about customer requirements, competition, and available technologies, etc., which run a risk of becoming obsolete, there are compelling reasons for avoiding further delays as soon as the specification has been set.

Turning to the second situational variable, product architecture, the integral architectures of cases Office and Automotive made decoupling of development tasks involving new technologies inherently difficult. In case Automotive, the multiple prototypes seem to have played a particularly important role. Functioning as critical milestones (Eisenhardt and Tabrizi, 1995), prototypes were important for creating a common understanding of the most critical technical problems and assuring that progress was made on the project. Furthermore, when tool design started before the final product design had been approved, product knowledge and production knowledge were continuously integrated on a system-embracing level in an iterative process. Not being exposed to the same amount of time pressure, case Office could follow a more sequential process, focusing initially on the technological concept, before moving to NPD and thereafter to production. The formalized handover between the NPD project and the production department served as an important point for integrating product and production knowledge on a system-embracing level.

Cases Home and Outdoor benefitted from modular product architectures and were able to manage the new technology introduction in a more modular fashion. This was particularly evident in case Outdoor, where engine development was clearly separated from the rest of the project. The strong time pressure in this case meant that the project had to be compressed. Therefore, engine technology development could be isolated to a specific module that was developed in parallel with other modules. This concurrent strategy allowed integration to occur on a more local module level. This strategy relied on a stable product architecture with clearly specified interfaces between the engine and other modules and on pre-specified test protocols to enable isolated verification of engine functionality and engine performance (cf. Baldwin and Clark, 1997).

The systems characteristics and time limits appear most beneficial in case Home, which enjoyed both modular product architecture and soft deadlines. Although the system was perceived and managed by forming a number of module teams and product and production knowledge were integrated on this local module level, the project still experienced significant integration problems, particularly between hardware and software development. This may be explained by the recent expansion of the product's software content, which resulted in significant challenges for the established R&D organization. Due to the strong software focus in the studied project, these challenges were particularly evident in this case. Software engineers experienced a lack of explicit routines for software technology development and considered that conceptual development was therefore organized as NPD project activities rather than as separate pre-development activities. Moreover, the consequences of hardware design adjustments for software design were not properly investigated during the project. The hardware could not be tested and verified until software was available. Hence, it seems as if modular product architecture to some extent was taken for granted in the project. Potential implications of the increased software content for the existing product architecture were not highlighted, and the issue of systems integration was downplayed. Based on the lessons learned from the project, two new systems engineers were therefore employed in the R&D department, with the aim of strengthening the organization's systems integration capabilities.

It is remarkable that all the case study projects except for case Outdoor experienced problems with production handover. In case Outdoor, it may have been assumed that the modular product architectures would facilitate team structures involving production engineers at an early stage. Such a cross-functional structure should have been beneficial for reviewing project information, resulting in a more smooth transition of the new product from development to production (Lynn et al., 1999). However, as the project gradually turned its focus from product to production system development, it had to integrate product and production engineering knowledge on a systems level. They achieved this by building a separate assembly line for production preparation. This test assembly line functioned as a valuable joint arena for problem solving, knowledge sharing, training, and learning. Moreover, the initial strong focus on deadlines seems to have spared the project from extensive time pressure in the later stages and enabled production preparatory activities to follow a very structured, emergent process. Consequently, if the logic of the production system differs from the logic of the product architecture, modular product architectures will not support design for assembly and manufacturability. Additional measures will then be required for knowledge integration between product engineering and production engineering.

We originally positioned the four case study projects to match the categories of knowledge integration processes, as depicted in our 2 × 2 matrix (Figures 6.1 and 6.2). However, none of the cases actually remained in the same square of the matrix throughout the execution of the project. The project managers were repeatedly forced to question their initial assumptions and reassess the knowledge integration mechanisms and processes that the projects used. They continuously had to find new and alternative ways to deal with new requirements. Figure 6.3 summarizes how the engineering knowledge integration processes changed in the case study projects.

The figure further describes how hard deadlines necessitate compression, which can be achieved by continuous interaction, while an integral product structure requires integration on a systems level. In contrast, more modular structures enable concurrent development of the modules and consequently knowledge integration on a module level. Extended time frames in cases of soft deadlines allow more sequential processes. In these sequential processes, the need for integration on a system-embracing level can be dealt with in the handover points between the different phases in NPD processes. In cases of modular product architectures, engineering knowledge can be integrated either by sequential integration in the handover points or by a more iterative integration, depending on how deadlines and product architecture characteristics change during the development process. Both can occur though on a local, module level.

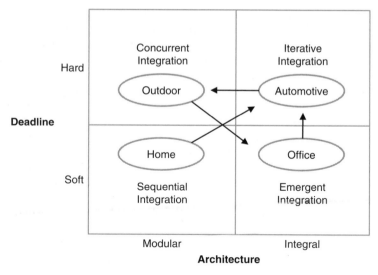

Figure 6.3 Changed knowledge integration processes in the case studies

6.6 CONCLUSIONS AND MANAGERIAL IMPLICATIONS

Our case studies illustrate that experimentation and iteration may take place on different levels, depending on the product architecture. Modular product structures allow the product to be decomposed. Consequently, iteration and experimentation will take place primarily on a local module level. In contrast, integrated product architectures require systems-level integration and iterations thus need to embrace knowledge integration on the systems levels as well as local knowledge integration on a modular level. Hard deadlines reinforce the necessity of iterative processes with high integration content. In these situations, working around the formal NPD processes, for instance by decomposing seemingly indecomposable integrated systems, may be a fruitful approach to gaining time. Soft deadlines enable emergent processes at the outset, but it seems that later in the project there is still an increased need for knowledge integration characterized by iteration and experimentation. These dynamics point to an important conclusion. By considering time as a situational characteristic rather than as a result variable (e.g. Eisenhardt and Tabrizi, 1995) or a control mechanism (Söderlund, 2002), we show that deadlines and perceptions of deadlines influence knowledge integration processes within projects. Product architectures show a similar dynamism.

Our case study findings further show how external conditions and an emerging understanding of the task may change initial perceptions during the course of an NPD project. Such retrospective interpretation of ongoing activities (Weick et al., 2005) can ultimately lead to an altered interpretation of the conditions surrounding deadlines and architectures and result in a need to revise knowledge integration processes to match emerging conditions. As perceptions of product architectures may change, calling for altered integration processes, designing processes for engineering knowledge integration in advance will be difficult.

Moreover, our study shows that some linkages exist between deadlines and product architectures. A transition from soft to hard deadlines can necessitate important reconsiderations of product architecture, in the direction of either more modular or more integral architectures. As a suggestion, this direction may depend on the focus on the product and production knowledge in the project. Hard deadlines impose challenges to decompose (at least parts of) seemingly integrated products into components that are more or less affected by technological uncertainty in the product design. Such reconsideration towards more modular architectures requires in-depth product knowledge. However, hard deadlines may also push perceptions towards more integral architectures. This is also affected by the stage of development and the degree of focus on product systems versus production. Product system modularity does not necessarily correspond to similar production system modularity. Hence, although modular product architectures may support isolated verification of performance, functionality, and manufacturability on the component level, integration processes relying on production system logic rather than product system logic may be required to assure manufacturability of the complete product system.

Modular product structures provide conditions for dealing with critical deadlines by front-loading production preparatory activities and integrating production knowledge at an early stage, which may free time later during the project. However, in both our cases with integrated product structures, deadlines became significantly harder towards the end of the project. An important reason for this is that integrated product architectures necessitate system-embracing knowledge integration processes which aggravate time management during the project. This implies that perceptions of the product architecture and the deadlines need to be challenged and reconsidered during the project. While there is still little freedom on an operative level to design product architectures and influence the characteristics of deadlines, the assimilation of knowledge about the product and the production system throughout the different project phases creates at least some room for interpretation. This necessitates consistent reconsideration of how the project can facilitate proper processes for engineering knowledge integration.

ACKNOWLEDGEMENTS

The chapter presents results from INTERFACE – Interfaces in Industrial Innovation Processes, a collaborative research project involving Linköping University, Jönköping University, and a number of manufacturing companies. The research was funded by the Swedish Agency for Innovation Systems (VINNOVA).

REFERENCES

Ali, A., Krapfel Jr, R. and LaBahn, D. (1995) Product Innovativeness and Entry Strategy: Impact on Cycle Time and Break-even Time, *Journal of Product Innovation Management*, 12: 54–69.

Baldwin, C. Y. and Clark, K. B. (1997) Managing in an Age of Modularity, *Harvard Business Review*, September–October: 84–93.

Bengtsson, L. and Berggren, C. (2008) The Integrator's New Advantage – Reassessing Outsourcing and Production Competence in a Global Telecom Firm, *European Management Journal*, 26: 314–24.

Biazzo, S. (2009) Flexibility, Structuration and Simultaneity in New Product Development, *Journal of Product Innovation Management*, 26: 336–53.

Calantone, R. J. and Di Benedetto, C. A. (2000) Performance and Time to Market: Accelerating Cycle Time with Overlapping Stages, *IEEE Transactions on Engineering Management*, 47(2): 232–45.

Clark, K. B. and Fujimoto, T. (1991) *Product Development Performance: Strategy, Organization and Management in the World Auto Industry*, Boston, MA: Harvard Business School Press.

Clift, T. B. and Vandenbosch, M. B. (1999) Project Complexity and Efforts to Reduce Product Development Cycle Time, *Journal of Business Research*, 45: 187–98.

Cooper, R. G. (1994) Third-Generation New Product Processes, *Journal of Product Innovation Management*, 11: 3–14.

—— (2008) Perspective: The Stage-Gate® Idea-to-Launch Process – Update, What's New, and NexGen Systems, *Journal of Product Innovation Management*, 25(3): 213–32.

Eisenhardt, K. M. (1989) Building Theories from Case Study Research, *Academy of Management Review*, 14(4): 532–50.

—— Graebner, M. E. (2007) Theory Building from Cases: Opportunities and Challenges, *Academy of Management Journal*, 50(1): 25–32.

—— Tabrizi, B. N. (1995) Accelerating Adaptive Processes: Product Innovation in the Global Computer Industry, *Administrative Science Quarterly*, 40: 84–110.

Eldred, E. and McGrath, M. (1997) Commercializing New Technology – II, *Research Technology Management*, 40(2): 29–33.

Filippini, R., Salmaso, L. and Tessarolo, P. (2004) Product Development Time Performance: Investigating the Effect of Interactions between Drivers, *Journal of Product Innovation Management*, 21: 199–214.

Grant, R. M. (1996) Toward a Knowledge-based Theory of the Firm, *Strategic Management Journal*, 17: 109–22.

Griffin, A. (1997) The Effect of Project and Process Characteristics on Product Development Cycle Time, *Journal of Marketing Research*, 34(1): 24–35.

—— (2002) Product Development Cycle Time for Business-to-Business Products, *Industrial Marketing Management*, 31: 291–304.

Henderson, R. and Clark, K. B. (1990) Architectural Innovation: The Reconfiguration of Existing Product Technologies and the Failure of Established Firms, *Administrative Science Quarterly*, 35(March): 9–30.

Iansiti M. (1995) Technology Integration: Managing Technological Evolution in a Complex Environment, *Research Policy*, 24: 521–42.

Kessler E. H. and Chakrabarti A. K. (1999) Speeding up the Pace of New Product Development, *Journal of Product Innovation Management*, 16(3): 2.

Langerak, F. and Hultink, E. J. (2006) The Impact of Product Innovativeness on the Link between Development Speed and New Product Profitability, *Journal of Product Innovation Management*, 23: 203–14.

—— —— Griffin, A. (2008) Exploring Mediating and Moderating Influences on the Links among Cycle Time, Proficiency in Entry Timing, and New Product Profitability, *Journal of Product Innovation Management*, 25(4): 370–85.

Lawrence, P. R. and Lorsch, J. W. (1967) *Organization and Environment: Managing Differentiation and Integration*, Boston, MA: Harvard University Press.

Levinthal, D. and March, J. G. (1993) The Myopia of Learning, *Strategic Management Journal*, 14(2): 95–112.

Lindkvist, L., Söderlund, J. and Tell, F. (1998) Managing Product Development Projects: On the Significance of Fountains and Deadlines, *Organization Studies*, 19(6): 931–51.

Lynn, G. S., Skov, R. B. and Abel, K. D. (1999) Practices that Support Team Learning and Their Impact on Speed to Market and New Product Success, *Journal of Product Innovation Management*, 16(5): 439–54.

McDermott, C. and Handfield, R. (2000) Concurrent Development and Strategic Outsourcing: Do the Rules Change in Breakthrough Innovation? *The Journal of High Technology Management Research*, 11(1): 35–57.

Mikkola, J. H. (2006) Capturing the Degree of Modularity Embedded in Product Architectures, *Journal of Product Innovation Management*, 23: 128–46.

Nightingale, P. (2000) The Product-Process-Organisation Relationship in Complex Development Projects, *Research Policy*, 29: 913–30.

Nobelius, D (2002) *Managing R&D Processes: Focusing on Technology Development, Product Development and Their Interplay*, PhD thesis, Göteborg: Chalmers University of Technology.

—— (2004) Linking Product Development to Applied Research: Transfer Experiences from an Automotive Company, *Technovation*, 24: 321–34.

Okhuysen, G. A. and Eisenhardt, K. M. (2002) Integrating Knowledge in Groups: How Formal Interventions Enable Flexibility, *Organization Science*, 13(4): 370–86.

Sanchez, R. and Mahoney, J. T. (1996) Modularity, Flexibility, and Knowledge Management in Product and Organization Design, *Strategic Management Journal*, 17(Winter Special Issue): 63–76.

Sehdev, K., Fan, I-S, Cooper, S., Williams, G. (1995) Design for Manufacture in the Aerospace Extended Enterprise, *World Class Design to Manufacture*, 2(2): 28–33.

Shenhar, A. J., Dvir, D. (1996) Toward a Typological Theory of Project Management, *Research Policy*, 25: 607–32.

Söderlund, J. (2002) Managing Complex Development Projects: Arenas, Knowledge Processes and Time, *R&D Management*, 32(5): 419–30.

Staudenmayer, N., Tripsas, M. and Tucci, C. L. (2005) Interfirm Modularity and its Implications for Product Development, *Journal of Product Innovation Management*, 22(4): 303–21.

Swink, M. (2003) Completing Projects On-time: How Project Acceleration Affects New Product Development, *Journal of Engineering and Technology Management*, 20(4): 319–44.

Takeishi, A. (2002) Knowledge Partitioning in the Interfirm Division of Labor: The Case of Automotive Product Development, *Organization Science*, 13(3): 321–38.

Takeuchi, H. and Nonaka, I. (1986) The New Product Development Game, *Harvard Business Review*, 64(1): 137–46.

Ulrich, K. (1995) The Role of Product Architecture in the Manufacturing Firm, *Research Policy*, 24: 419–40.

Vandevelde, A. and Van Dierdonck, R. (2003) Managing the Design-Manufacturing Interface, *International Journal of Operations and Production Management*, 23(11): 1326–48.

Veryzer, R. W. (1998) Discontinuous Innovation and the New Product Development Process, *Journal of Product Innovation Management*, 15: 304–21.

Weick, K. E., Sutcliffe, K. M. and Obstfeld, D. (2005) Organizing and the Process of Sensemaking, *Organization Science*, 16(4): 409–21.

Wheelwright, S. C. and Clark, K. B. (1992) *Revolutionizing Product Development: Quantum Leaps in Speed, Efficiency and Quality*, New York: The Free Press.

Wu, Y., Balasubramanian, S. and Mahajan, V. (2004) When is a Preannounced New Product Likely to Be Delayed? *Journal of Marketing*, 68(2): 101–13.

Yin, R. K. (1994) *Case Study Research: Design and Methods*, Thousand Oaks, CA: Sage Publications.

7

Knowledge Integration in Inter-firm R&D Collaboration: How do Firms Manage Problems of Coordination and Cooperation?

*Mattias Johansson, Mattias Axelson,
Cecilia Enberg, and Fredrik Tell*

This chapter shows that the interplay between problems of coordination, deriving from knowledge contingencies, and problems of cooperation, stemming from relationship factors, may explain both the extent of knowledge integration in R&D collaboration partnerships, and how the partnering firms set out to accomplish knowledge integration.

7.1 INTRODUCTION

Firms are rarely self-sufficient and therefore often need to integrate complementary knowledge of other firms in order to fully exploit their own resources and capabilities (Rothwell et al., 1974; Arora and Gambardella, 1990; Cassiman and Veugelers, 2006). This means that, to attain their goals, firms often need to collaboratively use and combine two or more organizations' knowledge bases. To accomplish this, firms have a multitude of mechanisms at their disposal, including cross-functional teams, knowledge brokers, and documents (Schmickl and Kieser, 2008). However, these mechanisms are not equally appropriate in every setting. This chapter addresses the challenges associated with creating an interface of mechanisms to support knowledge integration in the context of inter-firm R&D collaboration, an area where inter-firm relationships have grown considerably since the 1980s (Hagedoorn, 2002).

While it has become more important for firms to integrate external knowledge, the literature suggests that this is a challenging task (Kogut, 1989; Lam, 1997; Lhuillery and Pfister, 2009). There are at least two reasons for this. On the one hand, according to the literature, knowledge integration may be complicated by the characteristics of knowledge itself (Grant, 1996). For example, integrating specialists' know-how may be more difficult than integrating the knowledge they can explicate and communicate in words (e.g. Cohen and Levinthal, 1990; Kogut and Zander, 1992; Amesse and Cohendet, 2001). On the other hand, the literature suggests that the fact that knowledge integration increasingly occurs across firms, rather than within firms, means that integration is also affected by characteristics of the collaboration (Grandori, 2001). For example, if firms have divergent goals or interests, these may be more difficult to resolve between firms than within them (e.g. Hamel, 1991; Cyert and March, 1992; Chesbrough and Teece, 1996). To distinguish between these two sets of complications, the term 'problems of coordination' has been used to denote complications that stem from the characteristics of knowledge, while the term 'problems of cooperation' has been used to denote complications that result from relationship characteristics (Roberts, 2004; Postrel, 2009).

Although both types of problem have been identified as relevant to inter-firm collaboration, many studies tend to treat the problems independently. Knowledge integration mechanisms, for example, are often related only to characteristics of the knowledge to be integrated (Foss, 2007). While this may suffice in the context of within-firm knowledge integration, such a one-sided focus does not suffice in inter-firm collaboration. The reason lies in the tension that exists between the need to integrate knowledge in order to achieve objectives, on the one hand, and the risk of unintended leakage of valuable knowledge on the other (Heiman and Nickerson, 2004; Oxley and Sampson, 2004). Firms therefore need to consider safeguards against problems of cooperation in conjunction with the problem of coordination. This is clearly relevant to many inter-firm R&D collaborations, since the integration of partners' knowledge implies exposure to potential expropriation by the partner. Few studies, however, have enquired into how firms manage problems of cooperation and coordination simultaneously. It seems, therefore, that a detailed enquiry that takes both problems into account could increase our understanding of how firms create benefits from engaging in interorganizational R&D collaboration.

The purpose of this chapter is therefore to investigate how, in the context of three inter-firm R&D collaborations, firms manage knowledge integration in the face of problems of coordination and cooperation. The next section presents a conceptual framework based on relevant literature. Our empirical research strategy and methodology are discussed in Section 7.3, while Section 7.4 presents the three cases studied from the point of view of the conceptual framework. This is followed by an analysis in Section 7.5. Conclusions and a general discussion are provided in the final section.

7.2 THEORETICAL FRAMEWORK

This section first identifies two problems that firms may experience in inter-firm knowledge integration. Thereafter, the section presents proposals in the literature for dealing with each problem. Finally, the section seeks to explain how the two sets of problems may simultaneously influence how firms manage inter-firm knowledge integration.

7.2.1 Problems in inter-firm knowledge integration

Integrating knowledge across firm boundaries involves many problems, but generally these may be subsumed under two categories. The first category, here termed problems of cooperation, relates to how firms align their interests in the face of different inter-firm relationship characteristics. The second category, here termed problems of coordination, concerns how firms align competencies in the face of different knowledge characteristics, or knowledge contingency factors. The distinction is not clear-cut but most of the problems identified in literature are primarily assignable to one of these two categories.

Problems of cooperation

Although R&D collaboration does not necessarily involve the transaction of a good or a service in the sense of transaction cost economics (TCE), some of the factors that TCE stresses as problematic in relationships seem highly relevant for inter-firm R&D collaboration.

According to Williamson (1985), asset specificity is the 'big locomotive' for problems of cooperation. Asset specificity refers to assets (e.g. site, physical, and human) that cannot be redeployed to alternative uses, but which require specialized investments that incur a loss in the case of a failed agreement (Demsetz, 1991: 167). High asset specificity thus entails higher risks of losses. Since R&D may require specialized investments, such risks are highly relevant for the context of R&D collaboration, although firms may avoid the risk by engaging only in generic, non-firm-specific R&D collaboration (Nooteboom, 2000; Hagedoorn, 2002). Still, asset specificity itself may not influence a cooperative relation as much as it does when appearing together with other factors (Williamson, 1985).

Uncertainty is one important such factor that influences asset specificity, and which is also relevant in the context of R&D collaboration (Williamson, 1985; Folta, 1998). In relation to R&D, such uncertainty may, in line with Osborn and Baughn (1990), be associated with the technological intensity, or degree of novelty, of R&D work. Higher degrees of novelty are likely to reflect higher degrees of uncertainty. Whereas high uncertainty may lead by itself to problems of cooperation, such problems may be even more severe when high asset specificity is also involved, since there is then a larger potential for unsalvageable losses. As research is commonly associated with higher degrees of novelty than development, uncertainty problems of this type may be more latent in R&D collaboration at the 'front-end' (i.e. with a research orientation).

Conflicts of interest have been identified as a potential cause of inter-firm problems of cooperation in a wide range of studies. In TCE, it is a result of opportunism, that is, 'self-interest seeking with guile' (Williamson, 1985: 65). More generally, though, the fact that no two partners are alike and that actors are driven in part by self-interest and thus have partly different objectives provides sufficient grounds for potential conflicts. Such conflicts may occur as a result of, for example, difficulties in aligning objectives (Mora-Valentin et al., 2004), or for competitive reasons (Hamel, 1991). With regard to the latter, studies suggest that the risk for latent conflicts is greater in horizontal relations since competitors are less likely to be cooperative in sharing their knowledge (García-Canal, 1996;

Lhuillery and Pfister, 2009). Again, whereas a conflict of interest by itself may be a sufficient reason for problems of cooperation, the potential impact of such conflicts is greater in cases where a relation is also subject to high asset specificity. The reason is simply that with high asset specificity, more is at stake for one or several of the parties involved in a collaboration, thus making it more important to try to control and handle potential conflicts.

Problems of coordination

Like cooperation, coordination has been treated extensively in the literature. Commonly identified problems include those of knowledge differentiation, or degree of common knowledge (Mowery et al., 1998), interdependence (Gulati and Sytch, 2007), and the articulability or tacitness of knowledge (Zollo and Winter, 2002).

Firms need to integrate knowledge because the benefits of specialization render in-house production of all necessary knowledge virtually impossible. Still, to actually integrate external knowledge requires the existence of at least some common knowledge (Demsetz, 1991; Grant, 1996). Between firms, such common knowledge may consist of, for example, similar knowledge bases, common language, or other forms of symbolic communication such as statistics, theories, and practices. The presence of such common knowledge has been found to be important in technology alliances and R&D collaborations, suggesting that a lesser degree of common knowledge among firms is likely to increase problems of coordination in inter-firm R&D collaboration (Mowery et al., 1996; Lane and Lubatkin, 1998; Caloghirou et al., 2003; Cummings and Teng, 2003; Sampson, 2007).

Another important source of problems of coordination is task interdependence. Interdependence in this context refers traditionally to the number of elements to be integrated and the number of possible connections between them, so that a change in one element has repercussions on the state of all the others (cf. Thompson, 1967; Simon, 1976; Kauffman, 1993). Thompson (1967) identified three types of such interdependencies associated with increasing degrees of coordination problems. Firstly, pooled dependencies, in which activities are linked by making use of the same pooled resources; secondly, sequential interdependence, where the output of activity A is input for activity B; and thirdly, reciprocal interdependence, where the output of activity A is input for activity B as well as vice versa. In relation to knowledge and inter-firm R&D, such interdependence is relevant since input into the work performed by one specialist consists to various degrees of knowledge elements of other specialists. The intensity of such interdependence may thus influence the effectiveness of different means to integrate knowledge across organizational boundaries (Simonin, 1999; Grant and Baden-Fuller, 2004; Gulati and Sytch, 2007).

The articulability of knowledge refers to a commonly made distinction between explicit knowledge, which is expressible, and tacit knowledge, which reveals itself through its application (Polanyi, 1967). The distinction serves to highlight differences in transferability. Explicit knowledge is easier to transfer because it is articulated, whereas tacit knowledge is embodied and hence its transfer often requires close interaction or observation. By extension, this also affects the ability to coordinate and integrate knowledge. It has, for example, been argued that the close interaction required to transfer tacit knowledge limits the number of people that can effectively be involved in knowledge integration (Grant, 1996). Empirical studies also show how inter-firm R&D collaboration may be subject to coordination difficulties due to tacit knowledge (e.g. Lam, 1997).

Besides influencing cooperation, uncertainty is commonly suggested to be important in relation to coordination (Casciaro, 2003). This is because uncertainty makes it difficult to coordinate work through standardization and routines. Factors that contribute to task uncertainty have been argued to include the complexity of search processes, the time it takes to solve problems, and the extent to which tasks have knowable outcomes (Van de Ven et al., 1976). These factors seem to correspond well with the degree of novelty of R&D work. Research collaboration in early stages of R&D may hence face more uncertainty than collaborative development in later stages.

7.2.2 Inter-firm knowledge integration

A number of ways are proposed in the literature for how firms can deal with both problems of cooperation and problems of coordination in inter-firm relationships. However, these two sets of problems are generally managed differently. Problems of cooperation are generally managed through what will be referred to here as governance structures, whereas problems of coordination are often dealt with through what will be referred to as integration mechanisms.

Knowledge governance and problems of cooperation

Since problems of cooperation are often aggravated by the presence of high asset specificity, one way for firms to reduce the risks involved in inter-firm R&D is naturally to engage only in general-purpose joint R&D. This, however, is not always possible, or desirable, and firms have other options. One is to establish governance structures by means of legal contracts, monitoring, and safeguards that provide enough carrots and sticks to keep problems under control (Nooteboom, 2000). A variety of such governance structures exists, ranging from joint ventures that provide strong incentives for cooperation and opportunities for control to various forms of non-equity-based contractual agreements associated with weaker incentives. Equity forms of governance structures differ from non-equity-based in that they tend to produce complex, firm-like organizations (Casciaro, 2003). As such, they also provide more incentives to align objectives and room for administrative control, but are also considered more expensive to establish than non-equity-based structures. Still, the benefits of joint ventures have been argued to outweigh the costs in instances of high asset specificity (Kogut, 1988; Pisano, 1989).

However, uncertainty may make it impossible to anticipate all contingencies in contracts. Folta (1998), for example, argues that the cost of commitment in the face of technological uncertainties may even offset the administrative benefits of control that follow from, for example, joint ventures. But there are also other options for accommodating problems of cooperation. These include hierarchy and trust (e.g. Das and Teng, 1998). Hierarchy, however, has been seen as difficult to enforce between firms, although quasi-hierarchical arrangements such as joint ventures may provide room for its employment (Williamson, 1985; Grant and Baden-Fuller, 2004). Trust, in turn, may induce confidence and desirable behaviours, but generally develops out of interaction and may hence not be an option initially (Ring and Van de Ven, 1994).

Building on previous literature, we identify a continuum of four governance mechanisms, ranging from 'looser' contractual to 'tighter' equity-based ones (Oxley, 1997; Gulati and Singh, 1998; Narula and Hagedoorn, 1999). The most 'market-like' form of inter-firm governance is the unilateral contract, for example licensing of technology or short-term R&D contracts. A more integrated form of contract-based governance is bilateral contracting, for example cross-licensing or joint research agreements. Equity-based governance can either take the lesser integrated form of minority shareholding or the more integrated form of split ownership in a joint venture or in research corporations.

Knowledge integration mechanisms and problems of coordination

While governance structures may accommodate problems of cooperation to the extent that such problems can be anticipated, they are less appropriate for coordinating and integrating specialists' different knowledge bases. To that end, firms instead use various integration mechanisms. Grant (1996) differentiates between four types of such mechanisms: direction and rules, sequencing, routines, and group problem-solving and decision-making. The first three categories 'seek efficiency of integration through avoiding the costs of communication and learning' (Grant, 1996: 115). With regard to direction and rules, such efficiency can be achieved through the use of, for example, plans, rules, and standardized information, whereas, for example, modularization can help to achieve such efficiency in relation to sequencing and routines (Grant, 1996; Schmickl and Kieser, 2008). The last category, group problem-solving and decision-making, concerns mechanisms that allow for more personal interaction, and includes mechanisms ranging from formal meetings to liaison engineers, knowledge brokers, and integrated operational teams (e.g. Axelson, 2008; Schmickl and Kieser, 2008).

By allowing for more or less interaction, and being more or less standardized, these mechanisms also allow for the occurrence of different activities. The mechanisms required to integrate knowledge in R&D collaboration thus depend on the situation. In general, though, most coordination problems require mechanisms that promote interaction in one way or another. It has, for example, been argued that the more complex a task, the greater is the need to rely on non-standardized mechanisms that promote high interaction. Knowledge diversity has been suggested to call for integration mechanisms such as meetings, teams, or liaison engineers that can mediate and create a common platform of understanding (e.g. Tushman, 1977). Whereas direction and routines are efficient for coordinating pooled and sequential interdependencies, reciprocal interdependencies often necessitate the use of integrated, or cross-functional, teams that enable intense interaction (Grant, 1996). Similarly, whereas explicit knowledge may be conveyed in documents, tacit knowledge requires mechanisms such as teams that allow for observation and close interaction (Schmickl and Kieser, 2008).

Towards a framework of knowledge integration in collaborative R&D

The literature review suggests that both problems of cooperation and problems of coordination are important for inter-firm R&D collaboration. This is hardly surprising; the question is rather how these problems relate to and influence each other. Some clues may be derived from the literature on inter-firm relationship processes, which argues that firms first negotiate contractual arrangements that then form the context for interparty action (Ring and Van de Ven, 1994; Doz, 1996). As such, the knowledge governance structure would constitute a framework within which firms decide on the knowledge integration mechanisms to use, as depicted in Figure 7.1.

How problems of cooperation and coordination interact within such a framework is less clear, as is the associated question of how firms manage the two problems. While it has been argued that it is the combination of problems that is important in order to understand contractual arrangements (Williamson, 1985), studies that address the issue of how problems of cooperation and associated contractual structures influence the creation of the interface to deal with problems of coordination and knowledge integration tend to focus on only one. For example, Grandori (2001), arguing that situations characterized by problems of cooperation and problems of coordination require sufficiently tight initial contractual structures of the relationship for knowledge integration to take place, focuses only on the impact of conflicts of interest on those contractual structures. Heiman and Nickerson (2004) in turn focus only on the hazards of opportunism. Moreover, as governance structures are invariably incomplete, due to the impossibility of contracting for all contingencies (Williamson, 1985; Eisenhardt and Santos, 2002), governance structures alone may not provide enough of a framework to effectively resolve problems of cooperation.

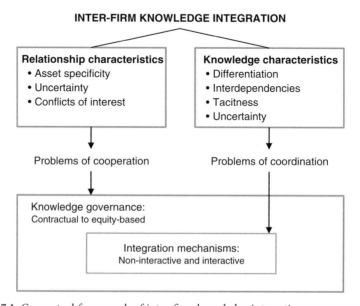

Figure 7.1 Conceptual framework of inter-firm knowledge integration

This should influence how firms manage knowledge integration, but the literature provides few details as to how.

Thus, a more detailed understanding is currently lacking of how both problems of cooperation and problems of coordination are relevant for knowledge integration in inter-firm partnerships. There thus seems to be much scope for improving our understanding of how firms establish mechanisms in relation to both these problems. To address these issues, a case study of three inter-firm R&D collaborations was conducted. The next section outlines the methodological foundation of this study.

7.3 RESEARCH DESIGN AND METHODOLOGY

Guided by the research focus, a multiple case study of three inter-firm R&D collaborations was conducted. A case study was considered appropriate since it allowed us to address the 'why' and 'how' of knowledge integration in R&D collaboration. The present research builds on an instrumental case-study approach, in that the cases have been instrumental in elucidating a particular phenomenon, here the process of knowledge integration in inter-firm R&D collaboration (Stake, 1995). The research is also an instance of a collective case-study approach, as several projects have been studied together with a focus on the specific and generic properties of knowledge integration in these projects.

The selection of cases was purposive, meaning that the cases were actively sought according to specified criteria in order to be able to elucidate the phenomena of interest and achieve theoretical focus (Glaser and Strauss, 1967; Eisenhardt, 1989). In the present study, the selection of cases was therefore based on the potential for problems of cooperation and problems of coordination, and on variation with regard to these problems. To that end, all cases concerned, for example, collaborations on complex systems as this implies a potential for coordinative problems, and the cases also included both horizontal and vertical collaborations (García-Canal, 1996).

The data collection has primarily consisted of face-to-face interviews, which were semi-structured and carried out with key project individuals. In all cases, members of each firm in the R&D collaboration were interviewed. The selection process for the interviewees basically followed a snowball sampling approach. Based on the initial discussions with the companies, we identified key participants in the projects, and then further persons were identified in the interviews with project participants. As a result of this process, a total of seventy-four persons were interviewed, distributed over the cases so that sixteen persons were interviewed in the Future Combat Air Systems (FCAS) project, thirty-three persons in the Explorer project, and twenty-five persons in the Automotive Sub-system (AS) project.

The analysis of the data was conducted accordingly. First, a single case history of each R&D collaboration was written and emerging themes in relation to the purpose of the study were noted. Second, these themes were compared and contrasted with prior literature on inter-firm governance and knowledge integration. Third, as the primary aim was to understand inter-firm knowledge integration in R&D collaboration, variation and similarities across the cases were used to analyse and help elucidate this particular phenomenon (cf. Eisenhardt, 1989).

7.4 THREE CASES OF R&D COLLABORATION

7.4.1 The FCAS project

The FCAS project forms part of a European technology acquisition programme and involves the armed forces, defence authorities, and industries of five European countries. The study presented here focused on the collaboration between the industrial partners.

The target of the collaboration was to identify and suggest advanced technologies for FCAS with the aim of reducing the risks and costs involved in combat air systems procurement. The time frame was post-2020 and at the time of the study, the focus was rather on building new technological competence than on developing a physical product.

While the companies involved were competitors, the initiation of the project served their interests well. They operated on a market characterized by consolidation and re-formation, where the prospects of acting alone in the future were poor from both a financial and a competitive perspective. Although some of the firms involved had experience of working together from former R&D collaborations, collaborating was described as just as complex as the technology.

When the technology acquisition programme and related R&D collaboration projects were initiated, governments signed a letter of intent and a memorandum of understanding. No joint venture or the like was created to govern the project. Instead, steering committees, with representatives from the industry partners, the defence authorities, and the armed forces, were created at the programme and project levels, respectively. What was referred to as 'a standard IP rights agreement' was signed.

The authorities acted as customers, defining the requirements of the FCAS under development, while the industry partners were responsible for conducting the operational work of identifying types of system and their related technology bases. Although one industry partner served as the contractor, the project was presented as a collaboration between equals, where each company had a representative on the project management board. Project members frequently used the project management board to solve disputes and misunderstandings; more generally, decisions were often shuffled up the hierarchy.

The FCAS project was organized in five interdependent work packages (WP). Further, the project was organized in phases and iterations such that in each phase there were a number of iterations between the WPs. There was an intricate interdependence between the various WPs, with some iterations following sequentially upon each other while others took place simultaneously. Many project members were simultaneously involved in several WPs.

All the companies involved in the collaboration had the ability, and thus the knowledge, to develop a combat air system in-house. Thus, the partnering firms' knowledge bases were substitutable to a certain extent but each firm was used to working with a specific technology and some firms were considered better than others within certain domains of expertise. Within the project, there was a division of labour such that each firm was responsible for managing one WP and one or several disciplines. All partnering firms were involved in all WPs. The project work has followed different logics at different phases, for example in some phases, all partners acted on all tasks while in other phases the tasks have been distributed such that each partner firm has been assigned the responsibility of a particular task.

Project members' various perspectives were regarded as 'the real challenges of collaborative project work', and project members gave numerous examples of instances when communication failed despite efforts to elaborate shared definitions.

> . . . for every step forward and as we reach a more detailed level, you realise that there are communication deficiencies, that we mean different things, we have different perspectives on the task and that's the biggest challenge. (Project member)

The project members were located at their respective home organizations for the duration of the project and the only occasion when project members from the different partners met was at the monthly project meetings, which took place interchangeably on the different partners' premises. At these meetings, the project leader of each WP chaired the various sessions where actions were followed up, the results and outcomes of work were discussed, and plans were made for the work to come. Although all the project members were gathered at the same location simultaneously, each WP had its own meeting. The project meetings were scheduled years in advance and the project members even knew in some detail what they were supposed to discuss at each meeting, since the meeting schedule also included an overall agenda. Generally, there were a number of documents that guided project work, whereof the statement of work was the one most often referred to by the project members, who considered the project to be very well planned. The statement of work defined the technical scope and duration of the project and also included detailed descriptions of the deliverables of each WP.

The project members emphasized that they were not actually working together with colleagues from the other partnering industries in the sense of doing practical work or solving problems together. Instead, they discussed the deliverables – both those which were finished and those which constituted new 'actions'. Project members also suggested that although discussions about the results were sometimes lively and took quite some time, they never asked each other about the models or methods applied in order to arrive at them. All they knew was that they were not applying the same processes, models, and methods in the different organizations.

> We've agreed on a way of working – we are supposed to exchange data with each other and then, how they have been arrived at, if you used a calculator or a supercomputer, that's of no importance. We can't question each other on these things, but each firm is responsible for its contribution. [. . .] You have to disregard these issues and trust each other's methods. We can't exchange methods because they constitute corporate confidential information. (Project member)

7.4.2 The Explorer project

The Explorer project was launched in late 2003 and involved seven European players in the defence industry. This case, however, concerns the project's first phase, which involved only two of the partners – here named Red Systems and Yellow Systems.

The aim of the project was to jointly develop a prototype of a new product platform, which could be described as a technological leap as the architecture would differ considerably from the existing versions. The intention was not to further develop the prototype into a product but to build new technological competence. The new competence was important both for each company's own products and for providing a basis for future projects. Although they were competitors, both companies' interests were served by this. Neither company would have been able to finance development by themselves. The market they operated in was characterized by consolidation, with poor prospects for any one firm to be able to continue entirely on its own. Both firms thus viewed the partnership as a strategically important way to build a competitive position that would enable more collaboration.

The Explorer project is an R&D consortium with Yellow Systems as the main contractor. Yellow Systems initially wanted full control over the platform's concept development phase. However, after tough negotiations and an assessment that Red Systems' ability to contribute was valuable, not least financially, Red Systems was allowed to participate in concept development. A contract for collaboration, signed in early 2005, explicitly stated that the two companies were jointly responsible for all deliverables, and it also involved an intellectual property (IP) rights framework of four levels, ranging from information open to both companies to information that both companies could see but not use. To lead and monitor development, the project organization included a senior board with members from each organization, and one project leader from each organization. Being the main contractor, Yellow Systems' project leader ultimately had the right to make decisions about the project. However, this right, as well as that of the board, was not used in daily work. Rather, all decisions were consensus-based.

The new product platform was based on the development of new technology and thus involved much uncertainty, not least with regard to how Explorer's product architecture and physical interfaces between subsystems should be defined. Much of the initial work therefore focused on reducing technological uncertainties, and defining the overall product architecture. This was complicated by differences in language and experience. Although both companies to a large degree had substitutable competencies, managers as well as engineers experienced frequent misunderstandings because of differences in company standards and terminology, as illustrated by the quote below. Initially, it was even difficult to identify when they did not understand each other.

> There are deep differences in the companies' conception of words, which are related to their history. (Senior engineer)

The communicative problems were exacerbated by the fact that both companies' engineers relied on their technological experience when making decisions:

> It is often really difficult to understand one another's points of view. For instance, when we argue that according to our experience certain integration of computers is impossible, they do not agree. They think they know what to do and so they just think we are wrong. This reflects our different experiences and they are difficult to share. (Project leader)

It was already clear during the early discussions that reducing uncertainties and clarifying interdependencies called for a substantial capacity for communication in the collaborative work. This anticipated need led to a decision to organize the project into a co-located integrated operational team just outside one of the company's plants. The team had some twenty members, eight of them from Red Systems. While more people were involved in development at the respective home organizations, their work was coordinated by the team, whose task was to create the base of common architectural knowledge. Work was regulated by a work breakdown structure, where smaller development groups of two to four persons were responsible for a technology area and for the specification of each package. This basic division of work did not change, although details and interfaces were gradually defined more clearly as a result of group interactions on such issues.

Both engineers and project leaders described the co-location as central to the accomplishment of the joint work tasks. This, not least because it promoted extensive interaction, allowed for daily face-to-face meetings, and contributed to ad hoc problem-solving. Everyday interaction also gradually enhanced the common understanding among the engineers of both firms.

7.4.3 The AS project

The AS project is an R&D partnership in the automotive industry between a systems integrator, SOM, and a subsystem manufacturer, USSM, located in different continents. The partnership was launched in 1989 but the present case focuses on a project that started in 2001 when relations between the two companies intensified and knowledge integration became a larger issue. The project ended in 2007 with the initiation of production.

The target of the partnership was to develop a new, technologically advanced subsystem for SOM's platform. The basic design of the subsystem built on an idea that had proven technologically feasible prior to the partnership; although outcomes of the further development were initially regarded as uncertain, the project leaned towards the development side of R&D. The partnership resembled a traditional buyer–supplier relationship, except that SOM had much more influence on the course of development. That influence not only provided part of the partnership's rationale in the first place but also caused frustration among SOM engineers, who complained that they were given final technological solutions without having a say in advance. However, it also meant that should the relation with USSM fail, SOM had few alternative uses for their investments since they had no intention of eventually developing these subsystems on their own. SOM consequently felt a great need to at least secure the ability to produce the system themselves. For USSM, the primary benefits resided in sharing the development costs of the subsystem, which they could also employ in other lines of business. Still, given SOM's specific requirements in relation to the platform, USSM needed to make specific adaptations of the subsystem in line with those requirements.

To govern the partnership, a contract was signed for joint development to take place in an independent project organization, financed equally by the two firms. A jointly owned company was also established to take care of IP rights, and a contractual clause was introduced that prohibited USSM from selling the subsystem to SOM's competitors. A fifty–fifty joint venture (JV) was established for production and later on the development part of the partnership was also brought into the JV. The project organization consisted of a board, with senior members from each organization, which dealt mainly with strategic issues; steering committees oriented towards operational issues; and various formally assigned project management roles. For SOM, it was important to have their own people in the right places in this structure because:

> At USSM, the informal decision making procedures are really important – then you've got to have a man on the inside. (Project manager)

Both firms' extensive knowledge in their respective fields made for a division of labour in the partnership, with USSM developing the subsystem and SOM providing specifications in terms of, for example, design, quality, and costs, and also feeding back test results. Still, it was not possible to just delineate the subsystem and develop it. For example, the new technology influenced other parts of SOM's larger system, and conversely, the subsystem's intended function in the larger system had consequences for USSM's development.

> In the beginning, they had little understanding for why we asked for the parameters we did. We, on the other hand, had little knowledge of what effects that would have on the sub-system. (Senior engineer)

Interaction between SOM and USSM also suffered from a lack of understanding of each other's work practices. For example, USSM relied on Six Sigma and statistics, whereas SOM relied on experience, or 'gut feeling', and small-scale tests. Moreover, SOM engineers were used to making decisions on lower hierarchical levels, whereas decisions at USSM were more often made at higher levels and based on statistics. This impaired the engineers' understanding of each other and on what basis decisions were made.

Given USSM's expertise in the subsystem, the project organization, and later the JV, was located on USSM's premises and primarily staffed by USSM's personnel. SOM initially supplied four liaison engineers and managers to the project organization, but a number of individuals located at SOM were also involved in telephone meetings with their USSM counterparts. SOM realized, however, that their on-site staffing was not sufficient to get the necessary oversight, and that telephone conferences could not substitute for face-to-face contacts:

> If you are to develop things as complicated as these, you have to meet physically at least a couple of times a year.... [At the moment, we also see that] those groups who meet the least also have the most problems. (JV board member)

To remedy this, SOM increased its on-site staffing, and both companies also temporarily exchanged people for periods of time, and arranged more regular face-to-face meetings. For SOM, these actions were highly important for accessing knowledge and developing personal relations with USSM's engineers. The latter also proved important for gradually improving communication:

> ... people started talking more and found more synergies. There was a whole new world of data that we could provide each other with. We dumped in a whole lot of new knowledge about test situations etc. to their development engineers. (Project engineer)

Moreover, encouraged by managers, such contacts led to the initiation of regular contacts between engineers regarding technological areas outside the formal contract.

The authority structure was also much used to support collaborative work, not least to enforce integration mechanisms that were needed at operational levels. In particular, SOM's engineers resorted to SOM's board members to enforce, for example, steering groups and work roles in response to specific problems. This procedure was a response to differences in culture and in responsibilities among engineers at the same hierarchical level. In addition, the partners have also worked much with shared artefacts. There has, for example, been a lot of work to create common servers in which drawings, test results, and the like are stored.

7.5 ANALYSIS

This section identifies some observations concerning the characteristics of each partnership context, the governance structures and integration mechanisms used, and how cooperation may relate to coordination.

7.5.1 FCAS

The partners in the FCAS case can be said to have faced potentially quite severe problems of cooperation. The competitive situation among them was intense in that all the partners were direct competitors, and FCAS also involved major uncertainties on account of the project's research nature, with goals far into the future. Both these characteristics were likely to stress the relationship since technological uncertainty increases the difficulties to control for contingencies and as relations between direct competitors bring out the risk of conflicts of interest (Lhuillery and Pfister, 2009). In fact, following Grandori (2001), the partners should have opted for a tight governance structure based on these considerations alone. Instead, FCAS arguably chose a fairly loose governance structure with a bilateral agreement that provided low incentives for closer alignment. There are various possible explanations for this. Firstly, FCAS may simply have opted for the wrong governance structure. Secondly, it may be argued that conflicts of interest and uncertainty were counteracted by comparatively low degrees of asset specificity. The knowledge and information derived by the partnering firms should be useful for their own assessments of future technological development regardless of the project's continuation. However, both explanations are gainsaid by the fact that the competitive situation and the uncertainty should have been sufficiently pertinent and clear for the partners to anticipate and be concerned about these problems. A third, more plausible, explanation may be that whereas a tighter governance structure could have been chosen, the project's current phase did not warrant the requisite investments. Given the project's great uncertainty, the mounting cost of commitment may have outweighed additional benefits of control (Folta, 1998). A better strategy for all parties may thus be an incremental approach, building commitment one step at a time.

The choice of governance structure also seems to explain the collaborative interface set up by the partners. The FCAS case relied exclusively on formal mechanisms that, apart from the joint monthly meetings, supported virtually no interaction between the partners. All work in between was highly formalized and structured, with detailed plans, standardized reports, and sequencing of work packages. Considering the vast complexity of combat air systems, though, it does not seem to have been a lack of problems of coordination that explain the absence of mechanisms to support interaction in FCAS. On the contrary, identifying a particular set of advanced technologies for future systems would seem to be a task that is not only highly uncertain but also one that requires extensive knowledge of interdependencies that such complex systems are likely to exhibit among their constituent parts, knowledge that furthermore may be embedded in the experience of specialists in each firm. In fact, rather than an evaluation of test results, it seems that what identifying advanced technologies for FCAS would require is an extensive exchange of knowledge of the technologies involved. However, in view of potentially high conflicts of interest and a governance structure that provides few incentives to align objectives, the strict focus on test results and a low amount of joint activities makes more sense. In fact, to limit the scope of integration seems to be a viable option under such circumstances (Simonin, 1999; Caloghirou et al., 2003; Oxley and Sampson, 2004).

7.5.2 Explorer

Explorer was similarly to FCAS, a partnership of direct competitors leaning towards the R-side of R&D, suggesting potential problems of cooperation. While the competitive situation suggests high risks of conflicts of interest, the collaboration was still very much in the strategic interest of both firms, which should have counteracted the latent conflicts of interest. However, the concept development nature of the project, concerning a new, technologically different platform architecture, still suggests fairly high levels of uncertainty. Furthermore, the consensus-oriented development likely implied adaptations to one another regarding the prototype. Whereas this most likely introduced some asset specificity into the R&D collaboration, the primary objective of the partnership was still to develop and build competence in a new area, something that would benefit both partners independently of each other. This more general purpose could thus be argued to have tempered the levels of asset-specific investments. To accommodate for these potential problems of cooperation, Explorer implemented a bilateral agreement.

The primary difficulties with regard to integrating knowledge resided in ambiguous tacit knowledge (Simonin, 1999). This was a challenge because the high uncertainty regarding the design of the product architecture meant high operational interdependence for solving everyday problems. In addition, there was a lack of common understanding. This stemmed more from differences in standards and language than from diversity of knowledge bases (e.g. Dougherty, 1992). A co-located, integrated operational team was chosen, allowing extensive and close interaction, which gradually led to an enhanced understanding. In fact, it may be argued that the project was almost bound to implement such a team considering the coordination challenges.

Given the extensive and close interaction between the firms, the choice of a bilateral agreement to govern the relationship seems somewhat odd considering the problems of cooperation. Because although this was a more general project, the potentially latent cooperation problems were by no means small, as the use of an integrated team might suggest they were (e.g. Grandori, 2001; Heiman and

Nickerson, 2004). That a tighter structure in the form of an equity-based agreement was not implemented may again be due in part to the uncertainty involved not justifying the higher costs of an equity-based form of JV (Folta, 1998). However, it also seems likely that the fairly independent project organization, the explicit focus on joint responsibility, and the structured IP rights agreement and formalized decision rights by themselves could provide enough additional incentives and controls to compensate for the lower levels of control that follow from bilateral agreements compared to equity-based ones. In fact, considering that the aim was limited to building knowledge through developing a demonstrator, not a saleable product, the latter explanation seems more plausible.

7.5.3 AS

The AS case was characterized by the partners being engaged in a non-competitive buyer–supplier relationship concerning the development of technology that was fairly close to production. Both these factors suggest fairly low problems of cooperation, and hence less need for a tight governance structure (Grandori, 2001). That a fifty–fifty equity-based form of agreement was formed nonetheless may largely be explained by the AS case involving high degrees of asset specificity. SOM in particular had few alternative uses for their investments, but USSM's investments may also be said to be specific since some adaptation was needed to SOM and because of the limitations on USSM's rights to sell the system. With asset specificity as a driving force for problems of cooperation, it may be argued, in line with Williamson (1985), that the relation was all the more sensitive to the conflicts and uncertainty that occurred. As indicated in the case, sources of such conflicts could relate to, for example, the technological solutions chosen and how they were chosen, and to the fact that since the project organization was largely synonymous with USSM's line organization, it was in practice heavily, albeit not deliberately, influenced by USSM. That SOM took additional measures to monitor development and protect their investment by assigning staff to managerial positions further strengthens this interpretation.

With regard to integrating knowledge, the greatest difficulties resided in uncovering the tacit knowledge of each partner's specialists, something made problematic by a lack of understanding for each other's work practices. Although regular meetings were important integration mechanisms for dealing with such contingencies, the liaison roles proved essential. The primary reason for choosing such liaison roles rather than using a more integrated team approach is arguably that the often tacit knowledge elements involved in the R&D collaboration involved many individuals and functional areas. Under such circumstances, an integrated team approach may have required the involvement of more people than cost considerations and efficient coordination would allow (Grant, 1996). In addition, USSM performed the bulk of development, whereas SOM needed to coordinate that development with efforts and requirements of the home organization. A consequence of this could be that while the specific technological solutions developed were naturally important to SOM, they may have been subordinate to the need for SOM to coordinate the more general course of development. This furthered the importance of oversight in many areas, and thus the use of liaison roles, which is also suggested by most liaison positions being managerial rather than development engineers. As mentioned above, these managerial liaison roles also coincide well with SOM's intention to monitor and control development. It is also worth noting that several of the changes to integration mechanisms, including the positions of liaison roles, were enforced via the JV board and authority structure. This structure accordingly played an important role not only for control but also for knowledge integration as such.

7.6 DISCUSSION AND CONCLUSIONS

The findings of this study suggest that in order to understand knowledge integration in R&D partnerships, problems of cooperation and problems of coordination should be treated simultaneously.

On the one hand, the present findings thus add to the knowledge integration literature by suggesting the importance of not only optimizing integration mechanisms according to the knowledge contingency factors involved, such as knowledge tacitness and complexity, but also considering the problems of cooperation. One reason for this is that integration mechanisms ideally needed from the perspective of dealing with coordination may require strong supportive governance structures to limit potential problems of cooperation. Such governance structures can, however, entail large costs in addition to those associated with the integration mechanisms. Indeed, some situations may require investments in governance structures to support optimal knowledge integration that exceed what resulting benefits and economic rationale would allow (Folta, 1998). In the present study, such an argument could explain the situation in the FCAS case.

Consequently, firms need to establish sufficient mechanisms and structures in relation to both problems of cooperation and problems of coordination, rather than optimal structures and mechanisms with regard to either problem by itself. This can be achieved in various ways. Firstly, if the costs of establishing optimal integration mechanisms and governance structures are too high for the problems in question, a viable alternative for firms is to limit the scope of the partnership (Simonin, 1999; Caloghirou et al., 2003; Oxley and Sampson, 2004). That is, to limit the 'amount' of knowledge integrated. Secondly, managers can sometimes use sufficient rather than 'optimal' integration mechanisms in exchange for other gains, as some integration mechanisms can be used to overcome both problems of coordination and problems of cooperation to some extent. As shown in the AS case, for example, integrator roles can facilitate knowledge sharing and thus integration while enabling the integrators to have some control over the process of knowledge integration. While such a mechanism may not be optimal to either problem alone, it may be sufficient for them together.

These findings may also help resolve those of Heiman and Nickerson (2004), who found that whereas increased knowledge tacitness and increased knowledge complexity by themselves were positively correlated to tighter governance structures, the simultaneous presence of both factors was negatively correlated with tighter structures. Based on the above reasoning, and assuming as Heiman and Nickerson did the presence of opportunism, this may be explained by the combined costs of highly interactive integration mechanisms and tight supporting governance structures being unjustifiably high. Under such circumstances, it may be more rational for many firms to opt for a limited partnership with looser structures.

The present research also adds more specifically to previous studies on inter-firm knowledge integration. In particular, the findings suggest a more complex interaction between problems of cooperation and problems of coordination than suggested by prior literature. Whereas Grandori (2001) and Heiman and Nickerson (2004) focus only on the impact of conflicts of interest and of opportunism on knowledge integration, the present cases suggest that other factors are also at play.

Firstly, uncertainty in inter-firm collaboration may help to explain the choice of governance structure and the scope of collaborative R&D. None of the three cases studied used unilateral contracting, but primarily relied on bilateral contracting or JVs. In line with Oxley (1997), we suggest that this may be due to the appropriability of knowledge spillovers generated by the R&D collaborations. These are also affected by uncertainty. Cassiman and Veugelers (2002) suggest that horizontal collaboration (such as the FCAS and Explorer cases) is subject to direct spillovers as they involve competing firms, while indirect spillovers (through supplying or buying firms) are dominant in vertical cooperation (such as the AS case). Assuming that direct spillovers create more of a hazard than indirect, we may expect tighter governance structures in FCAS and Explorer than in AS. Rather we found the opposite. However, this can be explained by the more mature stage of R&D in the AS case, where knowledge spillovers of joint R&D were more known and had to be safeguarded by the use of JVs and exclusive licensing. At the same time, outcomes were less known and much less specific in the other two cases.

Secondly, asset specificity may provide a partial explanation to the present findings. This is illustrated in the AS case, where the tight governance structure seems to have been motivated primarily by the need of SOM to protect its project-specific investment. As mentioned above, this in turn formed part of the reason for the integration mechanisms used. Conversely, the more general-purpose nature of the Explorer collaboration may aid in explaining the looser governance structures applied in combination with the highly interactive integration mechanisms.

Thus, whereas both conflicts of interest and opportunism are undoubtedly important factors, the present findings suggest, in line with Williamson (1985), that such factors may be even more important to consider in relation to the uncertainty and the asset specificity of the relationship. Indeed, rather than any factor alone, it is the combination of these factors that is important to consider in relation to problems of coordination when explaining the establishment of knowledge integration mechanisms.

In light of these findings, we can revisit the conceptual framework presented in Figure 7.1. As suggested by the framework, it is the combination of relationship characteristics that needs to be related to the characteristics of knowledge to be integrated. While firms need to manage these characteristics, the benefits of different governance structures and integration mechanisms also need to be related to their costs. As a result, firms may have to opt for sufficient rather than optimal structures and mechanisms. This can, however, be resolved in different ways, making it difficult to relate any one set of characteristics to any one set of structures and mechanisms. In line with the framework, it also seems that firms do construct initial governance structures that form the context within which they establish integration mechanisms. The findings, however, also suggest that problems may vary with the phase of R&D, and may only be recognized as time passes. Structures and mechanisms may therefore evolve over time.

7.6.1 Limitations and implications for further research

We have two observations across the cases regarding the dynamics of knowledge integration that we suggest imply a need for further research.

Firstly, while this study does not purport to provide such detailed data, it is interesting to note that the three cases largely concern different phases of development. This may indicate that the problems faced by firms in R&D collaboration vary over time and/or with the research phase. Given the comparative lack of research on how partners combine governance structures and integration mechanisms to support knowledge integration in static settings (Foss, 2007), a dynamic take on how such combinations evolve in response to specific problems could be an interesting venue for further research.

Secondly, recent literature has proposed that repeated interactions and historical collaborative experience influence the ability to integrate knowledge in R&D collaborations (Mayer and Argyres, 2004; Ryall and Sampson, 2009; Hoang and Rothaermel, 2010). While our study has not investigated the presence or absence of previous alliance experience, its findings suggest that such experience may well influence the conditions affecting both problems of cooperation and problems of coordination. More detailed studies on how collaboration-intense firms develop experiential capabilities over time for R&D collaboration and the influence of this experience on the selection of knowledge governance and knowledge integration mechanisms are, however, needed.

7.6.2 Conclusions

To conclude then, knowledge integration is not just about solving problems of coordination that result from characteristics of the knowledge to be integrated. In inter-firm R&D relationships at least, it is also important to take into account characteristics of the relationship, or problems of cooperation, when explaining the mechanisms established to support knowledge integration. Following Heiman and Nickerson (2004), the implication of these results for firms and research alike would be to not focus too much on either of the problems at the expense of the other (cf. also Agarwal et al., 2010). For firms, close integration (i.e. the problem of coordination) that disregards the associated problems of cooperation without an appropriate governance structure runs the risk of exposing the relationship to the hazards of conflicts, knowledge expropriation, and asset specificity. Too much focus on governance structure at the expense of problems of coordination runs the risk of creating tight and thus costly structures that may not be needed. For firms and managers alike, this implies a need to balance the benefits that may come from solving either of the problems of coordination and cooperation 'optimally' against the costs of dealing with both problems together.

ACKNOWLEDGEMENTS

The authors would like to express their gratitude to all those who have commented on the chapter. All the comments have been valuable, and Professor Lars Lindkvist deserves a special mention for making such frequent and helpful comments.

REFERENCES

Agarwal, R., Croson, R. and Mahoney, J. (2010) The Role of Incentives and Communication in Strategic Alliances: An Experimental Investigation, *Strategic Management Journal*, 31(4): 413–37.

Amesse, F. and Cohendet, P. (2001) Technology Transfer Revisited from the Perspective of the Knowledge-based Economy, *Research Policy*, 30: 1459–78.

Arora, A. and Gambardella, A. (1990) Complementarity and External Linkages: The Strategies of the Large Firms in Biotechnology, *The Journal of Industrial Economics*, XXXVIII(4): 361–79.

Axelson, M. (2008) *Enabling Knowledge Communication between Companies*, PhD thesis, Stockholm: Stockholm School of Economics.

Caloghirou, Y., Hondroyiannis, G. and Vonortas, N. S. (2003) The Performance of Research Partnerships, *Managerial and Decision Economics*, 24(2/3): 85–99.

Casciaro, T. (2003) Determinants of Governance Structure in Alliances: The Role of Strategic, Task and Partner Uncertainties, *Industrial and Corporate Change*, 12(6): 1223–51.

Cassiman, B. and Veugelers, R. (2002) R&D Cooperation and Spillovers: Some Empirical Evidence from Belgium, *The American Economic Review*, 92(4): 1169–84.

—— —— (2006) In Search of Complementarity in the Innovation Strategy: Internal R&D and External Knowledge Acquisition, *Management Science*, 52(1): 68–82.

Chesbrough, H. W. and Teece, D. J. (1996) When is Virtual Virtuous? Organizing for Innovation, *Harvard Business Review*, 74(a): 65–74.

Cohen, W. M. and Levinthal, D. A. (1990) Absorptive Capacity: A New Perspective on Learning and Innovation, *Administrative Science Quarterly*, 35(1): 128–52.

Cummings, J. L. and Teng, B-S. (2003) Transferring R&D Knowledge: The Key Factors Affecting Knowledge Transfer Success, *Journal of Engineering and Technology Management*, 20: 39–68.

Cyert, R. M. and March, J. G. (1992) *A Behavioral Theory of the Firm*, Cambridge, MA: Blackwell.

Das, T. K. and Teng, B. S. (1998) Between Control and Trust: Developing Confidence in Partner Cooperation in Alliances, *Academy of Management Review*, 23(3): 491–512.

Demsetz, H. (1991) The Theory of the Firm Revisited, in: O. E. Williamson and S. G. Winter (eds.), *The Nature of the Firm*, Oxford: Oxford University Press, pp. 159–78.

Dougherty, D. (1992) Interpretive Barriers to Successful Product Innovation in Large Firms, *Organization Science*, 3(2): 179–202.

Doz, Y. L. (1996) The Evolution of Cooperation in Strategic Alliances: Initial Conditions or Learning Processes? *Strategic Management Journal*, 17(Summer): 55–83.

Eisenhardt, K. M. (1989) Building Theories from Case Study Research, *Academy of Management Review*, 14(4): 532–50.

—— Santos, F. M. (2002) Knowledge-based View: A New Theory of Strategy? in: Pettigrew et al. (eds.), *Handbook of Strategy and Management*, London: Sage Publications.

Folta, T. B. (1998) Governance and Uncertainty: The Trade-off Between Administrative Control and Commitment, *Strategic Management Journal*, 19(11): 1007–28.

Foss, N. J. (2007) The Emerging Knowledge Governance Approach: Challenges and Characteristics, *Organization*, 14(1): 29–52.

García-Canal, E. (1996) Contractual Form in Domestic and International Strategic Alliances, *Organization Studies*, 17(5): 773–95.

Glaser, B. and Strauss, A. (1967) *The Discovery of Grounded Theory*, Chicago: Aldine.

Grandori, A. (2001) Neither Market nor Identity: Knowledge-Governance Mechanisms and the Theory of the Firm, *Journal of Management and Governance*, 5: 381–99.

Grant, R. M. (1996) Toward a Knowledge-based Theory of the Firm, *Strategic Management Journal*, 17(Winter Special Issue): 109–22.

—— Baden-Fuller, C. (2004) A Knowledge Accessing Theory of Strategic Alliances, *Journal of Management Studies*, 41(1): 61–83.

Gulati, R. and Singh, H. (1998) The Architecture of Cooperation: Managing Coordination Costs and Appropriation Concerns in Strategic Alliances, *Administrative Science Quarterly*, 43(1): 781–814.

—— Sytch, M. (2007) Dependence Asymmetry and Joint Dependence in Interorganizational Relationships: Effects of Embeddedness on a Manufacturer's Performance on Procurement Relationships, *Administrative Science Quarterly*, 52(1): 32–69.

Hagedoorn, J. (2002) Inter-firm R&D Partnerships: An Overview of Major Trends and Patterns Since 1960, *Research Policy*, 31(4): 477–92.

Hamel, G. (1991) Competition for Competence and Inter-Partner Learning Within International Strategic Alliances, *Strategic Management Journal*, 12: 83–103.

Heiman, B. A. and Nickerson, J. A. (2004) Empirical Evidence Regarding the Tension Between Knowledge Sharing and Knowledge Expropriation in Collaborations, *Managerial and Decision Economics*, 25: 401–20.

Hoang, H. and Rothaermel, F. T. (2010) Leveraging Internal and External Experience: Exploration, Exploitation, and R&D Project Performance, *Strategic Management Journal*, 31: 734–58.

Kauffman, S. (1993) *The Origins of Order*, New York: Oxford University Press.

Kogut, B. (1988) Joint Ventures: Theoretical and Empirical Perspectives, *Strategic Management Journal*, 9(4): 319–32.

—— (1989) The Stability of Joint Ventures: Reciprocity and Competitive Rivalry, *The Journal of Industrial Economics*, XXXVIII(2): 183–98.

—— Zander, U. (1992) Combinative Capabilities and the Replication of Technology, *Organization Science*, 3(3): 383–97.

Lam, A. (1997) Embedded Firms, Embedded Knowledge: Problems of Collaboration and Knowledge Transfer in Global Cooperative Ventures, *Organization Studies*, 18(6): 973–96.

Lane, P. J. and Lubatkin, M. (1998) Relative Absorptive Capacity and Interorganizational Learning, *Strategic Management Journal*, 19(5): 461–77.

Lhuillery, S. and Pfister, E. (2009) R&D Cooperations and Failures in Innovation Projects: Empirical Evidence from French CIS Data, *Research Policy*, 38: 45–57.

Mayer, K. J. and Argyres, N. (2004) Learning to Contract: Evidence from the Personal Computer Industry, *Organization Science*, 15(4): 394–410.

Mora-Valentin, E. M., Montoro-Sanchez, A. and Guerras-Martin, L. A. (2004) Determining Factors in the Success of R&D Cooperative Agreements between Firms and Research Organizations, *Research Policy*, 33(1): 17–40.

Mowery, D. C., Oxley, J. E., and Silverman, B. S. (1996) Strategic Alliances and Interfirm Knowledge Transfer, *Strategic Management Journal*, 17(Special Issue): 77–91.

—— —— —— (1998) Technological Overlap and Interfirm Cooperation: Implications for the Resource-based View of the Firm, *Research Policy*, 27(5): 507–23.

Narula, R. and Hagedoorn, J. (1999) Innovation Through Strategic Alliances: Moving Towards International Partnerships and Contractual Agreements, *Technovation*, 19(5): 283–94.

Nooteboom, B. (2000) Learning by Interaction: Absorptive Capacity, Cognitive Distance and Governance, *Journal of Management and Governance*, 4: 69–92.

Osborn, R. N. and Baughn, C. C. (1990) Forms of Interorganizational Governance for Multinational Alliances, *The Academy of Management Journal*, 33(3): 503–19.

Oxley, J. E. (1997) Appropriability Hazards and Governance in Strategic Alliances: A Transaction Cost Apporach, *The Journal of Law, Economics and Organization*, 13(2): 387–409.

—— Sampson, R. C. (2004) The Scope and Governance of International R&D Alliances, *Strategic Management Journal*, 25(8/9): 723–49.

Pisano, G. P. (1989) Using Equity Participation to Support Exchange: Evidence from the Biotechnology Industry, *Journal of Law, Economics and Organization*, 5(1): 109–27.

Polanyi, M. (1967) *The Tacit Dimension*, London: Routledge.

Postrel, S. (2009) Multitasking Teams with Variable Complementarity: Challenges for Capability Management, *The Academy of Management Review*, 34(2): 273–96.

Ring, P. S. and Van de Ven, A. H. (1994) Developmental Processes of Cooperative Interorganizational Relationships, *Academy of Management Review*, 19(1): 90–118.

Roberts, J. (2004) *The Modern Firm*, Oxford: Oxford University Press.

Rothwell, R., Freeman, C., Horsley, A., Jervis, V. T. P., Robertson, A. B. and Townsend, J. F. (1974) Sappho Updated: Project Sappho: Phase II, *Research Policy*, 3(3): 258–91.

Ryall, M. and Sampson, R. (2009) Formal Contracts in the Presence of Relational Enforcement Mechanisms: Evidence from Technology Development Projects, *Management Science*, 55(6): 906–25.

Sampson, R. C. (2007) R&D Alliances and Firm Performance: The Impact of Technological Diversity and Alliance Organization on Innovation, *The Academy of Management Journal*, 50(2): 364–86.

Schmickl, C. and Kieser, A. (2008) How Much do Specialists have to Learn from Each Other When They Jointly Develop Radical Product Innovations? *Research Policy*, 37(3): 473–91.

Simon, H. A. (1976) *Administrative Behavior*, New York: The Free Press.

Simonin, B. L. (1999) Ambiguity and the Process of Knowledge Transfer in Strategic Alliances, *Strategic Management Journal*, 20: 595–623.

Stake, R. E. (1995) *The Art of Case Study Research*, Thousand Oaks, CA: Sage Publications.

Thompson, J. D. (1967) *Organizations in Action*, New York: McGraw-Hill.

Tushman, M. L. (1977) Special Boundary Roles in the Innovation Process, *Administrative Science Quarterly*, 22(4): 587–605.

Van de Ven, A., Delbecq, A. L. and Koenig Jr, R. (1976) Determinants of Coordination Modes Within Organizations, *American Sociological Review*, 41(April): 322–38.

Williamson, O. E. (1985) *The Economic Institutions of Capitalism*, New York: The Free Press.

Zollo, M. and Winter, S. G. (2002) Deliberate Learning and the Evolution of Dynamic Capabilities, *Organization Science*, 13(3): 339–51.

8

Knowledge Integration in a P-form Corporation: Project Epochs in the Evolution of Asea/ABB, 1945–2000

Jonas Söderlund and Fredrik Tell

This chapter conceptualizes the organization of the firm as a function of its capability to solve complex problems through knowledge integration and argues that the project-based organizational form (P-form) is a specific configuration for such activities. The chapter describes the evolution and problem-solving capabilities of a P-form corporation, Asea/ABB, over a period of fifty years.

8.1 INTRODUCTION

For the last two to three decades, there has been an upsurge in the literature on knowledge-based theories of the firm. This literature argues that the explanation of firm existence and persistence as an economic institution is due to its capability to coordinate knowledge (see Teece, 1980; Winter, 1991; Kogut and Zander, 1992; Grant, 1996a, 1996b; Nickerson and Zenger, 2004). The organizational capability of the firm, that is, what a particular firm is capable to do well, is typically the focus of attention. Here, the organizational capability is what distinguishes the firm from other institutional arrangements for production of goods and services, for example markets. However, what are organizational capabilities and what role do they play in the organization and evolution of the firm?

In this chapter, following Grant (1996b: 377), we suggest that organizational capabilities are due to the integration of specialist knowledge to perform productive tasks. Accordingly, such capabilities represent learned and stable pattern of collective activity. As Kogut and Zander (1992) point out, organizational capabilities could be denoted 'combinative capabilities' since they primarily reside in the localized and path-dependent recombination of knowledge. Similar to Chandler (1992: 81), we consider organizational capabilities and economies of scale and scope essentially as depending 'on the organized human capabilities essential to exploit the potential of technological progress', that is, on knowledge, skill, experience, and teamwork. Chandler (1992: 86) also stressed both the importance of learning in specialized routines and the overarching organizational capability required to integrate such specialist knowledge: 'For the history of the industrial enterprise, learned routines are those involved in functional activities – those of production, distribution and marketing, obtaining supplies, improving existing products and processes, and the development of new ones. Even more important are those routines acquired to coordinate these functional activities.' These annotations thereby call attention to the organizational mechanisms relied upon to integrate specialized and complementary knowledge, especially concerning across functional activities.

8.1.1 The firm as an integrator of specialized and complementary knowledge: complexity and problem-solving

We conceive the major concern of knowledge integration to be the efficient combination of specialized yet complementary knowledge with the purpose of attaining specific objectives. One rationale for choosing this definition of knowledge integration is that it underlines the relation between complexity, knowledge integration, and organizational design. Framed this way, firms are institutions for integrating knowledge and there are different organizational mechanisms that they can rely on to achieve knowledge integration. According to Grant (1996*a*: 114–15), specialized knowledge can be integrated by (*a*) rules and directives, (*b*) sequencing, (*c*) organizational routines, and (*d*) group problem-solving and decision-making. While standardized rules and sequencing can be used in fairly simple situations, characterized by sequential interdependencies (Thompson, 1967), increasing complexity causes the firm to rely on organizational routines. Situations dominated by reciprocal interdependencies, uncertainty, and many exceptions may require the firm to use group problem-solving that caters mutual adjustment between specialized members of the organization, a relatively expensive alternative. This generally emphasizes the importance of the relationship between complexity and capabilities and the organizational mechanisms on which firms rely to economize on group problem-solving.

Various organizational mechanisms are available for the integration of specialized knowledge, and formal organizational structures also exert influence on search, problem-solving, and knowledge integration. Addressing the notion of complexity, in non-decomposable systems all parts are interrelated, constituting a tightly integrated system (Ulrich and Eppinger, 1995) and this, in turn, creates high-interaction problems (Nickerson and Zenger, 2004). On the other hand, a fully decomposable system is a system where subsystems are entirely independent, implying a modular structure (Baldwin and Clark, 2000), corresponding to low-interaction problems (Nickerson and Zenger, 2004). Many complex systems, however, are characterized by being 'nearly' decomposable: '(1) In a nearly decomposable system the short-run behaviour of each component sub-system is approximately independent of the short run behaviour of the other components;

(2) in the long run the behaviour of components depends in only an aggregate way on the behaviour of the other components' (Simon, 1996: 198). If the problem for an organization lies in understanding and solving complex problems, literature suggests that a viable strategy is organizational 'mirroring' of the decomposability of the system (Nickerson and Zenger, 2004; Colfer and Baldwin, 2010). Accordingly, Simon (1996) considered hierarchy to be an efficient organizational mechanism for problem-solving of complex problems precisely because it mirrors the hierarchical structure of nearly decomposable systems. Subsequent research has, however, pointed to the liabilities associated with learning in hierarchical structures characterized by specialized learning and distributed knowledge (e.g. Levinthal and March, 1993; Marengo, 1994; Siggelkow and Levinthal, 2003). While decomposition lies at the heart of bounded rationality, localized learning runs the risk of forsaking system-wide inferences for local optima. In Levinthal and March's phrasing (1993), organizations run the risk of overlooking distant times, distant places, and failures.

A hierarchical procedure for organizing a firm's activities can be exemplified by the grouping of organizational subunits. On the one hand, grouping into units constitutes a means for separating tasks into specialized groups, causing an increase in the differentiation of knowledge in the organization as a whole. This, in turn, increases the need for integration of these units – integration which can be devised by ascertaining units in different configurations such as the U-form (unitary form), M-form (multi-divisional form), matrix-form, and P-form (project form). On the other hand, grouping activities into units also serves as an integrating solution within the unit as it increases knowledge-base similarity (cf. Lindkvist, 2005), which in turn reduces the need for trans-specialist understanding within the focal unit (Postrel, 2002).

8.1.2 Knowledge integration and organizational design in the P-form corporation

Increasing interdependencies and complementarities among specialized knowledge reinforce the reason for grouping individuals in possession of that specialized knowledge in the same subunit (cf. Thompson, 1967; Teece, 1980). As documented in Chandler and Daems (1980), early industrial managerial hierarchies, such as the functional organization and the line-staff organization, relied heavily on organizing specialized individuals by function (Walker and Lorsch, 1968). Placing individuals and groups of individuals with similar knowledge of different aspects of the production process together generated economies of scale and throughput. With the proliferation of technologies and differentiated consumer demand in the mid-twentieth century, the M-form of organization started to diffuse (Chandler, 1962). By creating larger organizational units – divisions – based on products or markets where functions are duplicated across divisions, sequential interdependencies between different functional specializations were recognized (Mintzberg, 1979). Moreover, knowledge of, and responding to, market requirements increased in importance for the large industrial enterprise and became a guiding principle for the demarcation of divisional units. Still, pooled interdependencies were accommodated by creating central corporate units, for example R&D, accounting, and legal services. Despite the imposition of some market-based mechanisms for management control of divisions, the M-form still represented a hierarchical solution to unit grouping and problem decomposition.

Against this background, the rise of more recent developments in organizational forms, for instance matrix structures, process-oriented structures, and project-based structures, can be juxtaposed. With reports on increasing use in practice of project-based organizational forms (see Midler, 1995; Ekstedt et al., 1999; Whittington et al., 1999), conceptualizations of project-based organizational forms are offered in the literature (see e.g. DeFillippi and Arthur, 1998; Gann and Salter, 1998; Hobday, 1998, 2000; Lindkvist, 2004, 2005; Whitley, 2006; Söderlund, 2008; Söderlund and Tell, 2009, 2011). Such organizational forms are designed with the purpose of establishing lateral communication and integration mechanisms between specialist individuals and groups in organizations in order to accommodate a mounting complexity that is difficult to handle through hierarchy alone. In discussing project- and team-based organizational designs, Grant (1996*a*: 118) suggests: 'The recent vogue for team-based structures where team membership is fluid, depending upon the knowledge requirements of the task at hand, is one response to the deficiencies of hierarchy. The essence of a team-based organization is recognition that coordination is best achieved through the direct involvement of individual specialists and that specialist coordinators ('managers') cannot effectively coordinate if they cannot access the requisite specialist knowledge'.

Grant's observation generally suggests that project-based structures may serve as integrating devices between various functional specialists in organizations in situations where complexity is deemed to make managerial (hierarchical) intervention inefficient. Such increasing complexity and the subsequent applicability of team-based structures for knowledge integration may be due both to the increasing tacitness of knowledge, that is, 'epistemic complexity' (Grandori, 2001) and to 'computational complexity', that is, the number of elements and their interdependencies (Simon, 1962; Kauffman, 1993). In this chapter, we are particularly concerned with computational complexity. In order to solve problems in increasingly complex so-called 'rugged landscapes', organizational structures that enable the organization to draw inferences based on search processes taking place at organizationally dispersed locations need to be developed (Levinthal, 2000; Fleming and Sorensen, 2001). One particular feature of rugged landscapes, where organizations are modelled as solving problems through 'hill-climbing', is that there are many local optima, and that local 'peaks' may shadow a global optimum (i.e. whether an agent will see the highest peak depends on the position in the landscape). Using temporary constellations of specialized individuals, which is a common principle of project-based forms of organizing, recognizes the temporal aspect of problem-solving and knowledge integration, where it may be more effective for complex problem-solving to oscillate between centralized and decentralized search in order to detect system-wide interdependencies (see Siggelkow and Levinthal, 2003; Nickerson and Zenger, 2004; Enberg et al., 2006; Söderlund and Tell, 2010).

Project-based organizations in general are thus frequently adhered to in situations of high complexity (Clark and Fujimoto, 1991; Lindkvist et al., 1998;

Williams, 1999). The current interest in various types of cross-functional capabilities, such as new product development, systems integration, and project management, signals the importance and challenge of capabilities that require effective integration of many areas of expertise. Using the distinctions made by Hobday (2000) and Whitley (2006), we want to point out that the P-form is an organizational characteristic of certain permanence, and does not designate temporary inter-organizational constellations of activities. Of course, every project is unique to a certain extent, and likewise the causal ambiguity and heterogeneity may be severe (Zollo and Winter, 2002). Still, P-form corporations generate and implement projects on a repetitive basis; they develop routines and deep knowledge to handle complex and difficult problems and projects.[1]

Based on the discussion above, this chapter discusses two questions. First, how do the structure and capabilities of a P-form corporation evolve in response to changes in task complexity? Second, how do emerging organizational mechanisms and designs influence knowledge integration? In order to provide answers to these two questions, we conducted a case study of the evolution of a firm that we find representative of a P-form corporation: Asea/ABB.

8.2 AIM AND RESEARCH METHODOLOGY

As indicated above, our primary intention with this chapter is to investigate knowledge integration in project-based firms, particularly in firms displaying P-form characteristics. To allow for an evolutionary interpretation of the relationship between complexity and capabilities and thereby an improved understanding of the dynamics of knowledge integration at the firm level, we present a longitudinal study of how a P-form corporation has developed its organizational structure and problem-solving capability to adapt to increasing degrees of market and technological complexity. Our study focuses on major projects within Asea/ABB and in what organizational context they were embedded. The aim of the chapter is to analyse the relationship between task complexity (categorized as market complexity and technological complexity), knowledge integration, and organizational design. We also investigate the evolution over time. We argue that the conventional, often static, focus on organizational mechanisms for knowledge integration is far too restricted and needs to be addressed in an evolutionary perspective to fully acknowledge that organizational capabilities are due to the integration of specialist knowledge to perform productive tasks, such as in the case of Asea/ABB projects. Thus, the evolutionary perspective adopted in the present chapter would also be necessary to properly consider the path-dependent, learned, and stable nature of capabilities.

The chapter draws upon empirical data collected on Asea Brown Boveri (ABB) – the result of a merger in the late 1980s between Swedish Asea and Swiss Brown Boveri et Cie – and its Swedish predecessor Asea, covering developments from the

[1] For a more extensive conceptual analysis of the main contingencies and structural characteristics of the P-form corporation, see Söderlund and Tell (2011).

mid-1940s to the end of the 1990s. Secondary sources were utilized along with interviews with line managers, project managers, and senior managers. The present chapter primarily focuses on business projects in power engineering carried out by Asea/ABB and the formation of what we label new 'project epochs', that is, major shifts in the nature (markets, types, technologies), generation (formation, creation, development), and organization of projects (clients, partners, structures). This analysis was greatly facilitated by a large number of interviews and discussions with senior ABB managers.

The analysis of major changes was also informed by previous research on firm-level evolution and the role played by epochs in the transformation of a firm's internationalization process (Kutschker et al., 1997; Eckert and Mayrhofer, 2005). In our analysis of the evolution of Asea/ABB, we also identify changes in the market complexity and technological complexity. Our analysis led us to categorize the evolution of Asea/ABB into four primary project epochs, depending on changes in complexity and corresponding organizational arrangements.

8.3 EVOLUTION OF KNOWLEDGE INTEGRATION IN ASEA/ABB

The analysis presented here draws on the idea that in certain periods, there was a reliance on a particular logic of project organization. In the early days in our case study, the projects were mainly undertaken in the domestic market, initially in close collaboration with major customers, such as utilities (e.g. Vattenfall, then the Swedish State Power Board, SSPB), railway operators (e.g. the Swedish State Railways, SJ), or manufacturing industry (e.g. SKF or STORA). From the late 1950s and early 1960s, international projects played an increasingly paramount role and became a key driver for the growth of Asea. Asea gradually became an international company, mainly in the area of power engineering. Large projects were centralized and the organization had to cope with the dual challenges of manufacturing high-volume products and simultaneously supplying capital goods in increasingly complex international projects. Projects not only became larger but were also carried out at a higher frequency. These projects were placed centrally in the organizational structure and received extensive attention from senior management. Later, due to the effect of deregulation on many energy markets throughout the globe and expansion to markets with clients who possessed little knowledge in the field of power engineering, Asea and later ABB assumed even greater responsibility for the projects, including contract management and project management. Financial engineering slowly came into focus during the 1970s and had its definite breakthrough in the 1980s. From the late 1980s and during the 1990s, financial engineering played an increasingly important role for the management and organization of projects within ABB. In the following sections, we divide the evolution of Asea/ABB into four overall periods, referred to as 'project epochs' (Söderlund and Tell, 2009). The description of each epoch is structured according to (*a*) market complexity, (*b*) technological complexity, and (*c*) organizational structure.

8.3.1 The first project epoch: knowledge integration in collaborative embedded projects

This epoch primarily covered the late 1940s through the early 1960s. Project business during this epoch can be characterized by an increasing importance of scale in projects (for examples of major projects, see Table 8.1). After World War II, Asea was awarded a project for developing an aircraft jet engine to be used in military aircrafts (project Dovern). Although Asea managed to develop a competitive product, they lost the contract for supplying the engine. The knowledge and experience gained could however be utilized in developing a gas turbine for electricity generation (GT35). Hydropower plants with a capacity of more than 100 MW were developed and installed by Asea in Harsprånget in 1950 and in Stornorrfors in 1958. The world's first electrical 400 kV-High Voltage Alternating Current (IIVAC) transmission line, transporting electricity from the Harsprånget plant to Hallsberg in Sweden, a distance of approximately 1,000 km, was inaugurated in 1952. This project also signified the long-standing and important partnership with the Swedish state-owned utility company Vattenfall. The collaboration played a significant role in the successful completion of the first large transmission projects and thereby fostered the development of Asea's abilities to organize complex projects. The Gotland project, completed in 1954, was the world's first modern commercial High Voltage Direct Current (HVDC) power transmission system. Its completion was preceded by further joint development efforts by Asea and Vattenfall. In particular, these efforts concerned the ion-valves (rectifiers) to be used in the transmission system. The long-term partnership between Asea and Vattenfall, both in the research and development work on HVDC transmission technology and in the building of an operating utility for transmission, meant that Asea, as the first supplier in the world, held a reference plant for HVDC transmission. This project laid the foundation for the future internationalization of Asea's project business in power transmission equipment, with major installations initiated in the late 1950s and early 1960s, for example HVDC power transmission line across the English Channel (completed in 1961). Further, having participated in the electrification of the Swedish railways before World War II, Asea during this period focused on developing and supplying state-of-the-art electrical motorcars and locomotives, and also new equipment for industrial processes, both in close collaboration with domestic customers.

Table 8.1 Examples of important Asea projects during the first project epoch*

Power generation	Power transmission	Rail transportation	Industrial applications
Harsprånget (Hydro, Sweden, 1950), Stornorrfors (1958)	Harsprånget-Hallsberg (HVAC, Sweden, 1952)	Xoa7 (Electric railcar, Sweden, 1949)	Hagfors (electromagnetic stirring, Sweden, 1947)
Yngeredsfors/GT 35 (Gas turbine, Sweden, 1957)	Gotland (HVDC, Sweden, 1954)	Ma (Electric locomotive, Sweden, 1953)	Surahammar (Pressduktor, Sweden, 1954)
Kariba (Hydro, Zambia, 1959)		Ra (Electric locomotive, Sweden, 1955)	Quintus (Synthetic diamonds, Sweden, 1955)

* Year in parenthesis denotes year of completion.

Market complexity: domestic focus

While Asea was already heavily export-oriented in the early twentieth century (for instance, in the period 1928–30, 48 per cent of sold goods were exported), in 1946–55 exports amounted to no more than 21.5 per cent of total sales. The post-World War II markets were heavily regulated and preference was given to domestic suppliers. Despite this and negligible sales efforts abroad, infrastructure products like those provided by Asea were in huge demand. Thus, the company was able to attract international orders in the rebuilding of Europe's infrastructure and was also helped by the fact that the war had weakened international competitors.

In this period, Asea became increasingly involved in export markets. While domestic and European sales entirely dominated the first decade after World War II, the period 1956–66 saw increasing commitments abroad and, in particular, sales overseas (outside Europe) increased considerably. In particular, in the early 1960s, exports grew rapidly to countries in North America and Asia/Oceania. This was primarily due to the delivery of power system projects. In general, markets for power engineering products grew during this period and Asea's sales tripled from 1945 to 1959 (see Table 8.2). The main product markets for Asea and its subsidiaries consisted of power generation utilities (power generation, power transmission, and distribution equipment), industrial applications, transportation, and consumer products and appliances. Products delivered on the former markets were primarily defined as 'heavy products', while appliances, lighter motors, and electrical equipment were denoted 'light products'. In 1950-2, heavy products accounted for 66 per cent of sales and lighter components and products 34 per cent (Glete, 1983: 160).

Table 8.2 Asea's group revenues and employees, 1946–65

	Revenues (MSEK)	Employees in Sweden	Employees abroad
1946	406	24,163	3,093 (in 1944)
1947	431	24,974	N.A.
1948	525	25,995	2,587
1949	575	26,707	N.A.
1950	676	27,428	2,853
1951	884	29,106	N.A.
1952	1,022	28,447	N.A.
1953	975	27,186	N.A.
1954	1,045	28,520	N.A.
1955	1,133	30,300	N.A.
1956	1,209	30,562	N.A.
1957	1,258	31,940	N.A.
1958	1,332	32,242	N.A.
1959	1,222	28,428	N.A.
1960	1,353	30,681	N.A.
1961	1,612	30,928	N.A.
1962	1,742	33,356	3,204
1963	1,781	32,216	3,447
1964	2,082	33,398	3,946
1965	2,324	34,332	4,984

Source: Glete (1983: 220, 227).

Key customers were utilities, railways, and large industries. These groups placed 70 per cent of orders in 1942–55, and Asea was often involved in collaborations with their domestic customers regarding product implementation/installation, product improvement, or new product/technology development. On the domestic market, Asea was also the leading wholesaler of electrical equipment and served their customers with installations and technical services.

Technological complexity: complex products requiring control technologies

As indicated above, complex products constituted a lion's share of Asea's manufacturing in the 1950s. Industrial machinery for rolling mills, locomotives and trains, and power generation and transmission equipment were all products that required the integration of a complex set of components, apparatuses, and subsystems. In addition, Asea manufactured many components for such systems (e.g. relays, switchgear, valves), as well as lighter products (e.g. motors) for industrial use. Through acquisitions, the company also had subsidiaries manufacturing and selling products on consumer markets (e.g. appliances). The rate of technological change accelerated as the post-war economic recovery kicked in. Asea also developed new complex technologies in this period, a notable example being a jet engine for the emerging new series of Swedish military aircraft, which although never materialized led to the subsequent development of gas turbines. Moreover, some important control technologies developed before the war (e.g. power tubes and circuit breakers) were ripe for commercial application in power systems and electrical railway systems.

Organizational structure: functionally organized H-form

After World War II, Asea was organized as a complex holding company or corporate group with a number of more or less publicly known subsidiaries.[2] Moreover, the parent company was a substantial part of the corporation, with extensive manufacturing and sales activities, functionally grouped into departments (see Figure 8.1).

One problem for the firm was the organization of its subsidiaries. Most of them were 'product subsidiaries'; some of these operated quite independently from the parent company, while others became increasingly close to the parent company. Other subsidiaries again were 'vertical', providing supply (such as iron/steel) or demand (being utilities) for Asea's products. Finally, a couple of the subsidiaries constituted minor full-product-range, 'shadow' organizations of the parent company, as they produced and sold similar products. In essence, the activities of both subsidiaries and the parent company were organized in departments according to function. The parent company's organization was characterized by a centralized administration within each department, such as sales, design, manufacturing, etc. Hence, customers bought apparatus from various parts of the Asea group,

---

[2] Similar to the general development in, for example, France, see Cassis (1997) and Whittington and Mayer (2000).

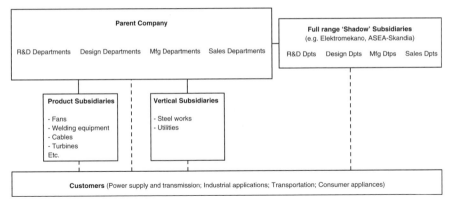

Figure 8.1 Asea's group organization after World War II

depending on which products they required, although many of Asea's more complex products were sold by the parent company. Such products, increasingly developed and delivered through projects, were thus primarily under the auspices of the parent company and did not involve coordination among subsidiaries.

As demonstrated in Table 8.2, Asea's organization was also primarily domestic. While revenues and employees grew rapidly during this epoch, the proportion of employees abroad seems to have remained around 10 per cent of the total workforce (though there is a shortage of data). It was not until the mid-1960s that employees abroad increased. With growing (international) sales and an increasing number of large projects, this holding form with its functionally grouped parent company and subsidiaries was increasingly difficult to manage, as few integrative devices existed.

8.3.2 The second project epoch: knowledge integration in increasingly international projects

As of the 1960s, Asea's business began to change. This development was accentuated with the entry of Curt Nicolin as new CEO in 1961.[3] Power plant capacity rapidly increased during this epoch, and Asea executed a number of projects pertaining to these developments (see Table 8.3). A new range of gas turbines were developed (GT120/GT200), the largest of their kind at the time. Moreover, Asea took part in the development of the Swedish Nuclear power programme, the first commercial power plant being delivered in 1971 (Oskarshamn). A number of international projects were also carried out in the course of the 1960s and 1970s. These included the Assuan dam in Egypt and Karun dam in Iran, both large hydroelectric power generation projects. Unlike the old state-owned utilities in the Western world, some customers did not possess the project management capabilities necessary to handle such complex projects. Asea was thereby forced to develop an international strategy.

---

[3] Although formally appointed in 1961, Nicolin was headhunted to rescue the ailing Scandinavian Airlines the same year and in effect was not operational in Asea before 1963.

Table 8.3 Examples of important Asea projects during the second project epoch

Power generation	Power transmission	Rail transportation	Industrial applications
GT 120 (Gas turbine, Sweden, 1960)	Cross-English Channel (HVDC, UK, 1961)	Stockholm underground (Electric railcar system, Sweden, 1961)	Hällefors (Asea-SKF Steel process, Sweden, 1965)
Otahuhu (Gas turbine New Zealand, 1968)	735 kV testbed (HVAC, USA/ Canada, 1965–8)	Rc1/Rc2 (Electric locomotive, Sweden, 1967–9)	Söderfors (ASP Alloy-Steel process, Sweden, 1971)
Assuan (Hydro, Egypt, 1970), Karun (Iran, 1976)	Pacific-Intertie (HVDC, USA, 1970)	Rb (Electric locomotive, Romania/ Yugoslavia/Austria, 1966–70)	ELRED (Iron ore reduction process, STORA Kopparberg, Sweden, 1971)
Oskarshamn (Nuclear, Sweden, 1971)	Skagerakk (HVDC, thyristor valve, Norway/Denmark, 1976)		

Asea gradually developed the capability to work more autonomously from Vattenfall on international projects. One example is the Pacific Intertie, a 1,362 km-long HVDC power transmission link, implemented in collaboration with General Electric, initiated in the early 1960s and completed in 1970.

In rail transportation and industrial applications, important new generations of products and industrial processes were developed in collaboration with highly capable customers, later to be exported. The major part of the projects during the 1960s was supplied to clients with in-house project management and to some extent also systems integration capabilities. The first epoch was dominated by collaborative projects in close cooperation with domestic customers; this was continued in the second epoch, for instance in industrial applications, but during the second epoch Asea also had to build up the capacity to operate abroad without key customers', such as Vattenfall's and SJ's, assistance. Asea was still very dependent on the technological and managerial capabilities of its clients to be able to supply these complex projects. While Asea was working on the projects that formed the basis for the second epoch, several projects in developing countries forced the company to develop its own capabilities to offer full-scale systems and related project management services.

Market complexity: growing international sales, increasing competition

This was an epoch characterized by a steady increase in international sales. From 28 per cent of revenues generated from exports in 1960, Asea went to 44 per cent in 1970 and 60 per cent in 1979 (see Table 8.4). Besides becoming more internationalized, the company was selling its products in almost every continent (see Table 8.5). In this epoch, however, Asea also went from primarily exporting from Sweden to enlarging its manufacturing abroad (for instance in Canada, Brazil, India, Mexico, the United States, and Greece), the main rationale being market access.

The importance of large projects for Asea's revenues is evident from the impact on export market revenues in this epoch of major projects in Zaire (Inga-Shaba

Table 8.4 Revenues, operating profits, and employees, Asea group, 1960–79

	Total revenues (MSEK)	Foreign revenues (MSEK)	Foreign share (%)	Operating profits (MSEK)	Operating profit margin (%)	Total employees	Foreign employee share (%)
1965	2,324	878	38	245	11	34,332	15
1966	2,447	988	40	162	7	34,413	14
1967	2,765	1,129	41	177	6	32,401	14
1968	2,728	1,218	45	191	7	32,726	14
1969	3,333	1,342	40	246	7	34,867	16
1970	3,690	1,611	44	252	7	36,591	17
1971	4,001	2,010	50	236	6	37,911	16
1972	4,996	2,314	46	264	5	38,651	16
1973	5,249	2,725	52	321	6	39,154	18
1974	6,917	3,192	46	432	6	41,217	18
1975	7,863	3,920	50	527	7	43,604	19
1976	8,400	4,379	52	685	8	44,194	19
1977	9,718	5,039	52	474	5	41,528	20
1978	9,814	5,301	54	426	4	40,574	23
1979	11,830	7,088	60	437	4	40,629	26

Source: Glete (1983: 227, 264, 345).

Table 8.5 Asea's largest export markets in 1966–70, 1971–5, and 1976–80

	1966–70		1971–5		1976–80	
	Country	Revenues (MSEK)	Country	Revenues (MSEK)	Country	Revenues (MSEK)
1	The United States	81	The United States	174	Brazil	174
2	The United Kingdom	52	Norway	141	Iran	141
3	Canada	50	Soviet Union	125	The United States	125
4	Denmark	49	Denmark	116	West Germany	116
5	Norway	36	Finland	85	Norway	85
6	Finland	35	Canada	84	Canada	84
7	Yugoslavia	32	Brazil	78	Mexico	78
8	Brazil	27	The United Kingdom	71	Australia	71
9	West Germany	25	Zaire	71	Denmark	71
10	Australia	24	South Africa	69	Finland	69

Source: Glete (1983: 265).

HVDC transmission system), Brazil (Itaipu hydropower station), and Iran (Karun hydropower station) (both completed in the 1980s, see Section 8.3.3).

Market development during this epoch was heavily influenced by the growth of the triad in international trade, that is, the regions North America, Europe, and Japan, with 70 per cent of world trade taking place in these regions. At the same time, the energy crisis, overcapacity and the continuation of national policies embracing national champion firms and domestic procurement preferences in the electrical engineering industry, placed heavy demands on driving down costs in order to survive. Table 8.4 also shows that Asea's profit margin declined in this period despite heavy emphasis on rationalization.

In the 1960s and 1970s, Asea's heavy products and projects were in great demand as the industrialized countries were building their power generation capacities. Moreover, industrializing countries, supported by international aid programmes, also wanted to build a modern infrastructure, such as power generation plants, auxiliary equipment, and electrified railways. Such countries had little previous knowledge of the technologies and designs involved, and complete turnkey solutions were increasingly sold. Accordingly, in this epoch, Asea went from a position of selling quite 'standardized' heavy products abroad to 70–80 per cent of exports being complete systems. Export markets increasingly contributed to Asea's overall sales volume. Moreover, manufacturing facilities were located abroad to a growing extent, mainly as a result of acquisitions.

Technological complexity: massive scale technologies

In an attempt to restructure the Asea group, the appliance subsidiary Elektro-Helios was divested, implying a decrease in technological diversification and certain market segments. Also the welding equipment business was transferred to Swedish manufacturer ESAB. At the same time, progress in some of Asea's core technologies and emerging related technologies still meant that, if anything, the number of technologies where Asea was active increased. There were a number of factors that made Asea become increasingly dependent on a growing number of technologies and therefore needed to invest heavily in product and technology development: (*a*) nuclear power development, (*b*) power electronics and semiconductors, (*c*) customers' heightened performance requirements, (*d*) size revolution in heavy machinery, such as transformers and generators, (*e*) standardization and modularization of components, (*f*) increased use of advanced materials, and (*g*) the emergence of turnkey solutions as a potential growth market.

Moreover, Asea continued its investments in forward vertical integration, with international expansion of the wholesaler subsidiary Asea-Skandia, and integrated backwards by acquiring cable suppliers. The developments were driven by the size revolution in power engineering technologies, where larger and more complex power generation units were designed, which in turn induced demand for more powerful and complex technologies for high voltage power transmission and distribution grids (Hirsh, 1989; Thomas and McGowan, 1990).[4]

---

[4] According to Hirsh (1989: 89), thermal efficiencies of state-of-the-art power plants went from 21.8 per cent in 1948 to 32.9 per cent in 1965, but then levelled out.

Organizational structure: sector organization

When Curt Nicolin took over, major organizational changes were put into effect. He set about creating a 'sector organization'. Design offices and factories for specific products were grouped together and co-localized in a range of Swedish towns. As a result, design, product development, and manufacturing were more tightly integrated, in accordance with basic principles of divisionalization. However, the responsibility for direct contact with most customers remained with the domestic sales offices, and international sales companies were not integrated in the various sectors. Departments for power, industrial, and traction products assumed responsibility for systems selling, engineering, and turnkey delivery, by buying components from the sectors at market prices. This organization meant that both sectors and sales-oriented departments were kept as separate profit-and-loss centres. Management's explanation for not completely divisionalizing and decentralizing the organization was that markets and technologies did not coincide in Asea's operations and that Asea was not sufficiently large to establish autonomous divisions. In total, thirteen sectors were established between 1962 and 1976; all of them with prime location in Sweden (see Table 8.6).

During this period, Asea developed a strategy for being competitive as a full-product-range supplier of power engineering products. The sector organization did not promote a profit focus in the organization (since units did not control both costs and revenues, they could not be assessed in these terms). Sectors were not responsible for sales; that responsibility resided with the sales unit (or foreign sales subsidiary). There were vice presidents for design, manufacturing, and sales. At this time, Asea was a technology-centred company run by engineers and accordingly technical design (function) was the primary focus, not profit. In particular, the J-sector, instigated in 1976, epitomized the technology-centred company, where a cadre of

Table 8.6 Asea's sector organization, 1962–80

Year of foundation	Letter	Name of sector and its main products	Location
1962	Y	Semiconductors and electronics	Västerås (Enköping)
1962	L	Power transmission products	Ludvika (Arboga)
1962	M	Small- and medium-sized alternating current machinery	Västerås
1962	H	Mechanical products	Helsingborg (Härnösand, Kristianstad)
1962	Ä	Forklifts	Härnösand
1962	Q	Diamonds	Robertsfors
1964	S	Apparatus	Västerås (Arboga)
1964	O	Direct current and large alternating current machinery	Västerås
1965	R	Relays	Västerås (Bollnäs)
1967	G	Semi-manufactured products	Västerås and other cities
1969	V	Services	Västerås and other cities
1976	T	Traction and marine	Västerås (Falun)
1976	J	Site solutions	Västerås

Source: Glete (1983: 252).

almost 1,000 engineers at corporate headquarters was responsible for centrally approving and designing all major plants and systems ordered. For instance, this meant that although important projects could be initiated locally at sales departments, systems engineering, integration, and project execution were centralized activities at the central sector level in the organization.

8.3.3 The third project epoch: knowledge integration in complex turnkey projects

The third epoch started in the late 1970s but management structures and organizational design were not changed until the early 1980s. The epoch lasted until the creation of ABB in 1988 and the subsequent implementation of new strategies and organizational structures. The third epoch is generally characterized by a growing importance of project management skills, and it gradually became more important for Asea to develop and use a broader range of technologies and capabilities. The projects were larger in scope and scale and were executed at a higher risk with clients who frequently lacked the engineering knowledge and experience of running advanced plants that were common among state-owned Western utilities. Important drivers behind the third epoch were the increased deregulation of markets and the declining influence of a selected number of state-owned utility companies. The deregulation of several markets in the Western world and the higher frequency of projects in industrializing countries generally spurred the introduction in the 1970s of what Asea referred to as 'complex turnkey projects' (see Table 8.7). The idea of supplying turnkey projects was also applied to other business areas, including automation, a business that later became an important part of Asea's international operations. For example, in the 1980s, Asea/ABB supplied sixteen large-scale international HVDC projects, compared to three similar projects carried out between 1969 and 1979. The effects of this project epoch included the transfer of managerial competence from clients to Asea. Asea started to emphasize the importance of project managers with the capacity to run 'really big business', with the skills to integrate technology, business, and management. A direct result of this was the implementation of project support offices and project management career paths, as well as subsequent development programmes for senior project managers.

Table 8.7 Examples of important Asea/ABB projects during the third project epoch

Power generation	Power transmission	Rail transportation
Harsprånget (Hydro, Sweden, 1980)	Inga Shaba (HVDC, Zaire, 1982)	Göteborg (Tramways, Sweden, 1982)
Sudirman/Mrica (Hydro, Indonesia, 1988)	Itaipu (HVDC, Brazil, 1985)	WAG6A (Locomotive, India, 1987)
	Gezhouba-Shanghai (HVDC, China, 1989)	X2000 (High-speed train, Sweden, 1990)

Market complexity: accessing global markets, deregulation, and restructuring

The key challenge for Asea was to gain further access to international markets, as the company's previous core markets were increasingly mature and larger volumes were needed to remain competitive in the fierce battle that would eliminate every 'minor league' competitor. Growth was occurring in emerging markets, where Asea had little previous experience or market presence. In order to exploit those markets, in the 1970s the company's management had already contemplated a transition from an international corporation towards a true multinational.

Between 1975 and 1990, there was a wave of corporate concentration in the electrical manufacturing industry (Tell, 2000). This shake-out was not just domestic; it involved the amalgamation of companies from different countries. In France, for instance, Alsthom-Atlantique emerged as the domestic leader and through international acquisitions became an important competitor to Asea. As many firms were aware of the new economic predicaments, this period was generally dominated by negotiations about mergers and acquisitions (as well as strategic pondering about divestments and exits) among the main firms in the heavy electrical manufacturing industry.

The oil crisis in the mid-1970s had a major negative effect on demand for power engineering products, but demand picked up again in the 1980s. Asea's ambition was to be one of the remaining firms in the consolidating industry, and the company managed to increase sales (see Figure 8.2) and win market shares from competitors, also helped by the devaluation of the Swedish currency (krona) in 1976–7 and 1981–2. This development coincided with an emerging trend in public policy to commence deregulation of electricity markets. The policies of national utilities and agencies for public infrastructure were slowly

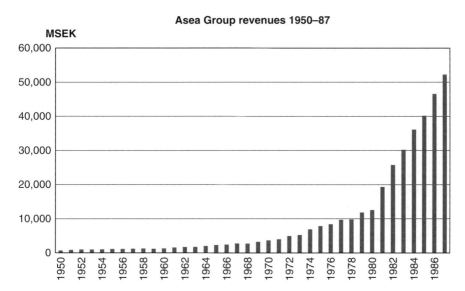

Figure 8.2 Asea group revenues 1950–87 (million SEK, current prices)
Source: Asea annual reports.

abandoned; cost recognition and the entry of new customers also implied increased cost competition between suppliers and less insistence on domestic preferences in procurement.

Technological complexity: the semiconductor revolution and controllable technologies

In addition to access to markets, there was a need to rationalize manufacturing and coordination of technologies in order to cut costs and gain economies of scale. While limits to size in some power technologies were recognized (concurrent with concerns over nuclear power technology), large systems were implemented on a global scale also in emerging economies. At the same time, the vulnerability of power systems had been highlighted during, for instance, the oil embargo and the Three Mile Island incident in Harrisburg: PA. This caused interest in developing and manufacturing more efficient and flexible power technologies, also using new sources of energy. Towards the late 1980s, large advanced gas turbine technology had been developed to utilize natural gas for electricity production on a grand scale, involving complex applications where gas turbines were combined with boilers and steam turbines to increase thermal efficiency.

The rapid advances in semiconductors contributed to the development of new power control devices such as thyristors, condensors, and static VAR compensators. Besides enhancing the efficiency of power systems, such devices could help to achieve greater controllability of an increasingly interdependent and international electrical power system. In conjunction with the computer technology evolution, control and surveillance technologies could be integrated, further accentuating the ability to control systems. As an alternative to oil dependence, electric rail transportation re-emerged as a state-of-the-art technology. In particular, high-speed trains became en vogue internationally and spurred new technological efforts. ABB was also awarded the contract for the Swedish high-speed train X2000 in 1987.

In line with these developments, Asea continued to become increasingly multi-technological as it sought to be a full assortment supplier of power technologies. The company needed to invest heavily in R&D to stay in the forefront in a large number of technologies identified as crucial for gaining and sustaining technological leadership in increasingly competitive markets.

Organizational structure: introducing the divisional form

Percy Barnevik was hired to be CEO of Asea as of 1 June 1980. In 1980–2, aided by some young Asea managers, he conducted a major reorganization of the company. Asea's immediate actions were first to discontinue units that had operating losses; second to reorganize the corporate bureaucracy; third to increase sales through new products; and finally to expand geographically to new markets.

The aim was to introduce a pure divisional structure that could work closer to the market than the previous sector organization had been able to do. In 1981, four divisions were created: Power Generation, Power Transmission & Distribution, Metallurgy, and Automation. The marketing department at headquarters was closed and marketing functions were decentralized to each division. Several other previously centrally organized departments were split up and deployed to the divisions. Central staff decreased from 1,655 employees to around 200. With this structure, each division could be held accountable for its profits, which drastically altered management accounting principles. Profit centres were created within each division. With the specific aim of decentralizing the company, but also to improve the integration of corporate functions, a matrix-like organization was established in 1981. Despite its ambiguities, this provided a framework for project organization and project collaboration, particularly in complex power engineering projects.

Besides establishing profit centres in the manufacturing organization, international companies were established with the aim of boosting exports from 50 to 75 per cent of sales. The organization was also divided into larger sections in the two dimensions: Business Areas, which were responsible for continuing R&D and technological development, and Regions, for regional strategies. In all, around twenty units were wound up. The bleeding steel works, Surahammars Bruk, was closed. Operations ceased in the factories in Brazil, Argentina, the United Kingdom, and Greece. Notwithstanding these withdrawals, the matrix organization was instituted with the aim of expanding Asea from an export company to strengthen its position as a multinational company to realize Barnevik's slogan: 'Be an insider, not an invader'.

8.3.4 The fourth project epoch: knowledge integration in globally engineered and financed total solutions

This epoch commenced with the ABB merger in 1988 and ended with the divestiture of ABB's 50 per cent share in Adtranz (a joint venture with Daimler-Benz in rail transportation established in 1996) in 1999 and its 50 per cent share in ABB-Alstom Power (a joint venture in power generation established in 1999) in 2000. Further, ABB's nuclear business was sold to BNFL the same year. Between 1960 and 1980, Asea's annual revenues rose almost tenfold (see Figure 8.2); after the merger in 1988, ABB's annual revenues exceeded MUSD 18,732 and employees numbered nearly 170,000 (see Figure 8.3). The company's size made it possible to get access to loans at a lower interest rate than many of its clients could obtain. Besides requiring skills in what was known internally as 'financial engineering', the financial solutions for complex, international projects emphasized other skills, such as risk management and business development. The financial services segment, launched several years earlier, now took an increasingly active role in the formation of the financial arrangements for large-scale international projects.

The fourth epoch, in addition to requiring the financing advantage and the critical role of risk management, included key activities for ensuring the flow of projects. For these reasons, the management team emphasized the importance of 'project development' and the capability to provide 'total solutions' from feasibility studies and engineering to total project management and financing. The first projects in this particular epoch were launched in the early 1990s and lasted throughout the 1990s and early 2000s (see Table 8.8); they are epitomized by the massive projects in Chandrapur-Padge (India), Leyte Luzon (Philippines) completed in 1998, and the Three Gorges project in China, commissioned in 2003. To be able to deliver complex power systems worldwide, ABB needed to collaborate

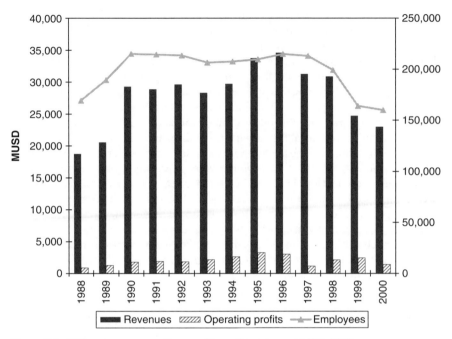

Figure 8.3 ABB revenues, operating profits, and employees, 1988–2000
Source: Asea annual reports.

Table 8.8 Examples of important Asea/ABB projects during the fourth project epoch

Power generation	Power transmission	Rail transportation
Värtaverket (PFBC, Coal, Sweden, 1991)	Quebec-New England (HVDC, USA/Canada, 1992)	Istanbul (Tramways, Turkey, 1992)
Roosecote (CCGT, Gas turbine, UK, 1991), Milford (USA, 1995)	Chandrapur-Padge (HVDC, India, 1998)	London underground stock (Metro trains, UK, 1992)
Helsingborg (GTX100, Gas turbine, Sweden, 1999)	Hällsjön (HVDC Light, Sweden, 1999)	WAP5 (Locomotives, India, 1995)

with competitors and suppliers in project consortia. Hence, ABB developed
capabilities to organize in-house projects (in the global matrix consisting of
1,000 subsidiaries) and manage large-scale projects across organizational boundaries together with external partners and subcontractors.

Market complexity: a deregulated global market with a few industry leaders

The ABB management started to draw a new world economic map to guide them
in understanding how markets and demand were developing. In essence, this map

amounted to a diagram with installed power on one axis and BNP/capita on the other, on which countries were plotted. The most interesting countries were deemed to be those that were moving upwards towards high levels of installed power and growing BNP/capita. This exercise emanated in a global structure of nine regions, which provided impetus for decisions on the localization of employees and management structures. Forty countries were singled out as 'home markets' for ABB, which entailed not just a marketing presence but also manufacturing establishment. During the global recession in the early 1990s, ABB responded by reducing the number in the First World and increasing it in the Third World in order to obtain access to growing markets and reduce costs.

According to the company strategists' market analysis, the emerging marketplaces where ABB competed were threefold: global, regional, and local. In dealing with these developments, ABB took up the multinational challenge. For their core products, top management realized that their home markets Sweden and Switzerland represented only 3 per cent of global demand. Hence, unlike some of its international competitors, ABB could not rely on being a preferred supplier on home ground but had to ponder how to achieve local diversity and ability to meet local customer demand with scale and technological leadership in manufacturing and product design. In 1993, 81 per cent of employees were to be found outside the home countries (Berggren, 1996).

At the same time, the 1990s was a period of globalization in demand and the deregulation of – in particular – mature markets. This meant that the main market growth was to be found in East Asia and the developing countries. Moreover, mature markets provided openings for market entry because many of the national champions in the heavy electrical manufacturing industry did not survive when a few select international giants conquered global markets. In addition, with new public management regimes, power and transportation systems lost some of their status as natural monopolies that should be controlled by the state; for instance, utilities and railways were privatized and operated under new principles. A new market for consultants arose as intermediaries between ABB and the customer. These consultants needed to be handled (as the customer) and influenced favourably towards the specific solution offered by ABB.

ABB's project business – including projects larger than SEK 100 million – grew to approximately SEK 70 billion, which represented more than one-third of the turnover in the mid-1990s. It became increasingly important for top management to know how many projects there were in the world and their size. As a result, the company developed elaborate systems and processes to keep track of the world market for projects. When it came to the largest projects, the SEK 1,000 million ones, there were only about 100 per annum in the world. To gain economies of scale in producing such units, increasing emphasis was placed on the modularization of components and subsystems to adjust to customers' demands at a reasonable cost.

Technological complexity: full range of complex technologies

After the merger, ABB management made efforts to create a technologically focused global giant in electrical power engineering. While this created opportunities for cutting down on unrelated products and technologies, ABB was still left with the most complex technologies from its parents, Asea and Brown Boveri.

Intense competition required landmark innovations when it came to improving performance. This, in turn, required further investments in, for instance, exploring and developing new materials and computer-based control and surveillance technologies. In addition, non-science-based technologies such as services and financing increased in importance, since new 'total solutions' (including, for instance, business development, risk management, and financial solutions) had to be invented to sell products and systems in emerging and deregulated markets.

ABB aimed at becoming the leading supplier in the heavy electrical engineering industry. This implied that besides providing a full assortment of technologies within the product segments where the company competed, it needed to be on top in each of these indeed complex technologies. For instance, in Power Generation this meant that ABB was active in seven to eight major product technologies, while some of its competitors focused on a more narrow range. Thus, it was not only in the execution of major installation projects that ABB needed to collaborate with other firms in consortia. In the development of advanced gas turbine technology, ABB tried to collaborate with several aircraft engine manufacturers to get access to important knowledge, albeit with only limited success (Bergek et al., 2008).

The trend in demand for both flexibility and efficiency in power systems and automation continued. Distributed and renewable energy generation was advocated, entailing developments in both generation (e.g. PFBC cleaner coal technology and the Powerformer HVDC generation range) and transmission (e.g. the HVDC Light systems and the so-called FACTS, i.e. flexible alternating current systems). At the same time, electricity generation and transmission programmes on an entirely new scale were planned and ordered in developing economies such as China, India, and Malaysia. Acquisitions of Combustion Engineering and International Combustion introduced new technologies in power generation, and ABB acquired an entirely new range of products in extended automation through the acquisition of Elsag Bailey in 1997. In effect, this emphasized the increasing technological demands on a manufacturer with full-range product assortment ambitions.

Organizational structure: the full-blown global matrix

With the creation of ABB in 1988, the global matrix (see Figure 8.4) developed into an essential managerial tool for 'being local worldwide' (cf. Bélanger et al., 1999). In conjunction with the merger, ABB embarked on an acquisition frenzy with the aim of becoming dominant in the four segments where it competed (power generation, power transmission, transportation, and automation), signified by the four slices of each letter in the ABB logotype.

The widely dispersed ABB organization (which, for instance, included more than twenty manufacturing plants for power transformers) with its trimmed corporate headquarters was held together by three main forces. First, at the helm, Percy Barnevik became famous for his relentless travelling in his attempts to coordinate and cheer on his troops. Second, the centralized management accounting system (ABACUS), developed in the early 1980s with the intention of standardizing all financial and accounting reporting to keep control and make units' performance comparable, was now used throughout the corporation. Third, large projects and project managers were emphasized by top management for the integration of the company. Many of ABB's products and systems were developed

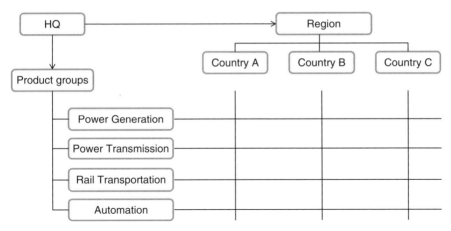

Figure 8.4 ABB's global matrix

and sold in projects with a large number of participants. If this was the business in which the company operated, it needed to excel in the management and execution of such projects. As a senior manager at ABB headquarters put it in the late 1990s: 'What most people did not realize when they discussed the in-built conflict between technology and markets in our global matrix was that projects constituted the third dimension in the ABB global matrix.'

During this period, managerial and leadership capacities also had to be increased. In interviews and various documents, the need to recruit and develop senior project managers was underlined. Barnevik, for instance, took measures to grow and nurture the cadre of 'global project managers' because, as he put it, 'managing a large-scale project is like being the president of a big company'. It was also stressed that the growth in the scale, scope, and complexity of such projects required more than 350 global project managers (Berggren, 1996). One basic idea was to keep corporate headquarters small and develop market 'sensors', business developers, and promoters throughout the world. This implied a trimmed sales organization and an emphasis on the execution of production in temporary projects, rather than in the line organization.

New functions were also incorporated into the matrix. For instance, financial services became a small but profitable unit that exhibited strong synergies with the management and execution of large-scale projects. In particular, the unit could make a profit out of the advances created by such projects if project designers, project managers, and financial experts managed to collaborate effectively in the project's early phases. Financial services thus became a natural part of setting up large projects and creating funding for them. The main leverage from an internal financial service unit came in the fourth project epoch,[5] where an increasing

---

[5] Respondents also stress that financial services, as part of the ABB organization, was partly made possible when Marcus Wallenberg, a key representative for the major shareholder family and also a major shareholder in one of the Swedish banks, died in 1983. Earlier, the policy had been for the company to use outside banks as far as possible and not set up competing financial institutions internally.

number of projects needed to be engineered financially on a par with their technical engineering, which also called for intense collaboration among engineers, risk managers, and financial expertise to sort out the risks involved and develop attractive financial solutions for their clients. In this period, a more elaborate association emerged with outside partners and competitors. The use of consortium agreements was one solution for improving collaboration with competitors to handle large-scale projects and ensure sufficient production capacities. Some cases involved partners representing such diverse businesses as rail systems and hydroelectric power systems. Collaboration with consultants in business development and market analysis to identify market opportunities early on was another measure for preparing and actively taking part in the formation of projects.

8.4 ANALYSIS

In analysing the evolution of each of Asea/ABB's project epochs, we first outline some major trends pertaining to market and technological complexity. We then discuss organizational designs used in different epochs and how they relate to the complexity faced.

8.4.1 Market and technological complexity and the evolution of project epochs

In line with Miller et al. (1995), Hobday (1998, 2000), and Magnusson et al. (2005), we conceive of Asea/ABB's power engineering business as competing in a Complex Products and Systems (CoPS) industry which exhibits a set of characteristics. Markets are characterized by oligopolistic competition, politicized markets, and extensive user–producer interactions. Significant for products and technologies are the multitude of sub-technologies, subsystems, and components in the artefact. Moreover, there are systemic relationships between components; hence, control systems are an important technology per se. It is therefore not very surprising that we find that a major firm in such an industry is involved in systems integration to deliver customized solutions in a project-based organizational form (Prencipe and Tell, 2001; Davies and Hobday, 2005). Partly in line with what this literature suggests, Asea/ABB's business over the period studied was a CoPS business both initially and at the end of the studied period. Hence, 'project epochs' do not denote radical shifts in the evolution of the corporation but rather evolutionary steps.

With regard to growth of markets and internationalization, we argue that Asea developed from being a (*a*) national small champion after World War II primarily competing on local and regional markets, that grew into a (*b*) 'small giant'[6] that competed globally with a small relative domestic home market in comparison to export, to (*c*) a globally leading company due to mergers, acquisitions, and organic

---

[6] Cf. Pacquier and Fridlund (1998) for a parallel analysis of Asea and Brown Boveri in the pre-World War I period.

growth. At the time of the ABB merger in 1987, one-third of Asea's revenues were generated in Sweden, one-third came from export to Sweden, and one-third by value-added in foreign operations. With the ABB merger, the last category five-folded. This also meant that customers and operations became more diverse, and the matrix structure was one means developed to cater for such heterogeneity. In addition, a global shake-out in conjunction with government deregulation of markets changed the competitive landscape and, as a result, market interdependencies increased. New markets opened up and since there were fewer suppliers competing for increasingly large projects, customer requirements and the size and time schedule of projects forced suppliers to cooperate in international consortia. The downsizing of many utilities led to less detailed engineering communication with customers. Over time, this had the effect that capabilities in systems integration and project management became part of the services that ABB offered to its customers.

This indicates that changes in market complexity influenced the evolution of Asea/ABB even to a higher extent than technological complexity. As indicated in the empirical account, the growing market complexity had rather profound effects on knowledge integration requirements and the capabilities ABB needed to deploy. Table 8.9 presents indicators of market complexity; it identifies three important factors of the market complexity that Asea, and later ABB, needed to absorb in its organizational configuration. The first factor relates to the internationalization of markets, the second to market interactions, and the third to project supply characteristics. The internationalization of markets is relatively straightforward, developing from a prime focus on the domestic market with primarily one, highly capable customer into a global and increasingly fragmented market, typically with customers lacking project management and systems integration capabilities in-house.[7] The second factor, market interactions, emphasizes

Table 8.9 Market complexity in the four project epochs

	Epoch I	Epoch II	Epoch III	Epoch IV
Internationalization of markets	Primarily focusing on domestic market with major customer	Selected international customers	Many international customers (developed and less developed countries)	Global market, fragmented demand
Market interactions	Little market competition; National champions	Increasing market competition; National champions	Intermediate consultants; Development initiatives	Deregulation; New customers
Project supply characteristics	Preferred supplier	Preferred supplier; Subsystem supplier	International consortia	International consortia; External network

[7] Although key domestic customers played an important role as test beds for new products all the way into the fourth project epoch identified.

the mounting market competition in the end market and, partly due to deregulation, the emergence of a new cadre of actors that influenced the procurement and collaborative processes, including the role of intermediate consultants and newly established customers. The third factor encompasses the evolution of collaboration from a few customers relying on vertical long-term, preferred supplier–customer relationships to horizontal consortium-type collaborations that customers wanted to use to lower price levels, and simultaneously, due to the size and time schedule of projects, were forced to implement.

Turning to technological complexity, a somewhat similar picture emerges. Asea/ABB was, like other players in this industry, throughout the studied period deeply affected by technological complexity. Not only was the company a true multi-technological corporation (Granstrand et al., 1997; Patel and Pavitt, 1997; Prencipe, 1997) ever since its inception, which required knowledge integration capabilities, it also engaged in related development of services, products, and financial offerings, which further accentuated technological complexity. In addition, there were a number of new and interdependent technologies in the post-World War II era, especially with regard to control technologies that considerably added to technological complexity. Moreover, the scale revolution in power engineering required the company to put heavy emphasis on R&D activities. As the company increased its product and service offering and range, a number of adjacent knowledge bases, such as financial engineering, became part of the organizational knowledge base. Hence, we also submit that technological complexity increased over time, albeit more gradually than market complexity.

Table 8.10 summarizes the key development patterns observed in the four identified project epochs. It considers three primary factors. The first, product characteristics, brings in the importance of the nature and characteristics of the products and the offerings. The second factor relates to relevant technological areas and the number of technologies that needed to be catered for in the

Table 8.10 Technological complexity in the four project epochs

	Epoch I	Epoch II	Epoch III	Epoch IV
Product characteristics	Complex hardware systems, typically integrated by clients	Complex projects, excluding financing, but including some installation and technical services	Turnkey projects, excluding financing, but including project management and systems integration services	Total solutions, including finance, business development, and risk management
Emerging technologies	Component and subsystem technologies	Component, subsystem, and materials technologies	Component, subsystem, materials, and computer hardware technologies	Component, subsystem, materials, hardware, and software technologies
Emerging system control technologies	Extension of pre-WWII converting and control technologies	Semiconductor-based converting and control technologies	Integrated converting, control, and surveillance technologies	Automated control technologies

organizational configuration. The third factor, system control technologies, emphasizes the interaction between technologies utilized in the offerings, and what technological solutions were developed to manage such interactions.

8.4.2 The evolution of organizational design and its influence on knowledge integration

So which organizational designs were used by Asea/ABB, and what role did projects and project-based organizing play in the organization? What were the main knowledge integration problems and how were these solved? We organize the subsequent discussion around the dominant organizational designs in the four epochs.

During the first epoch, projects were centrally governed in the Asea parent company. Due to the company's limited size and the limited number of large-scale projects, integration could be handled within the premises of the major plants in Västerås and Ludvika. The second epoch can be seen as a continuation of this centralization trend to coordinate development and installation projects. However, with the emerging sector organization, knowledge integration in major projects was specifically the task of the influential J-sector, which took on the responsibility for design and engineering of site solutions, and coordinated interactions with other sectors, but without much interaction with market-facing units. Furthermore, it is reasonable to assume that a major reason for establishing the J-sector was to allow for the evolution of systems integration capabilities and project management skills. Although every project to some extent was unique, there were still some overall similarities in terms of system architectures, specifications, technical designs, approval, and quality assurance. Accordingly, the J-sector represented an important solution to gradually build the capability to assume greater responsibilities for systems integration and project management skills. In particular, the J-sector allowed Asea to ensure a steady frequency of tasks that were needed to make sure these capabilities were sustained through their constant use.

The third project epoch signifies an important shift in attitude towards knowledge integration in major projects. By delegating responsibility to divisions for the execution of projects, more emphasis was placed on local initiatives. Thus, projects were primarily executed within divisions or in collaboration with the central R&D Lab. In addition, Asea began experimenting with a matrix-organization design in which projects became an important integrating device between markets and technologies. This also required a more elaborate form of knowledge integration which the sector organization could not facilitate. Additionally, the growth of technological complexity also made it increasingly difficult for the J-sector to sort out the knowledge integration problems involved. Instead, systems integration and project management skills had to be diffused within the organization and stronger capabilities to manage large-scale projects were built. At the same time, large-scale projects and the greater dependence on a rather volatile 'project market' called for managerial action. The growth strategy implemented by Barnevik seems to have played an important part in this respect. A reasonable interpretation is that the series of mergers and acquisitions were decisive steps to increase the likelihood of taking leading roles in large-scale projects and likewise sustain the integrative capabilities needed to supply products and subsystems to these projects. At the same time, they further matched the organization with the increasing size of projects and the obligations associated with them in terms of assessing market and technology risks and developing required services and products besides the hardware systems.

The fourth epoch epitomizes this development, when ABB emerged into 1,000 subsidiaries primarily coordinated in a global matrix in four main product segments. The merger as such could be seen as representing a solution for larger projects with a broader scope, requiring tapping into local knowledge to evaluate market and technological risks as well as coordination across markets and technologies to handle inter-market interactions and technological interdependencies. As the company was heavily reliant on its major projects for revenues, management emphasized project management and projects often mirrored aspects of the global matrix, albeit with an operational and time-limited focus. This also led to investments in leadership capabilities and the breeding of global project managers on a par with powerful subsidiary CEOs. Large-scale projects were also monitored regularly, both to identify market opportunities early on and also to track their financial performance and cash-flow during implementation. The collaboration across domains, for instance across experts in financial engineering, systems integration, and project management, seems to have been critical. The top management support received by these projects probably also contributed to the balance between decentralized, yet centrally monitored, subsidiaries and global projects, which was further underlined by Barnevik and his argument that the organization needed global project managers with particular kinds of managerial and leadership capacities. This signals that organizational capabilities, dependent as they are on the integration of specialist knowledge in situations of reciprocal interdependencies, rely heavily on the principle of 'remembering-by-doing' (Amsden and Hikino, 1994), indicating the importance of continuously using capabilities to make sure that they are sustained and stored appropriately.

To return to the issue of the relationship between organizational design and knowledge integration, the later project epochs in the evolution of Asea/ABB signified a concurrent use of matrix-form and P-form configurations that emphasize knowledge integration through group problem-solving in the conduct of large projects. Admittedly, there were also strong features of rules and directives, sequencing, and routines (Grant, 1996a). However, allowing for complex problem-solving through the integration of dispersed and specialized knowledge gradually became a decisive element of the P-form characteristics in Asea/ABB. Such structures allowed for the combination of local and global search patterns, and hence opportunities for decomposition and recomposition of the increasingly complex situations faced (Simon, 1996; Siggelkow and Levinthal, 2003; Yakob and Tell, 2009).

8.5 CONCLUSIONS AND IMPLICATIONS

We do not propose that there is a universal P-form corporation structure, but rather submit, in line with Hobday's analysis (2000), that such project-based configurations may have a variety of features. Our particular concern has been the relationship between complexity and project-based organizing from a knowledge integration perspective. We found that in its evolution, Asea/ABB faced increasing market and technological complexity and responded correspondingly. While we have not conducted a comparative study of competing firms, we still suggest that the firm was relatively successful in its endeavours. This claim we base on the rapid shakeout process in the industry in the 1980s, where ABB managed to survive. However, it is perhaps indicative that two of the four initial pillars of its business (transportation and generation) have been discarded, for different reasons.[8] Our focus on the power systems segment may thus be slightly biased, as it could be argued that the company was less successful in knowledge integration in the power generation segment (see Bergek et al., 2008).

Our study has shown that, on the project level, Asea/ABB was able to develop problem-solving capabilities by integrating increasingly specialized knowledge (generated by local search). Market complexity and technological complexity defined, in turn, 'market landscapes' and 'technology landscapes'. The market landscape in particular, but also the technology landscape, has at times emerged as quite 'rugged' and difficult to climb. By experimental search through 'vanguard projects' (Davies and Brady, 2000; Frederiksen and Davies, 2008), the firm was able to search for higher peaks in these landscapes. Certainly, organizational structures were not always conducive to such concurrent and coordinated local search, but rather, as suggested by Levinthal and Warglien (1999), organizational design in itself may be a constituent of the complexity faced.

The evolution of a P-form corporation allowed for experimentation and knowledge integration features of project-based organizing without all the liabilities of a completely temporary organization. We suggest that there are two important notions of temporality in conceiving project-based organizations and projects as mechanisms for knowledge integration: (*a*) On the project level, the temporary constellation of specialists allows for a unique opportunity to integrate knowledge that is emanating from highly differentiated and localized search processes. (*b*) On the firm level, a specific feature of the P-form corporation may be its ability to use projects for temporary decentralization (Siggelkow and Levinthal, 2003). By allowing temporarily decentralized project organizations/ teams to explore and solve high-interaction problems, for instance on vanguard

---

[8] We suggest that ABB stood at its peak as a P-form corporation in the fourth epoch identified in our empirical account. Within the original four segments of ABB (power generation, power transmission, rail transportation, automation), many of the large-scale projects (especially those conducted in consortia) belonged to the rail transportation and power generation segments. Those two segments were divested. This therefore constitutes the end of the fourth epoch, which was subsequently followed by the ousting of Swedish CEOs from ABB's top management (Tell, 2008). Much capability for running large-scale projects at the core of the business thus exited the company with these divestments, although some still remain in power transmission, such as HVDC transmission links and large power transformers. After the turmoil when ABB exited two segments, largely because of low growth rates and an idea that the company should enter new growth markets such as e-commerce at the millennium shift, CEO Jürgen Dormann publicly stated that ABB was not going to work with projects in the future (i.e. in any 'fifth' epoch of post-WWII ABB, the P-form characteristics are not as dominant as in the previous four – much due to the reliance on heavy and complex products that were sold on politicized markets).

projects, knowledge can be adapted and developed locally without consideration of central constraints. By only allowing for temporary decentralization, the organization may thus resume decision powers through recentralization and hence gain opportunities for organization-wide learning, a problem otherwise typically associated with project-based organizing.

This study has several limitations. We study only one case and provide rather crude measures of the market and technological complexity variables of how complexity influences organizational design. Despite, or perhaps thanks to, its drawbacks, we believe that much interesting research remains to be done in the area of knowledge integration, organizational design, and complexity.

REFERENCES

Amsden, A. H. and Hikino, T. (1994) Project Execution Capability, Organizational Know-How and Conglomerate Corporate Growth in Late Industrialization, *Industrial and Corporate Change*, 3(1): 111–47.

Baldwin, C. Y. and Clark, K. B. (2000) *Design Rules: The Power of Modularity*, Cambridge, MA: MIT Press.

Bélanger, J., Berggren, C., Björkman, T. and Köhler, C. (eds.) (1999) *Being Local Worldwide: ABB and the Challenge of Global Management*, London: Cornell University Press.

Bergek, A., Tell, F., Berggren, C. and Watson, J. (2008) Technological Capabilities and Late Shakeouts: Industrial Dynamics in the Advanced Gas Turbine Industry, 1986–2002, *Industrial and Corporate Change*, 17(2): 335–92.

Berggren, C. (1996) Building a Truly Global Organization? ABB and the Problems of Integrating a Multi-Domestic Enterprise, *Scandinavian Journal of Management*, 12(2): 123–37.

Cassis, Y. (1997) *Big Business: The European Experience in the Twentieth Century*, Oxford: Oxford University Press.

Chandler, A. D. (1962) *Strategy and Structure: Chapters in the History of Industrial Enterprise*, Cambridge, MA: MIT Press.

—— (1992) Organizational Capabilities and the Economic History of the Industrial Enterprise, *Journal of Economic Perspectives*, 6(3): 79–100.

—— Daems, H. (eds.) (1980) *Managerial Hierarchies: Comparative Perspectives on the Rise of the Modern Industrial Enterprise*, Cambridge, MA, and London: Harvard University Press.

Clark, K. B. and Fujimoto, T. (1991) *Product Development Performance: Strategy, Organization and Management in the World Auto Industry*, Boston, MA: Harvard Business School Press.

Colfer, L. and Baldwin, C. Y. (2010) *The Mirroring Hypothesis: Theory, Evidence and Exceptions*, Working paper, Harvard Business School.

Davies, A. and Brady, T. (2000) Organisational Capabilities and Learning in Complex Product Systems: Towards Repeatable Solutions, *Research Policy*, 29(7–8): 931–53.

—— Hobday, M. (2005) *The Business of Projects: Managing Innovation in Complex Products and Systems*, Cambridge: Cambridge University Press.

DeFillippi, R. J. and Arthur, M. B. (1998) Paradox in Project-based Enterprise: The Case of Film Making, *California Management Review*, 40(2): 125–39.

Eckert, S. and Mayrhofer, U. (2005) Identifying and Explaining Epochs of Internationalization: A Case Study, *European Management Review*, 2: 212–23.

Ekstedt, E., Lundin, R. A., Söderholm, A. and Wirdenius, H. (1999) *Neo-Industrial Organising: Renewal by Action and Knowledge Formation in a Project-intensive Economy*, London: Routledge.

Enberg, C., Lindkvist, L. and Tell, F. (2006) Exploring the Dynamics of Knowledge Integration: Acting and Interacting in Project Teams, *Management Learning*, 37(2): 143–65.

Fleming, L. and Sorensen, O. (2001) Technology as a Complex Adaptive System: Evidence from Patent Data, *Research Policy*, 30: 1019–39.

Frederiksen, L. and Davies, A. (2008) Vanguards and Ventures: Projects as Vehicles for Corporate Entrepreneurship, *International Journal of Project Management*, 26: 487–96.

Gann, D. and Salter, A. (1998) Learning and Innovation Management in Project-based, Service-enhanced Firms, *International Journal of Innovation Management*, 2(4): 431–54.

Glete, J. (1983) *ASEA under hundra år: En studie i ett storföretags organisatoriska, tekniska och ekonomiska utveckling*, Stockholm: Stenströms Bokförlag/Interpublishing AB.

Grandori, A. (2001) Neither Market Nor Identity: Knowledge-Governance Mechanisms and the Theory of the Firm, *Journal of Management and Governance*, 5: 381–99.

Granstrand, O., Patel, P. and Pavitt, K. (1997) Multi-Technology Corporations: Why They have 'Distributed' Rather Than 'Distinctive Core' Competencies, *California Management Review*, 39(4): 8–25.

Grant, R. M. (1996*a*) Toward a Knowledge-based Theory of the Firm, *Strategic Management Journal*, 17(Special Issue): 109–22.

—— (1996*b*) Prospering in Dynamically-Competitive Environments: Organizational Capability as Knowledge Integration, *Organization Science*, 7(4): 375–87.

Hirsh, R. F. (1989) *Technology and Transformation in the American Electric Utility Industry*, Cambridge: Cambridge University Press.

Hobday, M. (1998) Product Complexity, Innovation and Industrial Organisation, *Research Policy*, 26: 689–710.

—— (2000) The Project-based Organization: An Ideal Form for Management of Complex Products and Systems? *Research Policy*, 29: 871–93.

Kauffman, S. A. (1993) *The Origins of Order: Self-Organization and Selection in Evolution*, New York: Oxford University Press.

Kogut, B. and Zander, U. (1992) Knowledge of the Firm, Combinative Capabilities and the Replication of Technology, *Organization Science*, 3(3): 383–97.

Kutschker, M., Bäurle, I. and Schmid, S. (1997) International Evolution, International Episodes, and International Epochs: Implications of Managing Internationalization, *Management International Review*, 2: 101–24.

Levinthal, D. A. (2000) Organizational Capabilities in Complex Worlds, in: G. Dosi, R. R. Nelson and S. G. Winter (eds.), *The Nature and Dynamics of Organizational Capabilities*, Oxford: Oxford University Press.

—— March, J. G. (1993) The Myopia of Learning, *Strategic Management Journal*, 14 (Special Issue): 95–112.

—— Warglien, M. (1999) Landscape Design: Designing for Local Action in Complex Worlds, *Organization Science*, 10(3 Special issue): 342–57.

Lindkvist, L. (2004) Governing Project-based Firms: Promoting Market-like Processes within Hierarchies, *Journal of Management and Governance*, 8(1): 3–25.

—— (2005) Knowledge Communities and Knowledge Collectivities: A Typology of Knowledge Work in Groups, *Journal of Management Studies*, 42(6): 1189–210.

—— Söderlund, J. and Tell, F. (1998) Managing Product Development Projects: On the Significance of Fountains and Deadlines, *Organization Studies*, 19(6): 931–51.

Magnusson, T., Tell, F. and Watson, J. (2005) From CoPS to Mass Production? Capabilities and Innovation in Power Generation Equipment Manufacturing, *Industrial and Corporate Change*, 14(1): 1–26.

Marengo, L. (1994) *Knowledge Distribution and Coordination in Organizations: On Some Social Aspects of the Exploitation vs. Exploration Trade-off*, Laxenburg, Austria: IIASA Reprint 94-13.

Midler, C. (1995) 'Projectification' of the Firm: The Renault Case, *Scandinavian Journal of Management*, 11(4): 363–76.

Miller, R., Hobday, M., Leroux-Demers, T. and Olleros, X. (1995) Innovation in Complex Systems Industries: The Case of Flight Simulation, *Industrial and Corporate Change*, 4(2): 363–400.

Mintzberg, H. (1979) *The Structuring of Organizations*, New York: Prentice-Hall.

Nickerson, J. and Zenger, T. (2004) A Knowledge-based Theory of the Firm: The Problem-Solving Perspective, *Organization Science*, 15(6): 617–32.

Pacquier, S. and Fridlund, M. (1998) The Making of Small Industrial Giants: The Growth of the Swedish ASEA and the Swiss BBC through Crises and Challenges Prior to 1914, in: T. Myllyntaus (ed.), *Economic Crises and Restructuring in History: Experiences of Small Countries*, St. Katharinen: Scripta Mercaturae Verlag.

Patel, P. and Pavitt, K. (1997) The Technological Competences of the World's Largest Firms: Complex and Path-dependent, but not Much Variety, *Research Policy*, 26(2): 141–56.

Postrel, S. (2002) Islands of Shared Knowledge: Specialization and Mutual Understanding in Problem-solving Teams, *Organization Science*, 13(3): 303–20.

Prencipe, A. (1997) Technological Competencies and Product's Evolutionary Dynamics: A Case Study from the Aero-Engine Industry, *Research Policy*, 25(8): 1261–76.

—— Tell, F. (2001) Inter-project Learning: Processes and Outcomes of Knowledge Codification in Project-based Firms, *Research Policy*, 30: 1373–94.

Siggelkow, S. and Levinthal, D. A. (2003) Temporarily Divide to Conquer: Centralized, Decentralized, and Reintegrated Organizational Approaches to Exploration and Adaptation, *Organization Science*, 14(6): 650–69.

Simon, H. (1962) The Architecture of Complexity, *Proceedings of the American Philosophical Society*, 106(6): 467–82.

—— (1996) *The Sciences of the Artificial*, 3rd ed. Boston, MA: MIT Press.

Söderlund, J. (2008) Competence Dynamics and Learning Processes in Project-based Firms: Shifting, Adapting and Leveraging, *International Journal of Innovation Management*, 12(1): 41–67.

—— Tell, F. (2009) The P-form Organization and the Dynamics of Project Competence: Project Epochs in Asea/ABB, 1950–2000, *International Journal of Project Management*, 27: 101–12.

—— —— (2011) The P-form Corporation: Contingencies, Characteristics, and Challenges, in: P. Morris, J. Pinto and J. Söderlund (eds.), *The Oxford Handbook of Project Management*, Oxford: Oxford University Press.

Teece, D. (1980) Economics of Scope and the Scope of an Enterprise, *Journal of Economic Behavior and Organization*, 1: 223–47.

Tell, F. (2000) *Organizational Capabilities – A Study of Electrical Power Transmission Equipment Manufacturers, 1878–1990*, PhD thesis, Linköping: Linköping University.

—— (2008) ASEA – Managing Big Business the Swedish Way, in: S. M. Fellman, M. J. Iversen, H. Sjögren and L. Thue (eds.), *Creating Nordic Capitalism: The Business History of a Competitive Periphery*, Basingstoke: Palgrave/Macmillan.

Thomas, S. and McGowan, F. (1990) *The World Market for Heavy Electrical Equipment*, Sutton: Nuclear Engineering International Special Publications.

Thompson, J. D. (1967) *Organizations in Action*, New York: McGraw-Hill.

Ulrich, K. T. and Eppinger, S. D. (1995) *Product Design and Development*, New York: McGraw-Hill.

Walker, A. H. and Lorsch, J. W. (1968) Organizational Choice, Product versus Function, *Harvard Business Review*, November/December: 129–38.

Whitley, R. (2006) Project-based Firms: New Organizational Form or Variations on a Theme, *Industrial and Corporate Change*, 15(1): 77–99.

Whittington, R. and Mayer, M. (2000) *The European Corporation: Strategy, Structure and Social Science*, Oxford: Oxford University Press.

—— Pettigrew, A., Peck, S., Fenton, E. and Conyon, M. (1999) Change and Complementarities in the New Competitive Landscape: A European Panel Study, 1992–1996, *Organization Science*, 10(5): 583–600.

Williams, T. M. (1999) The Need for New Paradigms for Complex Projects, *International Journal of Project Management*, 17(5): 269–73.

Winter, S. G. (1991) On Coase, Competence, and the Corporation, in: O. Williamson and S. G. Winter (eds.), *The Nature of the Firm: Origins, Evolution, and Development*, New York, NY: Oxford University Press.

Yakob, R. and Tell, F. (2009) Detecting Errors Early: Management of Problem-Solving in Product Platform Projects, in: A. Gawer (ed.), *Platforms, Markets and Innovation*, Cheltenham, UK and Northampton, MA, USA: Edward Elgar.

Zollo, M. and Winter, S. G. (2002) Deliberate Learning and the Evolution of Dynamic Capabilities, *Organization Science*, 13(3): 339–51.

Part IV

Strategies and Outcomes

9

Knowledge Integration Challenges when Outsourcing Manufacturing

Lars Bengtsson, Mandar Dabhilkar, and Robin von Haartman

This chapter focuses on the balance between knowledge integration (KI) requirements and capabilities, explaining the tension between demands to outsource manufacturing to low-cost regions and the need to co-locate key functions and competencies in product development. It shows how different outsourcing strategies shape KI challenges and their effects on costs and performance outcomes.

9.1 INTRODUCTION

The trend towards internationalization of R&D and manufacturing strongly affects the basis for knowledge integration and innovation in technology-based firms. New economies in countries like China, Taiwan, and India not only offer low wages but are increasingly important as loci for knowledge-intensive work, and a major market for new products and services. Combined with the growth of other low-cost regions and the enlarged European Union, this trend has put severe pressure on firms in established industrial countries, resulting in a dramatic increase in the relocation and offshoring of manufacturing to the emerging economies. Outsourcing has consequently been a top-rank management concept for a number of years, driven by the high expectations of cost reduction, market expansion, or advantages gained from innovative suppliers (The Outsourcing Institute, 2005; Fifarek et al., 2008).

At the same time, there are strong arguments for integration within the globalized manufacturing networks. The development and industrialization of new products requires intimate communication and interaction between specialized knowledge bases. This knowledge goes beyond the organizational boundaries. Effective collaboration in innovative projects requires an overlap in knowledge of the product between the buyer and supplier (Brusoni et al., 2001; Takeishi, 2002). Advanced and complex product development calls for co-locating and integrating key activities such as design and manufacturing processes (Ulrich and Ellison, 2005). For rapidly changing products, integration capabilities seem particularly crucial for innovation capability, that is, the capability for rapid product industrialization and market introduction, and the knowledge for making proper sourcing decisions (Sturgeon, 2002).

Together, this creates a strong tension between the pressures of outsourcing and offshoring on the one hand and the needs of integration and co-location on the other. The tension presents a number of knowledge integration (KI) challenges that firms need to meet in order to be successful. In a recent global survey, McKinsey (2008) states: 'The top-rated challenge is the ability to share knowledge effectively across different manufacturing and sourcing locations'. More specifically, the challenges concern how firms can build up KI capabilities in order to meet the KI requirements that outsourcing manufacturing imposes.

To meet these challenges, there has been great interest in organizational mechanisms and forms for effective inter-organizational learning and collaboration (e.g. Myers and Cheung, 2008). But this is not just a question of external relationships. There is a need to further explore how the internal capabilities affect the capability to absorb and integrate knowledge from external sources and partners in the value chain (Cohen and Levinthal, 1990; Wagner and Boutellier, 2002; Lane et al., 2006). Studies indicate that manufacturing firms need to develop internal capabilities to be able to extract competencies from external sources and suppliers (e.g. Teece and Pisano, 1994; Brusoni and Prencipe, 2001; Azadegan et al., 2008). But few studies have empirically investigated how and to what extent manufacturing knowledge provides capabilities for external KI.

The purpose of this chapter is to explore KI challenges when outsourcing manufacturing. The challenges are expressed as the gap between KI requirements and KI capabilities and its subsequent effects on performance outcomes.

Three questions will be discussed. First, we will analyse how investments in manufacturing capabilities affect the performance outcomes of outsourcing and external integration. This relates to a strategic sourcing decision based on the potential of externalized knowledge-based processes compared to the potential of integrated internal processes. We will specifically explore how the combination of outsourcing and investment in in-house capability affects firm performance, given the altered KI requirements. We will argue that investments in manufacturing capability should be evaluated not only from their direct effects on performance but also from the capability they provide for meeting KI requirements derived from outsourcing manufacturing.

Second, we will scrutinize the character of the KI challenges in different types of outsourcing. We will specifically show how manufacturing-based outsourcing compares with component-based outsourcing under the influence of product characteristics. Based on this, we will illustrate that the different types of outsourcing have different effects on the KI capabilities of a firm, and thus on the potential to meet the transformed KI requirements.

The third question concerns the costs of KI when outsourcing. We will argue that outsourcing costs can turn up as hidden costs, performance trade-offs, or deteriorated cost reduction capability. Previous studies on outsourcing effects show that firms seldom obtain the declared benefits; the performance effects are rather mixed and contradictory (Gilley and Rasheed, 2000; Laugen et al., 2005; Espino-Rodriguez and Padron-Robaina, 2006; Bengtsson, 2008). We assert that one explanation why previous studies on outsourcing effects show mixed results is

that the need for integration and more specifically the gap between KI requirements and KI capability have not been taken into account.

The chapter is organized as follows. After this section, we define our core
concepts and conceptual model. In the following three sections, we explore the
three questions more closely and illustrate our reasoning by using empirical
results from our previous published studies on manufacturing outsourcing.[1] We
conclude the chapter by discussing the significance of manufacturing absorptive
capacity in understanding KI challenges when outsourcing manufacturing.

Although outsourcing concerns all firm activities and processes, in this chapter
we focus on the outsourcing of manufacturing. One point of departure is that
manufacturing knowledge and capabilities are of strategic importance for both
innovation and operation processes in technology-based engineering firms
(Brown et al., 2005). Successful innovation processes require an intimate relationship between product development, manufacturing, and marketing processes,
regardless of whether these are externalized or internalized.

9.2 CONCEPTUAL FRAMEWORK

9.2.1 Defining manufacturing outsourcing

We define manufacturing outsourcing as the process of transferring in-house
manufacturing activities to an external supplier. This definition stresses the
change process in an existing organization and is narrower than studies relating
to outsourcing as all activities performed by external parties (for further discussion of various definitions, see e.g. Gilley and Rasheed, 2000; Espino-Rodriguez
and Padron-Robaina, 2006). Our definition is further in accordance with Ulrich
and Ellison (2005), who regard outsourcing as a matter of externalizing activities
(outside an organization's boundaries), which has implications for how activities,
and knowledge, might be and need to be integrated.

There are several ways of classifying different types of outsourcing. One
common way is to distinguish between different motives for outsourcing. The
outsourcing literature has mainly focused on two types of outsourcing (Kakabadse
and Kakabadse, 2005; McIvor, 2005; Espino-Rodriguez and Padron-Robaina,
2006). The dominant motive has been cost reduction, driven by the suppliers'
economy of scale (Cachon and Harker, 2002) and lower labour costs (Choi, 2007).
The second type is strategic outsourcing driven by an ambition to become more
innovative, either by releasing resources to be spent on core competence and
innovation activities (Harland et al., 2005; Medina et al., 2005) or by getting access
to new competencies held by partners and suppliers (Baden-Fuller et al., 2000;

---

[1] The empirical data presented are based on both a survey and case studies. The survey covers 267
responses from a representative sample of Swedish manufacturing plants of engineering firms with
more than fifty employees (ISIC codes 28–35). Details of the survey are presented in, for instance,
Bengtsson et al. (2009). In addition, we use the results from our longitudinal study of outsourcing and
production strategies within the Ericsson, presented in Berggren and Bengtsson (2004) and Bengtsson
and Berggren (2008).

Quinn, 2000). In addition to these two main types, outsourcing to increase flexibility and capacity is rather common. Another type is based on organizational proximity and geographical proximity, where the former relates to ownership, similarity in organization and work procedures, common ICT systems, etc., and the latter concerns location. GAO (2004), for instance, defines four types of outsourcing by separating internal from external suppliers, and domestic from international outsourcing.

A third way of classifying outsourcing is to look at what is outsourced. While this relates to interdependencies between activities and processes, this type of classification is specifically interesting from a KI perspective. We can distinguish between process-oriented and product-oriented outsourcing. Firms that externalize only the manufacturing processes apply a process-oriented outsourcing, while keeping design and overall responsibilities for the product in-house. We will call this type *manufacturing outsourcing*. Firms that contract out both design and manufacturing (and related purchasing) of certain components or products implement what we will call *component outsourcing* (sometimes called black-box outsourcing). These two types of outsourcing seem to have clear relations to the motives for outsourcing. In our studies, we have found that outsourcing manufacturing is mostly driven by expectations of cost reduction, whereas outsourcing of entire components or products is motivated more by innovation and focus, that is, to benefit from external capabilities (Dabhilkar and Bengtsson, 2008; Bengtsson et al., 2009).

A related distinction is based on the strength of interdependencies. The needs of integration rooted in technological and organizational interdependencies have been well described in product development research that analyses the impact of product characteristics (see e.g. Ulrich, 1995). Several authors claim that developing complex products characterized by high interdependencies between various design process steps requires high levels of integration (Chesbrough and Teece [1996] 2002; Koufteros et al., 2005; Lakemond, et al., 2006). Based on the same reasoning, Huang et al. (2009) discerned the degree to which technology can be codified as one decisive factor for R&D sourcing strategies. In our analysis, we will also use the well-established distinction between modular and integral product architecture made by Ulrich (1995). Modular architectures are ideally characterized by well-defined interfaces between physical components and coherence between functions and physical elements, while integral architectures feature more complex interfaces and functions that are spread across components.

Building on this, Baldwin (2008) analyses how modularity in assembled products affects transaction costs and thus the organizational boundaries. She uses the expressions thin and thick 'crossing points' to describe the interdependencies between internalized and externalized tasks. If, for example, a component can be completely designed and manufactured before being supplied to the system owner, the crossing point is thin and transaction costs are low. Conversely, if the design of the system is dependent on the design of the component, externalizing the component will result in a thick crossing point. As a consequence, transactions (such as outsourcing) are more beneficial if located at module boundaries defined by thin crossing points. She also shows that product complexity (many components and relationships) strongly affects the trade-off between gaining benefits from externalizing tasks and adding transaction costs. One common conclusion from these studies is that outsourcing manufacturing of integral products, characterized by less codified knowledge and high task inter-dependencies, will likely be much more problematic than outsourcing more modular processes or products with the opposite features.

In our further analysis, we will distinguish between three main types of outsourcing:

1. *Manufacturing outsourcing.* This is a situation in which the manufacturing processes of certain components are externalized/outsourced, while the corresponding design and purchasing processes are internalized/kept by the focal firm. This situation is often driven by cost motives.

2. *Component outsourcing.* In this case, both the manufacturing and the related design processes for certain components are sourced from external suppliers. The outsourcing could be driven by focus and costs, but more by innovation and a desire to incorporate new knowledge from suppliers.

3. *Capacity outsourcing.* This represents a combined situation in which the firm keeps both manufacturing and design in-house but also contracts out the same processes to suppliers to gain capacity and flexibility to meet market volatility.

We will furthermore analyse how the KI challenges in these situations are affected by proximity/distance, product complexity, and modularization. We will also use the concept of thickness from Baldwin (2008) to characterize the KI requirements in each situation.

9.2.2 Defining knowledge integration capability

One of the most important features of a knowledge-based view is the insight that organizational borders and knowledge borders can differ (Prencipe, 2000). This affects the analysis of inter-organizational relations and integration processes. Brusoni et al. (2001), for instance, argue that efficient external collaboration requires that 'firms know more than they make'.

There are several ways to define KI and KI capability (see Chapters 1 and 2). We regard KI as a collaborative and purposeful process of combining complementary knowledge bases, which in turn leads to the creation of new knowledge used for the purpose. This is based on the reasoning by researchers who understand KI as the process of combining and applying dispersed and specialized knowledge in various organizational activities (e.g. Grant, 1996). A similar perspective is presented by Kogut and Zander (1992), who coined the expression 'combinative capabilities' to describe how firms generate innovations and new applications from existing knowledge.

The combinative approach does not fully explore how different kinds of innovation relate to various KI processes. Henderson and Clark (1990) distinguished between component- and architecture-based innovations, and described the corresponding KI processes. Similarly, Chesbrough and Teece ([1996] 2002) assert that systemic innovations require more extensive internal integration processes than do autonomous innovations. Given this variety of innovation processes, KI reflects a continuum between extreme points: KI as combination and coordination of component knowledge bases, and KI as the intensive interaction and creation of new knowledge by merging knowledge bases on a system level.

The various ways in which firms actually integrate knowledge can be supported by KI mechanisms. Grant (1996) mentions the following KI mechanisms and forms: transfer, sequencing, direction, routines, and group problem-solving and decision-making. Expanding on the notion of combinative capabilities, de Boer et al. (1999) specify systems capabilities as one type of capability that refers to the 'creation of new architectural knowledge through formal systems as codes, plans and procedures'. This capability is close to Nonaka's concept of combination (1994), which describes knowledge creation as a process of integrating explicit knowledge bases. De Boer et al. (1999) argue that firms can use these capabilities to develop component knowledge into new architectural knowledge, regardless of whether the component knowledge is located within the organization or externally. In this chapter, we will not focus on the KI mechanisms per se, but rather on a broader understanding of firms' KI capability, which includes a successful development and exploitation of KI mechanisms.

One important prerequisite for integrating knowledge is the need for common knowledge. Grant (1996) asserts that 'While these mechanisms for knowledge integration are necessitated by the differentiation of individuals' stocks of knowledge, all depend upon the existence of common knowledge for their operation. [. . .] The importance of common knowledge is that it permits individuals to share and integrate aspects of knowledge which are not common between them.'

This line of reasoning shares its argument with the concept of absorptive capacity when analysing firms' capability to integrate external knowledge. The seminal work by Cohen and Levinthal (1990) introduced the concept of absorptive capacity to explain how internal knowledge helps firms to exploit their external environment. They, along with many other authors, have shown that investment in R&D yields two distinct advantages: better technological knowledge and an ability to use external knowledge more efficiently. In line with suggestions by Cohen and Levinthal and others (e.g. Zahra and George, 2002), we assume that the same is true for investments in manufacturing.

In order to operationalize the concept, Lane and Lubatkin (1998) introduced the notion of 'relative absorptive capacity' to analyse the learning processes and the mechanisms for acquiring, assimilating, and exploiting external knowledge. Relative absorptive capacity stipulates that for knowledge transfers to be successful, there needs to be some degree of similarity of knowledge and organizational mechanisms between the collaborating firms. The presence of related knowledge and structures allows the firm to evaluate external knowledge, integrate the new knowledge, and exploit it for commercial gain. The more similar the two firms are, the easier it is to accommodate learning. This has a limit according to the authors. Even though knowledge tends to develop cumulatively and be path-dependent, attaining exactly the same knowledge before forming a learning alliance will reduce the scope for learning.

From this reasoning, the concept of absorptive capacity in manufacturing can be understood as a specific form of KI capability, based on two parts:

1. The knowledge assets, in terms of internal manufacturing capabilities.

2. The KI mechanisms applied in various phases of the KI process, including acquiring, assimilating, and exploiting knowledge. These KI mechanisms

might be materialized in strategy (e.g. strategic alignment), technology (e.g. information systems), or organization (e.g. cross-functional teams).

Even though the term absorptive capacity was initially coined to capture external integration, we will use it to describe the integration of knowledge between manufacturing and design, regardless of whether manufacturing is externalized or internalized. It is, however, important to stress that KI capability will differ in different outsourcing arrangements.

9.2.3 Conceptual model

The final conceptual model for analysing the KI challenges and the outcomes when outsourcing manufacturing is displayed in Figure 9.1. The main idea is that the chosen outsourcing strategy will affect the KI requirements. In accordance with the analysis by de Boer et al., (1999) and Lane et al., (2006), these KI requirements need to be met by certain KI capabilities, which are built up from knowledge assets and a combination of KI mechanisms in use. The gap between the KI requirements and current KI capability represents current KI challenges that will influence the performance outcomes of outsourcing. The costs of building the KI capability to close the gap can be seen as a factor that moderates the performance outcome of outsourcing, as expressed by Espino-Rodriguez and Padron-Robaina (2006). While knowledge assets potentially build up KI capabilities, these capabilities will be affected both by investments in manufacturing capabilities and by divestments in such capacity, that is, outsourcing.

In our analysis, we will also include three factors that moderate the impact of outsourcing (not displayed in Figure 9.1). Building on previous research, the impact of outsourcing on KI requirements is moderated by product complexity (see e.g. Olausson, 2009) as well as by the extent that components and processes are interdependent and modularized (see e.g. Baldwin, 2008). A factor of specific relevance for international outsourcing is proximity, which has been shown to

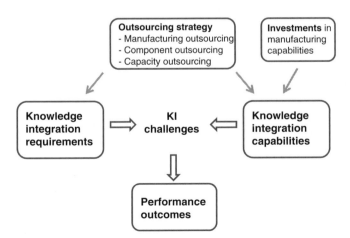

Figure 9.1 Conceptual model showing the KI challenges

have an impact on both the requirements and the capabilities to manage integration (see e.g. Mol et al., 2005).

To sum up, in the following, we will further explore the KI challenges, guided by the following questions:

- How are the outcomes of manufacturing outsourcing affected by investments in manufacturing capability? How may the KI requirements that follow from outsourcing be met by such investments?
- How do different types of manufacturing outsourcing affect KI requirements and KI capabilities and the subsequent performance outcomes?
- What are the costs of knowledge integration when outsourcing?

9.3 EXPLORING THREE KNOWLEDGE INTEGRATION ASPECTS OF OUTSOURCING

9.3.1 Investing in manufacturing capability when outsourcing

The first KI aspect concerns the strategic question of whether to make or buy. On a general level, this can be understood as a question of how to build firm capabilities. According to the resource-based view, core capabilities are built by investing in resources that are combined into distinctive and dynamic capabilities that form a basis for competitive advantage (Grant, 1996). Distinctive resources concern knowledge being hard to imitate due to firm specificity, social complexity, and causal ambiguity (Barney, 1991; Coff, 1999). Barney stresses that the decision about how to obtain unique capabilities depends on the degree of asset specificity and on the costs of developing or acquiring them externally. Thus, outsourcing constitutes a strategic dilemma. On the one hand, it is less costly to exploit highly specific and unique resources internally (Huang et al., 2009) and it is mostly more efficient to invest in existing capabilities (Mathews, 2003). In an outsourcing study, Espino-Rodriguez and Padron-Robaina (2006) conclude that the greater a firm's access to a set of valuable routines and processes, the lower will be the development cost and the greater the likelihood of obtaining a competitive advantage. On the other hand, since firms cannot possess all kinds of technology, they need to find efficient ways to capture new resources and internalize external knowledge (Quinn, 2000).

In a multiple case study on manufacturing outsourcing, Brusoni and Prencipe (2001) illustrate the significance of maintaining internal manufacturing competence in order to effectively involve suppliers in New Product Development (NPD). In a survey study, Rosenzweig et al. (2003) show that manufacturing-based competitive capabilities have a positive mediating role for supply chain integration and its impact on business performance. However, they use operational performance as a proxy for measuring capabilities and do not analyse underlying competencies.

One KI challenge is thus how to balance investment and divestment. There are many studies that build on arguments from the theory of transaction cost economics and a resource-based view on how to make the strategic choice to

Table 9.1 Regression models explaining performance outcomes by manufacturing investments and outsourcing

	Quality	Speed	Dependability	Mix flexibility	Volume flexibility	Cost
Core variables						
Manufacturing capability investment	0.43**	0.49**	0.53**	0.36**	0.41**	0.41**
Outsourcing intensity	−0.26*	−0.44**	−0.20*	−0.13	0.23*	0.16
Interaction effect	0.14	0.39**	0.18	0.22*	−0.07	−0.04
Contextual variables						
Company size	−0.05	0.03	0.02	−0.02	−0.06	0.04
Machining production system	−0.03	−0.07	−0.10	−0.05	0.00	−0.09
Assembly production system	−0.08	−0.12	−0.08	0.15*	0.15*	0.22*
Order fulfillment practice	−0.05	−0.09	−0.23**	0.06	−0.07	−0.14
Model fit						
ΔAdj R^2	*0.17*	*0.28*	*0.28*	*0.17*	*0.20*	*0.18*
Total variance explained	0.18	0.29	0.31	0.19	0.23	0.23
F (Full model)	9.22**	15.78**	17.26**	9.65**	11.69**	11.99**
N	255	257	254	261	254	254

Significant levels: * <0.05; ** >0.01.

make or buy, but few have empirically investigated the outcome of a combined strategy (Mathews, 2003). The outsourcing literature seldom considers the combined efforts, focusing rather on the outsourcing option.

The KI challenge will be illustrated by two of our previous empirical studies. The discussion is summarized in Table 9.1. The study by Dabhilkar and Bengtsson (2008) was designed to compare the effects of investing in manufacturing capability and outsourcing manufacturing. Manufacturing capability was defined by seven indicators describing improvements in manufacturing technology, team-based work, skills, and internal and external collaboration. The study focused on the extent of manufacturing outsourcing, that is, the share of value-added that has been outsourced during the past three years.

The results from the study show that there seems to be a greater potential for improvement in investing in, rather than divesting, the manufacturing function. Investments in higher manufacturing capability have overall positive effects on operating performance in terms of quality, speed, dependability, flexibility, and costs. Outsourcing intensity entails positive effects on volume flexibility and costs, but has negative effects on operating performance in terms of quality, speed, dependability, and mix flexibility. The interaction effect is either positive or close to zero. This means that negative effects for the most part are related to outsourcing when used as the main strategy to improve performance, while positive effects are more likely to be obtained if concurrent initiatives are used to develop manufacturing capability. This indicates that outsourcing is not beneficial as an isolated means for improving performance. Apparently, outsourcing's main value seems to be its use to free resources in order to invest in higher manufacturing capability.

In another study, we analysed how sourcing strategies that affect KI capability influence external collaboration efficiency. This question has been discussed in conceptual work by Azadegan et al. (2008), who suggest that a manufacturer's absorptive capacity, that is, its ability to use external knowledge, positively moderates the impact of supplier innovativeness on the manufacturer's performance. A study by von Haartman and Bengtsson (2009) well illustrates this expectation empirically. The companies were divided into two clusters defined by the level of manufacturing capability as measured by use of advanced technology, application of lean principles, and cross-functional teamwork. A correlation analysis was then conducted between performance indicators and the level of supplier involvement in product and process development. It was proposed that the companies with relatively higher manufacturing capability would show a clear correlation between supplier integration and performance, whereas the companies with lower capability would show little or no correlation (Figure 9.2). The companies with high capability were regarded as having higher manufacturing absorptive capacity so that they could translate supplier integration into real gains in performance.

The results confirm the proposed relationships and demonstrate that firms with greater manufacturing capability, and thus potentially improved KI capability, gain more from supplier integration than do firms with less manufacturing capability. For the 'high capability' clusters, there was a significant correlation between supplier integration and twenty of the performance indicators used, compared to only seven significant correlations for the 'low capability' clusters. The pattern is particularly strong for firms that have invested in advanced

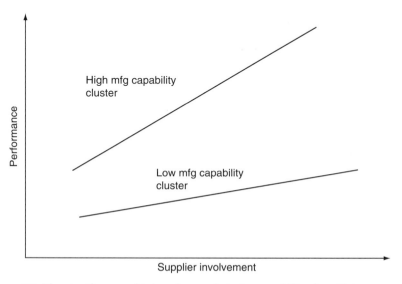

Figure 9.2 The significance of internal manufacturing capability for efficient external integration

Table 9.2 Knowledge integration challenges in different kinds of outsourcing

	Manufacturing outsourcing	Component outsourcing	Capacity outsourcing
Main motive and challenges			
Motives	Cost	Innovation and cost	Cost and flexibility
Key challenges	Exploit low-cost capability	Integrating distributed innovation processes	Exploit supply chain efficiency
KI requirements			
Complexity impact	Outsourcing complex products leads to increased KI needs in external mfg–design interface	Outsourcing complex mfg and related design reduces KI needs in the focal firm, while handled internally by supplier	Outsourcing complex mfg and related design does not change KI needs while still handled internally
Interdependency and modularity impact	Outsourcing mfg of both integral and modular products means increased KI needs and thick crossing points in mfg–design interface	Outsourcing parts of integral products means increased KI needs and thick crossing points, mainly in the design–design interface. Outsourcing modular products means unchanged KI needs between modules	The degree of modularity has a low effect on KI needs
Proximity	Distance in contrast to co-location increases KI requirements	Distance increases KI requirements	Distance affects the knowledge transfer process
KI capabilities			
Impact on manufacturing and KI capability	Outsourcing the mfg of complex and integral products decreases mfg capability. Outsourcing the mfg of simple and modular products has limited impact on mfg capability	Outsourcing the mfg and design of complex products, both integral and modular, decreases mfg capability	Limited impact on mfg and KI capability when kept in-house
KI challenges and expected outcomes			
	Outsourcing the mfg of complex and integral products to distant suppliers increases the KI challenges, which likely causes high transaction costs and negatively affects both costs and innovation capability. Outsourcing the mfg of simple, modular products to proximal suppliers causes few KI challenges that affect the outcome	Outsourcing parts of integral products, in contrast to modular products, increases the KI challenges, which likely causes high transaction costs and negatively affects both costs and innovation capability. Outsourcing parts of simple, modular products to proximal suppliers causes few KI challenges that affect the outcome	Few KI challenges occur. The performance outcomes are mainly modified by mundane transaction costs

Note: mfg = manufacturing, KI = knowledge integration.

machinery and achieved high utilization rates, whereas the results are more ambiguous for other types of manufacturing capabilities.

9.3.2 How do different outsourcing strategies affect knowledge integration capability and performance?

The second question concerns how various types of outsourcing affect KI requirements and capabilities, and in turn performance outcomes. Previous studies have shown that manufacturing can play a strategic role in internal NPD processes (Brown et al., 2005), such as when it comes to achieving a short time to market and low development costs. One main reason is that manufacturability is easier to secure if knowledge of manufacturing technology and capabilities is integrated into the product design process (see e.g. Swink, 1999). This integration is even more important when dealing with complex product development processes with high uncertainty (e.g. Lakemond et al., 2006).

Outsourcing has, however, many faces. We would therefore expect the KI challenges to differ significantly between different kinds of outsourcing. The greatest KI challenges likely occur when outsourcing manufacturing simultaneously entails rising KI requirements and deteriorating KI capability. Such situations will result in a widening gap that needs to be closed with compensatory investment in KI capability and mechanisms. In the following sections, we will analyse the types of outsourcing defined above and include the moderating effects of product complexity, interdependencies/modularization, and proximity. The discussion is summarized in Table 9.2.

Manufacturing outsourcing

The first type of outsourcing, manufacturing outsourcing, has commonly been driven by cost motives and increasingly means offshoring, in order to exploit the low-cost capability of suppliers located in low-cost regions. The most challenging situation, according to Ulrich and Ellison (2005), is when strong motives for internalizing design and externalizing manufacturing are combined with strong motives for integrating the two processes. Thus, outsourcing complex and integral products to distant suppliers creates the most dramatic increase in KI requirements. Such cases represent what Baldwin (2008) would call 'thick crossing points' in the interface between the outsourced manufacturing and the in-house design processes. The processes are characterized by complex and systemic interdependencies in the form of numerous related tasks across organizational and geographical borders. An offshore supplier adds further challenges to KI, while the conditions for organizing efficient communication and integration are deteriorating (Mol et al., 2005). In studies of complex industrialization processes, leading telecom firms stress the benefits of integrated internal processes when dealing with the development of new systems (Dankbaar, 2007; Bengtsson and Berggren, 2008). The challenge of KI in cases of complex industrialization concerns the combination of different kinds of knowledge of manufacturing technology, processes, and supply chain solutions. Internal solutions thus seem more beneficial compared to working with contract manufacturers with more standardized manufacturing approaches. If outsourcing is pursued in this situation, the resultant KI requirements increase, while this kind of outsourcing at the same time implies divestment in manufacturing capability. This could potentially endanger the firm's KI capability, which is needed to bridge the widening KI gap. Closing this gap would likely entail high transaction costs.

At the other end of the spectrum, outsourcing the manufacturing of less complex and integral products to co-located suppliers entails rather few KI challenges due to low KI requirements, even though the KI capability is affected negatively. The co-location of suppliers mitigates the negative effect of outsourcing while providing better options for intimate collaboration. This does not mean that this kind of outsourcing is free from transaction costs, but they do not relate to changes in knowledge requirements, rather to new logistics structures and challenges. Between the ends of the spectrum, there are of course several other outsourcing situations, which represent combinations of the KI challenges discussed.

Component outsourcing

The second main type concerns outsourcing of both manufacturing and related design activities (and most purchasing, too). This type can be driven by strategic reasons for cutting costs or refocusing business (McIvor, 2005) but it is often based on innovation motives (The Outsourcing Institute, 2005). In these cases, component outsourcing is regarded as a vehicle for facilitating the development of new products by getting access to new capabilities held by partners and suppliers (e.g. Quinn, 2000; Harland et al., 2005). The changes in KI requirements that follow from this kind of outsourcing strongly depend on the characteristics of the products and the proximity of the partner. Outsourcing manufacturing and related design of complex components of modular products will reduce the KI challenges within the focal firm, while a number of activities and processes will be managed by the new partner. Outsourcing modular components does not create any new KI demands in itself, while key product development and manufacturing are kept integrated both organizationally and spatially. Since this solution actually means a transfer of KI challenges to suppliers, the focal firm may experience lowered requirements. The idea of reducing problems in this way is also one of the driving forces behind what is sometimes called black-box outsourcing.

Outsourcing manufacturing and design of parts of integral products represents a more complicated KI challenge. The integral structure is characterized by strong task interdependencies, which cause thick crossing points in the interface between design of parts and design of the system (Baldwin, 2008). Distant suppliers would add to the KI challenge in these cases. This is supported by arguments in the product development literature for co-locating and integrating key activities, processes, and knowledge in product and manufacturing processes, at least in complex product areas (Ulrich and Ellison, 2005).

One overall problem in this case is that the outsourcing firm's knowledge of the outsourced component is reduced and so is their architectural knowledge, which requires knowledge about the components. It could be very difficult to maintain and nurture knowledge in areas that are outsourced (Sturgeon, 2002; Bengtsson and Berggren, 2008), which would result in notable transaction costs.

In conclusion, we would expect component outsourcing to outperform manufacturing outsourcing due to the high costs of KI, especially when dealing with cases of offshoring more complex and integral products and processes. This expectation was confirmed in a study that explicitly compared the outcome of component outsourcing with manufacturing outsourcing (Bengtsson and Dabhilkar, 2009). The results show that plants which choose to outsource design activities along with manufacturing (i.e. component outsourcing) exhibit stronger improvements in performance than plants that only outsource manufacturing activities and keep related design work in-house. This indicates that it is more beneficial to meet the integration needs between manufacturing and design in cases of complex and integral structures than to rely on possible improvements through outsourcing manufacturing while corresponding design is internalized. Co-locating suppliers could indeed be a strategy to improve the KI capabilities and in this way mitigate the effects of outsourcing (McIvor, 2005). But it is also clear that manufacturing outsourcing as an isolated strategy does not solve previous internal deficits; it is probably not easier to manage manufacturing externally than internally.

Capacity outsourcing

The third type, capacity-oriented outsourcing, is mainly driven by motives of cost and flexibility, which means that the most attractive capabilities concern efficiency in terms of cost reduction and higher flexibility along the supply chain. From a KI perspective, this mainly implies cloning knowledge bases to form several efficient supply chains. While the firm retains control and knowledge of the entire product and manufacturing process, the KI capability is unaffected and can be used not only to further develop but also to control the capacity suppliers' processes. This phenomenon is not affected by product characteristics. It is thus likely that this KI capability will contribute positively to the performance outcome.

Table 9.2 summarizes the possible impact of the three kinds of outsourcing manufacturing on KI requirements, KI capability, and their possible moderating effect on performance outcomes. The table follows the logic of the conceptual model presented in Figure 9.1. The cost aspects will be further elaborated in the next section.

9.3.3 The costs of knowledge integration when outsourcing

The third question concerns the costs of KI when outsourcing manufacturing. The different kinds of mismatch between the KI requirements and the KI capability explored in the previous section have consequences for the effectiveness of outsourcing in two ways: Firstly, that the intended benefits are not met, and secondly, that the efforts needed to bridge the gap with various KI mechanisms are not free. The size of these costs may vary but they will certainly affect the outcome of outsourcing. In the worst case, the benefits might be cannibalized by the costs for KI. The costs of KI can arise in at least three areas: as hidden costs of KI, as outsourcing trade-offs, and as a reduced cost reduction capability.

The hidden costs as costs of knowledge integration

Despite the great interest in outsourcing, empirical studies on outsourcing performance come to remarkably contradictory conclusions about the effects. Although most studies on outsourcing take the benefits expressed in motives for granted, not many studies actually show positive results. Most studies find a few, none, or even negative performance outcomes of outsourcing (see e.g. Gilley and Rasheed, 2000; Laugen et al., 2005; Espino-Rodriguez and Padron-Robaina, 2006). In our own survey of manufacturing outsourcing in the Swedish engineering industry, we also found that the effect of outsourcing on overall plant performance was negligible even though the direct effect was regarded as positive (Bengtsson, 2008; Dabhilkar and Bengtsson, 2008).

Several outsourcing studies have thus recognized a clear gap between the benefits expected in advance and the outcomes after outsourcing, even though few firms actually make the latter analysis. Some firms estimate these costs at 25 per cent of the manufacturing costs (see Jackson et al., 2001). With offshoring, this situation causes what Mol et al. (2005) describe as a balancing act between lower manufacturing costs abroad and lower transaction costs locally, a balance that is subject to constant change. In a recent recalculation, McKinsey (2008) claims that the total landed costs in 2008 compared to 2003 of producing servers in the United States versus in Asia had turned negative due to both less savings in wages and higher outsourcing costs.

Scrutinizing the costs of outsourcing, we find they fall into three categories: logistics, quality and risks, and project costs. The logistics costs are easiest to include in the cost analysis. The quality and risk costs, which relate to such things as reworking, warehousing, and currency exchange, could be harder to estimate and thus often become hidden costs (Hoecht and Trott, 2006). These costs do not, however, relate to cost of KI and could thus be treated as 'mundane transactions costs' (Baldwin, 2008). Often hidden in outsourcing decisions are the costs of carrying out the outsourcing project. This includes costs related to the project organization needed for transferring the product, as well as equipment and knowledge from the firm outsourcing to the contracted firm. To acquire, assimilate, and integrate this knowledge into the new organization requires substantial efforts by both the outsourcing firm and the supplier (Niss, 2002). The costs of these efforts could be seen as costs of knowledge transfer. But they can also be regarded as an estimate of costs for KI, while one of the major challenges in the transfer projects is to combine knowledge bases from two organizations when forming the new production systems.

KI as an explanation of outsourcing trade-offs

Another way to express the cost aspect of outsourcing is to look at the trade-offs from outsourcing. These trade-offs represent a choice that needs to be made when the KI requirements and efforts to meet them are not concurrent. One trade-off occurs between the motives of low cost and innovation. Previous studies assert that outsourcing for cost reasons may damage the capacity for industrialization (preparing new products for volume manufacturing) and thus the innovation capability of firms (Mol et al., 2004; Dankbaar, 2007; Bengtsson and Berggren,

Table 9.3 Mean value outcomes for different outsourcing clusters (analysis of variance)

Outsourcing strategy clusters	% of firms	Costs	Time to market	Functionality
1. Manufacturing outsourcing for low cost	38	0.43 [3*]	−0.11 [2**]	−0.20 [2**]
2. Component outsourcing for innovation	15	−0.16	0.76 [1**, 3**]	0.59 [1**, 3**]
3. Other types of outsourcing	47	−0.27 [1*]	−0.15 [2**]	−0.08 [2**]

Note: The group numbers within brackets [] indicate that the mean difference between groups is significant at either the 0.05 level (*) or the 0.01 level   (**); $N = 126$.

2008). One plausible reason for the trade-off is that the need for KI differs between low-cost-oriented outsourcing and innovation-oriented outsourcing, as described in previous sections. Outsourcing modular components for cost reasons likely represents fewer KI requirements, whereas innovation-oriented outsourcing of integral products requires several KI challenges that need to be met, as discussed above.

In order to explore this trade-off, we compare the outcomes of three types of outsourcing, reflecting both the intentions and the actions taken (Bengtsson et al., 2009):

1. Manufacturing outsourcing to low-cost regions results in lower costs.

2. *Component outsourcing for innovation.* This type was defined as outsourcing of high customer value and/or design processes to gain access to new knowledge by engaging suppliers with higher innovative capability.

3. *Other types of outsourcing.* This group includes capacity outsourcing but was not specifically in focus in this study.

The main results from this study show that the outsourcing strategies have distinctly different performance outcomes (see Table 9.3). Manufacturing outsourcing to low-cost regions results in lower costs, whereas component outsourcing for innovation reasons results in a reduction in time-to-market and increased product functionality.

Bengtsson et al. (2009) furthermore confirmed that manufacturing outsourcing is a trade-off between lowering costs and improving innovation capability. Firms applying a low-cost-oriented strategy performed significantly lower on time-to-market and improving product functionality than did innovation-oriented firms. Conversely, the latter group of firms have inferior cost performance. The study finally showed that only the innovation-oriented firms benefit from organizational integration that includes the manufacturing department in the product development process as well as early supplier involvement.

KI capability as a cost reduction capability

A third expression of how KI challenges affect outsourcing costs concerns a dynamic cost reduction capability. The learning effect is well recognized in the literature on manufacturing efficiency, showing that firms applying continuous improvements may obtain significant cost reductions over time (e.g. Boer et al., 2000; Bessant et al., 2003). Despite these insights, the basis for many outsourcing projects is a set of snapshots comparing the current prices of purchased components or processes with current internal manufacturing costs, while neglecting the impact of cost reduction capability. The outsourcing firm expects in such cases that the prices asked by the supplier will decrease over time, as a result of falling component prices and continuous improvements. One of the findings from our own study on Ericsson's outsourcing of radio base stations is, however, that the price reductions Ericsson gets from the contract manufacturer are small compared to cost reductions due to product redesign (Bengtsson and Berggren, 2008). When redesigning products, which included switching components, architectural changes, and re-evaluation of suppliers, Ericsson experienced cost reductions of up to 20–25 per cent annually. The study furthermore indicated that the key capability for this cost reduction redesign relied on Ericsson having control over and knowledge of the entire product development process. This means that the key cost reduction capability concerns the capability to redesign products, which in turn was based on the knowledge integration of manufacturing and design competencies.

9.4 DISCUSSION AND CONCLUSIONS

Globalization has created strong tension for industrial firms in developed countries between the high demands to outsource manufacturing to low-cost regions and the need to integrate and co-locate key functions and competencies in the product development chains. This tension is evident at firm level when promises to improve both efficiency and innovation capability come face to face with the problems and costs of outsourcing. They are to some extent rooted in the gap between knowledge integration requirements and capabilities. Finding ways to meet the knowledge integration challenges is crucial for maintaining competitiveness in many Western firms. To learn more about how to handle the challenges, in this chapter we have analysed three questions on KI when outsourcing manufacturing. One common point is that manufacturing absorptive capacity is a key concept in understanding KI challenges and their effects when outsourcing.

9.4.1 The significance of investing in manufacturing capability

We have argued that, by increasing absorptive capacity, investments in manufacturing capability may have a direct effect on performance as well as on efficiency in external integration. This was illustrated at two levels.

One is the strategic level. Investigating the strategic decision to outsource, we found that a combination of outsourcing and investing in manufacturing capability has positive performance effects. One obvious reason for this is of course that investments are made in more profitable areas while divesting processes with a lower performance impact. The motives of changing focus and freeing resources are common arguments for outsourcing (The Outsourcing Institute, 2005). Medina et al. (2005) also describe the benefits of releasing resources from noncore activities to spend them on innovation activities. Mathews (2003) further argues that a combined approach is more beneficial, since it allows continuing investment in successful areas while at the same time adding new capabilities.

However, another interpretation of the combination effect relates to KI. Outsourcing is not only about balancing motives with respect to internalizing and externalizing but also about recognizing the benefits of synchronic action that leads to activity integration. Investments in manufacturing capability may also make a firm better equipped for exploiting external relationships (Rosenzweig et al., 2003).

By extending the analysis to the need for manufacturing capability, we could also show on an operative level that investments are beneficial for external (supplier) integration. Investments in manufacturing capability and integration mechanisms provide the basis for external collaboration and in turn improve the performance outcomes. From a performance perspective, the combined strategy could thus be regarded as a strategy for increasing the firm's manufacturing absorptive capacity. This means that manufacturing absorptive capacity could be seen as the prerequisite for successful KI and performance. Our study thus provides empirical support to the study by Azadegan et al. (2008), who suggest that a manufacturer's absorptive capacity, that is, its ability to use external knowledge, positively moderates the impact of supplier innovativeness on the manufacturer's performance.

The findings must not, however, be over-interpreted. By itself, investing in manufacturing capability is unlikely to increase KI capability to manage KI challenges when outsourcing manufacturing. Such an increase in KI capability has at least two preconditions. To exploit the improved capability, firms need to build up technological and organizational mechanisms in parallel. Secondly, firms' investments in manufacturing knowledge need to be in areas that overlap their partner's knowledge base, as captured by the concept of relative absorptive capacity (Lane et al., 2006).

But in such cases, these results do have a clear implication. Usually, investments in manufacturing entail considerable costs for firms and are therefore hard to justify in terms of increasing innovation capability. But our study indicates that under the specified conditions, the rationale for manufacturing investments should be based not only on direct effects but also on the absorptive capacity they provide. This capacity gives a company the capability to acquire, assimilate, and commercialize external knowledge. In particular, resources may need to be invested internally, even in areas such as manufacturing that may have no direct contact with the sources of the knowledge. This finding is in line with Cohen and Levinthal's original propositions (1990), applied in the manufacturing area.

9.4.2 Knowledge integration capability varies with outsourcing type

The KI requirement and the effect displayed do, however, vary significantly with the type of outsourcing. The analysis summarized in Table 9.2 showed that the greatest KI challenges occur when outsourcing manufacturing of complex and integral products to distant suppliers. Such situations simultaneously imply rising

KI requirements and deteriorating KI capability. This is because such situations result in a widening gap that needs to be closed with significant investments in KI capability and mechanisms.

One conclusion from this analysis is that investments in manufacturing may build an important KI capability to meet these challenges and to be able to improve the performance outcome of outsourcing.

9.4.3 Knowledge integration challenges as an explanation of cost effects and mixed performance outcomes when outsourcing

It is well known that outsourcing entails integration requirements that must be dealt with together with the (new) supplier (McIvor, 2005). We argue that the costs of KI could be significant, especially when there is a large gap between the requirement and the capabilities for KI. We showed three types of costs that relate to KI. The first concerned the often hidden costs of outsourcing caused by the need to build new structures and processes for KI. The second concerned the outsourcing trade-off, where specifically the KI needs in innovation processes are hard to meet with low-cost outsourcing strategies. The third type of cost concerns the insight that a dynamic cost reduction capability in manufacturing requires product redesign, which in turn calls for effective KI capabilities realized by internal manufacturing capability. A part of these costs could be seen as the transaction cost of KI caused by investments in manufacturing absorptive capacity.

In line with previous studies, we argue that outsourcing manufacturing process-es with strong links to internalized manufacturing and/or design processes might be costly, due to the costs of integration and reduced cost reduction capability by redesign (Mol et al., 2004; Bengtsson and Berggren, 2008). This is also described by the theory of transaction cost economics (TCE), which suggests that the internali-zation of activities is characterized by high specificity (even though such an analysis in practice is accompanied by a high degree of uncertainty). TCE cannot, however, fully recognize cost dynamics and trade-off situations.

We have seen that outsourcing may widen the gap between current capabilities and the requirement for KI. As the cost of closing this gap might be substantial, there is a need for a dynamic KI capability that incorporates an in-depth understanding of how to balance the costs and benefits of KI when dealing with outsourcing.

Understanding the cost effects by using the concept of manufacturing absorp-tive capacity is also important when trying to explain the contradictory outcomes of outsourcing in previous studies. We argue that one possible explanation for these mixed outcomes is that KI tensions and requirements have not been taken into account. Few outsourcing studies have analysed the combined effects of outsourcing and investing in manufacturing capability, few have included strate-gies for integrating separated processes when analysing the resulting effects, and most studies have inadequately covered the need for internal manufacturing competence in the efficient external integration of knowledge. A second explana-tion is that any benefits from outsourcing need to be balanced against the KI challenges derived from outsourcing. KI has a price in terms of hidden costs, trade-offs, and cost reduction capability. We would argue that these KI costs explain why previous studies on outsourcing performance have come to such different conclusions.

A KI perspective may thus be useful to explain many of the problems experienced when outsourcing. Such insights are valuable as a basis for formulating ways out of the tension between the strong imperatives for externalization and the simultaneous integration needs that many industrial firms face today.

REFERENCES

Azadegan, A., Dooley, K. J. and Carter, P. L. (2008) Supplier Innovativeness and the Role of Interorganizational Learning in Enhancing Manufacturer Capabilities, *Journal of Supply Chain Management*, 44(4): 14–35.

Baden-Fuller, C., Targett, D. and Hunt, B. (2000) Outsourcing to Outmanoeuvre, *European Management Journal*, 18(3): 285–95.

Baldwin, C. Y. (2008) Where Do Transactions Come from? Modularity, Transactions, and the Boundaries of the Firm, *Industrial and Corporate Change*, 17(1): 155–95.

Barney, J. B. (1991) Firm Resources and Sustained Competitive Advantage, *Journal of Management*, 17: 99–120.

Bengtsson, L. (2008) Outsourcing Manufacturing and Its Effect on Engineering Firm Performance, *International Journal of Technology Management*, 44(3/4): 373–90.

—— Berggren, C. (2008) The Integrator's New Advantage – Reassessing Outsourcing and Production Competence in a Global Telecom Firm, *European Management Journal*, 26: 314–24.

—— Dabhilkar, M. (2009) Manufacturing Outsourcing and Its Effect on Plant Performance: Lessons for KIBS Outsourcing, *Journal of Evolutionary Economics*, 19(2): 231–57.

—— von Haartman, R. and Dabhilkar, M. (2009) Low-cost vs. Innovation: Contrasting Outsourcing and Integration Strategies in Manufacturing, *Creativity and Innovation Management*, 18(1): 35–47.

Berggren, C. and Bengtsson, L. (2004) Rethinking Outsourcing in Manufacturing: A Tale of Two Telecom Firms, *European Management Journal*, 22(2): 211–23.

Bessant, J., Kaplinsky, R., Lamming, R. (2003) Putting Supply Chain Learning into Practice, *International Journal of Operations & Production Management*, 23(2): 167–84.

Boer, H., Berger, A., Chapman, R. and Gertsen, F. (eds.) (2000) *CI Changes: From Suggestion Box to Organisational Learning. Continuous Improvement in Europe and Australia*, Aldershot: Ashgate Publishing.

de Boer, M., van den Bosch, F. A. J. and Volberda, H. W. (1999) Managing Organizational Knowledge Integration in the Emerging Multimedia Complex, *Journal of Management Studies*, 36(3): 379–98.

Brown, S., Lamming, R., Bessant, J. and Jones, P. (2005) *Strategic Operations Management*, Oxford: Butterworth-Heinemann.

Brusoni, S. and Prencipe, A. (2001) Managing Knowledge in Loosely Coupled Networks: Exploring the Links between Product and Knowledge Dynamics, *Journal of Management Studies*, 38(7): 1019–35.

—— —— Pavitt, K. (2001) Knowledge Specialization, Organizational Coupling and the Boundaries of the Firm: Why Do Firms Know More Than They Make? *Administrative Science Quarterly*, 46: 597–621.

Cachon, G. P. and Harker, P. T. (2002) Competition and Outsourcing with Scale Economics, *Management Science*, 48(10): 1314–33.

Chesbrough, H. W. and Teece, D. J. (2002, originally published 1996) Organizing for Innovation: When Is Virtual Virtuous?, *Harvard Business Review*, 80(8): 127–35.

Choi, E. K. (2007) To Outsource or Not to Outsource in an Integrated World, *International Review of Economics and Finance*, 16(4): 521–7.

Coff, R. W. (1999) When Competitive Advantage Doesn't Lead to Performance: The Resource-based View and Stakeholder Bargaining Power, *Organization Science*, 10(2): 119–33.

Cohen, W. M. and Levinthal, D. A. (1990) Absorptive Capacity: A New Perspective on Learning and Innovation, *Administrative Science Quarterly*, 35: 128–52.

Dabhilkar, M. and Bengtsson, L. (2008) Invest or Divest? On the Relative Improvement Potential in Outsourcing Manufacturing, *Production Planning and Control*, 19(3): 212–28.

Dankbaar, B. (2007) Global Sourcing and Innovation: The Consequences of Losing both Organizational and Geographical Proximity, *European Planning Studies*, 15(2): 271–88.

Espino-Rodriguez, T. F. and Padron-Robaina, V. (2006) A Review of Outsourcing from the Resource-based View of the Firm, *International Journal of Management Reviews*, 8(1): 49–70.

Fifarek, B. J., Veloso, F. M. and Davidson, C. I. (2008) Offshoring Technology Innovation: A Case Study of Rare-Earth Technology, *Journal of Operations Management*, 26(2): 222–38.

GAO (2004) International Trade: Current Government Data Provide Limited Insight into Offshoring of Services, Report No. GAO-04-932, US Government Accountability Office, Washington, DC.

Gilley, K. M. and Rasheed, A. (2000) Making More by Doing Less: An Analysis of Outsourcing and Its Effects on Firm Performance, *Journal of Management*, 26: 763–90.

Grant, R. M. (1996) Toward a Knowledge-based Theory of the Firm, *Strategic Management Journal*, 17(Special Issue: Knowledge and the Firm): 109–22.

Harland, C., Knight, L., Lamming, R. and Walker, H. (2005) Outsourcing: Assessing the Risks and Benefits for Organisations, Sectors and Nations, *International Journal of Operations & Production Management*, 2(9): 831–50.

Henderson, R. and Clark, K. B. (1990) Architectural Innovation: The Reconfiguration of Existing Product Technologies and the Failure of Established Firms, *Administrative Science Quarterly*, 35: 9–30.

Hoecht, A. and Trott, P. (2006) Innovation Risks of Strategic Outsourcing, *Technovation*, 26: 672–81.

Huang, Y.-A., Chung, H-J. and Lin, C. (2009) R&D Sourcing Strategies: Determinants and Consequences, *Technovation*, 29: 155–69.

Jackson, T., Iloranta, K. and McKenzie, S. (2001) *Profits or Perils? The Bottom Line on Outsourcing*, Arlington: Booz Allen Hamilton Inc.

Kakabadse, A. and Kakabadse, N. (2005) Outsourcing: Current and Future Trends, *Thunderbird International Business Review*, 47(2): 183–204.

Kogut, B. and Zander, U. (1992) Knowledge of the Firm, Combinative Capabilities, and the Replication of Technology, *Organization Science*, 3(3, Focused Issue: Management of Technology, Aug. 1992): 383–97.

Koufteros, X., Vonderembse, M. and Jayaram, J. (2005) Internal and External Integration for Product Development – The Contingency Effects of Uncertainty, Equivocality and Platform Strategy, *Decision Sciences*, 36(1): 97–133.

Lakemond, N., Berggren, C. and van Weele, A. (2006) Coordinating Supplier Involvement in Product Development Projects: A Differentiated Coordination Typology, *R&D Management*, 36(1): 55–66.

Lane, P. J. and Lubatkin, M. (1998) Relative Absorptive Capacity and Interorganizational Learning, *Strategic Management Journal*, 19(5): 461–77.

——— Koka, B. R. and Pathak, S. (2006) The Reification of Absorptive Capacity: A Critical Review and Rejuvenation of the Construct, *Academy of Management Review*, 31(4): 833–63.

Laugen, B. T., Acur, N., Boer, H. and Frick, J. (2005) Best Manufacturing Practices. What Do the Best-performing Companies Do? *International Journal of Operations & Production Management*, 25(2): 131–50.

Mathews, J. A. (2003) Strategizing by Firms in the Presence of Markets for Resources, *Industrial and Corporate Change*, 12(6): 1157–93.

McIvor, R. (2005) *The Outsourcing Process*, Cambridge: Cambridge University Press.

McKinsey Global Survey Results (2008) Managing Global Supply Chains, *McKinsey Quarterly*, July: 1–9.

Medina, C. C., Lavado, A. C. and Cabrera, R. V. (2005) Characteristics of Innovative Companies: A Case Study of Companies in Different Sectors, *Creativity and Innovation Management*, 14(3): 272–87.

Mol, M. J., Pauwels, P., Matthyssens, P. and Quintens, L. (2004) A Technological Contingency Perspective on the Depth and Scope of International Outsourcing, *Journal of International Management*, 10: 287–305.

Mol, M. J., van Tulder, R. J. M. and Beije, P. R. (2005) Antecedents and Performance Consequences of International Outsourcing, *International Business Review*, 14: 599–617.

Myers, M. B. and Cheung, M-S. (2008) Sharing Global Supply Chain Knowledge, *MIT Sloan Management Review*, 49(4): 67–73.

Niss, C. (2002) *Knowledge Brokering across the Boundaries of Organisations: An Interactionist Interpretation of a Temporary 'Mirror-organisation'*, Licentiate thesis, Stockholm: Royal Institute of Technology.

Nonaka, I. (1994) A Dynamic Theory of Organizational Knowledge Creation, *Organization Science*, 5(1): 14–37.

Olausson, D. (2009) *Facing Interface Challenges in Complex Product Development*, PhD Dissertation, Linköping University.

Prencipe, A. (2000) Breadth and Depth of Technological Capabilities in CoPS: The Case of the Aircraft Engine Control System, *Research Policy*, 29: 895–911.

Quinn, J. B. (2000) Outsourcing Innovation: The New Engine of Growth, *Sloan Management Review*, Summer: 13–29.

Rosenzweig, E. D., Roth, A. V. and Dean, J. W. (2003) The Influence of an Integration Strategy on Competitive Capabilities and Business Performance: An Exploratory Study of Consumer Products Manufacturers, *Journal of Operations Management*, 21: 437–56.

Sturgeon, T. J. (2002) Modular Production Networks: A New America Model of Industrial Organization, *Industrial and Corporate Change*, 11(3): 451–96.

Swink, M. (1999) Threats to New Product Manufacturability and the Effects of Development Team Integration Processes, *Journal of Operations Management*, 17: 691–709.

Takeishi, A. (2002) Knowledge Partitioning in the Interfirm Division of Labor: The Case of Automotive Product Development, *Organization Science*, 13(3): 321–38.

Teece, D. J. and G. Pisano (1994) The Dynamic Capabilities of Firms: An Introduction, *Industrial and Corporate Change*, 3(3): 537–56.

The Outsourcing Institute (2005) The Outsourcing Institute's Annual Survey of Outsourcing End Users, Available at http://www.outsourcing.com.

Ulrich, K. T. (1995) The Role of Product Architecture in the Manufacturing Firm, *Research Policy*, 24: 419–40.

——— Ellison, D. J. (2005) Beyond Make-Buy: Internalization and Integration of Design and Production, *Production and Operations Management*, 14(3): 315–30.

von Haartman, R. and Bengtsson, L. (2009) Manufacturing Competence – The Key to Successful Supplier Integration, *International Journal of Manufacturing Technology and Management*, 16(3): 283–99.

Wagner, S. M. and Boutellier, R. (2002) Capabilities for Managing a Portfolio of Supplier Relationships, *Business Horizons*, 45(6): 79–88.

Zahra, S. A. and George, G. (2002) Absorptive Capacity: A Review, Reconceptualization, and Extension, *Academy of Management Review*, 27(2): 185–203.

10

Trade-offs in Make–Buy Decisions: Exploring Operating Realities of Knowledge Integration and Innovation

Mandar Dabhilkar and Lars Bengtsson

This chapter argues that outsourcing manufacturing operations implies trade-offs, a matter that has not been discussed in the antecedent literature. These trade-offs are particularly relevant for firms that compete on innovation, and therefore try to integrate knowledge by involving their new contract manufacturers in innovation and development activities of outsourced parts.

10.1 INTRODUCTION

Management theories that inform make–buy decisions, such as transaction cost economies and the resource-based view, need to be extended to consider a knowledge-based perspective on integration and innovation. One reason is that while transaction cost economies help to decide which activities should be externalized, they provide little information about the boundaries of the firm, since activities still need to be integrated across firms (Brusoni et al., 2001; Ulrich and Ellison, 2005). Another reason is that firms also need to know more than they make. It therefore becomes increasingly difficult to specify what constitutes a firm's core competency. Brusoni et al.'s study (2001) of three aircraft engine manufacturers shows that although these firms outsource the design and manufacturing of the engine's control system, they still are very active in control system research and development. They further stress the need to maintain manufacturing knowledge in order to successfully integrate knowledge and processes after outsourcing.

The work of Brusoni et al. (2001) is written in an innovation management context. Their centre of attention is a firm's ability to introduce radical product and component innovations, and how this relates to outsourcing. However, the decision whether and what to outsource is also a distinct strategic choice in devising an operations strategy (Voss, 2005; Slack and Lewis, 2008). The innovation management and operations strategy interface is not fully compatible in this respect. While the former's focus is mainly on the processes for incremental and radical changes in products and processes (Tidd and Bessant, 2009), the latter's is mainly on trade-offs between competitive priorities, that is, cost, quality, speed, and flexibility (Slack and Lewis, 2008).

The point here is that radical product and component innovation implies a need to focus on competitive priorities such as flexibility and speed, in contrast to cost when devising an operations strategy. Therefore, statements such as 'firms aim to exploit flexibility and to cut costs by outsourcing the production and detailed design of modular components and subsystems', as argued in Brusoni et al. (2001: 599), oversimplify the issues involved. Hence, the purpose of this chapter is to further the work of Brusoni et al. (2001) into realities that emerge in an operations strategy context. Particularly by describing trade-offs that appear in make–buy decisions and exploring the role that strategies for integrating supplier knowledge may play in overcoming them.

This chapter is organized as follows. Section 10.2 summarizes the discourse on trade-offs in operations strategy and in consequence develops a notion of trade-offs in the decision whether to make or to buy. This notion defines the issues involved and explains why trade-offs occur. Section 10.3 describes the research methodology. The empirical analysis is based on survey data from 127 manufacturing firms in Sweden. Section 10.4 presents the findings of this study. Correlation analysis shows that trade-offs do exist in make–buy decisions, especially between cost and flexibility and between cost and speed. Moreover, integration strategies, where knowledge bases across firms are coupled in shared problem-solving efforts, play a limited role in overcoming them. While some trade-offs can be reduced, others are augmented by knowledge integration efforts. Our main point is that many of these trade-offs are unavoidable but since the antecedent literature has turned them a blind eye, we attempt to clarify implicated aspects. Section 10.5 concludes the chapter with a discussion of how these findings add to contemporary research on knowledge integration and innovation, and identifies avenues for further research.

10.2 THEORY DEVELOPMENT AND HYPOTHESES

The idea of trade-offs in operations strategy was introduced by Wickam Skinner in his seminal *Harvard Business Review* articles in 1969 and 1974. The US manufacturing sector was in crisis; in order to prevail, he argued, companies had to handle a set of competitive priorities, namely cost, quality, speed, and flexibility. Firms neglecting to do so, sacrificing performance in some objectives in order to excel in others, would simply end up second best in all. The underlying logic here is that manufacturing plants are viewed as technologically constrained systems, with inherent limitations in equipment, space, process technology, and other resources such as labour and capital. All of these limitations make trade-offs in the decision-making process inevitable. Therefore, to be competitive, a company has to focus its efforts and resources on one specific mission. This type of manufacturing strategy, known as the *focused factory*, advocates ranking strategic objectives and then targeting one objective at a time. The effectiveness of an operations strategy is determined by the degree of consistency among competitive priorities and corresponding decisions regarding operational structure and infrastructure.

However, Skinner's idea of having to make trade-offs when implementing operations strategy has been challenged since the mid-1980s (e.g. Nakane, 1986; Ferdows and De Meyer, 1990). Inspired by the experiences of successful Japanese firms such as Toyota, these scholars have argued that world-class manufacturing implies simultaneous excellence in a number of performance objectives, with no trade-offs between, for example, cost and quality (Schonberger, 1986). A special issue of *Production and Operations Management* (Benningson, 1996; Clark, 1996; Hayes and Pisano, 1996; Skinner, 1996) and two notes in the *Journal of Operations Management* (Schmenner and Swink, 1998; Vastag, 2000) have been instrumental in clarifying the issues involved. In summary, the main thrust of these arguments is that although trade-offs in operations strategy remain on an overall level, certain advanced manufacturing practices can still help to resolve conflicting objectives, such as cost and flexibility, simultaneously. The logic here is that a firm can indeed move from one performance frontier to another, more efficient frontier by world-class manufacturing practices without trade-offs. But as the firm arrives at the new performance frontier, it has to differentiate its offering to the marketplace by finding a unique position on the new frontier, and any move on the new frontier will create a trade-off. Schmenner and Swink (1998) and Vastag (2000) explain the theoretical underpinnings for this: A plant's proximity to its frontier indicates whether it may acquire cumulative capabilities or be subject to trade-offs among capabilities. Manufacturing plants may achieve multiple capabilities simultaneously when they are operating far away from their performance frontiers. However, as a plant approaches its performance frontier (i.e. becomes fully utilized), building capabilities requires more resources and intensifies the need for focus. Thus, the trade-off model is most applicable to firms operating near their performance frontier.

So why is there a need to further understand trade-offs in operations strategy? The above discussion shows that the cumulative and trade-off models coexist in industrial practice and theory. The cumulative model works for firms far away from their performance frontiers. As firms approach these frontiers, the trade-off model is more applicable, as has been empirically validated by Lapre and Scudder (2004). Moreover, there are another two motives for additional trade-off studies. First, despite the deeper understanding of the issues involved, the debate continues (see e.g. Rosenzweig and Roth, 2004). Second, and more important in view of the theme of this book, the trade-offs debate has so far had only an internal focus at a time when outsourced manufacturing has increased tremendously. The trend towards increased outsourcing drives a need to expand the scope of analysis in operations strategy research to a larger share of the supply chain (Hayes, 2002; Gupta et al., 2006). Not only focused factories, that is, focused internal manufacturing operations of the focal firm, but also focused sourcing decisions must be studied. Traditional make–buy literature, inspired by transaction cost economics or the resource-based view, only helps to decide which activities can be externalized, that is, outsourced. However, other outsourcing frameworks that place greater emphasis on integration and innovation aspects show that even though there may be strong reasons to externalize an activity, there are still very strong needs to integrate this activity with other activities, such as product design, within the focal firm (Ulrich and Ellison, 2005). One specifically interesting question is whether and, if so, how the ways firms manage integration requirements affect the trade-off situation. Does efficient external integration represent a complementary capability that mitigates trade-off problems?

The trade-off debate in operations strategy literature is analogous to the interest in innovation literature in finding ways to manage the contradictory requirements of exploiting existing capabilities and exploring new possibilities and solutions (March, 1999). Some assert the inconsistent logic and claim that firms need to build capabilities for either efficiency or innovation (compare the discussion above on cost efficiency versus flexibility as competitive priorities in devising an operations strategy). Others stress the importance of doing both at the same time and nurture the idea of 'dual' or 'ambidextrous' organizations (Birkinshaw and Gibson, 2004; O'Reilly III and Tushman, 2004). This implies that the way firms integrate and how this affects trade-offs may also increase our understanding of mechanisms for managing dual organizations.

The present research idea, to extend the debate over trade-offs in operations strategy into the theoretical domain of make-or-buy decisions, fits well with what constitute the key operations strategy decision areas today. In the work of Slack and Lewis (2008), for example, these decision areas are Capacity, Supply Networks, Process Technology, and Development and Organization. Make-or-buy decisions are a fundamental part of the Supply Networks decision area but, as mentioned earlier, previous studies have failed to consider that outsourcing may imply performance trade-offs. Most of the outsourcing literature is concerned with the advantages or motives for outsourcing, that is, to reduce costs, improve company focus, heighten product quality, increase flexibility, and take advantage of suppliers' greater innovation capability. However, outsourcing also has disadvantages. Outsourcing motives are sometimes in conflict, for example reduced costs and improved flexibility. The present study argues that trade-offs remain in make-or-buy decisions, as for internal manufacturing strategy decisions within the focal plant, and have to be considered when managers are contemplating outsourcing.

10.2.1 Make-or-buy decisions

The theoretical underpinnings for make-or-buy decisions can be traced back to both transaction cost economies (Williamson, 1975, 1985) and the resource-based view of the firm (Barney, 1991; Peteraf, 1993). The former specifies the economic conditions under which an organization should manage an exchange within its boundaries, and the economic conditions that are suitable for managing an exchange externally, that is, outsourcing. The latter views the firm as a bundle of resources that, if employed in distinctive ways, can create competitive advantage. Such distinctive resources are viewed as core business (Prahalad and Hamel, 1990) and should consequently be internalized, whereas non-core resources are candidates for being outsourced, if not too interwoven with core resources.

Make-or-buy decision frameworks that are based on these two theoretical underpinnings usually conclude with a set of decision factors to consider when outsourcing manufacturing: motives for outsourcing, supplier-operating capabilities, part characteristics, and supplier relationship strategies. See, for example, the outsourcing frameworks of Cánez et al. (2000), Holcomb and Hitt (2007), McIvor (2000), Venkatesan (1992), and Vining and Globerman (1999), all of which were reviewed for the present study in order to develop its theoretical framework and hypotheses.

Motives

Motives are dealt with primarily in the work of Cánez et al. (2000). They argue that the external environment, over which the company has little or no influence, usually creates situations that lead to motives for the make-or-buy analysis.

For instance, increased price competition in the marketplace can be viewed as a trigger that usually forces companies to reduce costs (a motive for outsourcing). Cánez et al. (2000) list a wide range of motives that can be grouped into five distinct subsets: reduce costs, increase focus, improve quality, increase flexibility, and increase innovation capability.

First, the cost motive: reduced costs can be achieved if the supplier provides goods or services to many customers, often referred to as external economies of scale. Lower costs are also achievable if, for example, the focal firm turns to suppliers that operate in countries with lower wages. Second, the focus motive: performance at the focal firm can be improved by outsourcing non-core activities to external suppliers and focusing more on core activities. Third, the quality motive: outsourcing partners generally have more experience manufacturing the specific parts and can therefore provide higher quality. Fourth, the flexibility motive inspires the focal firm to improve its responsiveness to variability in demand by outsourcing peak demand to suppliers. Fifth and finally, the innovation motive causes the focal firm to take advantage of the supplier's higher innovation capability, to improve the overall performance of its end product.

Supplier operating and innovation capabilities

All five of the reviewed outsourcing frameworks indicate that the supplier's operating capabilities are important to consider in the make-or-buy analysis, a natural consequence of the need in outsourcing to find a partner that complements the capabilities of the focal firm. Four such capabilities are identified: volume, design for manufacturing, purchasing scale, and low-wage operations.

If the supplier has a higher total volume of the outsourced parts, this can lead to lower fixed costs per unit. A common production platform that supplies several customers contributes to increased utilization of plant space and machinery, for example. This also implies that the supplier should be better able to cope with changes in individual customers' volumes, since demand is aggregated for several customers. Higher volumes can also lead to lower variable costs for the supplier, who learns from the experience. In addition, manufacturing the outsourced parts is often a core competence and prioritized activity at the supplier level. Therefore, the supplier should be able to achieve higher operating performance levels in areas such as product quality.

Engineering/design capability for outsourced parts can lead to lower variable costs. By designing the same kind of parts for several customers, the supplier can alter product design to incorporate cheaper and better components. Standardizing manufacturing processes in turn leads to additional possibilities for continuous improvements.

Purchasing capability for outsourced parts can lead to lower variable costs; the increased buying power allows the supplier to get pre-specified components for several customers at lower cost.

Operations in low-wage countries can lead to lower variable costs. However, this presupposes labour-intensive manufacturing.

Part characteristics

The reviewed frameworks highlight two types of part characteristics as critical to consider in the make-or-buy analysis: the degree of standardization and the level of complexity. Standard parts can be linked to having low asset specificity (Vining and Globerman, 1999). These parts are a clear case for outsourcing, which offers the potential for lower production costs for the product, as well as minimal bargaining. Complexity in manufacturing and design is linked to technological uncertainty, according to Holcomb and Hitt (2007). Increasing levels of uncertainty, they argue, entail growing information deficits that reduce cost economies and increase the difficulty of inter-firm collaboration.

Supplier relationship strategies

Three of the reviewed frameworks acknowledge the importance of developing supplier relationship strategies when outsourcing manufacturing (Cánez et al., 2000; McIvor, 2000; Holcomb and Hitt, 2007). Buyer and supplier interaction improves the likelihood of leveraging the supplier's operating capabilities. For example, McIvor (2000) asserts that the sourcing organization should adopt an appropriate relationship strategy, which will be influenced primarily by the potential for *opportunism* in the relationship (i.e. the supplier is taking advantage of the situation). Arms-length relationships are preferable in cases when the potential for opportunism is low, just as closer collaborative relationships are preferable when this potential is high.

Another aspect, not included in the scrutinized outsourcing frameworks, concerns how the needs and prerequisites of knowledge integration relate to different supplier relationship strategies. Previous studies have stressed the significance of establishing proper integration mechanisms across borders when dealing with interdependent processes (e.g. Ulrich and Ellison, 2005). Similarly, intimate and early involvement of suppliers has been shown to be effective for integrating activities and knowledge in complex product development processes (e.g. Clark and Fujimoto, 1991; Petersen et al., 2005; Lakemond et al., 2006). This analysis has been further advanced in modularity literature that makes a distinction between integral and modular products (Ulrich, 1995) and in studies on how the extent and character of interdependencies between different design and production stages affect the needs of integration (Baldwin, 2008). These studies imply that product characteristics and the extent and kind of interdependencies between activities outsourced and those maintained in-house have a strong impact on the need of knowledge integration and supplier involvement.

10.2.2 Trade-offs in make-or-buy decisions

In summary, exploiting capabilities at the supplier stage is a major issue in make-or-buy decisions. That is, the goal is to push the manufacturing process of outsourced parts as close as possible to a supplier's performance frontiers by leveraging the supplier's operating capabilities. This closeness to the supplier's performance frontiers makes trade-offs inevitable when outsourcing manufacturing. In addition, the discussion above about the need for assessing part characteristics in the make-or-buy decision shows that flexibility which involves enhancing value for customers through adding unique product features is likely to increase costs. The increased complexity inherent in demands for higher flexibility will generally reduce the supplier's ability to operate cost efficiently. Complexity dilutes the impact of reduced costs associated with other cost drivers, such as economies of scale. Therefore, customer demands for higher flexibility make it difficult to realize economies of scale, which is also why trade-offs remain in the make-or-buy decision.

Surprisingly, hardly any study in the previous make-or-buy literature investigates the issue of trade-offs. One exception is the work of Cáncz et al. (2000), which proposes a process for weighting and rating make-or-buy decision factors. Their work is an important first step but needs to be expanded to better fit the perception of trade-offs in the operations strategy literature and shift the focus from make-or-buy decision factors to performance objectives. In the operations strategy literature, a trade-off is perceived as a sacrifice in one performance objective in order to achieve excellence in another objective. Moreover, structural and infrastructural factors cause these trade-offs to occur as resources are constrained (Slack and Lewis, 2008: 54). The notion of trade-offs in make-or-buy decisions we propose here involves a definition of these trade-offs as well as an explanation for why they occur.

In order to excel in a particular performance objective when outsourcing manufacturing, companies have to sacrifice performance in other objectives to some extent. Trade-offs in make-or-buy decisions occur in two distinct ways: as a choice between different performance objectives, but caused by the same make-or-buy decision factor, or between different make-or-buy decision factors, but within the same performance objective. Make-or-buy decision factors that cause these trade-offs are mainly related to the supplier's operating capabilities or the characteristics of the outsourced parts. Improvements in one objective occur at the expense of another because supplier resources are finite. Exploiting supplier operating capabilities implies pushing the outsourced process as close as possible to the supplier's performance frontiers. In addition, certain characteristics of outsourced parts, such as complexity, dilute the impact of other performance drivers like economies of scale, which is also why trade-offs are inevitable in outsourced manufacturing.

One of the main points in the coming analysis is, however, that the trade-offs are affected by the supplier integration strategies applied. The reason is that these strategies may mitigate the knowledge integration requirements that follow from outsourcing decisions.

10.2.3 Hypotheses

This notion of trade-offs in make-or-buy decisions brings up two different kinds of hypothesis. One kind concerns whether or not outsourcing implies that improvements in one performance objective entail sacrifices in another objective. The other kind concerns how trade-offs are affected by the supplier integration strategies.

The first research question is: Does outsourcing imply trade-offs between performance objectives, and if so, between which performance objectives? Hypothesis development in this respect must start with acknowledging Krause et al.'s work (2001) on measures for competitive priorities in purchasing. Their research shows a need to add innovation to the more traditional competitive priorities of cost, quality, speed, and flexibility. But are there trade-offs between these performance objectives? Krause et al.'s work relates to a body of research on the importance of involving the purchasing function in strategic decision-making (Carr and Pearson, 1999; Shin et al., 2000; Narasimhan and Das, 2001; Chen et al., 2004; González-Benito, 2007). While this empirical research clearly shows that high involvement by the purchasing function contributes to improved manufacturing performance, to date it has overlooked the issue of trade-offs. As an example, Narasimhan and Das (2001) treat manufacturing performance as a composite construct, encompassing cost, quality, speed, flexibility, and innovation performance. Therefore, hypothesis development must be based on more conceptual research. Helpful here is the work of Cousins et al. (2008: 107), who argue that quality has become an order qualifier and implies a trade-off in strategic supply issues mainly between cost on the one hand and speed, flexibility, and innovation on the other. In consequence, four hypotheses are tested in the present study:

H1: When outsourcing manufacturing, there is no trade-off between cost and quality.
H2: When outsourcing manufacturing, there is a trade-off between cost and speed.
H3: When outsourcing manufacturing, there is a trade-off between cost and flexibility.
H4: When outsourcing manufacturing, there is a trade-off between cost and innovation.

The second research question concerns integration strategies. As elaborated in previous sections, it is likely that the adoption of appropriate supplier integration strategies expands the firm's capabilities and thus pushes the performance frontier. In this way, the supplier integration strategy may mitigate some of the trade-offs that appear at lower performance levels. The appropriateness of integration strategy is affected by product characteristics and the interdependences between separated activities. Two hypotheses will be tested:

H5: Identified performance trade-offs when outsourcing manufacturing are mitigated by the extent of supplier integration.
H6: The impact of supplier integration on trade-offs depends on product complexity.

10.3 RESEARCH METHODOLOGY

10.3.1 Sample and data collection approach

A postal survey was distributed to a disproportionately stratified random sample of 563 manufacturing plants that are part of Swedish engineering companies (see Table 10.1). This sampling technique is proposed when the population consists of subgroups of different sizes (Forza, 2002). After two reminders, 267 of the targeted plants returned the instrument, yielding an overall response rate of 47 per cent. However, the data analysis presented in this chapter is based on just the 136

Table 10.1 Sample characteristics and response rate

	Stratum (number of employees)					
	50–99	100–199	200–499	500–999	1,000+	$\sum$
Population (ISIC 28–35)	466	241	155	48	28	938
Target sample	188	144	155	48	28	563
Answered the survey	80	77	69	24	17	267
Response rate	43%	53%	45%	50%	61%	47%
Focus in this study: Has outsourced manufacturing operations during the last three years (No = 0/Yes = 1)	34	44	33	15	10	136
Omitted: Having incomplete responses on outsourcing, being a too influential observer or an outlier	1	4	2	1	1	127

Note: Key to ISIC codes: 28 = fabricated metal products; 29 = machinery and equipment; 30 = office machinery and computers; 31 = electrical machinery and apparatus not elsewhere classified; 32 = radio, television, and communication equipment and apparatus; 33 = medical, precision and optical instruments, watches, and clocks; 34 = manufacture of motor vehicles, trailers, and semi-trailers; 35 = other transport equipment.

manufacturing plants that responded as having outsourced manufacturing operations during the previous three-year period. Therefore, the actual response rate is 24 per cent. Outsourcing manufacturing was defined as having an external supplier provide parts or 'a family of parts' that formerly were manufactured internally (Cánez et al., 2000).

Statistics Sweden's *Business Register* 2003 of manufacturing plants with more than fifty employees within ISIC codes 28–35 was used as the sample frame. Data were collected during early spring 2004; in this article, the phrase *the studied three-year period* stands for the calendar years 2001, 2002, and 2003. The unit of analysis was manufacturing plants of engineering companies. In order to detect response bias, researchers tried to come in contact with a random sample of ninety-eight plants that after two reminders declined to fill in the form and return it. These plants were contacted by telephone. Thirty-four plants agreed to answer five key questions from the original instrument in the following three topic areas: the strategic role of the manufacturing function, the degree of outsourcing manufacturing, and plant performance. This enabled a comparison between those that participated in the survey and those that did not. No significant response bias was detected.

10.3.2 Measuring outsourcing performance

We measured five different outsourcing performance indicators (OPIs): cost, quality, speed, flexibility, and innovation. The question was posed as follows: 'What was the effect of your outsourcing initiative on the following performance indicators?' A seven-point Likert scale was used for each indicator (-3 = much worse, 0 = no effects, 3 = much better). Cost was measured as 'cost for outsourced part(s)', quality as 'quality', speed as 'lead time from order to delivery for your final product', flexibility as the 'ability to manage fluctuations in demand', and innovation as 'new functionality in outsourced part(s)'.

While this approach is a standard procedure for measuring performance in operations management research, it does have the major drawback of not guarding against the halo effect, which is a sort of rater bias (Thorndike, 1920). This bias arises from a rater's perception of a particular question being influenced by his or her perception of former questions in a sequence of interpretations. This means that, because of an overall impression, raters tend to rate performance generally high or low, with little differentiation. While there has been considerable discussion in the operations management literature on the need to improve constructs for measuring performance, there are still no established methods, which is why the standard procedure was used in this research. In order to counteract the impact of the halo effect, the present study used an approach developed by Boyer and Lewis (2002) that entails a transformation of the OPIs. The transformed OPI (e.g. cost) equals the difference between the untransformed OPI for cost and the average for all five OPIs, divided by the standard deviation for all five OPIs.

According to Boyer and Lewis (2002), this transformation leads to positive numbers for performance indicators that are above average and negative numbers for those that are below average. It also provides a more sensitive weighting of indicators by identifying the relative importance of various indicators for respondents whose ratings are very similar for all indicators (i.e. they tend to rate things similarly, within a tight cluster).

10.3.3 Measuring supplier integration

Supplier integration was estimated from the respondent's response to the following instruction: 'Please indicate how the following statements apply to the collaboration with your most important suppliers.'

(A) Our most important suppliers contribute early in the product development process.
(B) We pursue joint efforts to reduce costs.
(C) We give suppliers access to manufacturing plans and systems.
(D) They (suppliers) contribute to significant product improvements.
(E) We cooperate actively to integrate our manufacturing processes.

Each statement was measured on a five-point scale. A factor analysis revealed that all five variables load on the same factor (Cronbach's alpha 0.83).

10.4 FINDINGS

10.4.1 Results of performance analysis

In order to test the first four hypotheses, data were subjected to correlation analysis. Descriptive statistics for the outsourcing performance variables are

Table 10.2 Descriptive statistics for the outsourcing performance variables

	Descriptive statistics for untransformed data				Descriptive statistics for transformed data			
	Mean	Standard deviation	Min	Max	Mean	Standard deviation	Min	Max
Cost	4.95	1.44	1	7	0.55	0.99	−1.79	1.79
Quality	4.02	1.07	1	7	−0.34	0.71	−1.79	1.79
Speed	3.99	1.12	1	7	−0.31	0.78	−1.64	1.79
Flexibility	5.00	1.02	2	7	0.49	0.84	−1.23	1.79
Innovation	3.99	0.63	1	6	−0.39	0.55	−1.79	1.04

Table 10.3 Correlations among outsourcing performance objectives (transformed data and re-centred correlations)

	Cost	Quality	Speed	Flexibility	Innovation
Cost	1.00				
Quality	0.11	1.00			
Speed	−0.20	0.01	1.00		
Flexibility	−0.24	−0.10	0.17	1.00	
Innovation	0.01	0.07	0.09	0.18	1.00

Note: $^*p < 0.05$; $^{**}p < 0.01$ (two-tailed). Transformed data represent each respondent's response = (Performance objective − Respondent average)/Respondent standard deviation. The final correlations have been re-centred by taking the transformed correlations and subtracting the average correlation of transformed data in simulation (−0.25).

shown in Table 10.2. The results of the correlation analysis are shown in Table 10.3, which is confined to transformed variables that have been re-centred.

The results suggest support for Hypothesis 1: There is no trade-off between cost and quality when outsourcing manufacturing. They also suggest support for Hypothesis 2: There is a trade-off between cost and speed when outsourcing manufacturing. The negative correlation coefficient is well below 0 ($r = -0.20$). It would have been convenient to know whether this correlation coefficient is statistically significant but subtracting the re-centring value from the correlation coefficient prevents this. That is a drawback with Boyer and Lewis's approach (2002); further research is needed to overcome this. Meanwhile, one has to rely on intuition and related work, for example Dabhilkar et al. (2009), which clearly shows that the make-or-buy decision factor 'outsourcing to low-wage countries' improves cost performance but has a negative effect on speed.

Moving on, the results suggest support for Hypothesis 3: There is a trade-off between cost and flexibility when outsourcing manufacturing. This negative correlation coefficient is also well below 0 ($r = -0.24$). It is possible to trace this trade-off to the make-or-buy decision factor 'complexity in manufacturing' because firms that prioritize costs do not outsource complex manufacturing to the same extent as those which focus on improving flexibility. Firms whose dominant operations objective is flexibility tend to have products in early phases of the product life cycle. High customization and frequent design changes, which add complexity to the system, are important in winning orders, since competition is often based on novel products or specific part characteristics (Slack and Lewis, 2008).

Surprisingly, the study finds no support for Hypothesis 4: There is no trade-off between cost and innovation when outsourcing manufacturing, at least when we measure performance at component level. This result contrasts with the previous literature on strategic sourcing, which states unequivocally that innovation is an additional competitive priority that cannot be disregarded (Krause et al., 2001) and that it forms, together with speed and flexibility, the responsiveness end of Fisher's cost efficiency (1997) versus responsiveness spectrum (cf. Cousins et al., 2008). We speculate, in retrospect, that innovation is a distinct competitive priority that nevertheless need not be traded for cost. Suppliers should be able to offer both new functionality and improved cost if the parts are within their core competence and they are also operating with economies of scale. Thus, the point here is not whether or not there is a cost versus innovation trade-off but that cost and innovation are distinct competitive priorities when outsourcing manufacturing and they require different strategies. This interpretation is supported by Bengtsson et al.'s study (2009), which extracted firms with focus on either low-cost-oriented outsourcing or innovation-oriented outsourcing; the two groups had very different performance outcomes on costs and innovation. In addition, Dabhilkar et al.'s study (2009) shows that improved cost is predominantly associated with outsourcing non-complex products to low-wage countries, whereas innovation is associated with outsourcing standardized parts to suppliers with higher volumes and high engineering/design capability that are located near the focal plants (in the case of this study, in Sweden). Accordingly, there is no trade-off as defined in this study, that is, between cost and innovation performance. Nevertheless, a particular strategy is needed for each objective, a related issue that is outside the scope of this article.

On the whole, however, the study finds that the make-or-buy decision does involve trade-offs between different performance objectives. Also, this study's proposed definition of trade-offs in make-or-buy decisions has empirical support. Taken together with the empirical evidence in Dabhilkar et al. (2009) on how trade-offs occur in make-or-buy decisions, that is, between different objectives but caused by the same decision factor, or between different decision factors but within the same objective, the whole notion of trade-offs in make-or-buy decisions as proposed in this study has empirical support. The main implication of this is that current theory on trade-offs in operations strategy (e.g. Slack and Lewis, 2008) can be extended to the domain of make-or-buy decisions. Particularly pertinent are the trade-offs between cost and speed and between cost and flexibility.

10.4.2 The impact of supplier integration strategies

The second research question places a particular emphasis on knowledge integration and innovation. Since not all firms compete with innovation and therefore do not try to involve their suppliers in new product development, the statistical computations in the further analysis are limited to this sample.

Table 10.4 Effects of supplier integration on trade-offs

		Degree of supplier integration	
		Low	High
N	127	57	68
Cost vs. Quality	0.11	0.15	0.07
Cost vs. Speed	−0.20	0.01	−0.34
Cost vs. Flexibility	−0.24	−0.43	−0.10
Cost vs. Innovation	0.01	0.00	0.01

Note: Re-centred correlation coefficients are shown.

The hypothesis concerns whether or not supplier integration mitigates the identified trade-offs. A high degree of supplier integration means that suppliers contribute early in the process of developing new products, buyers and sellers make joint efforts to reduce costs, suppliers have access to manufacturing plans and systems, suppliers contribute to the improvement of products, and buyers and sellers integrate their manufacturing processes.

Table 10.4 shows the impact of supplier integration on the trade-offs. The results of statistical computations are, however, ambiguous and not easy to interpret. While a high degree of supplier integration increases the cost vs. speed trade-off, it reduces the cost vs. flexibility trade-off. The latter provides partial support for Hypothesis 5.

A possible explanation for the ambiguous results is that our supplier integration construct involves aspects of both new product development and mutual adaptation of manufacturing processes. It is possible that high integration in terms of close collaboration in new product development augments the inherent tension between cost and speed. This interpretation is supported by Swink's study (1999), which showed that too intimate and early supplier involvement may retard product development processes. On the other hand, high integration in terms of mutual adaptation of production processes may resolve the tension between cost and flexibility. Thus, the intensification of the trade-off between cost and speed seems to be related to collaboration in new product development.

It is likely that the reason why trade-offs remain in make–buy decisions is that while there may be good motives for externalizing a manufacturing activity, there is still a need for integration, for example, between R&D and manufacturing activities. To illustrate the latter, Table 10.5 shows how the cost vs. speed trade-off is increased when products are customized.

Table 10.5 shows that the correlation coefficient for the cost vs. speed trade-off becomes increasingly negative as the order fulfilment practice requires a growing element of design changes. This result provides some support for Hypothesis 6, while the process of design to order likely includes more complex and interdependent processes.

In conclusion, the results indicate that supplier integration may mitigate the trade-off between cost and flexibility, while the trade-off between cost and speed remains despite the integration efforts, and forces firms to make a choice.

Table 10.5 Order fulfilment practice and intensification of trade-offs

		Order fulfilment practice				
		Make to stock	Assemble to order	Produce to order	Configure to order	Design to order
N	127	27	26	59	11	3
Cost vs. Speed	−0.20	0.01	−0.17	−0.24	−0.34	−0.65
Cost vs. Flexibility	−0.24	−0.25	−0.07	−0.31	−0.24	−0.71

Note: Re-centred correlation coefficients are shown. Respondents were asked: 'Which of the following alternatives best describe operations at your plant?' Scale: 1 = Make to stock, 2 = Assemble to order, 3 = Produce to order, 4 = Configure to order, 5 = Design to order.

10.4.3 Assessing validity

The influences of plant size and process choice were controlled for in order to assess the validity of the findings. Plant size is measured according to the sample stratification and process choice following the example in Safizadeh et al. (2000).

Table 10.6 shows that the correlation coefficients remain negative for all size strata. Thus, it is possible to generalize to the whole sample. One exception is Cost versus Speed for plants with more than 1,000 employees, where the correlation coefficient is close to zero.

Tables 10.7 and 10.8 show that correlation coefficients remain negative and well below zero for almost all process types over both machining and assembly operations, enabling generalization to the whole sample. Exceptions occur in the Cost versus Speed trade-off in two situations: fixed position in machining operations and lines in assembly operations. The reason for differentiating between machining and assembly operations is that the survey instrument did not assume the same process choice for both kinds, even when they existed within the same plant. Therefore, two separate questions were posed, one for machining and the other for assembly operations.

10.5 CONCLUSIONS

While the debate over trade-offs in operations strategy has been restricted to date to inside the focal firm's factory walls, the present study extends this research to

Table 10.6 Controlling for plant size

		Plant size				
		50–99	100–199	200–499	500–999	1,000+
N	127	34	39	31	14	9
Cost vs. Speed	−0.20	−0.27	−0.18	−0.24	−0.30	−0.02
Cost vs. Flexibility	−0.24	−0.16	−0.28	−0.32	−0.12	−0.36

Note: Re-centred correlation coefficients are shown.

Table 10.7 Controlling for process choice in machining operations

		Process choice, machining operations				
		Fixed position	Functional workshops	Flow groups	Lines	N/A
N	127	5	44	47	10	18
Cost vs. Speed	−0.20	0.12	−0.30	−0.17	−0.22	−0.11
Cost vs. Flexibility	−0.24	−0.73	−0.31	−0.15	−0.05	−0.32

Note: Re-centred correlation coefficients are shown. Respondents were asked: 'Which process type is mainly used for your most important product in your machining operations?' Scale: 1 = Fixed position, 2 = Functional workshops, 3 = Flow groups, 4 = Lines, N/A = No machining operations exist.

Table 10.8 Controlling for process choice in assembly operations

		Process choice, assembly operations				
		Fixed position	Functional workshops	Flow groups	Lines	N/A
N	127	21	22	56	19	7
Cost vs. Speed	−0.20	−0.32	−0.32	−0.16	0.14	−0.42
Cost vs. Flexibility	−0.24	−0.16	−0.15	−0.30	−0.38	−0.21

Note: Re-centred correlation coefficients are shown. Respondents were asked: 'Which process type is mainly used for your most important product in your assembly operations?' Scale: 1 = Fixed position, 2 = Functional workshops, 3 = Flow groups, 4 = Lines, N/A = No assembly operations exist.

the supply chain, by addressing trade-offs in make–buy decisions. The chapter has shown the importance of understanding trade-offs in terms of operating realities for the kind of firms we target in this anthology, namely those that compete with innovation, and therefore try to integrate knowledge by involving their new contract manufacturers in the innovation and development activities of outsourced parts. For these firms, flexibility and speed are particularly important competitive priorities; when outsourcing is used to strengthen their competitiveness, gains in these areas are achieved at the expense of cost reduction. This is in sharp contrast to the antecedent literature, which mainly lists the advantages of outsourcing, that is, improvements in cost, quality, speed, flexibility, and innovation, but fails to consider that in real life these motives tend to conflict.

The reason why conflicts occur between outsourcing drivers is that even when an activity is externalized, that is, outsourced, it still has to be integrated across firms and fulfil a need in the buying firm. This reality is a blind spot in the traditional make–buy literature, which is mainly concerned with aiding decisions about which activities to externalize and which suppliers to select. A knowledge-based view of the firm brings it to the fore because that places greater emphasis on (re-)integration needs and innovation aspects.

The empirical analysis shows that trade-offs remain in make–buy decisions, especially between cost and flexibility, and cost and speed. It also shows, when different groups of firms are compared, that knowledge integration in terms of collaboration between outsourcing firms and their suppliers reduces some trade-offs but intensifies others. The cost vs. flexibility trade-off is reduced in this case, while the cost vs. speed trade-off is intensified. A possible explanation is that the construct measuring knowledge integration contains both operational and strategic aspects of supplier relationship strategies. Close operational collaboration, for example sharing production plans, can reduce the cost vs. flexibility trade-off. However, strategic collaboration aspects, for example joint new product development, intensify the already strained tension between cost and speed performance that is so common in the development of new products. It is important for future research to study integration mechanisms that aid in reducing the identified trade-offs when outsourcing manufacturing. In addition, research should examine the dynamics of these relationships to show whether and how the stage of the life cycle of the product (e.g. early vs. late) affects the nature and extent of the key trade-offs identified here.

In summary, our main point is that technology-based firms that compete with innovation often have to involve their new suppliers in the innovation and development activities of outsourced parts. However, when doing so, they have to consider that they cannot 'have it all' as the existing management literature often claims. As this chapter has shown, they may gain in speed, which is important to firms of this kind, but not simultaneously reduce the cost of outsourced parts. The management implications of these research findings are discussed in Chapter 12.

ACKNOWLEDGEMENTS

Christian Daum and Maryam Memarzadeh participated in early phases of this study and assisted in statistical computations and simulations.

REFERENCES

Baldwin, C. Y. (2008) Where Do Transactions Come from? Modularity, Transactions, and the Boundaries of the Firm, *Industrial and Corporate Change*, 17(1): 155–95.

Barney, J. (1991) Firm Resources and Sustained Competitive Advantage, *Journal of Management*, 17(1): 99–120.

Bengtsson, L., von Haartman, R. and Dabhilkar, M. (2009) Low-cost vs. Innovation: Contrasting Outsourcing and Integration Strategies in Manufacturing, *Creativity and Innovation Management*, 18(1): 35–47.

Benningson, L. (1996) Changing Manufacturing Strategy, *Production and Operations Management*, 5(1): 91–102.

Birkinshaw, J. and Gibson, C. (2004) Building Ambidexterity into an Organization, *MIT Sloan Management Review*, 45(4): 47–55.

Boyer, K. K. and Lewis, M. W. (2002) Competitive Priorities: Investigating the Need for Trade-offs in Operations Strategy, *Production and Operations Management*, 11(1): 9–20.

Brusoni, S., Prencipe, A., and Pavitt, K. (2001) Knowledge Specialization, Organizational Coupling, and the Boundaries of the Firm: Why Do Firms Know More than they Make? *Administrative Science Quarterly*, 46(4): 597–621.

Cánez, L. E., Platts, K. W. and Probert, D. R. (2000) Developing a Framework for Make-or-Buy Decisions, *International Journal of Operations & Production Management*, 20(11): 1313–30.

Carr, A. S. and Pearson, J. N. (1999) Strategically Managed Buyer-Supplier Relationships and Performance Outcomes, *Journal of Operations Management*, 17(5): 497–519.

Chen, I. J., Paulraj, A. and Lado, A. A. (2004) Strategic Purchasing, Supply Management, and Firm Performance, *Journal of Operations Management*, 22(5): 505–23.

Clark, K. (1996) Competing through Manufacturing and the New Manufacturing Paradigm: Is Manufacturing Strategy Passé? *Production and Operations Management*, 5(1): 42–58.

—— Fujimoto, T. (1991) *Product Development Performance: Strategy, Organization and Management in the World Auto Industry*, Cambridge, MA: Harvard Business School Press.

Cousins, P. D., Lamming, R., Lawson, B. and Squire, B. (2008) *Strategic Supply Management: Principles, Theories and Practice*, Harlow, UK: Pearson Education.

Dabhilkar, M., Bengtsson, L., von Haartman, R. and Åhlström, P. (2009) Supplier Selection or Collaboration? Determining Factors of Performance Improvement when Outsourcing Manufacturing, *Journal of Purchasing and Supply Management*, 15(3): 143–53.

Ferdows, K. and De Meyer, A. (1990) Lasting Improvements in Manufacturing Performance: In Search of a New Theory, *Journal of Operations Management*, 9(2): 168–84.

Fisher, M. L. (1997) What Is the Right Supply Chain for Your Product? *Harvard Business Review*, 75(2): 105–16.

Forza, C. (2002) Survey Research in Operations Management: A Process-based Perspective, *International Journal of Operations & Production Management*, 22(2): 152–94.

González-Benito, J. (2007) A Theory of Purchasing's Contribution to Business Performance, *Journal of Operations Management*, 25(4): 901–17.

Gupta, S., Verma, R. and Victorino, L. (2006) Empirical Research Published in *Production and Operations Management* (1992–2005): Trends and Future Research Directions, *Production and Operations Management*, 15(3): 432–48.

Hayes, R. H. (2002) Challenges Posed to Operations Management by the 'New Economy', *Production and Operations Management*, 11(1): 21–32.

—— Pisano, G. (1996) Manufacturing Strategy at the Intersection of Two Paradigm Shifts, *Production and Operations Management*, 5(1): 25–41.

Holcomb, T. R. and Hitt, M. A. (2007) Toward a Model of Strategic Outsourcing, *Journal of Operations Management*, 25(2): 464–81.

Krause, D. R., Pagell, M. and Curkovic, S. (2001) Toward a Measure of Competitive Priorities for Purchasing, *Journal of Operations Management*, 19(4): 497–512.

Lakemond, N., Berggren, C. and van Weele, A. (2006) Coordinating Supplier Involvement in Product Development Projects: A Differentiated Coordination Typology, *R&D Management*, 36(1): 55–66.

Lapre, M. A. and Scudder, G. D. (2004) Performance Improvement Paths in the US Airline Industry: Linking Trade-offs to Asset Frontiers, *Production and Operations Management*, 13(2): 123–34.

March, J. G. (1999) *The Pursuit of Organizational Intelligence*, Oxford: Blackwell Business.

McIvor, R. (2000) A Practical Framework for Understanding the Outsourcing Process, *Supply Chain Management: An International Journal*, 5(1): 22–36.

Nakane, J. (1986) *Manufacturing Futures Survey in Japan: A Comparative Survey 1983–1986*, Tokyo: Waseda University.

Narasimhan, R. and Das, A. (2001) The Impact of Purchasing Integration and Practices on Manufacturing Performance, *Journal of Operations Management*, 19(5): 593–609.

O'Reilly III, C. A. and Tushman, M. L. (2004) The Ambidextrous Organization, *Harvard Business Review*, 82(4): 74–82.

Peteraf, M. A. (1993) The Cornerstones of Competitive Advantage: A Resource-based View, *Strategic Management Journal*, 14(3): 179–91.

Petersen, K. J., Handfield, R. B. and Ragatz, G. L. (2005) Supplier Integration into New Product Development: Coordinating Product, Process and Supply Chain Design, *Journal of Operations Management*, 23: 371–88.

Prahalad, C. K. and Hamel, G. (1990) The Core Competence of the Corporation, *Harvard Business Review*, 68(3): 79–91.

Rosenzweig, E. D. and Roth, A. V. (2004) Towards a Theory of Competitive Progression: Evidence from High-Tech Manufacturing, *Production and Operations Management*, 13(4): 354–68.

Safizadeh, M. H., Ritzman, L. P. and Mallick, D. (2000) Revisiting Alternative Theoretical Paradigms in Manufacturing Strategy, *Production and Operations Management*, 9(2): 111–27.

Schmenner, R. W. and Swink, M. L. (1998) On Theory in Operations Management, *Journal of Operations Management*, 17(1): 97–113.

Schonberger, R. (1986) *World Class Manufacturing: The Lessons of Simplicity Applied*, New York: Free Press.

Shin, H., Collier, D. A. and Wilson, D. D. (2000) Supply Management Orientation and Supplier/Buyer Performance, *Journal of Operations Management*, 18(3): 317–33.

Skinner, W. (1969) Manufacturing: Missing Link in Corporate Strategy, *Harvard Business Review*, 47(3): 136–45.

—— (1974) The Focused Factory, *Harvard Business Review*, 52(3): 113–20.

—— (1996) Manufacturing Strategy on the 'S' Curve, *Production and Operations Management*, 5(1): 3–14.

Slack, N., and Lewis, M. (2008) *Operations Strategy*, Harlow, UK: Financial Times, Prentice-Hall.

Swink, M. (1999) Threats to New Product Manufacturability and the Effects of Development Team Integration Processes, *Journal of Operations Management*, 17(6): 691–709.

Thorndike, E. (1920) A Constant Error on Psychological Ratings, *Journal of Applied Psychology*, 4(1): 25–9.

Tidd, J. and Bessant, J. (2009) *Managing Innovation: Integrating Technological, Market and Organizational Change*, Chicester: John Wiley & Sons.

Ulrich, K. T. (1995) The Role of Product Architecture in the Manufacturing Firm, *Research Policy*, 24: 419–40.

—— Ellison, D. J. (2005) Beyond Make-Buy: Internalization and Integration of Design and Production, *Production and Operations Management*, 14(3): 315–30.

Vastag, G. (2000) The Theory of Performance Frontiers, *Journal of Operations Management*, 18(3): 353–60.

Venkatesan, R. (1992) Strategic Sourcing: To Make or Not to Make, *Harvard Business Review*, 70(6): 98–107.

Vining, A. and Globerman, S. (1999) A Conceptual Framework for Understanding the Outsourcing Decision, *European Management Journal*, 17(6): 645–54.

Voss, C. (2005) Paradigms of Manufacturing Strategy Re-Visited, *International Journal of Operations & Production Management*, 25(12): 1223–7.

Williamson, O. E. (1975) *Markets and Hierarchies*, New York: Free Press.

—— (1985) *The Economic Institutions of Capitalism: Firms, Markets and Relational Contracting*, New York: Free Press.

11

Creative Accumulation: Integrating New and Established Technologies in Periods of Discontinuous Change

Anna Bergek, Christian Berggren, and Thomas Magnusson

This chapter provides insights into the characteristics of the process of creative accumulation and the challenges of acquiring and integrating new knowledge with the evolving base of established knowledge when responding to technological discontinuities.

11.1 INTRODUCTION

What happens when industries enter eras of uncertainty, triggered for example by changing selection environments such as new regulations or new technological opportunities? Existing literature provides us with two, partly conflicting, answers. On the one hand, it tells us that technological discontinuities often have dramatic effects on established industry structures. In situations where new technologies require existing firms to make major changes to their products or processes to stay competitive, competitive patterns may break down and intensified technological competition may ensue (Abernathy and Clark, 1985; Anderson and Tushman, 1990; Utterback and Suárez, 1993). Leading firms thus find themselves in situations where the existing values, norms, and structures, upon which they traditionally have built a competitive edge, turn into rigidities that limit their ability to innovate (Leonard-Barton, 1992). A process of *creative destruction* (Schumpeter, 1942/1994) unfolds in which established knowledge becomes obsolete and 'attackers' have an advantage over incumbents (Foster, 1986). This process eventually leads to the demise of established firms. On the other hand, the literature emphasizes the cumulative nature of technological development and the persistence of established firms as important innovators (Pavitt, 1986; Granstrand et al., 1997; Cefis and Orsenigo, 2001). This is a process that some authors refer to as *creative accumulation*, that is, the process where incumbent firms persistently and successfully exploit innovations built on established knowledge. Creative accumulation seems to be more common than creative destruction, yet it has received far less attention in research.

Whereas previous literature recognizes that established companies often have severe difficulties in handling destructive patterns of innovation, it is implicitly assumed that incumbents have little trouble dealing with processes of creative accumulation. Because of the general lack of interest in creative accumulation, we know little about how firms deal with this process, that is, what strategies they use, what challenges they face, and what methods they employ to handle these challenges. It seems in particular that the sourcing of new knowledge and the integration of this knowledge with established but evolving knowledge bases present important challenges, as creative accumulation requires firms to link new with existing knowledge. As illustrated by the two industry cases analysed in this chapter, innovations that expand established knowledge in mature industries may result in huge difficulties for incumbents, in the extreme case even in 'late shakeouts' of large companies.

The first case concerns the race, from the mid-1980s to the early 2000s, to launch efficient and reliable gas turbines, primarily for combined-cycle gas turbine (CCGT) applications. The second case is about the competition to develop fuel-efficient automotive power-trains, a race that started in the late 1990s and is ongoing. Both these cases comprise technological developments that can be characterized as discontinuous and that have had a spectacular effect on industry structures. Industry leaders with a 100-year legacy of technological accumulation have lost their positions, and some large firms have even been pushed out of business. Moreover, both cases are concerned with products that can be characterized as complex. They build upon several interdependent fields of technological knowledge, and consist of a large number of interacting subsystems and components. However, these cases also differ. While the advanced gas turbine is a complex capital good characterized by high unit costs, customization, and low production volumes (Miller et al., 1995; Hobday, 1998; Bergek et al., 2008), the automobile is a mass-produced consumer good, with many standardized interfaces and a strong focus on unit cost.

The overall aim of this chapter is to build on these cases in order to advance the understanding of creative accumulation. More specifically, the chapter will explore (*a*) what types of innovation established companies may opt to develop (the creativity aspect), (*b*) how companies may source – develop and/or acquire – new knowledge and handle it in relation to their existing knowledge base (the accumulation aspect), (*c*) the knowledge integration challenges implied by these two aspects, and (*d*) the implications for industry-level competition and firm-level organizational structure.

The chapter is outlined as follows. Section 11.2 reviews the existing literature on creative accumulation. Section 11.3 presents the two industry cases. This is followed by a comparison of key aspects of the creative accumulation processes displayed by the leading contenders in these two cases (Section 11.4). The concluding section 11.5 summarizes the main observations, relating them to existing literature and outlining a number of general themes and implications which emerge from the studies.

11.2 CREATIVE ACCUMULATION AND KNOWLEDGE INTEGRATION

11.2.1 Innovation patterns in mature industries: creative destruction vs. creative accumulation

It was Joseph Schumpeter who first used the concept of creative destruction, which he described as '. . . a process of qualitative change . . . of revolutions . . . of industrial mutation . . . that incessantly revolutionizes the economic structure from within, incessantly destroying the old one, incessantly creating a new one' (Schumpeter, 1942/1994: 83). In particular, he recognized the effect of this process on established companies:

> It is not that kind of competition [price competition] which counts but the competition from the new commodity, the new technology, the new source of supply, the new type of organization . . . – competition which commands a decisive cost or quality advantage and which strikes not at the margins of the profits and the outputs of the existing firms but at their foundations and their very lives. (Schumpeter, 1942/1994: 84)

This and later work in the same tradition emphasize the 'attacker's advantage' (Foster, 1986) over incumbents: 'the "creation" is usually accomplished by invaders – new firms or entrants from other industries – while the "destruction" is suffered by the incumbents' (Rosenbloom and Christensen, 1994: 656).

In contrast, other researchers argue that technological innovation is not primarily characterized by creative destruction but rather by what they refer to as *creative accumulation*, where incumbent firms innovate on the basis of cumulative development and deployment of established knowledge and capabilities (cf. Pavitt, 1986; Granstrand et al., 1997). It is this process, where established firms play the role of the most important innovators (Cefis and Orsenigo, 2001), that is the focus of this chapter.

However, most of the scientific articles that result from a keyword search for 'creative accumulation' only mention the concept in passing.[1] Others tend to be descriptive studies (often based on patent data) of the characteristics of innovative patterns, for example their degree of cumulativeness of knowledge (e.g. Malerba and Orsenigo, 1996; Breschi et al., 2000). Few empirical studies describe how the process unfolds over time or identify specific challenges for the companies involved.

The literature that considers creative accumulation in more detail offers two main perspectives. One of them focuses on the industrial organization of innovative activities and defines creative accumulation as an innovation pattern in which incumbent firms play the dominant role (e.g. Kavassalis et al., 1996; Baaij et al., 2004; Corrocher et al., 2007). Such a pattern is sometimes denoted 'Schumpeter Mark II' (cf. Winter, 1984; Malerba and Orsenigo, 1996) after the pattern

---

[1] We searched the fulltext databases Scopus ('all fields'), Science Direct ('full text'), and J Stor ('full text') and found a total of thirty-one scientific articles, excluding duplicates and obviously unrelated articles (e.g. two biomedical papers on 'creatinin accumulation'). Of these, fifteen articles only mention creative accumulation in passing or refer to definitions provided by other articles on the list. An additional eight articles focus on other concepts (e.g. 'innovation persistence') after briefly mentioning creative accumulation.

described by Schumpeter (1942/1994).[2] The second, more common perspective focuses on the knowledge processes involved in creative accumulation and on the cumulative feature of these processes. According to this perspective, the defining feature of creative accumulation is that the creation of new knowledge builds on existing knowledge and expertise, rather than replacing it (Pavitt, 1986; Hobday, 1990; Granstrand et al., 1997; Cefis, 2003). This perspective has clear similarities with the idea of 'competence-enhancing innovation' discussed by Tushman and Anderson (1986); these authors, however, do not relate their concept to the discussion of creative accumulation.

These two perspectives on creative accumulation both capture the concept's cumulative aspect, but the *creativity* aspect tends to be disregarded, making 'creative accumulation' more or less equivalent to 'incremental innovation'. For example, Granstrand et al. (1997: 22) describe creative accumulation as a 'careful, step-by-step accumulation and enhancement of corporate competencies' (cf. also Kash and Rycroft, 2002; Hopkins et al., 2007). Perhaps this is due to the connection that some researchers make between creative accumulation and the 'specific' (or mature) phase of the industry life cycle (e.g. Breschi et al., 2000), which according to the literature is characterized by incremental improvements in products and processes (Utterback and Abernathy, 1975).

We would argue that much of the generative value of the concept of creative accumulation is precisely its inherent critical tension between the creativity aspect, implying responses 'outside of the range of existing practice' (Schumpeter, 1947: 150), and the accumulation aspect, implying knowledge creation that builds on existing practices. Taking the knowledge-based perspective on creative accumulation as a starting point, the remainder of this theoretical section will explore its creative and cumulative aspects in more detail. This provides a basis for the subsequent empirical analysis, where we will highlight some of the features and implications of such patterns of 'non-destructive' – but still creative – innovation.

11.2.2 Creativity and accumulation aspects of innovation in complex products

According to the knowledge-based definition of creative accumulation, *the accumulation aspect* implies that innovation is competence-enhancing rather than competence-destroying, that is, it builds on previous knowledge rather than substituting for it (cf. Abernathy and Clark, 1985; Tushman and Anderson, 1986). As a consequence, a type of 'kinship' exists between new and previous products, due to cumulative learning over product generations and even, in some cases, through the sharing of physical components (Jones, 2003).

As previously mentioned, the empirical focus in this chapter is on complex (or 'bundled') products, that is, products composed of a large number of components and technologies. The development of reliable and cost-competitive complex

---

[2] The labels Schumpeter Mark I and Mark II derive from the two quite different innovation patterns described by Schumpeter in *The Theory of Economic Development* (Schumpeter, 1934) and *Capitalism, Socialism & Democracy* (Schumpeter, 1942/1994), respectively.

products involves the design, engineering, sourcing, and integration of both physical components and subsystems as well as the integration of a diverse set of scientific and engineering knowledge bases and capabilities (Rycroft and Kash, 2002). Improving the performance of combustion engines, for example, requires a combination of technological competencies from fields of knowledge as varied as mechanics, materials, heat transfer, combustion, fluid flow, electronics, computer-aided design, etc. (Granstrand et al., 1997). The requisite knowledge may be related to individual components and subsystems, and also to 'architectural' knowledge, that is, knowledge of how to integrate various components and relevant engineering knowledge bases (Henderson and Clark, 1990; Henderson and Cockburn, 1994; Takeichi, 2002). Thus, for complex products, knowledge kinship can exist both on the component level and on the product architecture level. Product generations also frequently share physical components and subsystems.

From earlier literature, we know that an important R&D challenge for firms operating as integrators of complex products is to address the critical balance between deep component-related knowledge and broad systems-related architectural knowledge (Takeichi, 2002). In particular, it has been emphasized that a certain degree of component-level knowledge is required to maintain the required level of architectural knowledge (Brusoni et al., 2001; Becker and Zirpoli, 2003). The concept of creative accumulation adds another dimension to this challenge. According to Mendonça (2009: 479), this concept implies that new knowledge is linked with existing knowledge 'in a complementary and enhancing fashion'. Companies must thus balance not only component/subsystem knowledge and architectural knowledge but also the use of existing knowledge against new knowledge on both these levels. They must be able to source new knowledge and integrate it with existing knowledge into a functioning whole. This challenge is a central theme in the empirical study, where we will investigate what types of old and new knowledge firms need to develop various 'creative responses', what strategies they use to source new knowledge, and how they handle the relationship between different sets of knowledge when developing new technologies and products.

Let us now turn to the *creative aspect* of creative accumulation. In the context of innovation, creativity essentially has to do with the degree of novelty involved, implying changes in the price/performance of the product/process and related changes in the physical structure or software content of the product/process itself (Ehrnberg, 1995).[3] With regard to changes in performance, a distinction can be made between *incremental* innovation, which is an efficiency-oriented process of puzzle-solving actions in small steps (Tushman et al., 1997), and *discontinuous* innovation, which implies either 'drastic' (Arrow, 1962) order-of-magnitude improvements in cost, performance, or quality over previous technologies or products or a 'disruptive' introduction of new performance criteria, that is, '. . . a different constellation of costs and benefits, in which neither old nor new dominates the other' (Rosenbloom and Christensen, 1994: 659). We would argue that the concept of *creative* accumulation is most relevant in relation to discontinuous

---

[3] Ehrnberg (1995) also mentions a third dimension – changes in the competence and other resources needed for designing and producing the product – but this dimension primarily refers to the distinction between competence-enhancing and competence-destroying innovation as described previously.

innovation, since this can be expected to expose companies to substantial challenges both in terms of mastering 'an untested and incompletely understood product or process' (Tushman and Anderson, 1986: 444) and of acquiring and integrating new types of knowledge.

With regard to product changes, previous literature has distinguished between changes on the architectural level and changes within architectures, that is, in terms of new components (cf. Ehrnberg, 1995). Some researchers have indicated that modular innovation (changes in components) tends to follow architectural innovation in a sequential fashion (cf. Henderson and Clark, 1990). By contrast, the Tushman and Anderson (1986) model of competence-enhancing discontinuities discusses a process with parallel developments along a number of different technology trajectories. The sequencing and variety of responses will be further explored in our empirical study.

In the context of complex products, which are the centre of interest in this chapter, innovations requiring substantial changes in the product tend to imply significant integration challenges. This is mainly because of the high dependency between system-level performance and the performance of the subsystems, which in turn are dependent on the performance of the underlying components (Prencipe, 1997). These interdependencies imply that the development of any single technological component or subsystem is related to the availability and integration of other components/subsystems (Rycroft and Kash, 2002). Since components and subsystems develop at unequal rates, product innovation requires coordination of the development and design of component and subsystem in order to avoid performance imbalances between them (Prencipe, 2000). This is particularly difficult to achieve when different sectors and firms are responsible for different components and subsystems (Tidd, 1995). The magnitude of these interdependencies depends in part on strategic decisions about the choice of integrated or modular product architectures (Ulrich, 1995): if firms can decompose the system into composite parts with clear interfaces, the challenges outlined above will be easier to handle; on the other hand, close interaction between different components in the product system means that modular innovation is likely to affect other parts of the system as well (Prencipe, 1997). In some cases, the relationships between components and subsystems are so complex that it may even be difficult to achieve modularization in the first place (Rycroft and Kash, 2002).[4] Thus, the successful development, launch, and sales of new complex products can be seen as an indicator of knowledge integration capability.

To sum up, we have defined creative accumulation as a process in which existing knowledge continues to develop but is complemented and integrated with knowledge from new sources in order to develop novel products or processes with major improvements in performance. To aid an understanding of the challenges of creative accumulation, we will now turn to an analysis of the two industry cases. First, we will consider the creativity aspect, analysing the firms' different technology choices and their implications for changes in components,

---

[4] These relationships may change over time, however, from being highly interdependent in an early phase of system development to becoming more modular with increasingly standardized interfaces at a later stage of technological maturity.

product architectures, or both. This will make it possible to discuss the pattern of innovation: is it a sequential process where one firm's radical or architectural innovation is followed by modular innovations at competing firms, or does it involve a parallel development of different types of innovation by different companies? Second, we will discuss the accumulation aspect, that is, how the companies involved source and handle new knowledge in relation to their existing knowledge base. Third, we will analyse how the competing firms reconcile the tension between accumulation and creativity, and the implications of this tension for the knowledge integration challenges faced by the competing firms. Fourth and finally, we will discuss the effects of creative accumulation on the structure of the industries involved. One important question is whether all incumbents are proficient in the art of creative accumulation (as the literature on competence-enhancing innovation implicitly assumes), or whether there may be substantial differences across companies, resulting in lasting consequences for the evolving industry structures.

11.3 COMPETITION IN GAS TURBINES AND AUTOMOTIVE POWER-TRAINS: CASE BACKGROUNDS[5]

11.3.1 Two types of complex product

As they are built up of several interacting and interdependent subsystems linked via technical interfaces, both automobile power-trains and gas turbines can be characterized as complex products (Tushman and Rosenkopf, 1992). Gas turbines are primarily used for power generation and are, thus, often part of even more complex structures, comprising also steam turbines and auxiliary equipment. A modern gas turbine consists of four main subsystems: a compressor, which compresses air from the air inlet; a combustor where the compressed air is heated; turbine blades and vanes, through which the hot, compressed air expands, together with a cooling system; and a rotor connected to a generator that produces the electric power (Bergek et al., 2008). Organizations active in the development of advanced gas turbines need expertise in a variety of fields of engineering, including mechanical engineering and material integrity, combustion technology, aerodynamics, and software (Magnusson et al., 2005).

Similarly, automobile design and production are characterized by multiple dimensions of complexity:

> An automobile is composed of thousands of functionally meaningful components, each requiring many production steps. The technological sophistication of each component may be somewhat lower than that found in some high tech products, but subtle trade-offs and tight interdependence among many components makes internal coordination of the total vehicle extremely challenging. Small size makes layout coordination for some cars quite difficult. Use of common parts across products

---

[5] For more details on the industry cases, see: Bergek et al. (2008), Berggren et al. (2009), and Magnusson and Berggren (2011).

complicates inter-project coordination. (. . .) The automobile is also externally complex; the customer-producer interface is generally subtle and multifaceted, and a vehicle can satisfy customers in a number of ways beyond basic transportation, not of all of which are clearly recognized by the customers themselves. (Clark and Fujimoto, 1991: 10)

The focus of the automobile case will be on technological competition in the core system of the complete product, that is, the automotive power train, which incorporates several interacting parts, such as engine, ignition system, transmission, etc. The design of the power train determines some of the vehicle's most important properties, including speed, acceleration, reliability, and fuel economy.

Because it is difficult to maintain expertise in every field, manufacturers of advanced gas turbines and of automotive power-trains both tend to operate as systems integrators, sourcing the design and production of many components and subsystems from external suppliers, while maintaining control of the overall product architecture. However, to understand interdependencies in the product system and cope with imbalances due to unequal rates of technological progress in different components, these systems integrators still retain a broad technological knowledge base. In other words, they need to know more than they make (Brusoni et al., 2001).

Although automotive power-trains and gas turbines display similarities in terms of product complexity, they are polar cases in terms of production volumes. Major car manufacturers normally produce several hundred thousand of each power train annually, whereas the annual worldwide production of advanced gas turbines is only a few hundred units. With a strong focus on mass production, cost-cutting, and process innovation, the car sector can be characterized as 'scale intensive' (Pavitt, 1984). By contrast, even though the advanced gas turbine industry has reached a so-called mature stage in the industry life cycle, low production volumes mean that process innovation is generally downplayed in favour of a high degree of customization (cf. Miller et al., 1995).

11.3.2 Industry backgrounds

New technologies and increased competition in the advanced gas turbine industry

Modern gas turbines are a key building block in CCGT applications, which combine gas and steam turbines to achieve electrical efficiencies that are almost 50 per cent higher than those of other fossil-fuel power stations. Before the market for advanced gas turbines took off in the late 1980s, there was a long period of gestation that goes back to the first successful experiments at the Swiss firm Brown Boveri in the late 1930s and a number of British and American manufacturers shortly after World War II (Constant, 1980; Watson, 1997, 2004). The first attempt to sell the gas turbine innovation to electricity utilities in the late 1940s failed because at that time the new technology was still outperformed by the incumbent technology (steam turbine power plants).

The development of CCGT continued throughout the 1970s and 1980s, encouraged by governmental R&D programmes that aimed to find ways of burning fossil fuels more cleanly and efficiently, to deal with the problems of high oil prices and environmental pollution. Trends in economics, environmental performance, and reliability combined to increase the advantages of CCGT over other alternatives. Most importantly, the capital costs of CCGT fell in the 1980s and 1990s, in contrast to those of competing technologies such as coal and nuclear. At that time, gas turbines were being offered by several companies, including General Electric (GE) and Westinghouse in North America; Siemens, ASEA, Brown Boveri, GEC, and Alsthom in Europe; and Toshiba, Mitsubishi, and Hitachi in Asia. However, few of them were able to achieve a substantial stock of orders.

During a period of transformation and restructuring in the 1980s, several of these heavy electrical engineering firms disappeared, and the industry consolidated around a few internationally operating corporations: GE and Westinghouse in North America, Siemens and Asea Brown Boveri (ABB) in Europe (Bélanger et al., 1999; Tell, 2000). It was generally assumed that after this sweeping restructuring, competition between the survivors would become more stable and predictable. However, as the total market for electric power generation equipment grew only slowly in the late 1980s and early 1990s, sales of advanced gas turbines for CCGT applications suddenly took off when GE introduced its 'Frame 7F'. With this innovative design, GE increased the thermal efficiency of combined-cycle applications to 54 per cent, far above that of any other fossil-fuel technology. From just a small fraction of installed power generation capacity in 1987, CCGTs increased their share of the market for new electric power plants to over 35 per cent in 1993.

To cope with this expansion and the challenge from GE, all its competitors invested heavily. Westinghouse was the first to respond with its own 'F' turbine, developed in collaboration with Mitsubishi. In 1990, Siemens followed with its V94.3 machine and in 1992 ABB was the last of the incumbents to launch a turbine comparable to GE's Frame 7F. Only one year later, however, ABB took the technological lead by introducing the GT24/26, which triggered yet another stream of product launches from the other incumbents: Westinghouse in 1994 and Siemens and GE in 1995.

Two features of the CCGT market are particularly important in this context. One is that a superior technology in terms of efficiency and reliability effectively displaces all old technological solutions. Operating costs, defined by fuel efficiency and availability (uptime), are much more important for customer choice than the purchase cost of the new equipment. The other feature is that the market is thoroughly international – the same technology is sold globally with no major regional differences.

As can be seen from Figure 11.1a, in this early phase of the new era the leading firms on this global market had fairly similar market shares. The top three competitors were GE, Siemens, and ABB. However, the battle over technology was intense and the firms' fortunes differed dramatically. Innovative machine concepts were introduced, building on recent advances in such technologies as heat resistant materials, computerized fluid dynamics, and finite element calculations. The final outcome was that both Westinghouse and ABB left the field, leaving GE as the obvious leader and Siemens as a distant second (see Figure 11.1b).

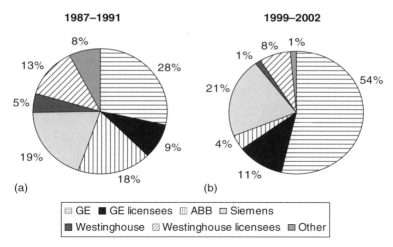

1987–1991   **1999–2002**

(a)   (b)

| ▤ GE ■ GE licensees ▥ ABB ☐ Siemens |
| ■ Westinghouse ▨ Westinghouse licensees ■ Other |

Figure 11.1 Global market share based on total CCGT orders in 1987–91 vs. 1999–2002
Note: GE licencees are primarily Alstom; Westinghouse licencees are primarily Mitsubishi.

An emerging era of ferment in automotive power-train development

Few sectors display such stability in their incremental improvements of core technologies as the car industry. Researchers have repeatedly foreseen an end to this stable pattern in favour of radical departures, for example in the aftermath of the two oil shocks in the early 1980s (Altshuler et al., 1984), growing environmental concern (Nieuwenhuis and Wells, 1997), or the Californian zero emissions vehicle (ZEV) mandate (Pilkington and Dyerson, 2005). Instead, the industry's incremental trajectory prevailed, adding equipment for emissions treatment and efficiency enhancement, but maintaining conventional power-train architectures. Moreover, in contrast to the power generation industry, the structure of the car industry remained regional: American firms dominated in the United States, European firms in Europe, and Japanese firms in Japan. For many decades, General Motors (GM) was the world's overall top producer.

Since the late 1990s, however, this pattern of technological and industrial stability has been changing. There are several reasons for this, including pressure from rising fuel prices, new stringent legislation such as the EU mandate to reduce CO_2 emissions for new cars, which will come into operation in 2012, and the opportunities offered by a range of new technologies. This has initiated fierce technological competition, based on innovations in the core of the vehicle: the automotive power train. One of several alternatives to significantly improve fuel efficiency and reduce CO_2 emissions is the hybrid-electric power train (Hekkert et al., 2005; Schäfer et al., 2006). Hybrids are considerably more complex than battery electric cars, but offer key advantages in terms of driving range, cost, ease of charging, etc. However, to combine the virtues of combustion engines and electric drives, hybrid-electric vehicles require innovation in components (e.g. batteries, power electronics, and electronic control systems) as well as in the power train's overall architecture. In 1997, Toyota was the world's first auto producer to launch a series-produced hybrid

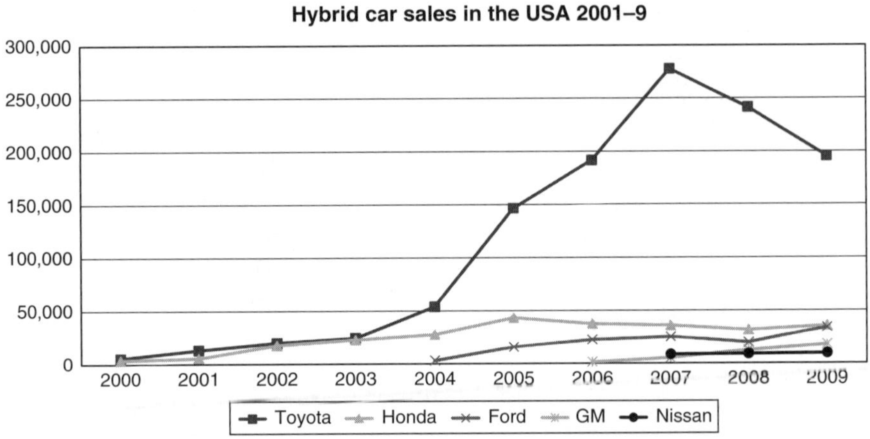

Hybrid car sales in the USA 2001–9

Figure 11.2 Hybrid car sales in the United States 2001–9
Source: Hybridcars.com.

car – Prius – for standard customers. Initial sales were poor, but soaring fuel prices and a rising public awareness of global warming made Prius a symbol of the modern environmental car (Sperling and Gordon, 2009). Toyota sold 53,992 hybrid cars in the United States in 2004 and as many as 277,633 three years later. By that time, Toyota had launched several new hybrid models, and announced plans for annual global sales of 1 million vehicles by 2010.

The American competitors reacted slowly to the introduction of hybrids and their early R&D in the field did not give rise to actual products. When hybrid sales gained market shares, GM and Ford ramped up their technological activities and presented their own hybrid cars, but their sales were minuscule compared to those of Toyota (see Figure 11.2). In 2008, following the collapse of its profitable SUV and light truck segments and a general downturn in the domestic market, the previous leader, GM, was in a disastrous financial situation and had to appeal for government subsidies to survive.

In contrast to the United States, European hybrid sales were very small. In 2006, hybrid-electric vehicles had less than 0.2 per cent of the market. Whereas GM and Ford belatedly tried to launch their own hybrids, the European car manufacturers eschewed architectural innovation, such as hybrid power-trains, in favour of 'accelerated incrementalism', characterized by efforts to increase the performance of the established internal combustion engine, in particular the diesel engine. This diesel evolution can be seen as a case of modular innovation, involving significant redesign and addition of components, but no change in the basic product architecture. The improvements in fuel efficiency, power, and driveability resulted in rapidly increasing sales; in 2007, more than 50 per cent of new cars in Western Europe were powered by diesel engines. Within Europe, Volkswagen (VW) emerged as a leader in this accelerated development of established technologies. However, in North America, with its tradition of low fuel prices and the relatively high cost of diesel compared to gasoline, sales of diesel engines remained very low, hovering around 3 per cent of the car and light truck market. In 2008–9, European manufacturers, led by VW and Mercedes-Benz, launched several new 'clean diesel' cars in the United States, which sold above expectations, albeit from a very low starting point.

Thus, in contrast to the case of gas turbines for CCGT applications, competition between efficient automotive power-trains takes place on regional markets with distinctively different sales patterns. New technological solutions have to compete with improved versions of established technologies which command more attractive prices, and this variety of alternatives is expanding. In the power generation industry, CCGT was a key application for every firm, and market shares here were a good indicator of corporate positions. In the automotive power-train case, market strength in one power-train technology is not a reliable competitive measure. The best available indicator is overall market share in the two historically most important regions, Europe and the United States. As can be seen in Figure 11.3, there are not only strong regional differences but also a

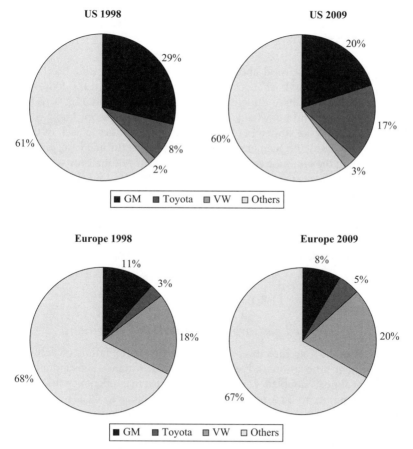

Figure 11.3 Market shares for three leading firms in the US and European car markets in 1998 and 2009 (cars and light trucks)

Source: Adapted from EAMA (2010).[6]

---

[6] In terms of global production, GM was No. 1 in 1998. In 2008, Toyota occupied this place, with Volkswagen as No. 2 in car production and No. 3 for cars and LCVs combined. No figure is yet available for 2009 (see OICA, 2009).

consistent pattern of change across regions: GM lost around 30 per cent of its market share in both regions from 1998 to 2009, Toyota increased its share by 60–100 per cent, and VW by 10–60 per cent.

This dramatic change reflects the competitive positions of the firms' overall product portfolios. However, GM's failure in both America and Europe is strongly related to its lack of ability to launch competitive fuel-efficient cars (Sperling and Gordon, 2009); in Europe, Opel/GM lost out against VW's new generations of turbocharged, direct-ignition gasoline and diesel engines; in the United States, GM was unable to match either the advanced Prius or the cost, efficiency, and reliability of conventional Toyota cars.

11.4 CHALLENGES IN CREATIVE ACCUMULATION AND KNOWLEDGE INTEGRATION: A COMPARISON

The two industries discussed above represent cases of intensified technological competition and dramatic changes in corporate positions. In the following sections, we will use the three dimensions presented in Section 11.2 – technology choices, technology and knowledge sourcing, and challenges for knowledge integration – to discuss the strategies of three prime competitors in each of these two industries: GE, ABB, and Siemens in the advanced gas turbine case; and Toyota, GM, and VW in the automotive power-train case. Our rationale for selecting these six companies for a deeper analysis is that they all had leading positions in terms of market share in their respective industries during significant parts of the periods in focus. As discussed in more detail below, these firms developed very different strategies in their efforts to cope with the increased technological competition. There was also a significant variation in outcomes, related to the six companies' different abilities to exploit the new technological options.

11.4.1 Technology choices

Advanced gas turbines: leapfrogging ambitions

With the Frame 7F architecture, GE launched a combination of architectural and component innovations, which improved performance substantially: power output was almost doubled (150 MW) and thermal efficiency increased by 2 percentage points to 34.2 per cent (and much higher in CCGT applications). This advance was closely related to GE's efforts to be the undisputed technological leader of the field. Accordingly, GE invested in a higher level of R&D activities than its competitors, as indicated by patenting records. Figure 11.4 shows the huge disparity between GE and ABB in this area. It also shows how Siemens increased their R&D activity in the late 1990s, in an effort to catch up with the leader.

Faced with GE's early mover advantage, Siemens followed with its V94.3. This new machine comprised many advanced component features, such as supersonic blades in the compressor and cooling in three of the four turbine blade stages. It was larger (200 MW) and also slightly better in terms of thermal efficiency than

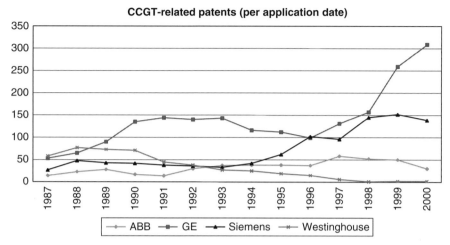

Figure 11.4 Total number of patents in combined cycle gas turbine-related areas (per application date)

GE's 7F turbine (35.7 per cent). ABB's first response, the GT13E2 turbine, corresponded to Siemens' turbine in terms of thermal efficiency, but had a smaller capacity (164 MW). ABB subsequently tried to leapfrog the performance of the competitors' turbines, launching GT24/26. This was a very different machine, featuring a new sequential combustion chamber design and a new type of compressor with increased efficiency which gave another 2 percentage point increase in thermal efficiency (to 37.5 per cent). It sold very well initially but after a few years, it ran into disastrous difficulties because the new components could not stand full-load, high-temperature operations for the required length of time. ABB's attempted creative response, offering both a new architecture and new components, failed and sales of the 'GE killer' had to cease. The other companies launched new generations of turbines in 1995 with thermal efficiencies ranging from 38 (Siemens' V84.3 in 1995) to 39.5 per cent (GE's Frame 7G in 1995). Unlike ABB's architectural innovation, these turbines were largely based on component improvements such as blade design, materials, and cooling configurations within the existing product architecture.

Automotive power-trains: leaders with contrasting strategies

The picture of R&D competition in the development of hybrid-electric power-trains is rather different (see Figure 11.5). Toyota pioneered hybrid patenting in the United States in the early 1990s, but after these initial years, Toyota has not been in the lead. Nevertheless, their consistency is striking. Honda outperformed Toyota in the early 2000s in an effort to catch up with the market leader but has not been able to maintain its patenting activity in recent years. Apart from Renault-Nissan, European manufacturers are virtually non-existent in this field.

Compared with its two main rivals in terms of overall market share, GM and VW, Toyota is the undisputed hybrid patent leader. After a very late awakening, GM tried to catch up in 2006–7 as accelerated efforts were made to develop

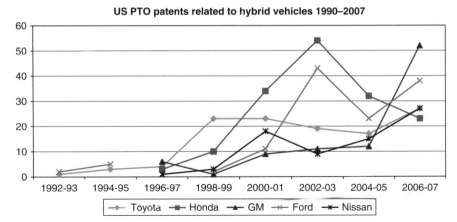

US PTO patents related to hybrid vehicles 1990–2007

Figure 11.5 Total number of US patents in hybrid electric vehicle technology 1990–2007 – the five most active firms

technologies for the next round of hybrid evolution, plug-in hybrids, that is, cars with extended battery capacity that can be charged from the electric grid. Volkswagen, on the other hand, had not entered the hybrid race by the end of the studied period; instead, it stepped up its efforts to launch more powerful conventional engines – both diesel and gasoline – introducing features such as direct injection and supercharging.

Increased engine power output paves the way to downsizing, which is a key to reducing fuel consumption (Schäfer et al., 2006). Figure 11.6 shows mean engine output (kW) per unit of engine size (litre) for all gasoline and diesel engine alternatives offered by Volkswagen in six consecutive generations of their Golf model (Mk1–Mk6). The graph illustrates a gradual trendwise improvement in engine performance.[7] However, it also reveals a few significant jumps in performance as a result of new engine concepts. In particular, this relates to the broad introduction of turbocharged direct injection (TDI) diesel engines in the fourth Golf generation (produced 1998–2005), and to the introduction of the combined turbo- and supercharger gasoline engine concept (TSI) in the fifth Golf generation (produced 2003–9). Volkswagen offers a broader range of TSI engines in the sixth Golf generation and has thus achieved another significant improvement in the output/size ratio.

Volkswagen has also increased its efforts to innovate in additional fuel-saving components and subsystems such as dual-clutch transmissions and start-stop systems to eliminate idling. One of the results is the Golf Mk6 generation from 2008 with a broad range of power-train configurations, which reduced fuel consumption and CO_2-emissions by 11–16 per cent compared to the previous generation.

However, Volkswagen is not alone in this race. A brief comparison with Opel Kadett/Astra and Toyota Corolla/Auris, two of VW Golf's prime competitors in

---

[7] Compared to other Golf generations, the engine line-up for the second generation (Mk2) included a disproportionate number of engine alternatives for high-performance Golf models such as GTI and G60. This may explain the higher mean output/size ratio for this generation compared to the third generation (Mk3).

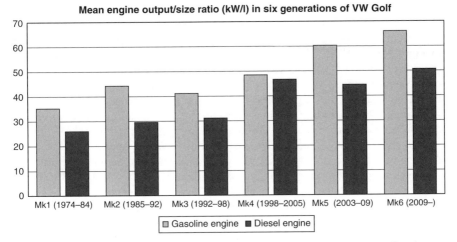

Figure 11.6 Mean output/size ratio for gasoline and diesel engine alternatives offered in six generations of VW Golf

the compact car segment, shows a similar trend of gradual improvement. Incrementally advancing the output/size ratio of internal combustion engines thus appears to be a prerequisite for keeping up with the competition. In particular, this relates to the European market, which compared to the US market traditionally has had a much greater predilection for smaller engines. Moreover, competition on the European market has almost exclusively driven the substantial improvements in diesel engine performance. The car manufacturers' corresponding engine development trends indicate that these manufacturers have essentially relied on a similar set of technologies.[8] This points to the key role played by specialized suppliers such as Bosch and Denso. For example, these suppliers' fuel injection systems have been paramount in improving engine performance. Automotive power-train development is due just as much to the R&D efforts of these specialized suppliers as to the car manufacturers themselves.

11.4.2 Technology sourcing strategies

Gas turbines: the challenge of knowledge sourcing

The key to the improvements in the thermal efficiency and power output of GE's 7F was a significant increase in firing temperature and compressor airflow, which required advanced materials and blade cooling techniques. Crucial elements of the new knowledge were developed not by component specialists but in a related industry field: aircraft jet engines. Due to high levels of government support for military and civil jet engine programmes, aircraft engine companies were far

---

[8] As Volkswagen appears to have taken the lead in terms of output/size ratio for gasoline engines in the two most recent Golf generations, their combined turbo- and supercharger concept TSI could be an exception to this.

ahead of their industrial counterparts in the 1990s (Watson, 1997). Thanks to its incorporation of both an industrial gas turbine and a jet engine division and a large technology base, GE was in a unique position here (as previously illustrated by Figure 11.4). When GE introduced its 'F technology' industrial gas turbines in the late 1980s, it was keen to stress the use of jet engine technology in key aspects of the new vintage. Many technologies transferred to the GE Frame 7F can be traced back to the 'high bypass' jet engine programmes of the late 1960s (Makansi, 1995) including turbine blade cooling configurations and aero-engine design techniques for transonic compressor stages (Boardman et al., 1993).

ABB chose a different technological path for its GT24/26 models; one reason was the lack of direct access to the knowledge developed in the aero-engine industry. However, despite of a rather weak knowledge base (cf. Figure 11.4), ABB still tried to develop key technologies internally. They recruited jet engine specialists from the former Soviet Union, acquiring the Moscow-based design office Uniturbo in the mid-1990s. In addition, the Swiss-Swedish firm tried external sourcing through technology alliances. These efforts were not very successful. ABB was the first to negotiate an alliance with an aero-engine company – Rolls-Royce in 1988 – but the partnership was dissolved four years later due to a difference of opinion about the 'way forward' (Mukherjee, 1995). ABB also tried to exploit compressor technology from Motoren- und Turbinen Union (MTU), a German jet engine company (Watson, 1997), but the problems with the GT24/26 compressor design indicate that this partnership was a limited success, too.

In contrast, a fruitful alliance with Pratt & Whitney in 1990 'gave Siemens exclusive rights to Pratt & Whitney's technology in so far as it can be applied to heavy-duty land-based gas turbines' (Baxter, 1995). This alliance was a key factor behind the performance improvements embodied in the gas turbines that Siemens introduced in 1994 and 1995. The acquisition of Westinghouse in 1998 enabled Siemens to source turbine-relevant knowledge developed in the American military R&D context (Curtis, 2003). The major increase in internal R&D, described above, complemented the external sourcing strategy.

A comparison of the different approaches shows that integration of new and specialized knowledge fields, developed in different contexts, is a highly demanding task. Siemens demonstrates that an alliance strategy may be feasible, but ABB's unsuccessful efforts show how difficult this route can be. This mature technology-intensive industry offered just a few external sources of knowledge, giving firms limited chances of success.

Automotive power-trains: different kinds of innovation – different sourcing strategies

In the case of hybrid-electric power-train development, a key element in Toyota's competence-building strategy was to accumulate deep knowledge both in the new technologies involved in hybrid power-trains and in critical component manufacturing. Many components of the hybrid power train were originally developed for low-volume applications and had not been exposed to the process innovation required to reach competitive prices in the car industry. So Toyota had to become a significant mass producer of electric motors. With this strategy, the company seeks both to ensure functionality and reduce costs. For the crucial development of battery systems, Toyota selected the same supplier as for electric vehicle batteries, Panasonic. As the battery is integrated in the hybrid power train, with complex interfaces to other components, intimate collaboration was required. The companies formed a joint venture and during the development project Toyota located a significant number of vehicle engineers at Panasonic. At a later stage, Toyota acquired a controlling interest in this joint venture.

The basic rationale for Toyota's strategy is that systems level restrictions, such as comfort, safety, serviceability, reliability, and cost, make it necessary to optimize all of a car's components. This is particularly demanding in the case of hybrid development. A fuel-efficient cost-competitive hybrid car cannot carry any excess capacity in power, energy storage, control systems, etc. Toyota's sourcing strategy indicates that when the requisite knowledge base changes, developing new technical insights at the R&D level does not suffice. To optimize the system, the company needs to access knowledge involved in manufacturing and its cost structures and therefore may find it necessary to in-source component production.

In contrast to Toyota's collaboration with a single battery supplier, in its efforts to catch up in the hybrid vehicle race GM has used several. Between 1995 and 2008, GM's electric car and hybrid car programmes used nine different battery suppliers, accompanied by a declared ambition to create in-house capabilities to develop and manufacture battery systems for plug-in hybrids (Pohl and Yarime, 2010). GM's use of several competing suppliers may be taken as an indicator of a short-term cost-cutting focus, as opposed to Toyota's long-term collaborative learning strategy in battery R&D and manufacturing.

Finally, Volkswagen relies mainly on in-house development of its traditional core technologies. For new functions, they use a modular strategy, sourcing new components from key outside suppliers in an effort to exploit their economies of scale. Start/stop systems, for example, are offered by the component specialists Valeo and Bosch, who expect the market for these systems to reach 2.5 million units in 2010. A key assumption behind Volkswagen's strategy is that new automotive power-trains will evolve in a modular direction, which reduces the innovation and creativity burden on car manufacturers (Christensen et al., 2002).

11.4.3 Knowledge integration challenges

Gas turbines: challenges of integration and reliability in untested systems

Developing new gas turbines requires a truly multidisciplinary process; if one discipline assumes a commanding role without considering the implications from other disciplinary perspectives, the result could be a disaster. As explained by the manager of industrial gas turbine development at Siemens, Sweden:

> It could be the case that, e. g., a specialist in thermodynamics sits down to make a new machine layout, optimizing like bloody hell and making all these detailed drawings, but never understands that this design is impossible. . . . He can invent anything, but it won't work. . . . All these decisions have to be made in a group [of specialists], and there is a problem if one of them is too communicative and dominant. There has to be a balance. If an expert in, e. g., solid mechanics starts telling people what to do in

thermodynamics, it's getting dangerous.... Often no single expert has the answer. We had a difficulty in integrating various parts of the burner, and the experts offered seven different solutions to deal with the problems of NOx emissions, vibrations and acoustics. Seven! What could we do? We built prototypes for each of them and tested, and not one of them was right. To me, that is a real case of complexity. So we had to start all over, but now we had more data to build on. (Interview March 2008)

Balancing and integrating expert knowledge is not the only challenge in this development process. A particular factor that makes innovation in advanced gas turbines much more uncertain than innovation in automotive power-train development is the very high unit cost of a new machine and the large facilities needed to run full-load tests of new machines. This makes it difficult for engineers to verify the real-world performance and reliability of their new product, possibly leading to highly negative experiences for customers once a product is put into use.

Introducing advanced products is therefore not enough. Every company that entered the gas turbine race studied here was able to launch successive generations of turbines at about the same rate and performance. However, they all also suffered from difficult periods of customer-experienced problems with their machines. During the development process, the firms introduced a range of new methods, materials, and manufacturing technologies. This opened up possibilities in terms of more heat-resistant turbine blades, more optimized designs, and more intricate cooling systems. But such things as elevated compression ratios, higher turbine inlet temperatures, and lean combustion processes, used to attain higher efficiencies and lower NO_x emissions, gave rise to entirely new problems.

The novelty of these problems meant that the engineers could not foresee them in their simulations or laboratory tests. So when the machines were delivered to the first customers, the problems had not been recognized and had to be overcome after the turbines had been commissioned. Solving after-delivery problems and safeguarding high operational reliability in these complex machines was the real moment of truth, requiring on-the-field application of both specialized and integrated knowledge approaches. When reports of turbine problems began to surface in the mid-1990s, GE reacted very determinedly. Faulty turbines were decommissioned and returned to the United States; problem-solving teams were assembled with experts from relevant divisions. In this way, GE was able to use its long experience in this technological domain, in both aero engines and stationary gas turbines. Reports on problem-solving activities at ABB are more difficult to come by. Although the company was aware of problems with the new GT24/26 design, it continued to sell these turbines until that was no longer possible. With hindsight, ABB was clearly overambitious in its hurried introduction of this design, perhaps because it was the last company to launch an F-class product. It was this, together with new and unique architectural and component designs, that lay behind the problems that emerged. The company never managed to rectify the technical problems and had to exit from the entire power generation industry.

From a knowledge and innovation perspective, it may be argued that GE was able to master both the creation and the accumulation aspects of its innovation process. The company embedded the creative elements – the Frame 7F design with its new components – in a broad, deep pool of knowledge and experience. This also provided a basis for its superior problem-solving abilities. ABB, on the other hand, suffered from a lack of knowledge depth and integrative capabilities at key R&D positions. Its GT24/26 design, with a sequential, two-stage combustion process, involved large technical risks that could not be validated in its in-house facilities. Despite insufficient accumulated knowledge, a risky sales process was launched, without back-up in deep problem-solving abilities. The result was a massive innovation failure. In contrast to ABB, the new V84.3A turbine from Siemens was largely based on the previous vintage, with increased temperature and compressor airflow to improve efficiency. Pratt & Whitney also added some new technology, such as blade designs, high temperature materials, and cooling configurations. Siemens subsequently reported vibration problems associated with its new turbines, and the cost of rectifying these problems meant that the entire power generation segment lost money in 1999. However, a few years later the company had solved these problems and could remain a strong No. 2 on the market, with a share of just over 20 per cent.

Automotive power-train case: challenges of innovation, integration, and cost

In terms of successfully launching and mass-producing a car embodying a distinctively new power train, Toyota Prius represents a prominent innovation case in the car industry. However, this success was preceded by the deployment of massive resources, for manufacturing investment and for meeting the challenges of knowledge acquisition and knowledge integration. As Toyota Europe's Executive Vice President of R&D explained:

> We don't believe in black box design, where suppliers have all design responsibility and design insight. We want to know all the details of new important technologies. With black box design, the OEM (the car company) cannot do anything if there is a problem. To develop hybrid systems is about integration. Then you need to have detailed knowledge of key components. After we have acquired this detailed knowledge it is possible to subcontract production. (Interview 7 November 2006)

A specific challenge in the Toyota strategy, when competing with enhanced versions of established technologies, is the high cost of its hybrid system. The integrated approach, developing both a new architecture and new specialized components in-house, has resulted in significant improvements in performance, but restricted the opportunities for taking advantage of industrial specialization and external economies of scale. This means that Toyota has to carry the major cost burden when its hybrid offering is expanded from a niche presence to the cost-sensitive mass market.

When the hybrid segment started to expand rapidly on its home market, GM was forced to respond; ten years after Toyota launched Prius, GM introduced several hybrid models, albeit with very limited sales success. Considering Toyota's accumulated production experience, in excess of 1 million units, and well-developed supplier base, GM's prospects on entering the field were indeed bleak. GM Powertrain Europe's Vice President for Product Engineering acknowledged the difficulty of reaching a competitive cost level for hybrid car production, claiming that it was virtually impossible to sell hybrids without significant losses (interview 4 May 2007). The subsequent collapse of the US car market, followed by falling oil prices, made long-term investment in production learning even more difficult to justify. Still, as of 2009, GM has clung to their plan to be the first to introduce plug-in hybrids on the market. However, since the extended battery capacity required by plug-in hybrids currently implies a considerable additional cost, at present, these plans appear to be a highly uncertain venture commercially.

By contrast, Volkswagen has been able to offer enhanced versions of its core models, such as the Golf programme, at prices that are highly competitive in relation to their performance. A key reason is the company's modular strategy. This also reduces the knowledge integration aspect of its development process. However, when innovative components are required from outside suppliers, even Volkswagen encounters a genuine knowledge acquisition problem, as explained by its Vice President of Group Research:

> We have worked two years with suppliers and we see that beyond a certain level these suppliers won't give us detailed information on things like the value chain for the raw materials for batteries, what are the cost prognoses, what are the chances of reducing production cost, etc. These are key questions that companies won't tell us, because this is proprietary knowledge, competitive knowledge. But we need to know this to make the right decision internally. So it seems that the only way to get answers to these questions is to build up your own competence. (Interview 4 July 2008)

Compared with Toyota, Volkswagen's overall knowledge development process tends to emphasize accumulation more than creation and integration. While this has provided cost advantages so far, such an approach meets difficulties when the company aspires to smoothly incorporate new components that entail high system interdependency. A case in point seems to be Volkswagen's first hybrid car, the hybrid version of the SUV model Touareg, launched to the market in 2010. A comparison between VW Touareg Hybrid and Toyota's Hybrid SUVs (Highlander Hybrid and Lexus RX 450h) shows that the Toyota models have about 50 per cent better fuel economy in city traffic (manufacturers' specification, EPA standard-testing). Consequently, it appears difficult for Volkswagen to catch up. An efficient hybrid system will require an integrated approach which stands in marked contrast to Volkswagen's strategy based on incremental and modular advancements.

11.5 CONCLUSIONS: CHARACTERISTICS AND CHALLENGES OF CREATIVE ACCUMULATION

In this chapter, we have explored the concept of creative accumulation, defined as a process by which existing knowledge is combined with new types of knowledge in order to develop new products or processes with substantially improved or changed performance. In the theory section, we emphasized that innovation researchers have been much more interested in creative destruction than in creative accumulation. Further, when the literature does discuss the latter process, it tends to conflate it with incremental innovation, stressing the aspect of accumulation much more than that of creation. Thus, we found it important to empirically explore the duality involved in creative accumulation and its particular and sometimes contradictory challenges in concrete industry settings. More specifically, the chapter set out to explore (*a*) what types of innovation established companies may opt to develop (the creativity aspect), (*b*) how companies may source – develop and/or acquire – new knowledge and deal with it in relation to their existing knowledge base (the accumulation aspect), (*c*) the knowledge integration challenges implied by these two aspects, and (*d*) the implications for industry-level competition and firm-level organizational structure. Our major conclusions with respect to items (*a*), (*b*), and (*c*) are summarized below, while the conclusions for (*d*) are presented in Section 11.5.6.

11.5.1 Creative accumulation may involve a variety of creative responses

When mature industries enter phases with technological discontinuities, there is room for a variety of corporate strategies in spite of the similar contingencies faced by firms in such industries (Bonaccorsi et al., 1999). This general observation has been illustrated both in the gas turbine and in the automotive power-train cases reported above. As is evident from these cases, creative responses may come in a variety of forms, with different emphasis on the creative and cumulative aspects, and in a matrix of different combinations of both new and evolving old technologies. Furthermore, the overall pattern of innovation may vary. In the case of gas turbines, GE introduced a new architectural innovation, which was followed first by modular innovations by Siemens and ABB and later by a new architectural innovation by ABB. In the power-train case, Toyota and GM developed competing architectural innovations, whereas Volkswagen focused on modular innovation, expanding on the basis of its established technology domain. Thus, creative accumulation can take the form both of sequential innovation, as in the gas turbine case, and parallel innovation, with modular and architectural innovations pursued simultaneously, as in the power-train case. In contrast to the suggestions of Tushman and Anderson (1986), these industry cases show that discontinuous innovation in existing industries does not have to result in a new technology cycle.

11.5.2 Creative accumulation is mainly of a sustaining nature

A second observation is that most of the innovations in the two cases resulted in improvements along established performance trajectories rather than the introduction of fundamentally new performance parameters. This was even true in the case of electric-hybrid power-trains, which could have been a candidate for disruptive innovation if new performance criteria had been offered. To gain acceptance on established markets, however, the innovators had to comply with existing customer criteria and performance requirements. This indicates that creative accumulation is more about sustaining than disruptive innovation, probably due to the predominance of incumbents with a strong customer base in this type of industry competition (cf. Christensen and Rosenbloom, 1995).

11.5.3 Creative accumulation implies a challenge to get new technologies from new sources

Creative accumulation does not destroy the existing knowledge base but builds on it. In the industries studied, creative accumulation also involved searching for and acquiring new knowledge outside established relationships. In the gas turbine case, firms had to acquire complementary knowledge about new materials from the aircraft engine field. In the car industry, hybrid development is making electrotechnical engineering a new core competence. The need for new knowledge concerns not only the product as such but also new manufacturing processes. This implies difficult decisions regarding sourcing and competence building: to invest in internal knowledge development – R&D and product engineering as well as process/manufacturing engineering – or to invest in and sustain knowledge-generating alliances with outside partners. Due to the oligopolistic nature of many of these industries, partner choices are highly limited and sourcing investments need to be strategic, in terms of making alliances productive and of building capabilities to absorb and integrate the new knowledge.

11.5.4 Creative accumulation also means a challenge to keep abreast with accelerating developments in old domains

Another intrinsic aspect of creative accumulation is the need for companies to maintain deep knowledge in established technologies, where the pace of improvement and innovation tends to increase significantly in eras of uncertainty and technological competition. This is illustrated by the accelerated development of technologies for conventional automotive power-trains. Competition between technologies is well known in the history of technology (Pistorius and Utterback, 1997), and is often referred to as the 'sailing-ship effect', first discussed by Gilfillan (1935), who showed that nearly all the components and materials of the 'old' sailing ships were improved when steamships were developed in the nineteenth century. Referring to more recent cases, Cooper and Schendel (1976: 67) argued that '[i]n every industry studied, the old technology continued to be improved and reached its highest stage of technical development *after* the new technology was introduced', but eventually the new technology carried the day: 'Sales of the old technology may continue to expand for a few years, but then usually decline, the new technology passing the old in sales within five to fourteen years of its introduction' (Cooper and Schendel, 1976: 61).

Creative accumulation implies a very different case of competition between technologies. Instead of leaving the stage, the 'old' technology continues to improve rapidly. Moreover, it is combined in various complex configurations with new technologies. This means that firms cannot choose to follow only one technological track but have to pursue several – and integrate them again and again.

11.5.5 Creative accumulation implies substantial challenges for knowledge integration

The characteristics of creative accumulation as described above make it a highly demanding process in terms of knowledge integration. Technological disciplines and areas of expertise have to interact in novel ways to develop products with substantially improved or changed performance. New fields of knowledge also have to be aligned with existing, rapidly evolving, technologies. There is no Archimedean fixed point – both the 'old' and the 'new' domains evolve and interfere with each other. This implies that the process of knowledge integration required by creative accumulation is itself a continuous process of learning; firms need to learn not only where to acquire and source new knowledge and how to hone their existing knowledge base but also how to integrate these diverse sets of knowledge into functioning processes and products that survive the competition in the market place.

11.5.6 Implications of creative accumulation for competition and organizational structure

Far from displaying any 'attacker's advantage' (Foster, 1986), the intense techno-logical competition in the mature technology-based industries studied here involved only a small number of large incumbents. Neither in the gas turbine nor in the automotive power-train case did any successful new competitor emerge. This circumstance underlines the barriers to entry which the cumulative character of the relevant knowledge implies, even in times of discontinuous change. In the case of the gas turbine industry, no new firms entered during the 1990s in spite of a rapidly expanding market involving entirely new customer segments. The automobile industry has time and again witnessed new entrants' endeavours to launch new power-trains, building on specialized technological expertise (e.g. in electrical engineering). To date, however, no firm has succeeded in integrating this expertise with the evolving knowledge base and capital invest-ments of established power-train technologies, to build a major market presence.

Still, the creative aspects of this process have the power to disrupt an industry. Both our industry cases are characterized by late shakeouts. In the gas turbine case, ABB and Westinghouse had to exit the gas turbine market completely. In the automotive power-train case, after being the industry's No. 1 for eighty years, GM lost significant market shares in both the United States and Europe, and went virtually bankrupt in late 2008 as a result of failures both to keep abreast of the process-based competition on costs, and in the technology-based search for new power-trains. Consequently, established firms have no guarantee of stable market positions. The creative aspect of the accumulation process may indeed destroy companies.

Creative accumulation, as perceived in these cases, involves the process of developing and refining a number of different technologies. Our discussion has focused on firms developing and manufacturing complex products, in which product innovation could be analysed in terms of components and architectures. However, creative accumulation may also be a fruitful concept when analysing developments in other sectors, for example materials-processing industries, where the challenges of creativity and accumulation involve different types of interaction, and the most critical process tends to be the integration of product and process knowledge.

Understanding the process of creative accumulation may have important consequences for how firms organize their operations. The conventional advice to managers faced with discontinuous technological change is to isolate their efforts to explore these new options, using small independent units that may focus on serving the market niches that appreciate the particular performance attributes that the new technology brings (Bower and Christensen, 1995). In essence, managers are advised to create the so-called 'ambidextrous organizations', where units running the existing businesses are separated from units in charge of emerging businesses (O'Reilly and Tushman, 2004). In this way, development based on discontinuous new technologies may coexist with ongoing operations that rely on established knowledge and structures. However, these arguments do not apply in cases of creative accumulation. As creative accumulation relies on the knowledge embedded in existing organizations, it cannot be accomplished in isolation. Still, it does challenge existing organizations and creates tensions between the established and new fields of knowledge. In fact, this is its creative aspect. Thus, from a managerial standpoint, creative accumulation involves an inherent dilemma that goes far beyond simple organizational formulae. There is a range of possible strategies for addressing the challenges of creative accumulation, and coherent choices must be made in terms of organization, technology acquisition, and internal technology development. It is this complexity, tension, dynamism, and duality that make creative accumulation an important reference point for innovation studies, and a demanding arena for knowledge integration.

REFERENCES

Abernathy, W. J. and Clark, K. B. (1985) Innovation: Mapping the Winds of Creative Destruction, *Research Policy*, 14(1): 3–22.

Altshuler, A., Anderson, M., Jones, D., Roos, D. and Womack, J. (1984) *The Future of the Automobile: Report of MIT's International Automobile Program*, Cambridge, MA: MIT Press.

Anderson, P. and Tushman, M. L. (1990) Technological Discontinuities and Dominant Designs: A Cyclical Model of Technological Change, *Administrative Science Quarterly*, 35: 604–33.

Arrow, K. J. (1962) Economic Welfare and the Allocation of Resources for Inventions, in: R. Nelson (ed.), *The Rate and Direction of Inventive Activity: Economic and Social Factors*, Princeton, NJ: Princeton University Press.

Baaij, M., Greeven, M. and van Dalen, J. (2004) Persistent Superior Economic Performance, Sustainable Competitive Advantage, and Schumpeterian Innovation: Leading Established Computer Firms 1954–2000, *European Management Journal*, 22(5): 517–31.

Baxter, A. (1995) Birthday in Berlin, *Financial Times*, Survey of Power Generating Equipment, 16 May: VII.

Becker, M. C. and Zirpoli, F. (2003) Organizing New Product Development: Knowledge Hollowing-Out and Knowledge Integration – The Fiat Auto Case, *International Journal of Operations & Production Management*, 23(9): 1033–61.

Belanger, J., Berggren, C., Björkman, C. and Koehler, C. (1999) *Being Local World-Wide. ABB and the Challenge of Global Management*, Ithaca, NY: Cornell University Press.

Bergek, A., Tell, F., Berggren, C. and Watson, J. (2008) Technological Capabilities and Late Shakeouts: Industrial Dynamics in the Advanced Gas Turbine Industry, 1986–2002, *Industrial and Corporate Change*, 17(2): 335–92.

Berggren, C., Magnusson, T. and Sushandoyo, D. (2009) Hybrids, Diesel or Both? The Forgotten Technological Competition for Sustainable Solutions in the Global Automotive Industry, *International Journal of Automotive Technology and Management*, 9(2): 148–73.

Boardman, R., White, A. and Wusterbarth, M. (1993) Seoinchon Comes on Line in Record Time, *Modern Power Systems*, 13(8): 49–57.

Bonaccorsi, A., Pammolli, F., Paoli, M. and Tani, S. (1999) Nature of Innovation and Technology Management in System Companies, *R&D Management*, 29(1): 57–69.

Bower, J. L. and Christensen, C. M. (1995) Disruptive Technologies: Catching the Wave, *Harvard Business Review*, January–February.

Breschi, S., Malerba, F. and Orsenigo, L. (2000) Technological Regimes and Schumpeterian Patterns of Innovation, *The Economic Journal*, 110(463): 388–410.

Brusoni, S., Prencipe, A. and Pavitt, K. (2001) Knowledge Specialization, Organizational Coupling and the Boundaries of the Firm: Why Do Firms Know More than They Make? *Administrative Science Quarterly*, 46: 597–621.

Cefis, E. (2003) Is There Persistence in Innovative Activities? *International Journal of Industrial Organization*, 21(4): 489–515.

—— Orsenigo, L. (2001) The Persistence of Innovative Activities: A Cross-Countries and Cross-Sectors Comparative Analysis, *Research Policy*, 30(7): 1139–58.

Christensen, C. M. and Rosenbloom, R. S. (1995) Explaining the Attacker's Advantage: Technological Paradigms, Organizational Dynamics, and the Value Network, *Research Policy*, 24: 233–57.

—— Verlinden, M. and Westerman, G. (2002) Disruption, Disintegration and Dissipation of Differentiability, *Industrial and Corporate Change*, 11(5): 955–93.

Clark, K. B. and Fujimoto, T. (1991) *Product Development Performance: Strategy, Organization, and Management in the World Auto Industry*, Boston, MA: Harvard Business School Press.

Constant, E. W. (1980) *The Origins of the Turbojet Revolution*, Baltimore/London: Johns Hopkins University Press.

Cooper, A. C. and Schendel, D. (1976) Strategic Responses to Technological Threats, *Business Horizons*, 19(1): 61–9.

Corrocher, N., Malerba, F. and Montobbio, F. (2007) Schumpeterian Patterns of Innovative Activity in the ICT Field, *Research Policy*, 36(3): 418–32.

Curtis, M. R. (2003) *The Innovation of Energy Technologies and the U.S. National Innovation System – The Case of the Advanced Turbine System*, Washington, DC: Office of Policy and International Affairs, U.S. Department of Energy.

EAMA (2010) Data Supplied by the European Automobile Manufacturers Association, URL: www.wardsauto.com (Accessed 26-01-2010).

Ehrnberg, E. (1995) On the Definition and Measurement of Technological Discontinuities, *Technovation*, 15(7): 437–52.

Foster, R. (1986) *Innovation: The Attacker's Advantage*, New York: Summit.

Gilfillan, S. C. (1935) *Inventing the Ship*, Chicago, IL: Follett Publishing Co.

Granstrand, O., Patel, P. and Pavitt, K. (1997) Multi-Technology Corporations: Why They Have 'Distributed' rather than 'Distinctive Core' Competencies, *California Management Review*, 39(4): 8–25.

Hekkert, M. P., Hendriks, F., Faaij, A. P. C. and Neelis, M. (2005) Natural Gas as an Alternative to Crude Oil in Automotive Fuel Chains: Well-to-Wheel Analysis and Transition Strategy, *Energy Policy*, 33(5): 579–94.

Henderson, R. and Clark, K. B. (1990) Architectural Innovation: The Reconfiguration of Existing Product Technologies and the Failure of Established Firms, *Administrative Science Quarterly*, 35: 9–30.

—— Cockburn, I. (1994) Measuring Competence? Exploring Firm Effects in Pharmaceutical Research, *Strategic Management Journal*, 15: 63–84.

Hobday, M. (1990) Semiconductors: Creative Destruction or US Industrial Decline? *Futures*, 22(6): 571–85.

—— (1998) Product Complexity, Innovation and Industrial Organization, *Research Policy*, 26: 689–710.

Hopkins, M. M., Martin, P. A., Nightingale, P., Kraft, A. and Mahdi, S. (2007) The Myth of the Biotech Revolution: An Assessment of Technological, Clinical and Organisational Change, *Research Policy*, 36(4): 566–89.

Jones, N. (2003) Competing after Radical Technical Change: The Significance of Product Line Management Strategy, *Strategic Management Journal*, 24(13): 1265–87.

Kash, D. E. and Rycroft, R. (2002) Emerging Patterns of Complex Technological Innovation, *Technological Forecasting & Social Change*, 69: 581–606.

Kavassalis, P., Solomon, R. J. and Benghozi, P-J. (1996) The Internet: A Paradigmatic Rupture in Cumulative Telecom Evolution, *Industrial and Corporate Change*, 5(4): 1097–126.

Leonard-Barton, D. (1992) Core Capabilities and Core Rigidities: A Paradox in Managing New Product Development, *Strategic Management Journal*, 13: 111–25.

Magnusson, T. and Berggren, C. (2011) Entering an Era of Ferment – Radical vs. Incrementalist Strategies in Automotive Power Train Development, *Technology Analysis and Strategic Management*, 23(3): 313–30.

Magnusson, T., Tell, F. and Watson, J. (2005) From CoPS to Mass Production? Capabilities and Innovation in Power Generation Equipment Manufacturing, *Industrial and Corporate Change*, 14(1): 1–26.

Makansi, J. (1995) Personal Communication from the Editor of *Power Magazine*, New York.

Malerba, F. and Orsenigo, L. (1996) Schumpeterian Patterns of Innovation Are Technology-specific, *Research Policy*, 25(3): 451–78.

Mendonça, S. (2009) Brave Old World: Accounting for 'High-tech' Knowledge in 'Low-tech' Industries, *Research Policy*, 38(3): 470–82.

Miller, R., Hobday, M., Leroux-Demers, T. and Olleros, X. (1995) Innovation in Complex Systems Industries: The Case of Flight Simulation, *Industrial and Corporate Change*, 4: 363–400.

Mukherjee, D. (1995) Interview, ABB Power Generation: Baden, Switzerland.

Nieuwenhuis, P. and Wells, P. (1997) *The Death of Motoring?: Car Making and Automobility in the 21st Century*, Chicester: Wiley.

OICA (2009) *2008 Production Statistics*, Published by The International Organization of Motor Vehicle Manufacturers (Organisation Internationale des Constructeurs d'Automobiles), URL: http://oica.net/category/production-statistics.

O'Reilly III, C. A. and Tushman, M. L. (2004) The Ambidextrous Organization, *Harvard Business Review*, April: 74–81.

Pavitt, K. (1984) Sectoral Patterns of Technical Change: Towards a Taxonomy and a Theory, *Research Policy*, 13: 343–73.

—— (1986) 'Chips' and 'Trajectories': How Does the Semiconductor Influence the Sources and Directions of Technical Change? in: R. MacLeod (ed.), *Technology and the Human Prospect*, London: Frances Pinter, pp. 31–54.

Pilkington, A. and Dyerson, R. (2005) Gales of Creative Destruction and the Opportunistic Hurricane: The Case of Electric Vehicles in California, *Technology Analysis & Strategic Management*, 17(4): 391–408.

Pistorius, C. W. I. and Utterback, J. M. (1997) Multi-Mode Interaction among Technologies, *Research Policy*, 26: 67–84.

Pohl, H. and Yarime, M. (2010) Relationships between Battery Suppliers and Automakers for Knowledge Base Development during Paradigmatic Shifts in Technology, Paper Presented at the International Conference on Organizational Learning, Knowledge, and Capabilities (OLKC), Boston, 3–6 June 2010.

Prencipe, A. (1997) Technological Competencies and Product's Evolutionary Dynamics: A Case Study from the Aero-Engine Industry, *Research Policy*, 25(8): 1261–76.

—— (2000) Breadth and Depth of Technological Capabilities in CoPS: The Case of the Aircraft Engine Control System, *Research Policy*, 29(7–8): 895–911.

Rosenbloom, R. S. and Christensen, C. M. (1994) Technological Discontinuities, Organizational Capabilities, and Strategic Commitments, *Industrial and Corporate Change*, 3(3): 655–85.

Rycroft, R. W. and Kash, D. E. (2002) Path Dependence in the Innovation of Complex Technologies, *Technology Analysis & Strategic Management*, 14(1): 21–35.

Schäfer A., Heywood, J. B. and Weiss, M. A. (2006) Future Fuel Cell and Internal Combustion Engine Automobile Technologies: A 25 Year Life-Cycle and Fleet Impact Assessment, *Energy – The International Journal*, 31(12): 1728–51.

Schumpeter, J. A. (1934) *The Theory of Economic Development*, Cambridge, MA: Harvard Economic Studies.

—— (1942/1994) *Capitalism, Socialism & Democracy*, 5th ed., New York: Routledge.

—— (1947) The Creative Response in Economic History, *The Journal of Economic History*, 7(2): 149–59.

Sperling, D. and Gordon, D. (2009) *Two Billion Cars*, Oxford: Oxford University Press.

Takeichi, A. (2002) Knowledge Partitioning in the Interfirm Division of Labor: The Case of Automotive Product Development, *Organisation Science*, 13(3): 321–38.

Tell, F. (2000) *Organizational Capabilities – A Study of Electrical Power Transmission Equipment Manufacturers, 1878–1990*, PhD thesis, Linköping: Linköping University.

Tidd, J. (1995) Development of Novel Products through Intraorganizational and Interorganizational Networks: The Case of Home Automation, *Journal of Product Innovation Management*, 12(4): 307–22.

Tushman, M. L. and Anderson, P. (1986) Technological Discontinuities and Organizational Environments, *Administrative Science Quarterly*, 31: 439–65.

—— Rosenkopf, L. (1992) Organizational Determinants of Technological Change: Toward a Sociology of Technological Evolution, *Research in Organizational Behavior*, 14: 311–47.

—— Anderson, P. C. and O'Reilly, C. (1997) Technology Cycles, Innovation Streams, and Ambidextrous Organizations: Organizational Renewal through Innovation Streams and Strategic Change, in: M. L. Tushman and P. Anderson (eds.), *Managing Strategic Innovation and Change: A Collection of Readings*, Oxford: Oxford University Press, pp. 3–23.

Ulrich, K. (1995) The Role of Product Architecture in the Manufacturing Firm, *Research Policy*, 24: 419–40.

Utterback, J. M. and Abernathy, W. J. (1975) A Dynamic Model of Product and Process Innovation, *Omega*, 3(6): 639–56.

—— Suárez, F. F. (1993) Innovation, Competition, and Industry Structure, *Research Policy*, 22(1): 1–21.

Watson, W. J. (1997) *Constructing Success in the Electric Power Industry: Combined Cycle Gas Turbines and Fluidised Beds*, PhD thesis, Falmer: University of Sussex.

—— (2004) Selection Environments, Flexibility, and the Success of the Gas Turbine, *Research Policy*, 33: 1065–80.

Winter, S. G. (1984) Schumpeterian Competition in Alternative Technological Regimes, *Journal of Economic Behavior & Organization*, 5(3–4): 287–320.

Part V
Conclusion

12

Lessons and Insights for Managers

Michael Hobday and Anna Bergek

> This chapter summarizes the conclusions from the book. It examines insights gained, challenges to conventional management thinking, and, above all, lessons for practicing managers. It also assesses the future of knowledge integration in academic research and business practice.

12.1 NEW INSIGHTS INTO KNOWLEDGE INTEGRATION

This book has provided the first comprehensive, multilevel understanding of the knowledge integration (KI) processes. In Chapter 2, we set the stage by identifying three core areas of deficiency in the treatment of KI in previous research. These areas were then assessed both conceptually and empirically to illustrate the nature and dynamics of KI and to draw out practical lessons for managers tasked with the difficult challenges of carrying out KI in different contexts. The three areas were as follows:

- Part I examined the human dimension of KI by analysing how *people and processes* are organized to meet KI needs and challenges.
- Part II provided new evidence on how KI challenges are managed through *projects and partnerships*, the principal organizational forms of KI efforts, within and beyond the firm.
- Part III examined *strategies and outcomes*, describing not only the part played by KI in achieving organizational success, especially in delivering new products, systems, services, and processes, but also the costs and trade-offs intrinsic to KI.

In this final chapter, we focus on the implications for managers and strategists. The empirical focus of the book is technology-based business firms and the lessons learnt from our research are, in consequence, especially relevant in such contexts. We believe that many of the KI challenges and solutions presented in this book may be relevant also in other contexts where the effective integration of increasingly diverse knowledge and expertise is a key to success, for example in other types of business firms and many public organizations. That, however, is outside the scope of this chapter. Below, we present the key findings of the research, focusing on new insights which challenge conventional management wisdom. Thereafter, we detail practical lessons for managers and strategists charged with integrating knowledge in knowledge-intensive (and often high-technology) contexts. Finally, we look to the future of academic research and business practice in the KI area.

12.2 CHALLENGES TO CONVENTIONAL MANAGEMENT THINKING

12.2.1 People and processes

Part I of the book filled a major gap in the field, regarding the role of individuals and groups in KI and the creativity involved in this process. In contrast to much conventional research on problem-solving routines and capabilities, we showed that while KI involves many different kinds of routine problem-solving activity, it is also a creative non-routine act, which requires imagination, the generation of alternative solutions, and the reframing of 'given' problems. In fact, KI is one of the heartland creative processes that go on within the firm.

We also showed that two types of individuals are particularly important agents in KI and, thus, in the innovation process. First, in many large, technology-based companies, a few highly inventive (in terms of patenting) individuals tend to play a key role in the 'micro-processes' of KI. The contribution of these individuals is not primarily to master internal politics or manage innovation projects, as emphasized in previous research, but rather to overcome knowledge-related challenges, build knowledge networks in the organization, and collaboratively test and refine inventive ideas. Second, a special breed of 'mobile' engineers, capable of dealing with the complex demands of KI, are essential to the business of KI, as they move in and out of projects, learning special, often rare, personal competencies while earning reputation and trust, both within and outside individual firms. An important characteristic of both these types of individuals is that they move around and between projects. For the purpose of KI, processes, teams, and projects should therefore not be seen as closed but rather as 'permeable' entities, embedded in a web of more or less informal collaborative practices.

12.2.2 Projects and partnership

Part II of the book examined the critical question of which organizational forms are needed to underpin successful KI. This part provided an in-depth knowledge of organizational options and challenges, including the way successful KI processes are organized in practice and the key roles of different types of projects. We showed that to be successful, KI must occur on many different levels, both within the project and the firm and across all the external organizations involved. When KI goes beyond the boundary of a single firm, this poses challenges for setting up suitable organizational structures for dealing both with the coordination of diverse knowledge and tasks, and with the cooperation required to handle conflicts of interest, including the possible loss of intellectual property.

The management of KI obviously goes beyond conventional project management and planning techniques and tools, such as gateways, milestones, and work breakdown structures. KI in complex product technology and product development requires not only formal systems and tools, but also flexible approaches and inspirational management that embrace experimentation, interaction, and learning alongside adapted project planning. Moreover, KI management cannot be fixed or 'set in stone' but must be iterative and itself creative. KI activities and deadlines can shape the required management structure and approach, and KI management needs to change according to the stage of the project and the changing character of the deadline and product architecture. We also saw that KI requires firms to engage in a balancing act, making sure that projects are creative and generate space for innovative activities while, at the same time, ensuring that learning diffuses into the wider structures of the firm through special arrangements such as 'project-led organizations'.

12.2.3 Strategies and outcomes

Part III examined KI strategies and outcomes, dealing with the hard choices firms need to make, the costs of 'getting it wrong', and the benefits to be gained from building up strong KI capabilities. One key corporate challenge is how to partner with a network of suppliers via outsourcing. Outsourcing, although often unavoidable, presents both difficulties and paradoxes that have yet to be fully understood or addressed by most analysts and strategists. On the one hand, outsourcing is often both desirable and necessary. On the other, everything outsourced needs to be reintegrated – and the cost of this can be significant and depends crucially on specialized investments in in-house KI capabilities (or 'absorptive capacity'). Therefore, when designing an outsourcing strategy, the benefits of outsourcing (including direct cost reductions, for example in manufacturing, and access to specialized external skills and technologies) need to be set against not only the explicit and direct costs of outsourcing but also the hidden, less obvious costs of building the necessary skills and capabilities, structures, and processes needed for this extended knowledge reintegration.

Another key challenge is how to manage innovation in fields characterized by 'creative accumulation', where new products or processes with substantially improved or changed performance are the result of a combination of existing knowledge and new types of knowledge. While previous research has emphasized the advantage of industry incumbents in such fields, we showed that the sourcing and integration of new technologies with established and continuously evolving 'old' technologies creates tensions within the organization, which require careful consideration also for incumbents to stay in business and prosper. In particular, traditional organizational solutions that keep new developments separate from old ones will not work, since there is a need to integrate the old and the new, over and over again.

12.3 LESSONS AND INSIGHTS FOR MANAGERS

Given this set of difficult challenges, this section deals with lessons and implications for managers and businesses involved in KI. Against each of the three themes covered (people and processes, projects and processes, and strategies and outcomes), we examine (*a*) what managers need to understand about their area in relation to KI, (*b*) the shifts in thinking a KI perspective might entail, (*c*) the new approaches that are being adopted by leading firms, (*d*) how managers can best support KI, and (*e*) what they should not be doing if they want to develop successful KI processes. In short, this section develops specific lessons for managers, based on the research. While there can be no single best practice or strategy for KI, insights from leading firms and practitioners may well prove useful for other managers facing the challenge of KI. Against each area, we present 'headline' lessons, followed up with detailed explanations and advice gained from the businesses studied.

12.3.1 People and processes

KI is a creative, trial-and-error process

The basic message of Chapter 3 was that KI is, above all, a creative, evolving process which occurs in projects that, over time, generate increasingly useful knowledge. In the traditional view of project management, progress is often seen as dependent on careful goal formulation, risk estimation efforts, milestones, and tollgate assessments. While project managers no doubt find these kinds of measures valuable, for example, as a benchmark against actual progress, they also need to appreciate that knowledge growth in projects relies on learning under conditions of uncertainty and on trial and elimination of errors.

The evolutionary approach presented in Chapter 3 highlighted that KI in a project context is a learning process, in which the project goal creates a shared focus, but that often relatively little is known initially. Because of uncertainty, managers may be unable to predict outcomes with much accuracy. Managers and project members must often act on the basis of limited knowledge and without recourse to any heavy front-loading effort geared at gathering information. In order to deal with uncertainty, they then need to change their assumptions, conjectures, and actions through time as new knowledge is revealed. Long-term goals and plans for a project therefore have an inevitable 'visionary', searchlight dimension involving good judgement and experience (even guesswork), which sooner or later will be changed and adapted to incorporate new experience.

Insight, imagination, and experience are essential in KI

A second important lesson for managers from Chapter 3 was that the act of creating something beyond what we presently know is often a matter of 'unexpected variation' from what has happened before. This requires a process building on both insights and imagination. Such processes are seldom unconstrained. Even in very early, explorative project sessions, structures such as goals, norms, and rules will be operating simultaneously. Individuals, project groups, and social groups of various kinds are key sources of imagination and novel ideas. The challenge for project managers is therefore to design and enable arenas and opportunities for practitioners to engage in task-related communications that will allow them, knowingly or unknowingly, to inspire each other as their 'unfathomable' knowledge is being circulated and collaboratively refined. In doing that, project managers need to account for the fact that such processes are a matter of both imagination and discipline, often enhanced by hard-won experience in previous projects.

The project team helps moderate and shape individuals' creativity . . .

Chapter 3 also showed that project managers should rely heavily on collective modes of knowledge creation and assessment. While individual contributions are a key to the creative process, individuals often tend to be strongly inclined to seek verification for existing beliefs rather than trying to change or falsify them. On their own, they have great difficulty seeing 'what is wrong' with their conjectures and find it difficult to change their interpretations. Managers need to recognize these human features and design collective gatherings where critical enquiry prevails. Participants in projects need to be encouraged to compare their emerging conjectures and solutions regularly with other perceptions that may emerge during the project. Collective feedback is a crucial enabler for achieving a progressive knowledge process, and the role of milestones and tollgate meetings can be reinterpreted more positively in the light of this background, for example using them as benchmarks to compare with what 'actually' happens.

. . . but sometimes a few key individuals can make all the difference

Formal teams and project structures are important for focusing effort and creativity, but as Chapters 4 and 5 demonstrated, inventive and collaborative individuals can play a major role for innovative achievements and KI. Chapter 4 revealed the role of individual inventors as knowledge integrators. Its central message was that in many large, technology-based companies, a few, highly productive (e.g. as indicated by patenting measures) individual inventors often play critical roles also in KI processes. These individuals act as both idea generators and knowledge integrators in the wider organization, operating within and outside project structures. The contribution of these individuals is not so much to address internal politics or manage projects but rather to build new knowledge networks in the organization, to use them for various 'pre-development' activities, and to act as mentors for younger, less experienced engineers and researchers. They generate and help to refine inventive ideas, using their special skills to fuse their own specialized knowledge with knowledge from other fields, including customer needs, throughout the innovation process. They do this not in conflict with formal projects but in parallel to them.

Managers therefore need to identify and support individual inventors as important agents in the KI process and, thus, in the overall innovation process. They should not be seen as 'lone heroes', playing their own game, but rather as key team players in collaboration with others. In a time when many companies are investing in highly structured project processes, there is a need to allow and encourage, certainly not prevent, these individuals to pursue unplanned creative activities in parallel with formal projects. In this unplanned space, which often exists between the lines of the formal organizational chart, individual inventor–innovators can explore the unexpected and combine knowledge in new ways.

Projects should be seen as part of a wider innovation ecology

These findings have important implications for the way managers see projects. Projects should be viewed as permeable entities rather than closed systems. Project leaders may wish to allow inventors to be part of several different types of groups and projects and encourage them to engage in a broader web of goal-directed, but not formally planned creative activities, where these individuals can come up with new solutions to difficult problems. Managers should create possibilities for key individuals to participate in the entire innovation process, from idea generation to customer launch, involving dialogue with people in related fields, such as manufacturing, service, and sales. This may seem easy on the face of it, but in many organizations it may entail a complex balancing act between formal project structures, process-mapping and time-based controls, and less formal practices, driven by curious, creative, and collaborative individuals.

Improve the effectiveness of knowledge collectivities by supporting mobility of engineers

Building further on the idea of permeable projects, Chapter 5 looked into the role of key individuals in the form of mobile engineers. A substantial, perhaps increasing, amount of KI is performed in projects that resemble knowledge collectivities, where people come and go on a continuous basis. Part of the modern project manager's job is, therefore, to learn how to handle the mobile and flexible nature of work and learning and become an inspirer of KI. Managers need to understand the nature and role of such mobile individuals in order to reward and manage them effectively. Firms need to recruit, retain, and enhance the skills of individuals so that they are enabled to move from project to project, from team to team, and even from one client organization to another, so that they can enter decisively into the KI collectivity and operate skilfully even if they do not have solid roots in one particular team or department. Important issues include building the mobile engineers' reputation within the client's organization, upgrading their task-related technical skills and abilities, and making networks of relationships and resources available to particular engineers. By considering these needs of mobile engineers, managers of various kinds can help improve the effectiveness of knowledge collectivities as arenas for the creative and complex problem-solving dimensions of KI.

12.3.2 Projects and partnerships

Part II of the book identified various ways in which leading firms organize KI. This is not a trivial task as KI occurs on various levels, both in projects across the organization and, increasingly, in partnerships with external organizations.

KI needs to be managed both on module and system architecture levels

The evidence from Chapter 6 showed that managers need to be aware that the experimentation and iteration required for successful KI may take place on various levels, depending on the product architecture. On the one hand, modularized product structures allow the product to be decomposed. Consequently, iteration and experimentation will take place primarily on a 'local' module level. On the other hand, integrated product architectures require systems-level integration, and iterations then need to be managed primarily at the 'global' firm or inter-firm KI level.

Deadlines can be used to shape project strategy and processes

Chapter 6 also showed that deadlines, and perceptions of deadlines, deeply influence KI processes within projects. Hard (i.e. strict) deadlines reinforce the necessity of iterative processes with a high integration of product- and production-related knowledge. In these situations, project managers and engineers often have to work around the formal product development process by, for instance, decomposing seemingly non-decomposable integrated systems. This proves to be one valuable strategy for gaining time. In contrast, soft deadlines enable sequential processes at the outset, but later on in the project the need for experimental and iterative KI increases anyway. These dynamics mean that alongside the product's architecture, deadlines should be taken into account when framing the strategy for KI. Managers need to see time both as a situational characteristic and as a control mechanism.

Deadlines and architectures are interdependent and change over time

To make matters even more complex, and despite previous assumptions to the contrary, time limits and product architectures are not mutually independent. Indeed, Chapter 6 showed that some linkages exist. For example, a transition from soft to hard deadlines can necessitate important reconsiderations of the product architecture in the direction of either more modular or more integral structures. Generally, this direction depends on the focus of the product and production knowledge in the project. If projects are highly time-critical, then managers and engineers may need to sacrifice some functionality in order to decompose products that had previously been conceived as tightly integrated and separate those components that are less affected by technological uncertainty from those that are directly affected by changes in the overall product design.

Alongside this type of consideration, managers also need to be aware that external conditions and a deeper understanding of the task may change initial perceptions during the course of new product development (NPD) projects, resulting in a need to revise KI processes to match emerging conditions. During a development project, some global KI processes may become more local and local processes may become more global. Soft deadlines can be turned into hard deadlines and vice versa. Similar to Chapter 3, Chapter 6 thus found strong elements of learning in KI.

This implies that it is difficult to design a precisely planned mechanism for integrating product- and production-related knowledge in advance. Instead, good judgement is called for, based on experience of what will and will not work under circumstances of some uncertainty. Conventional process planning alone will not enable practitioners to respond rapidly to the requirements of KI. To manage this process, perceptions from different angles on both product architectures and time limits need to be discussed, challenged, and reconsidered during the project life cycle. There can be no 'one best' plan when managing creative processes under conditions of uncertainty, confirming the results of other chapters.

Problems of cooperation and of coordination interact in cross-firm partnerships

Inter-firm collaboration in KI is becoming increasingly common, given the specialist and deepening knowledge sets held within different organizations. Chapter 7 focused on KI in the context of inter-firm R&D collaborations, looking at both benefits and costs. Managers need to solve problems of inter-firm coordination related to differences in knowledge bases and firm-specific expertise. However, they also need to handle problems of cooperation that are related to conflicts of interest, different corporate goals and the specificity of investments. The findings of Chapter 7 indicate that the interaction of these two problems is more complex than suggested by prior literature. Consequently, firms need to establish sufficient mechanisms and structures in relation to both problems of cooperation and problems of coordination, rather than optimal structures and mechanisms with regard to either problem by itself.

The (hidden) cost of KI in cross-firm collaborations can be large

A general implication for managers from Chapter 7 is that they need to conduct an expanded analysis of costs and benefits before entering into inter-firm R&D collaboration. That is, they need to identify the factors that are critical in the project, and then compare the costs of mitigating the risks relative to the benefits that follow. This is a complex assessment to make and often relies on good judgement and experience. However, neglecting this analysis runs the risk of either investing too much in administrative structures and mechanisms which may negatively affect KI progress or, conversely, of losing control of intellectual property rights that are vital strategic assets.

In particular, managers need to identify the hidden costs of integration mechanisms and support structures when integrating knowledge across organizations. Mechanisms that promote close interaction ideally involve strong governance structures to limit the risks of expropriation (e.g. the gaining of a partner's intellectual property). Such structures can, however, incur large costs. In addition, if the problems of cooperation are intense, it may be difficult to anticipate all the contingencies in contracts even if much effort is put into establishing a strong governance structure. Indeed, investments in governance structures to support KI may exceed the resulting benefits, undermining the economic rationale for the project. In such cases, managers need to fall back on informal assessments and mechanisms and build up trust with partners through close communication helping to ensure that risks do not materialize. Finally, due to the interaction between problems of coordination and cooperation, firms have to balance the benefits that may come from solving these problems against the costs involved. That is, given the efforts associated with inter-firm KI, managers need to think in terms of sufficient rather than optimal KI. This can be achieved in different ways. For example, if the costs of close coordination appear too high, one possible alternative is to limit the amount of knowledge being integrated by limiting the scope of the partnership. Or, managers can sometimes use integration mechanisms that handle both problems sufficiently (rather than optimally) well, thereby facilitating knowledge sharing at the same time as they get reasonable control over the process of KI.

Project-led organization is conducive to knowledge integration when complexity is high

In many industries, project-based forms of organizing have emerged as one way of dealing with increasing complexity and highly demanding technological, market, and task environments. Rather than structuring organizations in semi-permanent departments grouped according to functions or markets, project-based organizing entails a concomitant and temporary structuring to meet these changing needs. However, as Chapter 8 showed, a 'project-led organization' (i.e. a combination of a permanent or semi-permanent organizational structure and major projects) is even better positioned to cope with two of the main challenges in managing KI, namely market complexity and technological complexity. Project-led organization allows for strong experimentation and has the KI features of project-based organizing without all the liabilities of a completely temporary organization. In particular, with the globalization of competition in capital-goods industries, partly the result of deregulated markets, large high-technology corporations need to develop integrated customer solutions based on an advanced project capability for integrating knowledge from a variety of fields.

Path-creating projects contribute to building firm-level KI capabilities

Project-led capabilities can be nurtured by developing path-creating projects that serve as experiments in creating new systems and services for challenging markets. By resisting the temptation to resort to a standard permanent (e.g. departmental) structure and, instead, letting projects operate on a temporary basis within more permanent organizational structures, there are opportunities for managers to learn from 'rare' experiments and improve the systems and services under development, so as to create new categories of products and markets. At the same time, this approach enables the integration of the knowledge gained from such experiments into the more slowly evolving knowledge base of the permanent organization, represented, for instance, by divisional or matrix structures. In essence, the development of a P-form (project-form) of organization, utilizing temporary decentralization, oscillating between decentralized and centralized authority in the organization, is a strategy which major systems integrators should consider under rapidly changing, complex technological and market circumstances.

12.3.3 Strategies and outcomes

Part III of the book examined KI strategies and outcomes, dealing with the hard choices firms need to make when partnering with other companies, the costs of 'getting it wrong', and the benefits of building up strong KI capabilities, particularly when outsourcing processes and engaging in innovation characterized by creative accumulation.

Outsourcing should be viewed as a strategic value chain activity

Analysing outsourcing from a KI perspective opens up several new lines of thought. Chapter 9 showed that outsourcing is a major challenge facing knowledge integrators and demonstrated the importance of recognizing the double KI effect of outsourcing. The data indicated that outsourcing is mostly driven by ambitions to exploit low-cost alternatives or to get access to suppliers' unique knowledge or competencies.

However, firms that focus solely on costs when outsourcing do not always realize that outsourcing alters internal KI requirements and that the interdependencies between separated functions and processes need to be handled, together with the new supplier. The managerial task should, thus, not just be confined to questions of how to select the right process to externalize and the right supplier to involve, but should also include the strategic question of how the firm as a whole can meet the need to integrate and co-locate key functions, knowledge, and capabilities along the extended product–service value chain.

Outsourcing should be matched with internal reintegration capability

Externalizing functions also affects the in-house capability to integrate along the development chain. Very few firms currently understand how outsourcing affects their KI capability. Chapter 9 showed on an operative level that efficient utilization of external knowledge requires investments in in-house manufacturing capability that overlaps the knowledge base of the outsourcing partner. Together with technological and organizational integration mechanisms, they provide the basis for external collaboration and, in turn, improved performance outcomes. A first implication of this is that managers should identify any gap between KI requirements on the one hand and in-house KI reintegration capability on the other, so that they can benefit from lower integration costs as well as improved innovation capability. A key managerial challenge when outsourcing is therefore to address the gap between KI requirements and in-house KI capability.

A second implication is that outsourcing and manufacturing capability investments should not be considered as two distinct options. Instead, a combined strategy should be seen as a way to increase the firm's manufacturing absorptive capacity and its ability to manage KI challenges when outsourcing manufacturing. The rationale for manufacturing investments should, therefore, be based not only on cost and output effects but also on the capability (or absorptive capacity) it provides. This capability enables a company to acquire, assimilate, and commercialize external knowledge. Therefore, internal investments may be needed in capability, even in areas such as manufacturing that may have no direct contact with the sources of the knowledge. In other words, investments in manufacturing capability should be evaluated not only from their direct effects on performance but also from the perspective of the capability they provide for meeting KI requirements which accompany outsourcing.

The long-term costs and benefits have to be considered when partnering

Another lesson is that any benefits from outsourcing need to be balanced against the KI challenges derived from outsourcing. In addition to the obvious costs of logistics and project organization, KI has a price in terms of hidden costs (including the costs of implementing integration mechanisms, as discussed in Chapter 7), trade-offs, and a deteriorated in-house cost reduction capability that needs to be taken into account to provide a robust basis for decisions on outsourcing. Chapter 9 argued that these KI costs explain why previous studies on outsourcing performance have come to such different conclusions. An important lesson for managers is that the KI challenges vary significantly with the kind of outsourcing undertaken. For example, outsourcing parts of the manufacturing process can be very complicated and costly, due to various interdependencies, compared with, say, component- or modular-based outsourcing.

KI strategy should always be a core dimension of outsourcing

Building on the findings of Chapter 9, Chapter 10 took a strategic view on how firms can best manage trade-offs involved in make-or-buy decisions. It showed that when outsourcing manufacturing, there are trade-offs between the performance objectives cost and flexibility and between cost and speed. This implies that managers have to understand that they cannot 'have it all' but instead need to appreciate and balance these trade-offs and to establish congruence between firm competitive strategy and outsourcing motives. For example, firms that compete with low prices would probably outsource primarily for cost reduction reasons, while firms that compete on differentiation may use outsourcing to improve their responsiveness to customer needs.

However, Chapter 10 also showed that these trade-offs are influenced by the degree of supplier integration in terms of early supplier contributions in the NPD process of outsourced parts, joint efforts to reduce costs, supplier access to manufacturing plants and systems, and integration of manufacturing processes.

The cost–flexibility trade-off is mitigated by higher supplier integration, whereas a high degree of supplier integration increases the cost–speed trade-off. A possible interpretation of the first of these results is that mutual adaptation of production processes (e.g. through the sharing of production plans) resolves the tension between cost and flexibility. A well-considered KI strategy can, thus, reduce the cost–flexibility trade-off in manufacturing in outsourcing. By developing greater KI capability, managers will be able to assess where they should expect performance improvements and how these relate to responsiveness.

A possible interpretation of the intensified cost–speed trade-off is that very close and early collaboration in NPD of outsourced parts can result in significantly improved speed, which on the one hand is very important for these kinds of firms and on the other is extremely difficult to achieve together with cost reductions. The chapter showed some support for this interpretation as the cost–speed trade-off increased with increasing degrees of product customization. This seems to imply that firms have to choose between cost reduction and speed when deciding the degree of supplier integration when outsourcing manufacturing and involving their suppliers in NPD of outsourced parts. However, a well-developed KI initiative that enables the reintegration of design and development knowledge within the outsourcing firm and the contract manufacturer is important in developing competitive advantage, and more research is needed on how to design integration mechanisms that aid in overcoming trade-offs when outsourcing manufacturing.

New technologies often build on and need to be integrated with existing ones

As Chapter 11 showed, one of the most difficult strategic challenges of KI occurs during periods of dramatic technological and market change. Based on case studies of discontinuous developments facing two established and technologically complex industries, this chapter demonstrated that such developments impose severe challenges for strategists and R&D managers also in previously very successful companies. This is because the new technologies need to be acquired and then integrated with established technologies, which themselves are evolving and improving, often at an accelerated pace. The cumulative nature of technological advance often gives industry incumbents advantages. However, there are no guarantees for the incumbents' survival. Instead, careful responses are required for firms to stay in business and to renew their approaches. In particular, the dual requirement to master both the sourcing of new technology and the rapid development of old technology often creates a tension within the organization, which managers need to address. This and other challenges can be understood and managed by applying the concept of 'creative accumulation' developed in this chapter.

Innovative activities should not be separated from traditional lines of business

To succeed in creative accumulation, managers may need to explore new technological options and question established routines and practices. However, the need to integrate old and new technologies, which are both evolving, means that KI cannot be accomplished in isolation from the traditional line of business. Conventional wisdom that managers should keep new developments separate from old will not work. Instead, managers need to orchestrate a continuous process of learning and innovating, which addresses issues such as how to source new knowledge, how to hone the existing knowledge base, and how to integrate these diverse sets of knowledge into functioning processes and products that survive intense competition in the market place.

It is important to balance internal knowledge development and technology sourcing from external partners

Creative accumulation implies a challenge to search for and source novel technologies. This implies difficult decisions regarding sourcing and competence building: to invest in internal knowledge development – R&D and product engineering as well as process/manufacturing engineering – or to invest in and sustain knowledge-generating alliances with outside partners (as also discussed in Chapters 7, 9, and 10). Such sourcing investments need to be strategic, both in terms of making alliances productive and in terms of building capabilities to absorb and integrate new knowledge (both internally developed and acquired) with existing knowledge.

There is room for variety in creative responses

In contrast to the suggestions in some previous literature, Chapter 11 showed that there is room for strategic variety as firms respond to this type of discontinuous innovation. In particular, there are various options with regard to which product system level to innovate within (system architecture, components, or both) as well as to the mix between new and evolving established technologies. However, the choices made influence KI challenges and options. Coherent choices must be made in terms of organization, technology acquisition, and internal technology development and it is this complexity, tension, dynamism, and duality that make creative accumulation a demanding arena for KI.

12.4 THE FUTURE OF KNOWLEDGE INTEGRATION

Leading firms would already have learned some of the specific insights and lessons presented above. They will understand the importance of conceptualizing, managing, and learning more about the complex processes of KI and how these relate to business success. However, many firms and other organizations – even some of the most successful firms described in this book – have yet to produce a strategic and coherent approach to KI.

In contrast to the case of relatively simple hardware and systems production, where there are well-known management methods, tools, and best practices, the processes of KI are still poorly understood as a strategic and operational function within high-technology business. There is far less agreement on how best to approach KI, how to measure KI progress, and how to integrate KI within the strategic and operational functions of business. Many traditional management tools (e.g. total quality management, IT-based project management techniques, capability maturity management, and ISO-based approaches) are not suited to the tasks of KI that involve creativity and learning, search and revision, context specificity, and strategic choice. In other words, KI approaches cannot always be formally planned at the outset. They need to be tailored to specific cases and individual firms, and they may need to be adapted during the emerging stages of the life cycle of the delivery of the high-technology system or product in question. Failure to understand the basics of KI can lead to huge losses and missed opportunities. However, the initial lessons above provide some guidance to both the strategic challenges and the operational tasks of KI across a range of industries.

As this book has shown, there are several cases of success and failure and many lessons to be learned. These are not only useful for current projects but could also create new opportunities for firms willing to take on board the lessons and insights of others. By explicitly addressing the challenges of KI and building broad KI capabilities within and beyond the organization, particular firms can gain new advantages in the competitive race. Managers in many high-technology industries, with little experience of KI strategies and KI modes of organization, can potentially benefit a great deal by learning the lessons of the more successful KI practitioners.

In the future, knowledge creation and KI will be increasingly recognized as a key organizational challenge and a fundamental component of innovation strategy. Therefore, managers should be prepared to consider how best to integrate KI within their business models and strategies. They will need to question conventional tools and systems, especially those designed for hardware rather than knowledge and for decomposable processes rather than interactive, evolutionary knowledge creation.

While there can be no single 'best practice' for the treatment of KI in business, new KI challenges offer an opportunity to (*a*) develop novel and effective approaches to understand and manage the intangible, (*b*) harness the creativity of key individuals and groups, (*c*) create and re-create the organizational structures needed and support business leaders, and (*d*) treat KI as a strategic resource capable of delivering competitive advantage. Each new project involving KI can help businesses and researchers learn more about how to apply KI to competitive strategy and innovation. Further studies of KI in practice will also aid a better understanding of the methods and approaches best suited to this task and provide more evidence for managers and practitioners engaged in meeting the challenges of KI.

Looking to the future, academic researchers can, through careful empirical research and by building on the insights presented in this book, develop new models of KI, elevating KI to its rightful place as a key strategic and operational function within the firm. We need to know more about KI capabilities, how to measure them, and how to build them. Researchers need to identify in more depth the nature and meaning of KI capability, showing precisely which attributes underpin the skills, knowledge, and experience that make up KI capability; how these capabilities are built up and put into use through the activities of individual inventors, engineers, and managers; and how they are exhibited in improved organizational structures, in the strategies undertaken by business leaders, and in the processes which firms use to conduct their business. Only then will business managers and leaders be confident in how to understand and improve the overall level of KI capability of the firm.

Researchers also need to explain why the innovation environment is driving businesses further towards knowledge creation and knowledge intensity and what this means for education and training. Increasingly, firms face the task of developing service-intensive systems and solutions for customers who are much more demanding of their technology and system suppliers. As we have shown, accessing external knowledge via outsourcing can be a response to these increasing pressures but, to be effective, outsourcing itself requires a strong in-house KI capability, including the skill to work creatively with partners across a diverse, changing, and complex supply network.

In understanding how to deploy new KI approaches, researchers and managers need to move beyond the traditional approach of core capabilities, which are more suited to the existing operational needs of firms. Instead, firms need to understand how to manage and unleash the creative processes of individuals, teams, projects, and external partners. This could well mean breaking down routines and challenging existing capabilities. KI also demands that we move beyond the traditional mindsets of operational efficiency and cost reduction. While these are obviously critical, KI, as a creative function, is also central to long-term business innovation, capability building, and corporate strategy. Efficiency planning, on its own, can therefore undermine longer term capability building.

However, as some of the chapters in this book have shown, there can be limits to the benefits of KI, and there is reason to believe that in some contexts the direct and indirect costs of KI can be very high. This implies that in some situations, firms may be better off trying to reduce the need for KI, by, for example, developing modularized products with standardized interfaces when dealing with supplier partnerships. More research is clearly needed on how to identify and handle these strategic choices.

Because each project involving KI will have its own features and its own distinctive lessons, firms that explicitly manage KI activities so as to learn and benefit from these experiences will be far more effective in creating new technologies, products, and solutions and handling new complex challenges emanating from radical economic or ecological changes. Ultimately, these firms will learn to capture the rewards of successful KI, creating new forms of competitive advantage in existing markets and leading positions in the new markets of the future.

Index

absorptive capacity 13, 16, 23, 32, 114, 207, 210–11, 214, 221–3, 279, 287
actionable knowledge 62, 63
activities 9, 46, 67, 71, 92, 115, 119, 126–7, 171, 174, 207
  bracketing 63
  core 232
  creative *see* R&D
  externalization of *see* outsourcing
  foundational 91
  functional 171
  internalization of 223
  interrelated 100, 105–6, 113–17
  joint *see* cooperation
  organizational 37, 178–9, 209
  production preparatory 135, 141, 142–3, 145
  routine 4, 78
  see also knowledge integration; knowledge sharing
ÅF 97
agency 101
ambidextrous organizations 231, 270
analogical reasoning/thinking 108, 109, 115, 117
analysability 29
application of knowledge 36
architectural innovation 7, 13, 23, 40, 44, 47, 159, 210, 217, 221, 250, 256, 258, 259, 264, 267
articulability of knowledge 151
Asea/ABB 170–201, 254
  collaborative projects 176–9
    complex projects 178
    domestic focus 177–8
    H-form projects 178–9
  employees 181, 188
  export markets 181
  international projects 179–84
    market complexity 180–2
    sector organization 183–4
    technological complexity 182
  KI evolution 175–92
  revenues 181, 188
  total solutions 187–92
    deregulated market 188–9
    deregulation 188–9
    global matrix 190–2
  turnkey projects 184–7
    divisional form 186–7
    global markets 185–6
    semiconductor revolution 186
assignment specifications 112
automotive industry 252–8

downsizing 260–1
hybrid cars 256, 259–61
KI in 265–6
market shares 257
new technology 255–8, 259–61
technology sources 262–3

Barnevik, Percy 186, 190
BIS project 159–61, 163–4
black-box outsourcing 208, 209

capability 9–10, 209–11, 251, 285, 290
  combinative 170, 209
  innovation 6, 232–3, 239
  integrative 40, 43, 45, 47
  manufacturing 212–16, 221–2, 286–7
  as strategic issue 9–10
  supplier operation 232–3
capacity outsourcing 209, 211, 215, 218, 220
capital 116
  activation 115
  analogical 117
  role 117
  social 32
case studies
  Asea/ABB 170–201, 254
  automotive industry 252–8
  Combitech 96–121
  gas turbine industry 252–8
  inter-firm collaboration
    BIS project 159–61, 163–4
    Explorer project 157–9, 162–3
    Future Combat Air Systems project 155, 156–7, 161–2
  new product development 133–41
client organizations 97, 100, 102, 107, 108, 110, 114, 116, 282
collaboration *see* inter-firm collaboration
collaborative emergence 70
collaborative processes 91
collaborative projects 176–9
combinative capabilities 170, 209
Combitech case study 96–121
common knowledge 12, 22, 25, 27, 31, 96, 151, 210
competence-enhancing innovation 249, 250, 251
competencies 12, 97, 105, 114, 115, 136, 150, 158, 206, 212, 221, 249, 250
  core 5–6, 207, 228, 232, 239, 268
competitive advantage 4, 8, 10, 11, 14, 127, 212, 231, 288, 290
  see also creative accumulation